Blu Greenberg

Gloria Greenfield

Miriam Hawley

Melanie Kaye/Kantrowitz

Amy Kesselman

Irena Klepfisz

Marya Levenson

Cheryl Moch

Jane Pincus

Judith Plaskow

Letty Cottin Pogrebin

Adrienne Rich

Esther Rome

Vivian Rothstein

Susan Schechter

Susan Weidman Schneider

Alix Kates Shulman

Marilyn Webb

Naomi Weisstein

Ellen Willis

JEWISH RADICAL FEMINISM

THE GOLDSTEIN-GOREN SERIES IN AMERICAN JEWISH HISTORY

General editor: Hasia R. Diner

Jewish Radical Feminism

Voices from the Women's Liberation Movement

Joyce Antler

NEW YORK UNIVERSITY PRESS
New York

NEW YORK UNIVERSITY PRESS
New York
www.nyupress.org

References to Internet websites (URLs) were accurate at the time of writing.
Neither the author nor New York University Press is responsible for URLs
that may have expired or changed since the manuscript was prepared.

Library of Congress Cataloging-in-Publication Data
Names: Antler, Joyce, author.
Title: Jewish radical feminism : voices from the women's liberation movement /
Joyce Antler.
Description: New York : New York University Press, [2018] |
Series: The Goldstein-Goren series in American Jewish history |
Includes bibliographical references and index.
Identifiers: LCCN 2017045030 | ISBN 9780814707630 (cl : alk. paper)
Subjects: LCSH: Women in Judaism. | Jewish women—United States. |
Feminism—Religious aspects—Judaism. | Gender identity—Religious
aspects—Judaism. | Feminism—United States—History—20th century. |
Feminism—United States—History—21st century. | Queer theory.
Classification: LCC BM729.W6 A58 2018 | DDC 305.42089/924073—dc23
LC record available at https://lccn.loc.gov/2017045030

New York University Press books are printed on acid-free paper,
and their binding materials are chosen for strength and durability.
We strive to use environmentally responsible suppliers and materials
to the greatest extent possible in publishing our books.

Manufactured in the United States of America

10 9 8 7 6 5 4 3 2 1

Also available as an ebook

To Tillie and Max

CONTENTS

Introduction

The women's liberation movement that began in the United States in the late 1960s may have been the most important social movement of the last century, challenging gender inequality in myriad forms and participating in what soon became a global movement to transform women's lives. Although the movement began with the formation of several small collectives in rapid succession, historians often cite Chicago's West Side Group as the first women's liberation group in the country. Formed in late 1967, that group shared the ecstasy and exhilaration of creating a movement that was "ready to turn the world upside down," in the words of Naomi Weisstein, one of its key members. Every subject was a topic of intense discussion, Weisstein recalled. "We talked incessantly . . . about our pain, . . . our righteous anger, . . . our orgasms. Then we felt guilty for talking about our orgasms. Shouldn't we be doing actions?"[1] And act they surely did, to stunning effect. The power and joy of their deep involvement in the women's movement is reflected in the image of Weisstein that adorns the cover of this book.

The one issue that the group never talked about was the Jewish backgrounds of the majority of its dozen members. "We *never* talked about it," Weisstein admitted to me and to several West Side friends when, some forty-five years after the group's founding, I brought them together to probe the issue. "It was so embarrassing to have so many Jews around," Weisstein acknowledged. "There was even a silent agreement that we didn't bring it up because it was counter to the universalist vision of that time. . . . It was sort of a whiff of anti-Semitism."[2]

Even in the decades after the demise of the Chicago Women's Liberation Union, the citywide group the West Side women had helped to create, they did not discuss their Jewish identities. The same was true for most Jewish women who joined women's liberation groups in other cities in the 1960s and 1970s. While a few individual Jewish women have been acknowledged for their work as women's liberationists, for the most part, Jewish women's impact on the movement *as Jews* seemed to be unimportant, a matter ignored by participants in the movement and historians alike. This neglect also characterized the post-1970s phase of women's liberation, sometimes referred to as feminist identity politics, which drew together specific groups of women on the basis of shared racial, ethnic, sexual, or other backgrounds. Radical feminists who identified Jewishly found themselves to be outsiders in the increasingly multicultural landscape fashioned by the politics of identity.

Yet the place of Jewish women in women's liberation is highly significant. Jewish women were leaders, helping to start several of the first radical feminist groups in the country, among them the Chicago Women's Liberation Union, New York's Redstockings and New York Radical Women, and Boston's Bread and Roses. Eight out of the dozen founders of the Boston Women's Health Book Collective, one of the most long-lasting women's liberation projects in the country, were Jewish.

Jewish women in second-wave feminism helped to provide the theoretical underpinnings and models for radical action that were seized on and imitated throughout the United States and abroad. Their articles and books became classics of the movement and led the way into new arenas of cultural and political understanding in academe, politics, and grassroots organizing. Even a partial honor roll of Jewish women's liberation pioneers must include such figures as Shulamith Firestone, Ellen Willis, Robin Morgan, Alix Kates Shulman, Naomi Weisstein, Heather Booth, Susan Brownmiller, Marilyn Webb, Meredith Tax, Andrea Dworkin, Linda Gordon, Ellen DuBois, Ann Snitow, Marge Piercy, Letty Cottin Pogrebin, and Vivian Gornick.

Despite historians' acknowledgment of the salience of Jewish women in earlier social movements, their prominence within radical feminism failed to attract much attention. Well-known histories of second-wave feminism, including those by Sara Evans, Alice Echols, Ruth Rosen, and Susan Brownmiller, do not identify the contributions of Jewish women to the women's liberation movement. Benita Roth's study of black, Chicana, and white pathways toward feminism does not accord a distinct place to Jewish women but subsumes them under whiteness. Winifred Breines's study of black and white women in second-wave feminism refers to many radical feminists who are Jewish but treats them simply as white and does not explore differences within that category.[3]

By making the Jewish component of the radical feminist movement visible, I hope to offer a deeper understanding of the complexities of feminist activism and the multiple political issues in which feminists inevitably became involved as the movement developed and feminist consciousness expanded. This excavation is necessary because Jewish women's participation in this movement has been hidden for several generations. To recover this history, the book documents and assesses the depth and diversity of Jewish women's participation in a wide range of feminist activities and actions within the second wave of the women's liberation movement broadly defined. It examines both the early women's liberation movement and the later, more self-consciously identified "Jewish feminist" movement that arose in the 1970s and 1980s to address Jewish religious and secular life. Analysis of these two groups offers a fuller picture of second-wave feminism and an enhanced understanding of the relationship of Jewish women's liberationists and Jewish feminists to their non-Jewish counterparts. Even though, at first glance, the objectives, politics, and profiles of Jewish women's liberationists and Jewish feminists may seem divergent, their stories are interrelated. Interrogating the connections between these two branches of feminist endeavor will help to revise what Sara Evans has criticized as the "homogenized" narrative of the second wave and to create what Stephanie Gilmore describes as a "capacious definition of feminism."[4]

To foster such an understanding, I brought forty representatives of the two branches of Jewish-inflected feminism together for a two-day conference titled "Women's Liberation and Jewish Identity" at New York University in April 2011, asking the women to reflect on their personal motivations for activism and the role of Jewishness in their lives and the movement.[5] A number of these women had created the first radical feminist groups in the country, including women's liberation groups in Chicago, Boston, New York, and Atlanta; others represented the subsequent wave of explicitly Jewish-identified feminists who initiated significant social change in Jewish-based secular and religious life. Over the ensuing decades, many leaders in both groups pursued their activism in striking ways: increasing women's participation in religious and communal life; organizing for improved health care and reproductive rights; advocating for consumer, welfare, and housing rights; protecting the homeless, the aging, and low-income workers; and much more.

Those who became writers and scholars are responsible for landmark works in women's art, culture, politics, and history.[6]

But by and large, the two groups that attended the conference—the women's liberation feminists who are Jewish and the Jewish-identified feminists—had not met each other or directly interacted before. Most of the women's liberationists had not been involved in activities within the Jewish community, nor had most of the Jewish feminists participated in broader movement activities. My goal in convening the conference was to introduce and probe the stories of these two groups of feminists in relation to each other and to larger narratives of feminist and Jewish activism and to place these accounts on the historical record.

While some of the speakers were wary about participating in an event that segregated Jewish feminists from their non-Jewish allies, they found themselves deeply engaged in conference dialogues and excited to learn from feminists with different experiences and perspectives. The diversity of views about Jewishness and radical feminism exhibited at the conference mirrored the main themes of this book: that Jewishness and feminism profoundly impacted each other and the revolutionary feminist movement of our time. Separately and together, they are complex amalgams, modified and reinterpreted over time but building on customs, values, and traditions that grew out of particular heritages as well as changing social locations. Conference presenters demonstrated the multiple ways in which, from these beginnings, feminism unfolded over the course of their lives, offering a vivid portrait of political and social activism that is astonishing in its breadth and originality.

The book's chronicle of Jewish radical feminism correlates with the main thrust of second-wave feminism, from the late 1960s through the mid- to late 1980s. The women who shaped this movement were a distinct "political generation," according to sociologist Nancy Whittier. Whittier believes that those who entered the movement at about the same time "identified as belonging to a common group" that set them apart from later feminists and thus constitute a "mini-cohort"—"a group with distinct formative experiences and collective identity that emerged at and shaped a particular phase of the women's movement."[7] My analysis suggests that in addition to the particular time at which women entered the movement, the racial, religious, and ethnic factors embedded in their activism differentiates their collective identities from other second-wavers and from each other.

Recovering the Jewish stories of second-wave radical feminists can help us to understand the varied meanings of Jewish life in late twentieth- and early twenty-first-century America, when traditional modes of religious and community belonging have given way to more personal and varied affiliations and choices.[8] These stories also provide crucial links in the chain of Jewish women's activism over time. Exposing the shared cultural values that drew Jewish women in numbers disproportionate to the population into these social movements connects "the feminist and the Jew," as leading feminist organizer Heather Booth said at a conference at Brandeis University. It is a way of passing on the "legacy to change the world"; we can "reinforce what drives us forward and correct what holds us back."[9] Such markers of identity, reflecting positive aspects of Jewish social values, should have substantial appeal to young twenty-first-century Jews as they seek to construct individual and collective meanings of Jewishness in a world where identity is increasingly chosen voluntarily.

The feminist activism of Jewish women builds on the legacy of the past. Jewish women participated in and led successive movements for social change in America—as garment workers, trade unionists, suffragists, campaigners for birth control and reproductive rights, anarchists, socialists, communists, civil rights workers, peace activists and antiwar protesters, and more.[10] Their numbers in these radical movements far exceeded their numerically small representation in the population at large, paralleling or surpassing those of their male coreligionists as well as those of U.S.-born and other ethnic women. Jewish women's participation in second-wave feminism is similarly compelling, not only because of the prevalence of these women in feminist ranks but because of the formative impact of Jewish background and values on them, even when not consciously acknowledged, and on the movement as well. Although Jewish women struggled with their own ambivalence and anger about Jewish religious and social customs that tended to marginalize them, they were inevitably shaped by their inheritance.

The generational chasm between these women and their parents and grandparents may well have been narrower than it was among other young radicals during the 1960s, since many Jewish rebels were strongly motivated by their parents' radical backgrounds and their moral and religious values.[11] Although the story of Jewish feminist activism is fundamentally one of gender rebellion, it is also about an intergenerational Jewish legacy. At the same time, clashes over Jewish norms, religious traditions, and family patterns motivated other Jewish radical feminists and helped shape their political identities. Post-1960s radical feminism differed markedly from Jewish women's activism before the 1960s, which historian Melissa Klapper describes as an organic fusion of Jewish identity and women's organizational affiliations that flowed from the gendered ideology of maternalism, which celebrated the civic values of motherhood in both the private and public spheres.[12] Most Jewish radical feminists, to the contrary, engaged in a no-holds-barred struggle against maternalism.[13] The confluence between Jewishness and activism served as a driving force for some radical feminists, but it is more difficult to locate and gauge in this later period.

How and why young women related to this powerful, transformative movement and what role Jewishness may have played in their activism are questions that can illuminate the influences of gender and ethnic inheritance on social activism and feminism.[14] These explorations can also elucidate the many ways that Jews, as a minority ethnic group in a postmodern, postethnic world, chose and constructed their identities. As we explore these issues, context becomes extremely important. Geographic location, family background, class position, religious affiliation, the place of the Holocaust, views of Zionism and experiences in Israel, civil rights and New Left involvements, new ideas about gender, sexuality, and activism—all were important determinants of the interactive and dynamic influences of Jewishness and Judaism on women's liberationists and, through them, on the movement itself.[15] This story forms a critical counterpart to that of the disproportionate presence of Jewish youth in the civil rights and student movements of the 1960s.[16]

In addition to creating a richer portrait of second-wave feminism, I hope that this book expands our understandings of American Jewish history, which historian David Hollinger has characterized as unnecessarily narrow due to the neglect of "dispersionist" aspects of Jewish history in favor of a single-minded focus on Jewish "communalist" history. By "dispersionist," Hollinger refers to the lives of all persons with "ancestry in the Jewish diaspora," no matter what their extent of "declared or ascribed Jewishness." As opposed to such "scattering," "communalist" history focuses on the "organizations and institutions that proclaim Jewishness" and the "activities of individuals who identify themselves as Jewish and/or are so identified by non-Jews with the implication that it so matters." Hollinger cites the failure of scholars to probe the Jewish origins of radical feminism as the primary example of the deficient historical analysis that he observed. Calling for an "ethnoreligious demography of feminism" that can anchor an "expanded compass," he argues that if "Jewishness were as central to our histories of feminism as Protestantism is to our studies of the civil rights movement," then the contributions of Jews might be better "integrated into our mainstream histories.[17] Jewish women's activism as second-wave feminists can serve as a prototype for a new and vital reconsideration of American Jewish history.

Liberal, Radical, and Jewish Feminism

"Women's liberation," though often broadly applied to second-wave feminism, in fact refers to the radical wing of the movement, as distinguished from "liberal" or "equal rights" feminism, the feminism of Betty Friedan and the National Organization of Women (NOW). Whereas liberal feminists called for increasing women's opportunities for individual independence and meaningful careers, women's liberationists demanded a complete restructuring of society and culture, including the abolition of normative, constricting definitions of masculinity and femininity—and, for some leading radical feminists, of the nuclear family and gender differentiation itself. These two types of feminists also differed in their organizational profiles, strategies, and tactics. Based in organizations such as NOW and state commissions for equal rights, liberal feminists pursued traditional forms of protest such as lobbying, picketing, marches, and lawsuits; nevertheless, they highlighted individual change. As women's liberationists sought to transform the root structures of society, they joined in more fluid, "amoeba"-like consciousness-raising groups, creating theory that brought together the "personal and the political" and engaging in creative, often dramatic forms of direct action.[18] Although by the mid-1970s the two branches converged around many ideas and strategies, different orientations remained, often across a generational divide.

The second wave of feminism was composed of distinct currents of activism. Several of them, including liberal feminism, included Jewish participants (according to one estimate, about 12 percent of the women in NOW were Jewish).[19] The Jewish pioneers of women's liberation were conspicuous in the earliest groups of radical, as opposed to liberal, feminists. I have found that in some collectives in large cities, two-thirds to three-quarters of women's liberation participants may have been Jewish. The Jewish makeup of several of these collectives was an open secret for some participants, suspected but not explicitly recognized. Jewish identity usually remained invisible, ignored, or thoroughly rejected. Nowhere did Jewish-identified women's liberationists participate as an organized group within the movement.

In the early 1970s, a second stream of feminism developed, representing the newly self-conscious "Jewish feminist" movement. Consisting of religiously and secularly identified Jews, these women helped to transform ideas about and practices of gender within and beyond the Jewish community. Using lessons learned from women's liberationists, Jewish-identified feminists called for immediate redress of inequalities in religious and Jewish communal life.[20] While religiously based Jewish feminists generally saw a basic harmony between Judaism and women's liberation, some at first dissented from prominent feminist themes, particularly regarding the nuclear family and reproductive rights. Feminism's embrace of radical individualism was generally absent from Orthodox Jewish feminism, although not from most liberal denominations. While some people in Orthodox Jewish feminists' communities saw the women as "radical fanatics," these feminists considered themselves as authentic religious Jews and as activists and change agents.

In embracing the demand for expanded rights and obligations for women, Jewish feminists promulgated an agenda consonant with that of second-wave feminism.[21] They were directly influenced by the work of second-wave radical feminists and personal encounters with them. Some religious feminists were closer to the liberal stream of women's liberation than to the self-identified radical one, but these women, too, dedicated themselves to changing gender norms that subordinated women within Jewish community life and religious texts and traditions.

I use the term "radical feminist" in a capacious, open-ended way to refer to all the women in this book who sought such transformations.

In contrast to religiously Jewish feminists who targeted inequality in the synagogue and seminary, secular Jewish feminists waged all-out war on what Aviva Cantor, a Radical Zionist, called "the assimilation game," asserting the need for Jewish women to proclaim their distinctiveness as Jews rather than to blend into the mainstream. For these women, trying to "pass" meant committing "cultural suicide."[22] While promoting Jewish identification, they linked their struggle as Jewish women fighting patriarchal institutions to larger efforts to eradicate capitalism, racism, and sexism. To be fully aware of themselves as Jewish women was a first step toward combating the multiple causes of social oppression.[23] But this commitment included supporting the liberation of Jews along with that of other subjugated groups.[24]

Jewish lesbian feminism was another vital component of radical Jewish feminism. For Evelyn Torton Beck, who edited the landmark 1982 collection *Nice Jewish Girls: A Lesbian Anthology*, becoming visible as a Jew within the feminist movement paralleled the process of coming out as a lesbian.[25] Beck and her contributors descried the invisibility of Jewish women in the movement, especially lesbians, speaking to the fear and dangers Jewish women experienced when identifying themselves as Jewish feminists. Worse yet, they remained vulnerable to anti-Jewish feelings within that movement. "Writing as a Jew," Beck observed, "the feminist takes the risk of losing her place."[26]

Jewish lesbian feminists also had to fight against the homophobia within Jewish communities. Neither Jewish space nor lesbian space offered them a haven. Because LGBT people were not welcome in synagogues, dozens of lesbian and gay groups were created across the country. Publicly claiming their identities as Jewish lesbian feminists became part of the campaign to challenge the universal oppressions of women and minorities.

In the early years of Jewish feminism, assertions of identity politics tended to separate feminists from others in the Jewish community who saw their strong stance on gender issues as potentially threatening to Judaism. Women's liberationists either rejected separatist Jewish feminism or ignored it. But increasingly, as religious Jewish feminists successfully critiqued ancient patriarchal customs, women's liberationists supported their attempts to overhaul masculinist systems within Jewish religious and community life. "If we are able now to speak as feminists in the Jewish community," Alisa Solomon wrote, "it's only because we first learned to speak as Jews in the feminist community."[27]

A sudden explosion of concern about anti-Semitism in the women's movement in the late 1970s that continued through the 1980s became another site for the acknowledgment and development of Jewish feminist identity that this book chronicles. At a time when historians and many Jewish communalists pronounced anti-Semitism to be of declining importance within the United States, radical feminists faced contentious debates about this issue at conferences and meetings at home and abroad and in the feminist press.[28] These controversies raged among Jewish women, as well as between them and non-Jewish feminists and Third World women.[29]

The issue of anti-Semitism within the women's movement surfaced at three UN World Conferences on Women held in Mexico City, Copenhagen, and Nairobi during the UN Decade for Women, 1975–1985. A "Zionism is racism" plank passed at the Mexico City conference in summer 1975 set the stage for the Zionism-is-racism UN General Assembly resolution a few months later, shocking many previously unidentified American Jewish feminists into a new awareness of their Jewishness. At the International Women's Conference in Copenhagen in 1980, anti-Zionism and anti-Semitism resurfaced in even more blatant forms, with openly anti-Semitic attacks on Jewish women from Third World delegates and the passage of a resolution calling for the elimination of Israel. Although a Zionism-is-racism resolution was defeated at the UN World Conference on Women in Nairobi five years later, harsh condemnations of Israel and ubiquitous anti-Zionist and anti-Semitic rhetoric alarmed Jewish attendees and colleagues in their home countries.[30]

Tensions over these issues escalated within the United States as well, with accusations of anti-Semitism and racism splitting apart longtime alliances, including many African American and Jewish women. These difficult conflicts spurred consciousness-raising about the intersections of ethnicity, race, religion, sexual identity, class, and other differences. Many Jewish women discovered themselves as Jewish feminists for the first time. Unlike many earlier women's liberationists and Jewish feminists, they adopted a dual agenda composed of struggles against both sexism and anti-Semitism.

A smaller group of Jewish women saw these issues differently. Allying themselves with Third World anticolonialists and antiracist struggles, they opposed Zionism as a project of military occupation and state force and did not support Israeli nationhood. Prioritizing the political goals of anti-imperialism, anti-Zionism, and solidarity with Palestinian and Third World struggles, they began to debate issues of anti-Semitism, Zionism, and anti-Zionism with Jewish-identified feminists.[31]

Such opposing perspectives might have reflected what Deborah Dash Moore calls "Jewishly inflected identity politics," which had grown out of Jewish involvement in the New Left. "No longer could one claim an identity as a Jew and then adopt whatever politics one desired," Moore explained. "Politics and identity were intertwined."[32]

Jewish Universalism versus Jewish Particularism

The women's movement acted as a crucible for change both in society at large and in the Jewish community, providing opportunities to channel values inherited from Jewish tradition, especially those promoting social justice and *tikkun olam* (repair of the world). For many women, feminism opened the door to activism by addressing feelings of marginality that Jewish women had experienced growing up. Yet, like the white women who went south on Freedom Rides in the 1960s, most radical feminists did not self-consciously identify as Jews.[33] At a time when the vision of a common sisterhood took primacy within the movement, the claims of any particular ethnic or religious group, especially one identified with white privilege, could not hold sway. Even when radical feminists acknowledged their Jewish roots in a manner that historian Matthew Frye Jacobson identifies as part of a wider "ethnic revival," they refrained from explicitly asserting that ancestral inheritances drove the momentum for change.[34]

Movement activists especially held back from making such a connection. "Our identification with the outside world, in opposition to our parents' narrow . . . views, was rebellious and progressive, a response against the broader society's divisions by ethnicity and religion," said

Vivian Rothstein, a member of the West Side Group and a founder of the Chicago Women's Liberation Union. "Why would we identify ourselves as Jews when we wanted to promote a vision of internationalism and interfaith and interracial solidarity?" "We identified as universalists," agreed Paula Doress-Worters of the Boston Women's Health Book Collective. "We were afraid of seeing ourselves as too driven by our particularities; it wouldn't have been proper to call ourselves radical Jews. But that is exactly what we were."[35]

Yet the embrace of universalism over particularism was itself very Jewish. As Ezra Mendelsohn points out, for many Jewish adherents of universalism, "the very vision of the essential unity of mankind . . . was a Jewish vision, invented by the greatest humanists of all, the Hebrew prophets."[36] Like universalism, secularism was important to modern Jewish social thought. "Jewish secularism is a revolt grounded in the tradition it rejects," argues David Biale, citing Isaac Deutscher's often-quoted remark about "the non-Jewish Jew," made in a 1954 speech. The "Jewish heretic who transcends Jewry belongs to a Jewish tradition," Deutscher asserted.[37]

Although Deutscher had his eye on European intellectuals, including Spinoza, Marx, Freud, Trotsky, and Rosa Luxemburg, the same could be said of American radical thinkers and activists such as Emma Goldman, who celebrated the Day of Atonement, the holiest night of the Jewish year, at the anarchists' festive Yom Kippur Ball. Individuals such as these moved beyond the confines of Jewry, crossing boundaries they considered too narrow. "Their minds matured where the most diverse cultural influences crossed and fertilized each other," Deutscher wrote. They lived on the margins or in the nooks and crannies of their respective nations. "They were each in society and yet not in it, of it and yet not of it."[38] Like their European forebears in this tradition, pioneer Jewish women's liberationists in the U.S. were well assimilated into the culture of their times, but nevertheless, in disclosures to this author and at public events related to this project, they acknowledged a sense of difference based on their ethnicity and gender. This otherness helped take these activists "beyond the boundaries of Jewry," in Deutscher's words, enabling them to "rise in thought above their societies, above their nations, above their times and generations . . . to strike out mentally into wide new horizons and far into the future."[39]

Jewish women had been prominent in social movements, both in Europe, where they constituted one-third of the membership of the eastern European socialist bund in the early twentieth century, and in the United States, where disproportionate numbers of Jewish immigrant women played active roles in the socialist, anarchist, and trade union movements.[40] While Jewish women mixed with like-minded men and women from other ethnic and racial groups, more often than not they agitated alongside other Jews, their proximity a natural outcome of common upbringing and beliefs as well as their concentration in neighborhoods and occupations. Jewishness was a factor that supported the universal goals of these social justice movements, but often with conflict and ambivalence. As Tony Michels elaborates in his study of New York City Yiddish socialists, questions of Jewish identity, culture, and community were problematic for radicals trying to reconcile competing claims of Jewish group identity and wider spheres of community in the early twentieth century. Their struggles brought into sharp focus a major issue facing Jews in the modern world: "How should Jews define themselves in relation to the larger society and community of nations in which they live?"[41]

The issue was particularly acute for Jewish women, who encountered deep-seated prejudice from male radicals and co-workers, even from other Jews, and confronted an invidious gender division of labor in the workplace and political organizations. To be a Jewish woman radical meant to question the place of the individual in regard to the state, the shop floor and factory, and the synagogue and religion, as well as to interrogate the presumed boundaries between domestic and public life and fundamental inequalities of gender and power.

Many Jewish women in the early twentieth century flocked to reform as well as radical causes, working to alleviate the infirmities of class, injustice, and poverty suffered by their immigrant coreligionists, alongside a host of other campaigns to improve the lives of Americans. They were sometimes motivated by non-Jewish women's activism in the public sphere, but the acknowledgment of special Jewish interests and the taint of Christian women's organizations' anti-Semitism led them to form their own organizations, such as the National Council of Jewish Women and Hadassah, and to join alliances of Jewish women's groups, such as the World Council of Jewish Women. Many of these women identified as Jewish feminists but found little difficulty in affiliating with secular as well as Jewish women's organizations. They could locate their primary allegiance in the Jewish community but still recognize themselves as "sisters" who banded with other women in search of solutions to the vexing problems of women's lives.[42]

In both the interwar and postwar eras, once seen as periods when feminism was "in the doldrums," Jewish women engaged in multiple activist causes, including women's rights, birth control, and international peace, which according to Melissa Klapper provided them opportunities for "gendered activism without abandoning Jewish meaning."[43] For members of the National Council of Jewish Women, the National Federation of Temple Sisterhoods, the Workmen's Circle, and other organizations, Judaism and Jewishness were sources of activism, compelling the women's involvement in wider causes. Klapper sees little discontinuity between Jewish women's organizations and secular ones.

I believe that the connection between Jewish women's activism and explicit Jewish motivations was much less explicit in the social movements of the 1960s than in the earlier period. The Jewishness of Jewish men and women involved in the civil rights, student, antiwar, and New Left movements took diverse forms, but at the time, most young Jewish student activists did not consider their ethnicity or religion to have motivated their social action. Although Jewish women made up a considerable proportion of the women who participated in sit-ins and Freedom Rides, Debra Schultz argues that these young women did not identify Jewishly, even though Jewish values and backgrounds were positive influences on them. Rather, their antiracist activism was "one expression of a universalist concern with justice that has roots in Jewish history, ethics, and political radicalism."[44]

Universalist concerns propelled Jewish student activists in other 1960s social movements. Jews accounted for about one-quarter of the white Freedom Riders and a significant proportion of volunteers who journeyed to Mississippi to register voters. Approximately one-third to one-half of New Left activists were Jewish, including the membership of Students for a Democratic Society (SDS). They were highly represented in the free speech movement that arose at the University of California at Berkeley and in the student-led antiwar movement. Even when compared to the relatively high proportion of Jews in the university population (10 percent among the general college population), these numbers suggest the degree to which Jewish youth were overrepresented in New Left activism.[45] But few identified Jewishly at the time, preferring to see themselves as socialists, internationalists, and civil rights and human rights workers.[46]

Like New Left activists generally, liberal feminists in the second-wave feminist movement included many Jewish women. Particularly notable was Betty Friedan, who made little of her Jewish (and left-wing) origins until the mid-1970s, and Bella Abzug, elected to Congress in 1970, who with Friedan, Gloria Steinem, and others founded the National Women's Political Caucus. Although Abzug had a more pronounced connection to Zionism and the Jewish community than Friedan did, her Jewish identity and connections played a less direct role in her championship of women's causes than in her lifelong peace activism. Steinem, whose father was Jewish, has said that she identifies as a Jew "whenever there is antisemitism."[47]

The Jewish radical feminists who helped create the women's liberation movement of the late 1960s had even less reason to emphasize their Jewish upbringings than did the Jewish women of NOW, the National Women's Political Caucus, and other liberal second-wave organizations. A full generation or younger than Friedan and Abzug, they had grown up in postwar rather than Depression America, their Jewish families generally well integrated into the mainstream. Most had made it into the middle class, though some occupied its insecure lower rungs. Beginning in the late 1940s, anti-Semitism began to decline, and although it never disappeared completely, Jewish children generally grew up without facing the open prejudice that some members of the previous generation had encountered. Coming of age in a world where religion increasingly seemed to be a private matter, particularly and symbolically after the election of John F. Kennedy as president in 1960, the rising feminists of the late 1960s did not fear the stigma of Jewishness—or pay much attention to their Jewish identity at all.

They believed that the struggle that they had to engage concerned their place as women in a world of pervasive gender inequality. It was sexism, and not the limits of ethnicity, that called them into battle.

The Ambiguities of Racial, Class, and Cultural Belonging

The revolutionary potential of radical feminism lay in the way it channeled women's feelings of otherness into a protest against the social structures and prejudices that marginalized and excluded them. Women from many racial, ethnic, and class backgrounds participated in the assault against the patriarchal status quo. As social historians continue to correct the more monolithic accounts of this uprising, we see that a movement originally characterized as racially white and economically middle class was much more varied in its leadership and constituencies than previously recognized.[48]

The combination of gender marginality with racial, class, ethnic, and sexual otherness led to accumulated experiences of subordination and difference, fueling women's anger and channeling their insights. On the edges of the majority society, these women were more motivated to see the flaws in the conventional structures of society than many others were. Despite the high achievements of Jewish women and the successful assimilation of many of their families into the American mainstream, many perceived themselves as part of a minority group and shared feelings of alienation.

Yet Jewish women's liberationists were more likely to have experienced the personal impact of privilege than of social and economic deprivation. Scholars such as Karen Brodkin have suggested that Jews transitioned over the course of the twentieth century from "racial other" to "not-quite-white" to "white," distinctly American categories that were socially constructed on the basis of the racial binary between blackness and whiteness but also carried class implications.[49] For Brodkin, becoming fully "white" allowed a previously marginalized minority to reap the rewards of power and material success but came at the price of adopting mainstream social norms, particularly regarding gender, about which Jewish women were ambivalent.

Some Jewish youth dissociated themselves from the culture of prosperity in which they had been raised. "By being radicals we thought we could escape our Jewishness," commented Mark Rudd, who led the 1968 student uprising at Columbia University. "Left-wing radicalism was internationalist, not narrow nationalist; it favored the oppressed and the workers, not the privileged and elites, which our families were striving toward." Jewish radicals retained a sense of themselves as never quite blending in. "We Jews at Columbia—and I would guess at colleges throughout the country—brought the same outsider view to the campuses we had been allowed into. We were peasant children right out of the shtetls of New Jersey and Queens," Rudd said. Although he did not recall a single conversation in which radicals discussed their Jewishness, he said, "all of us were Jewish": "[SDS] was as much a Jewish fraternity as Sammie."[50]

Many second-wave feminists sensed that as Jews, their backgrounds differed from those of other movement activists. Childhood encounters with anti-Semitism and the experience of McCarthyism, which targeted Jewish political and labor activists, and especially the influence of the Shoah imparted a powerful sense of difference. Some radical feminists had direct experiences with the Holocaust as the children of refugees or as child refugees themselves, while others had close relatives who had perished or been displaced. A generation of young women who grew up in the lingering shadow of World War II instinctively grasped the importance of collective action as a bulwark against violence and victimization.

For some Jewish women's liberationists, the legacy of social justice bequeathed to them as children of Yiddishists, anarchists, socialists, and communists served as the most powerful springboard to activism. Their activism demonstrates that the link to the radical tradition of Jewish life did not end when a majority of Jews left the working class and that Jewish women, who had been prominent in social movements in the first half of the twentieth century and in the later civil rights movement, continued to play a vital role in social justice movements.[51]

The women's movement enabled many Jewish women to escape from the suburban, parochial, confined environments where they had been brought up as well-behaved, acculturated daughters of the middle class.[52] Some of these rebels from materialism and conformity, a stance that prevailed among those who would most readily fit Brodkin's description of the postwar Jews who became "white," ardently declared war on sexism, class and gender inequality, and homophobia as well.

Even though these women might have been "insiders," as a matter of background and style, the women often felt like "outsiders." "The consciousness-raising movement made it okay to be different," commented one woman at the NYU conference. For example, "it normalized being loud, bookish, talking with your hands"—the outward characteristics that others frequently saw as Jewish.[53] Jewish women's feelings that they stood outside the dominant culture's frame of womanhood may have increased their sense of otherness, but it also shaped their abilities to critique patriarchy and encouraged new theoretical stances and innovative problem solving.

The range of motives for political and social protest associated with Jewish roots was thus quite varied. For radical feminists, it could be associated with religious beliefs; a set of attitudes toward social justice; a tradition of intellectual debate; emotions and feelings involving marginality and insecurity; a leadership style marked by assertiveness and articulateness; or a set of affiliations to schools, camp, synagogue, shul, or parents. These influences were combined in different ways, ebbing and flowing in consonance with individual and group experiences. For most of the Jewish women's liberationists, attitudes concerning gender discrimination were much more salient at the time than were Jewish influences, even though these had unacknowledged significance.

Yet many radical feminists who might be considered "non-Jewish" Jews utilized Jewish culture and political traditions to promote goals of the women's movement. Against the backdrop of Jewish patriarchy, they were empowered by examples of strong, nurturing Jewish parents or other role models and by Jewish secular and religious values handed down through generations. "Believing in freedom and justice and the struggle for freedom itself was a Jewish value," Heather Booth remarked. Booth explained what Judaism came to mean: "I valued the struggle for freedom and felt tied to a people who had an obligation to continue that struggle."[54]

Maximalists, Minimalists, Intersectionalists

Those who initially identified as Jewish feminists came to embrace Jewish particularism as an essential step on the road to their own liberation. When, in the early 1970s, the first idealistic understandings of gender universalism began to evaporate and were soon replaced by an emphasis on differences among women, these Jewish feminists began to pay attention to the markers of ethnic or religious identity. They viewed themselves as "maximalists" in regard to Jewish identity, as opposed to more "minimalist" women's liberationists.[55] For them, Jewishness signified personal identity, inherited values, and community.

Goaded by radical feminism's powerful attack on patriarchy, Jewish-identified feminists mobilized explicitly as Jews and began to carry on the fight against sexism within Jewish religious and community life. Despite the fact that women's liberationists provided them with useful tools they could wield in their fight against patriarchal oppression, their struggles could be painful and divisive. Could they be revolutionaries, be committed Jews, *and* navigate the gender divide in ways that would break the back of centuries of Jewish patriarchy? Would they lose standing in the Jewish community? Would they become isolated or marginalized within the feminist movement?

For both Jewish women's liberationists and Jewish-identified feminists, identity was never single themed. Given that all persons have multiple identities and that power dynamics exist on multiple grids simultaneously, as political scientist Marla Brettschneider puts it, oppression is not "crystallized into one single aspect of our group identity."[56] In Audre Lorde's powerful words, "There is no such thing as a single-issue struggle because we do not lead single-issue lives."[57]

Like the African American women whose widely influential 1977 Combahee River Collective Statement asserted that women's identities were marked by multiple, linked oppressions, Jewish women who identified Jewishly, apart from the wider feminist movement, shared a similar unease with universalist feminist models.[58] Jewish women noted the pioneering work of women of color in creating a new intellectual feminist framework, acknowledging that the new consciousness had emboldened them to explore their own multiple identities.

Critical legal studies scholar Kimberlé Crenshaw coined the term "intersectionality" in 1989 to describe how different power structures interact in the lives of minorities, especially black women, causing "compound and overlapping" discrimination.[59] For Crenshaw, a key idea was that each group needed to go beyond critique to consistently explain its own experiences and create its own theories, "so it's incorporated within feminism and within anti-racism."[60] The term immediately gained a toehold in the field of feminist and critical studies, but for the most part, Jewish women's position was excluded from consideration in relation to the interlocking issues of race, class, gender, and sexuality that framed this discourse.

While some Jewish feminists acknowledged the opportunities that their race and economic circumstances provided, they saw their invisibility within these new discourses as itself a symptom of "radical otherness."[61] In similar ways, Jews who attempted to become part of what Eric Goldstein calls the "multicultural rainbow of minority groups" had also met with resistance. Sharing a sense of "alienation and disengagement," some Jewish women protested that the notion of "undifferentiated whiteness" did not apply to them. They preferred to view themselves as an "off-white" race, constructing their identity from a "double vision" that came from what Karen Brodkin called "racial middleness."[62] Still other Jewish women's liberationists resisted the assertion of Jewish distinctiveness. In their view, an attitude of "Jewishness first" masked the privileges of whiteness that many midcentury Jews enjoyed.[63] Yet entering the world of American whiteness meant more than privilege, Goldstein explains; it could involve the loss of communal cohesion and a concomitant increase of alienation and psychic pain.[64]

Like attitudes toward race, ethnicity, color, and culture, Jewish women's choice between maximalist or minimalist approaches to Jewish feminist identity was a matter of background and personal predilection. These choices could seem baffling, irrelevant, or of deep significance. Moreover, the decision as to where to place oneself on the spectrum of Jewish feminist identity could change over time and vary in different circumstances. For example, feminist antipornography activist Andrea Dworkin, who never affiliated with a Jewish group, told an interviewer in 1980, "Everything I know about human rights goes back in one way or another to what I learned about being a Jew." She recalled a time in childhood when she witnessed the collapse of a concentration-camp survivor who had been in the midst of narrating her experiences to Dworkin's family. "Later, when I began to think about what it means to be a woman," Dworkin asserted, "it was that experience that I called on. Everyone's history is central to the way they think. . . . In my particular case, my Jewishness is the background that's most influenced my values."[65] Yet her opinions on Israel, Jewishness, and Judaism remained ambivalent and fluid.

The difficult task of locating Jewishness as a contributing factor to feminism and its salience in personal and public identity unfolded in a conversation between Fran Moira, an editor of the women's liberation magazine *off our backs*, and Jewish lesbian feminist writer and scholar Evelyn Torton Beck in 1982. "I don't know how my voice as a Jewish woman is different from my voice as a woman," Moira told Beck. "It's not that one's background doesn't make any difference," said Moira. "I feel a close identification with Jewish history, with certain ways of being, ... but ... I don't see where all that matters to what we're doing now, how we relate to one another, and what we want. I see us all being equally aware of what we would consider the injustices in the world." "There's a big difference between just being Jewish and being consciously Jewish in the world," Beck replied. "In a way, it changes our whole experience."[66]

That conversation encapsulates the varied experiences of Jewish radical feminists recounted in this book. The rich and diverse set of narratives that emerges highlights a multiplicity of identity patterns and activist engagement during these formative decades.

Life Stories of Feminists and Their Collectives

The story of Jewish women in radical feminism may be seen as simultaneously diachronic, evolving over time and incorporating issues of legacy and roots, and synchronic, occurring at a particular moment because of strategies, tactics, and opportunities taken by specific individual actors and collective groups. In contrast to the continuous historical developments that characterize diachronic history, synchronic understandings emphasize the structure of the present and the interrelations between groups. Both modes—the historical and temporal, describing how individuals and their generational cohort change over time, and the sociological, portraying the demographics and social structure at a particular moment—help to convey the richness and variety of Jewish women's radical feminist activism and its underlying causes. Another framework employed in this book, which is applied both to individuals and to generations, focuses on the dynamic, psychological process of identity formation over the life course.

Taken together, these perspectives illuminate why and how Jewish women shaped women's liberation and how they in turn were shaped by it. As historian Linda Gordon observes, change happens "through a group process that provides a sense of belonging in a new community."[67] These narratives reveal how the "belonging" that came from Jewish values and traditions played a complementary role in creating identity and social change.

The notion of Jewishness in constant development, shaped by relationships, feelings, beliefs, and actions, as well as by broader social changes over time, parallels feminist emphases on individual autonomy and transformation, as well as postmodern or "postethnic" ideas about Jewish identity described by such scholars as David Hollinger, David Biale, and Shaul Magid.[68] For Bethamie Horowitz, Jewish identity was not a unitary, fixed factor but "multifacteted and multi-dimensional."[69] This notion of fluidity, which goes against the grain of the inherited or behavioral measures of Jewish identity, accords well with Erik Erikson's classic psychological perspective, which defines identity formation as a process experienced as an individual moves through the life course. The emphasis on flux and change is also central to the idea of "cultural identity" articulated by Stuart Hall, the influential Afro-Caribbean scholar who founded critical cultural studies in Britain. For Hall, "cultural identity" entails "becoming" more than "being." Identities can "undergo constant transformation," he wrote. "Far from being eternally fixed in some essentialised past, they are subject to the continuous 'play' of history, culture and power."[70]

In my book *The Journey Home: How Jewish Women Shaped Modern America*, I used the notion of "journey" to encapsulate the ways in which over the course of the twentieth century, American Jewish women movers and shakers frequently found themselves guided "home" by influences from their Jewish heritage. These were often powerful but unacknowledged. Bethamie Horowitz similarly considers Jewish identity to encompass "how Jewishness unfolds and gets shaped by the different experiences and encounters in a person's life. Each new context or life stage brings with it new possibilities. A person's Jewishness can wax, wane, and change in emphasis. It is responsive to social relationships, historical experiences and personal events" as individuals navigate "interior journeys" in subjectively meaningful ways.[71] The stories in this book show flux since they include retrospective accounts of previously unexamined Jewish backgrounds. While such themes may not have reached conscious levels of examination in the 1960 and 1970s, they emerged as salient to life choices and values when women were prodded by later events or my own inquiries.

In addition to the idea of identities-in-flux, this book highlights the notion of collective struggle and collective identities. Radical feminists drew attention to the multiple ways that group affiliations serve as markers of women's lives. They brought to their movement a sense that while the individual was a starting point for remedying injustice, only shared experience would overcome the demons in the outside world and in women's own heads that denied them respect and agency. When the individual is linked integrally with the collective, the "personal is political" and "sisterhood is powerful."[72]

For women's liberationists and Jewish feminists, belonging to a collective unit was fundamental to the perception of self. Rather than being dichotomous with individual identity, collective identity provided mutual respect, an understanding of the social world, and the strength to act efficaciously.[73] Historically, Jews located the individual's basic identity within the larger entity of the Jewish people; Rabbi Hillel's admonition not to "separate yourself from the community" remained a guiding ethical principle through the ages.[74] Similarly, second-wave feminists recognized that the deepest wellsprings of selfhood derived from shared experience in the group. As Linda Gordon wrote of the women's movement, "'collective' was a sacred liturgical word and 'individualist' a damnation."[75]

Bringing together the individual and the collective, this book embeds the personal narratives of dozens of Jewish women's liberationists and Jewish-identified feminists within the framework of the small group or collective, the organizational structure that typified the women's movement. While for centuries, the minyan of ten adult Jewish males required for public worship has been essential to traditional Jewish religious and communal life, the all-female women's collective served as the engine of feminist community building in the late twentieth century. Perhaps it is no coincidence that the paradigmatic feminist collective studied in this book consisted of approximately ten members.

As Kimberlé Crenshaw has emphasized, women need to "tell their stories," to document, explain, and theorize about the interlocking themes, meanings, and oppressions of their lives, restoring what has been invisible and erased so as to articulate "what difference the difference makes."[76] Telling the stories of Jewish women who became feminists from the late 1960s through the 1980s is the project of this book. It is my hope that in presenting these stories, the individuality of the actors, along with the ties that bound them to each other, emerges intact. These multiple yet intertwined narratives provide a catalogue of Jewish women's diverse pathways to feminist activism. Their accounts and viewpoints create an intersectional history of lives-in-process, taking us beyond binary categories and oversimplified theories. Rather than a template that presents set patterns, the women emerge as a polyphony of voices encapsulating the distinctiveness, individuality, and fluidity of diverse experiences. By speaking to "what difference the difference makes," they enable us to understand the multidimensional significance of being both Jewish and feminist during this formative period.

To collect these stories, I interviewed Jewish women involved in women's liberation and Jewish feminism in several major urban centers and convened the NYU "Women's Liberation and Jewish Identity" conference in 2011.[77] These women's recollections and reflections, supplemented by archival and print research about their lives and times, anchor this book.[78] I include a few additional individuals whose trajectories intersect with the women and collectives discussed and whose viewpoints provide additional perspectives. Among them are several non-Jewish founders of the Boston Women's Health Book Collective, who offer especially valuable insights. While the book focuses on collectives in Boston, New York, and Chicago, the outlooks and histories that emerge can elucidate the choices and perspectives of Jewish radical feminists in other cities and regions. The varied stories of these activists bear witness to the heterogeneous experiences of Jewish women and their influence on second-wave feminism.

Based on unstructured interviews that enabled narrators to reflect on their own choices and histories, these biographies take us deep into the construction of identities, providing "thick descriptions" of lives in motion. They immerse us in unique journeys of feminist activism, chronicling influences, motivations, turning points, conflicts, and struggles that the women regarded as Jewish related. Whichever aspect each woman may have placed as primary, she lived at the nexus of multiple identities. From converging locations of gender, ethnicity, class, sexuality, religion, race, age, and region, the narrators traveled to the social movements that drew in so many others of their cohort, providing a basis for joint action.

A part of the second-wave cohort (birth years 1936–1955), the majority of subjects in the book were born in the 1940s. A good many belonged to the minicohort that Nancy Whittier labels "the initiators," inaugurating the earliest phase of the movement; other second-wave minicohorts included founders (1970–1973), joiners (1974–1976), and sustainers (1977–1984).[79] According to Whittier, the time of joining the movement determined participants' collective identity even more than age did, reflecting shared social circumstances, political messages, and other synchronic factors. The narrators in this book came into the radical feminist movement at various moments during the heyday of the second wave, carrying with them the particular perspectives that stemmed from the context of their everyday lives and the outside world. But they also brought heritages from family and ethnic backgrounds that influenced their political socialization and coming of age.

I begin this history in 1967, a moment in time that marked divergent directions for radical women and radical Jews. Tumultuous meetings of the New Left's National Conference for New Politics (NCNP) over Labor Day weekend in Chicago that year left in their wake two failed resolutions relating to women and to Jews. The refusal to consider a resolution developed by Shulamith Firestone, Jo Freeman, and their Women's Caucus set the stage for Firestone's and Freeman's creation of West Side, the first women's liberation group in the United States. With other early groups, West Side helped to spawn the rapidly expanding feminist movement throughout the country. By a three-to-one margin, the convention did pass a resolution condemning the 1967 Arab-Israeli conflict as an "imperialist Zionist War"; this resolution was introduced—and then rescinded—by the Black Caucus.[80] For some feminists, the popularity of the anti-Zionist resolution at the NCNP harbored a troubling anti-Semitism and made it difficult for them to identify as Jewish women on the left.

I see this moment in 1967 as inaugurating disparate yet often converging paths to complex Jewish and feminist identities. Over the next two decades, women's liberationists and their successors shaped and refined an autonomous radical movement, and secular and religious

Jewish feminists prompted a sweeping transformation of Jewish life. Each group was influenced by varied amalgams of heritage, background, networks, and relationships. The book ends in the late 1980s, with the First International Feminist Conference for the Empowerment of Jewish Women in Jerusalem and other emblems of the new global directions of Jewish feminism.

The book treats the two branches of Jewish radical feminism as distinct though interconnected. Part 1 tells the stories of approximately twenty Jewish women in women's liberation collectives, including Chicago's West Side Group, New York's Redstockings and New York Radical Women, and Boston's Bread and Roses and the Boston Women's Health Book Collective. Part 2 presents narratives of another twenty women in the religious feminist group Ezrat Nashim, the Jewish Student Network, the Brooklyn Bridge and Chutzpah collectives, and the Jewish lesbian feminist collective Di Vilde Chayes. The final chapter of part 2 takes the development of Jewish feminist identities to locales across the nation and globe, chronicling tensions around anti-Semitism, racism, and anti-Zionism. The conclusion and epilogue assess the varied pathways to feminist and Jewish identities during these decades and provide thumbnail sketches of six younger women whose lives demonstrate changing amalgams of gender and Jewish identity.

For a good number of the women whose Jewish and feminist lives are chronicled in this book, the conversations and conference led to a renewed exercise in consciousness-raising. Indeed, at the conference, West Side Group member Vivian Rothstein described me as an "instigator" as well as a historian for asking women's liberationists to excavate the Jewish influences in their lives that had remained buried. But she and almost all other narrators were enthusiastic about reclaiming this past and placing it for examination alongside other feminist stories. For some, the excursion into the Jewish aspects of their histories was unfamiliar and potentially uncomfortable, yet they ventured into this arena with keen interest. In inviting the women to remember, I hoped to encourage them to pursue memories and to try out ideas, rather than determine the directions they might follow. As "reminiscing subjects," they framed their own narratives in interaction with my prompts, constituting themselves in multiple ways as participants in this mosaic of ethnic feminist history.[81]

While demonstrating individual influences and motivations, the stories also reveal themes that result from common social locations and shared beliefs. In the life story, as Janet Giele explains, "the subject passes through thick and thin to emerge a distinctive individual, driven by a unique identity that is interactively shaped by the culture of origin and subsequent social forces."[82] Focusing on shared sociocultural contexts, such narratives represent more than isolated, idiosyncratic accounts. In this book, they offer clues to factors that determined Jewish and feminist identifications, among them historical location, social relationships, personal motives and individual traits, and adaptation to major life events.[83]

Using life stories in this collective fashion, the book evokes prosopography, an investigation that relies on "writing history in sets of multiple biographies." A primary means of studying marginal groups, prosopography is especially applicable to the history of Jewish women because it emphasizes a "catalogue of lives side by side" as well as the life narratives of individual women. In this way, it can bring out "affinities or traditions," with the assembled biographies representing both "the individual and the group."[84] Informed by subjects' memories and reflections, the composite stories create a framework for analysis of multiple, overlapping, feminist identities, which today we recognize as intersectional. Sometimes dominant and definitional, at other times crosscutting or conflicting, the women's collective identities as feminists and Jews responded to social context variables as well as individual experiences and histories. While these hybrid identities were not always uppermost at the time, they served important social, psychological, and political functions and demonstrate distinctiveness, meaning, and historical resonance.[85] These multiple stories become keys to an expanded history of second-wave feminism and a more complex understanding of Jewish identity.

"What would have changed if you acknowledged your Jewish identity at the time?" historian Alice Kessler-Harris asked women's liberationists at the NYU conference, an admittedly counterfactual question.[86] A question that might have been posed to the Jewish-identified feminists there is equally counterfactual: what would have changed if you had not been forced to struggle for validation of your identity within the feminist and Jewish communities? Or if anti-Semitism had been less of a present and frightening force at home and abroad, both among feminists and in the wider world? While such hypothetical questions have no answers, the memories and perspectives of these women tell us a great deal about the way that history did in fact happen. Their stories and those of other Jewish second-wave feminist activists offer fresh perspectives on a movement that did so much to change the ways that we understand and imagine our world.

Connections to both the individual and collective struggles of these pioneering feminists can provide a framework for understanding contemporary struggles for belonging and usable models of inquiry and social change. At a moment in time fraught with increasingly complex personal and political challenges for Jews and feminists, the chronicle of these sometimes frayed but often linked bonds offers pathways for claiming meaningful identities and for comprehending the dynamic social movements that have shaped our lives.

PART I

"We *Never* Talked about It"

Jewishness and Women's Liberation

1

"Ready to Turn the World Upside Down"

The "Gang of Four," Feminist Pioneers in Chicago

This chapter highlights the story of four young Jewish feminists—Amy Kesselman, Heather Booth, Naomi Weisstein, and Vivian Rothstein—who were in the vanguard of the women's liberation movement in Chicago as it took shape in the late 1960s. At the time of their involvement with the first glimmerings of women's liberation, none of these pioneering radical feminists recognized themselves or acted as "Jewish" women seeking a revolution in sex and gender roles. Like the Jewish women who went south to participate in the civil rights struggle a few years earlier, they "just didn't think of it then."[1] The powerful ideology of the new women's movement drew them and colleagues of other faiths and backgrounds into a common endeavor that they hoped would radically change society.

The women chronicled their experience as radical feminists and their remarkable friendship in the article "Our Gang of Four: Female Friendship and Women's Liberation," published in *The Feminist Memoir Project*, a 1998 anthology.[2] All four were part of the West Side Group, the nation's first sustained women's liberation group, which began in Chicago in 1967.[3] Friendships such as those that developed among Heather Booth, Amy Kesselman, Vivian Rothstein, and Naomi Weisstein formed a pivotal part of second-wave feminism; they were "central to the energy and insights that emerged among women's liberation activists in the 1960s," the Gang of Four wrote.[4] Female friendships empowered women and the movement, becoming the matrix for its revolutionary ideas.

"Our Gang of Four" focuses on the women's family histories and their involvement in the social movements of the 1960s. The one feature that is not mentioned, except in the case of Rothstein, the daughter of Holocaust refugees, is the women's Jewishness. Until I contacted

Amy Kesselman, the four friends had never spoken about their Jewish backgrounds to each other—neither in the article nor in forty years of friendship. Perhaps this was because they perceived little commonality to their Jewish identities or because the issue had never arisen in their feminist work. Or perhaps the women sensed an antagonism between the particularities of ethnicity and religion and the dream of universality that guided the women's movement. Because they were secular Jews or atheists, the meaning of Jewishness in their lives had been camouflaged by the cultural association of Jewishness with religion and, for some, with middle-class striving and privilege. In the views of some in the group, American Jews had seemed to turn away from a commitment to a social justice agenda. Also problematic was that Judaism did not offer women a central role. Like others in women's liberation, the four friends focused their attention on class and race as they intersected with the problems of sexism. It was unclear how the constituent elements of American Jewish life fit into this framework.[5]

As a consequence, the bond of Jewishness among the women remained invisible, though implicit, in their friendship. Only when I came to the four with questions about Jewish identity and its relation to women's liberation did they begin to explore Jewishness as a personal and political issue. We conducted two long telephone conversations, one about the women's backgrounds and beliefs as Jews and feminists and the other about the Holocaust, and also shared correspondence on these topics. The stories that emerged point to the significance of Jewishness in these women's lives, influences that were melded with value systems that developed from the women's participation in the social networks of their cohort.

Although at the time of the women's involvement in the movement, they did not acknowledge Jewish influences on their activism, the Gang of Four came from significant but different Jewish backgrounds: secular Yiddish / Communist Party radicalism; Orthodox-Conservative suburban; outsider refugee. Each had some Jewish education, whether formal (Yiddish shul, synagogue, and Hebrew school) or informal (Jewish community centers or Labor Zionist camp). Heather Booth framed it this way: "Many of the elements of Judaism were consciously part of my upbringing." While several would have specified an antireligious Jewishness rather than Judaism, they might well have shared her appraisal.

For each of the four, ethnic/religious background came together with other elements of personal and collective identity that molded the early women's liberation movement. "I couldn't say where one [part of my identity began and one] ended," Booth said. "Was I who I was because I was in a loving family, because we shared common values, because I was a woman, because I was white, because I was in Brooklyn? They were all part of a common definition." Fluid and multiple, the varied aspects of identity intermingled, becoming more or less salient over time, depending on social context and the life course. For these women's liberationists, Jewishness was one of the primary constituents of this mix.

The story of Marilyn Webb forms a coda to this chapter. In graduate school at the University of Chicago, Webb met the Gang of Four and other Chicago feminists and joined the movement to liberate women from the oppressive beliefs and structures of their lives. Moving to Washington, D.C., she was instrumental in starting D.C. Women's Liberation, one of the most vital of early movement groups. With Shulamith Firestone, Webb participated in a foundational moment of radical feminism at the Nixon counter-inaugural rally in Washington in 1969. Like other Jewish women's liberationists, she disregarded her Jewish identity during her movement years, only connecting to her roots decades later.

Amy Kesselman, Heather Booth, Vivian Rothstein, Naomi Weisstein: "Our Vision of Beloved Community"

In 1966, fifty women, including Heather Booth and Marilyn Webb of Chicago, attended a national conference of the radical organization Students for a Democratic Society (SDS), at the University of Chicago.[6] For three days, the women discussed a memo written the previous year by Mary King and Casey Hayden about sexism in the Student Nonviolent Coordinating Committee (SNCC). The first to publicly air grievances against male superiority in the civil rights movement, the memo encouraged the women to think about their own experiences with SDS's sexual politics, but they were not yet ready to break with the male-dominated New Left.[7]

The following year and through 1968, groups of young women's liberationists spontaneously formed throughout the country, organizing to protest the sexism they confronted in everyday life, including on the

New Left. Shulamith Firestone, a twenty-two-year-old former Orthodox Jew from St. Louis, was one of the Jewish women whose actions helped to stimulate the rise of women's liberation in Chicago; other early centers of women's liberation activism included Seattle, Detroit, Toronto, and Gainesville, Florida.[8] Memos and workshops that grew out of SDS and the civil rights movement had been precursors to the formation of these groups.[9]

Firestone, a young artist studying at the Chicago Art Institute who was unknown to other Chicago activists, came into the spotlight during a weekend convention of the National Conference for New Politics (NCNP) held in Chicago on Labor Day 1967. About two thousand activists had gathered at the conference to debate the Vietnam War, black nationalism, and whether to run a third-party ticket headed by Martin Luther King, Jr., the convention's keynote speaker, and one of the radical youths' most admired figures, Dr. Benjamin Spock.[10]

Backroom conniving mixed with pandemonium on the ballroom floor at Palmer House, where the convention was held. A women's caucus met for days, framing a minority report that called for free abortion and birth control; an overhaul of marriage, divorce, and property laws; and an end to sexual stereotyping in the media. But conference chairman William Pepper refused to accept the women's report, calling it insignificant. He told them that in any event, he already had one from a women's group, Women's Strike for Peace, even though theirs addressed peace issues, not gender. Allowing a young man to address the NCNP about a Native American resolution, Pepper refused to permit women's caucus representatives to speak. "Infuriated, we rushed the podium," activist Jo Freeman recalled, "where the men only laughed at our outrage. When Shulie reached Pepper, he literally patted her on the head. 'Cool down, little girl,' he said. 'We have more important things to do here than talk about women's problems.' Shulie didn't cool down and neither did I. . . . The other women responded to our rage. We continued to meet almost weekly, for seven months. . . . We talked. And we wrote."[11]

Following the incident, Firestone and Freeman organized the Chicago West Side Group, so named because it met at Freeman's house on the west side of the city. In addition to Freeman and Firestone, members included Amy Kesselman, Fran Romanski, Laya Firestone (Shulamith's sister), and Heather Booth and Naomi Weisstein, whose course on women at the Free University at the University of Chicago, first taught in 1966, served as a catalyst for Freeman.[12] Vivian Rothstein, Sue Munaker, and Evelyn (Evi) Goldfield came six months later, with Linda Freeman and Sara Evans Boyte joining within the year. These dozen women were the regulars, although another dozen or so variously attended meetings.[13] The West Side Group used the phrase "women's liberation" in an early article and in its newsletter, the *Voice of the Women's Liberation Movement*, published from 1968 through 1969, helping to spread the goals of the movement around the country.[14]

"Ready to turn the world upside down," in Naomi Weisstein's words, the West Side women "talked incessantly": "We talked about the contempt and hostility that we felt from the males on the New Left, and we talked about our inability to speak in public. Why had this happened? All of us had once been such feisty little suckers. But mostly we were exhilarated. We were ecstatic."[15] It was as if the NCNP "had broken a dam," Sara Evans wrote in *Personal Politics*, one of the first histories of the movement. When the Chicago women heard the message— "sometimes in the form of the words 'women's liberation'—their first response, over and over again, was exhilaration and relief."[16]

Jo Freeman gave Heather Booth credit for spinning off new women's liberation groups in Chicago, where several new groups formed. Through the New Left, "she had the connections," Freeman recalled, "and she had the commitment."[17] Shulamith Firestone, who left Chicago for New York a month after the founding of West Side, helped organize the first women's liberation meeting in New York two months after the Labor Day conference in Chicago. By the next spring, Firestone had prodded the New York group, which took the name New York Radical Women, into producing its first collection of writings, *Notes from the First Year*. When Kathie Amatniek (later Sarachild), another New York feminist activist, visited Boston, she persuaded her childhood friend Nancy Hawley to join the growing women's liberation movement. The following year, Hawley was part of an informal women's group that would write the revolutionary women's health book *Our Bodies, Ourselves*.

The Jeannette Rankin Brigade Protest, a January 1968 peace action in Washington, D.C., organized by the West Side Group and New York

Radical Women, helped to promote the movement and, in a flier created by Kathie Sarachild, introduced what was to become its trademark
slogan, "Sisterhood Is Powerful."[18] The movement was spreading like
"wildfire," commented Ann Snitow, a member of New York Radical
Women. "We called ourselves brigades and we founded a whole bunch
of other brigades; we cloned ourselves."[19]

By April 1968, approximately thirty-five small radical women's
groups concentrated in big cities were on the map; by the end of the
first year, there was "hardly a major city" without one or more.[20] The
groups formed spontaneously, as women sought each other out for support and to discuss specific abuses.[21] While focused on general women's
liberation issues, each group reflected the overall emphases of the area
in which it formed.[22] "New York City is the culture capital. Chicago,
heavy industry. We were the edge, you the heartland," Rosalyn Baxandall of New York City wrote to Naomi Weisstein, pointing to one of the
regional differences that shaped early radical feminist groups.[23]

To create a wider coalition, Marilyn Webb and several colleagues
organized the first nationwide gathering of women's liberationists at
Sandy Springs, Maryland, in August 1968. There, twenty participants
spent a tense fall weekend arguing about whether men or capitalism was
the greater enemy and castigating themselves for the failure to involve
black women in the incipient movement. As an outcome of the meeting, Webb, with Laya Firestone of Chicago and Helen Kritzler of New
York, organized a conference to commemorate the 120th anniversary of
the first women's rights convention at Seneca Falls. Due to their efforts,
two hundred women came together at a YWCA retreat in Lake Villa,
outside Chicago, during Thanksgiving week, but this larger meeting was
also wracked by controversies between "politicos" (arguing from the
New Left position that women's oppression derived from capitalism)
and pro-woman "radical feminists" (urging an autonomous women's
movement since men were the ultimate oppressors).[24]

In Chicago, the West Side women wrestled with their allegiance
to the male-dominated Left but believed that their group marked an
important step away from the masculinist emphases of SDS. After years
of being "judged and humiliated" by New Left men, Amy Kesselman
exulted in the fact that she had comrades with whom she could openly
develop her ideas. But separating from the New Left was extremely

difficult—like "divorcing your husband," she said. Several members of West Side were in fact married to SDS "heavies": Heather to Paul Booth, a former SDS vice president; Naomi to historian Jesse Lemisch, a member of the original SDS at the University of Chicago and then Northwestern University; Vivian to activist Richie Rothstein.[25]

Nonetheless, the Chicago women felt that their position inside SDS was "no less foul, no less repressive, no less unliberated" than outside: "We were still the movement secretaries and the shit-workers."[26] They tried to find a balance between the socialist perspectives they shared with male leftists and their conviction that it was essential to challenge male supremacy. The attempt to find a middle ground is reflected in an April 1968 paper, "Toward a Radical Movement," by Heather Booth, Evi Goldfield, and Sue Munaker, which argued that "there is no contradiction between women's issues and political issues, for the movement for women's liberation is a step toward changing the entire society."[27]

Yet Jo Freeman believed that more than any other city, Chicago had a women's movement "bound by the leftist mentality." Years later, in an unpublished memoir, Weisstein admitted, "our ties to the male New Left really retarded our progress, tied up our creative energies, restricted our freedom in thinking and doing."[28] This view was shared in New York, where radical feminists believed that the Chicago Women's Liberation Union (CWLU) women "were under the thumb of the male SDSers."[29] Sara Evans believes that Chicago feminists resisted the divide between the two orientations. Although West Side was "decidedly politico" at first, historian Alice Echols agrees, organizing around such non-gender-specific issues as opposition to the Vietnam War, the group became women-centric.[30]

As West Side members sought to develop their own political agenda, Kesselman, Booth, Rothstein, and Weisstein looked to each other for "political support and guidance, consulting each other about almost everything [they] did."[31] Each of the four had come to Chicago for different reasons. After Weisstein completed her doctorate in psychology at Harvard, she took a postdoctoral position at the University of Chicago and then, briefly, a faculty position at Loyola University. Rothstein had participated in the Mississippi Freedom Summer Project in 1965 and then went to Chicago to be an organizer with the SDS project JOIN Community Union, to "build a multi-racial movement of the poor."[32]

Kesselman, who had become an activist at City College in New York, moved to Chicago because it seemed to her "like the belly of the beast: the perfect place to build a revolutionary movement."[33] Booth studied at the University of Chicago, where she founded the first campus women's movement organization and started Jane, an underground abortion service that assisted more than eleven thousand women end their pregnancies prior to the legalization of abortion with *Roe v. Wade*.[34]

After the creation of the citywide CWLU in October 1969, Rothstein became the organization's first (unpaid) staff member, responsible for developing a workable structure, and a contributor to many of the organization's theoretical writings; she inaugurated the Liberation School for Women, which offered skills-based and subject-matter courses relating to women and families. With Weisstein, she organized the CWLU Speakers' Bureau. Booth helped organize CWLU's Action Committee for Decent Childcare (ACDC) and brought women into the CWLU to work with Jane. Trained by doctors who had performed the abortion procedure for Jane, after a time, women of the collective began to do the procedure themselves. Kesselman used her background as an SDS organizer to develop CWLU's workgroups, one of its distinctive features. Weisstein had the idea for the Speakers' Bureau and, in 1970, created the Chicago Women's Liberation Rock Band, feminism's first rock group, which aimed to liberate rock from "sexist evil" and create a "revolutionary women's culture."[35] Although the band lasted only three years, Weisstein believed that it presented "an image of feminist solidarity, resistance, and power," offering "absolute democracy, the players and the audience together in a beloved community, . . . a world without female suffering or degradation."[36] The band produced one album, *Mountain Moving Day*, with two songs written by Weisstein, the title track and "Papa, Don't Lay That Shit on Me." Weisstein, who loved comedy and came "*this* close to running off" with Chicago's famed Second City troupe, gave the band its distinctive performance style and comic tone.[37]

The CWLU became a model for sixteen other socialist-feminist women's liberation groups throughout the country. At its peak, the organization counted fifty core members, with two hundred participating in workshops and chapters and another one hundred members at large. Hundreds of others took classes at the Liberation School, came to the pregnancy-testing clinics, or called the rape hotline; its mailing list reached nine hundred by the end of the 1970s. Most members were young, white, middle class, and highly educated, a pattern typical of women's liberation groups at the time. As Margaret Strobel discovered in her interviews with forty-six CWLU leaders, the homogeneity of the group extended even further: all but one of her sample were of European descent and included a noteworthy proportion—43 percent—of Jewish women.[38] Consonant with its socialist-feminist framework, the CWLU focused on building solidarity with working women, continually attempting to extend its outreach to poor, working-class, and minority women through its service projects and the Liberation School. The large number of Jewish women in its membership went unnoticed, but Jewish women were among those who most vociferously attempted to diversify the organization.

"We Hit the Glass Ceiling on the Left": The Route to Chicago

Born in 1939 (Weisstein) and in 1944–46 (the others), the members of the "Gang of Four" grew up in the golden age of the "feminine mystique": Heather Booth in Bensonhurst, Brooklyn; Amy Kesselman in Jackson Heights, Queens; Naomi Weisstein on the West Side of Manhattan; and Vivian Rothstein in Los Angeles. While the messages that they received from their parents were often positive and purposeful, the values of the surrounding society left them, in Kesselman's words, "feeling alienated from just about everything." Kesselman absorbed "political consciousness" from her left-activist parents, but "in the fearful atmosphere of the McCarthy era," such messages seemed "muted and confused." She became an activist, organizing a high school discussion group even though she was told that "politics, sex, or religion" were forbidden topics. In her senior year, Kesselman was suspended for several days for protesting the civil defense drills that perpetuated the belief that "standing against the wall could save us if a nuclear bomb dropped on New York City."[39]

Naomi Weisstein's high school experience was little better. After two years in an all-girls school, she transferred to the prestigious Bronx High School of Science, and her world "collapsed": "All my music, my art, my writing, my acting in plays, my power, standing, and popularity, that I enjoyed in the first fourteen years of my life vanished in a day, as it became clear that the only thing that girls were judged on was their ability to negotiate the world of heterosexuality. . . . I can still feel my resentment, rage, and despondency at this state of affairs, especially because it seemed as if my future were closing down on me."[40] Like Kesselman, Weisstein had grown up "in the church of socialism." Intuitively, she recognized that politics would be a part of what she did with her life, while even in this prefeminist era, she assumed that the domestic "mystique" would not. "I knew that my life could not be devoted to husband and children," Weisstein wrote in *The Feminist Memoir Project*, "that I must have a career, and it wouldn't be such a bad thing if I didn't marry at all." But in that "harsh, repressive, and wildly woman-hating decade" (Weisstein was "ten in 1950, twenty in 1960"), she could not openly proclaim her beliefs. Thus, she said, "I was in the closet most of the time on two accounts—my socialism and my feminism."[41]

High school also presented a challenge to Heather Booth, whose family moved from Brooklyn to Long Island when she was a teenager. Booth became head of several high school clubs but could not find a way to engage the values of social responsibility passed on by her parents. Like Weisstein and Kesselman, she began protesting even before college, dropping out of the school sorority and one of the cheerleading teams "when it was clear that they discriminated against blacks and girls who did not fit some standard definition of 'pretty.'" Like the others, she was ready for other meaningful activity.[42]

As a child of German Jewish immigrants who fled from the Nazis in the late 1930s, Vivian Rothstein's coming-of-age years differed from those of her friends. Because her parents were refugees from Nazi Germany, she had a "keen sense" that she was a "person potentially at risk": "they could come after us at any time." Rothstein acknowledged that it was this fear that led her to gravitate toward other groups at risk: "not just to help them out, but to protect myself." This feeling, combined with the absence of her father (who had separated from her mother), made Rothstein feel "like an outsider looking into mainstream America." She, too, was a "ripe candidate" for 1960s activism.[43]

The moment came soon enough. Amy Kesselman entered City College in 1962, interested in "read[ing] Marx instead of doing homework." Soon she was president of the campus committee against the war in

Vietnam. Yet with her male colleagues, Kesselman felt "stupid and inadequate," her activism filled with "petty humiliations and frustrations."[44] After college, she moved to Chicago to work with an organizing project with high school students, but she again found herself stymied by male leaders' hostility to women peers.

Vivian Rothstein became a scholarship student at the University of California at Berkeley, a member of the first generation in her family to go to college. While a student, she participated in mass civil disobedience actions organized by CORE, then dropped out of school to become a full-time organizer, first in Mississippi and then for JOIN Community Union in Chicago. But neither the civil rights nor New Left movement welcomed her as a "leader or as an intellect." There seemed to be room for her "only as a body going limp in mass demonstrations."[45]

Naomi Weisstein flourished in Wellesley's all-female atmosphere but had a difficult time studying for her Ph.D. in Harvard's psychology department, where she faced sexism and the "heterosexual juggernaut." Moving to New Haven for her dissertation work, she joined CORE but was shocked to find that she was terrified to speak publicly. "I didn't understand it at all," she recalled. "I didn't understand it until Chicago, until Heather and I started talking about women's position in these movements for social change."[46]

In 1960, still in high school, Heather Booth joined the effort to aid CORE's sit-ins to support African American students' boycott of Woolworth's. At the University of Chicago, which she entered in 1963, she joined SNCC and went on the Mississippi Freedom Summer Project the next year. In 1965, after learning that a friend from the Summer Project had become distraught over an unwanted pregnancy, she began the Underground Abortion Collective, Jane.[47] Booth chafed at the sexism in the student movement around her. At one large meeting, when a male student told her to "shut up," she did. But, she said, "that was the beginning of our own organization, the Women's Radical Project (WRAP), which became one of the most dynamic groups on campus."[48]

As Vivian Rothstein recalled, "We had hit the glass ceiling on the left and there was nowhere for us to go. We were hungry for political discussion with others who took us seriously, and slowly we began to find each other."[49] Weisstein and Booth met at a University of Chicago sit-in in 1966; they "shared their consternation about how few women were speaking and talked about their own struggles and frustrations."[50] They then co-taught a course at the University of Chicago organizers' school. The following year, Kesselman met Booth at a draft counseling office. After their first two-hour conversation, Kesselman felt as if she "had been awakened from a deep sleep": "together we figured things out." Later she met Weisstein, who was "astounded" by Kesselman's comments about the importance of agency in people's lives. "I wanted to talk to Amy forever," Weisstein recalled.[51] Rothstein met Booth at the 1965 SDS conference in Champaign-Urbana, which held the first separate meeting of women radicals. She met Kesselman through the Chicago Organizers Union. In 1967, Booth, Kesselman, and Rothstein came together to discuss tactics for getting involved in justice campaigns.[52]

"Throughout 1966 and '67," Kesselman wrote, "Heather, Naomi, and I talked about what it meant to be female in our society at every possible opportunity. Each time we talked, we generated new insights. The world seemed to be coming dramatically and miraculously into focus."[53] "The best part of the group was that we all took each other seriously," Weisstein agreed. "We had become so used to the usual heterosexual chill that it was a giddy and slightly terrifying sensation to talk and have everybody listen. All of a sudden we were no longer inaudible . . . the joy! Unbelievable. The sound system had just been turned on. We couldn't wait to go to meetings."[54] After Rothstein joined the West Side Group, she became the fourth member of the "gang," the others drawn to her "sense of moral purpose, her intelligence, and her unshakable commitment to organizing."[55]

"Our appreciation of each other was like fertilizer," Kesselman recalled, "liberating energy long stifled by the sexism of the male leadership of the new left."[56] "We were so different," Booth remembered. "We were so similar. We were so courageous. We were so insecure. We called forth the best in each other. We called forth what we did not even know was there. We were more than the sum of our parts."[57]

As the women's movement spun off other new projects and ideas, the friendship of these four women flourished. There was none of the ambivalence that Kesselman felt about her female friendships at the male-dominated City College, where women seemed to accept their marginality.[58] In Chicago, the friends came together to talk, study, organize, and protest, emboldening each other as they joined a larger group to start a feminist revolution. How did they come to take this path together? Did Jewishness have anything to do with it?

Growing Up Jewish: Yiddish Radicals, Jewish Mothers, the Holocaust, and Israel

Growing up Jewish during the years of the postwar feminine mystique influenced each woman's maturation into left activism and feminism. Despite the lack of any explicit Jewish identification, the influence of Jewish values and experience was significant.

For Amy Kesselman, growing up as the child of secular left-wing Yiddishists was a formative influence on her developing political views.

> My parents were . . . communists until the 50s. They had both rejected the religion of their immigrant parents but in the wake of the Holocaust they embraced their Jewish identity as a political act and were determined to communicate a secular Jewish identity to their children. We never went to synagogue except when visiting my grandparents who spent the high holidays at a Jewish Old Age home. But we did celebrate Chanukah and Passover. The menorah always stood at the window to show people in the neighborhood that we were Jews and we sang the spiritual Go Down Moses at our seder. After the war my parents joined with other secular, progressive Jews to organize a "shul" in our community that would teach their children Jewish history, Jewish folksongs and the rudiments of Yiddish, all of which was infused with progressive politics—a hatred of dictators and Jew haters, a belief in struggle. I think the shul achieved its primary goal: making us identify as Jews and to feel a connection with down trodden people. It was less successful in teaching us Yiddish.[59]

The heritage of secular Jewishness played a role for Naomi Weisstein as well, though her Yiddish skills remained similarly undeveloped. "My mother was very atheist, and her father, my grandfather, who had come from Russia, used to sit on the steps of shul on Yom Kippur, eating a ham and cheese sandwich. They had a sort of positive commitment to secular Jewishness and a rabid anticlericalism. But they did send me to Yiddish school, not Hebrew school, so that I could learn the folkways of my people. I couldn't stand it because I am very bad at languages.

Finally Mrs. Lerner called my mother and asked, 'Is Naomi retarded?' My mother took me out. Why pay for this?"[60] Although Weisstein identified as a "red-diaper" baby, she commented that given her mother's anarchist radicalism and her father's nonpolitical stance, she might more accurately be labeled a "purple and white polka dot baby." Samuel Weisstein, a lawyer, was dedicated to his clients in Harlem, for whom he worked for "pennies," but Naomi considered him "racist" in his belief that "black people were poetry" and "childlike," needing his protection. Then there was the influence of her maternal grandparents, her Menshevik grandfather and Bolshevik grandmother. Because of these forebears, Weisstein acknowledged, "I am infused with the Jewish radical tradition."[61]

Also identifying as "secular Jewish," Heather Tobis Booth absorbed the Judaic values of social justice in her childhood and adolescence. This tradition became a vital lens with which she interpreted the world.

> Many of my mother's family were Orthodox, some Hasidic, and lived in walking distance of each other in Bensonhurst. My mother married someone who was Conservative. When another relative married outside of Orthodoxy, the father sat shiva for the daughter. But my father was going to be a doctor. Also [my mother] was sort of a loved child with many loving members of her extended family. My father's family was also very loving and close.
>
> My mother became anti–organized religion. But many, many of the elements of Judaism were consciously part of my upbringing, so I couldn't say where one [part of my identity began and one] ended. . . . I thought being Jewish meant sharing values—believing in freedom and justice and the struggle for freedom itself. The holidays were very important— what is Passover but the struggle for freedom that ends up being successful? This is true for many of our holidays, celebrated in many of our traditions—standing up for what is just and right. Even the Bible says, "justice, justice shalt thou pursue." Twice it says "justice," because it is that important.[62]

Once asked how she got to be the way she was, Booth responded, "some people get to be radicals by having [to] break from the past, whereas we felt very consistent with it."[63]

Vivian Leburg Rothstein believed that her "Jewishness played a role" in her "ability to be a critic of American culture and in becoming a feminist." "My parents fled Nazi Germany and already felt at risk and outsiders in the U.S. So I naturally shared some of their sense of alienation and separateness. Plus I was aware that their European social values clashed with the Puritanical American standards of the general society."[64] For Rothstein, "fear of persecution, separation from mainstream American society, identification with 'outsiders,'" coupled with "a need to find others who shared [her] story, . . . to coalesce . . . for mutual protection," propelled her activism.[65] Although her apolitical parents did not question much about American life, they were deeply concerned about moral issues, especially "what happened to Jews" and the possibility of fascism. Rothstein absorbed their values and understood the experience of minorities well.[66] But as the child of immigrants, with the added stigma of divorced parents, she felt excluded from mainstream American life. At school, she was treated as "something a little odd," "foreign" and "deprived," isolated by school administrators. Rothstein's sister reacted to the same circumstances by becoming mainstream.[67] Rothstein became a lifelong radical.

In addition to parental models, the education provided in synagogues and more informally through community centers, camps, and travel impacted the women's social values. Rothstein's family went to synagogue for the High Holidays but were not synagogue members. She grew up in the Jewish Center community, "which offered an alternative Jewish life. That way Jewish children could have an identity that was anti-religious but not ritualistic—camps, after school sports programs, etc." The Jewish Center gave Rothstein a community-based opportunity for Jewish engagement outside temple membership, connecting her to Jewish culture, rituals, and holidays. This was particularly important for young girls not offered the bat mitzvah experience and so lacking the mentoring provided by that training. The center's focus on community service was equally important. Rothstein learned to function as part of a group and became comfortable in group life, lessons she carried with her to her lifelong work as activist and organizer. For Rothstein, and later for her children, Jewish community centers offered education about Jewish traditions and values without being intensely religious. They became building blocks of identity.[68]

Rothstein's involvement in the Labor Zionist camp Hashomer Hatzair, to which she went for about three years, reinforced these experiences. The organization was "actively recruiting and training young people to fight for the state of Israel and be prepared for kibbutz life." Rothstein described what the Jewish youth learned: "to overcome our fears and be brave (breaking into school grounds, crossing borders with 'forged passports'); seeing ourselves as fighters who make personal sacrifices for a larger goal." Hashomer Hatzair emphasized the need to share resources and "take action rather than being acted upon," introducing Rothstein to the concept of a "movement" and "being part of something larger than [oneself]." Its communal/socialist/Zionist values promoted equality between girls and boys. "I think the place I got my feminism from in terms of the Jewish community was Hashomer Hatzair. . . . Hashomer Hatzair was very radical and had a Sabra mentality; it did not believe in sex roles. We were not allowed to wear lipstick. Equality between the sexes was valued. They taught us to use rifles (never loaded), and to staff guard towers. We were supposed to go to Israel. Our leader wound up marrying an Arab guy. For this left-wing Zionism at the time, Arab culture was considered very cool."[69]

Heather Booth was deeply influenced by confirmation studies, a trip to Israel, and her progressive rabbi.

We finally ended up in a synagogue with a very progressive rabbi after some bad experiences. By this point we moved to the North Shore [of Long Island]. The rabbi played a very important role for me and I wanted to be a rabbi. Of course I was told women couldn't be rabbis (at that time), couldn't be bat mitzvahed. But I was confirmed, and my confirmation study was the Book of Amos—"let justice flow like a river and righteousness like a mighty stream"—comes from Amos. And we really studied and understood what a prophetic tradition is in order to live by its precepts. And in '63 to accompany a friend of mine who was going to Israel I lived on a kibbutz in the northern Negev. And supported an Arab who was running for mayor in a nearby city. So the tradition [was] sort of reaffirmed. It was part of who I was and what I believed in. I considered living in Israel, but returned to be part of the civil rights movement in the States.[70]

Visiting Yad Vashem, Israel's Holocaust Museum, had a "transforming effect" on Booth. The memorial to Jews who died in World War II was so horrifying to her that she went through profound emotional change. "I promised myself that in the face of injustice I would struggle for justice."[71] "I felt you never go down unless you're fighting. Never let someone else go down unless you fight for them."[72] "Judaism came to mean that I valued the struggle for freedom and felt tied to a people who had an obligation to continue that struggle."[73]

But the peer culture inhabited and shaped by Jewish men clashed with many of the positive values bequeathed by Jewish family and community. Amy Kesselman explained:

> As I became involved in politics at male dominated city college, I started resenting Jewish men, who, I told my friends, "had their penises in their heads." Men asked the five-paragraph questions in the classrooms and dominated the political movements that I was involved in. When women's liberation erupted in my life, I looked back critically on the dynamics in my family and the way they enshrined my father as the political and intellectual superior whose approval I always sought but never felt that I fully gained. . . . So my Jewishness bequeathed a mixed legacy—a commitment to social justice and anger at the sexism embedded in Jewish culture.[74]

Role models offered by Jewish mothers were a further source of confusion. Like the influence of family and community life generally, the impact of Jewish mothers was profound, yet it pulled in opposite directions. Some women's liberationists, such as Vivian Rothstein, whose refugee mother raised her as a single parent, greatly admired and respected their mothers' examples of strength and autonomy. In these women's eyes, Jewish mothers seemed more empowered than other postwar females were. Rothstein's mother offered a different model from the outset, one definitely not defined by the postwar "feminine mystique." "I grew up with just my mother," Rothstein explained. "She was the head of our family. She had left my father when I was born. I had great total respect for my mother. I was completely connected to her. I was totally in love with her." In Rothstein's opinion, most refugee mothers, such as her own, bore much of their families' financial burden. "Their husbands had been middle-class businessmen in Europe, like my father, but in postwar America, they were déclassé and couldn't find similar work. In this community, men were supposed to be the strong ones, but women ran the finances. It wasn't the feminine mystique model at all." But although her mother was self-sufficient "to an extent," Rothstein identified with her "isolation and limited role options."[75]

These women's effectiveness, as well as their nurturing and caring attitudes—"really loving kindness," as Booth phrased it—shaped daughters' values and initiated them into the Jewish tradition of social and community concern. Booth elaborated:

> I viewed my mother as sort of the mother—the mothering-ing person, which she was—and my father as the intellectual who made activity in the world. My mother's father believed women shouldn't go to college. And though she had won a scholarship to go to Hunter—she had been valedictorian in her high school—he told Hunter not to accept her, that he wouldn't accept the scholarship. So she didn't go to college until we were in high school. And then got her master's, became a special ed teacher. . . .
>
> It turns out that she also was an activist as a young person. Before World War II, part of her valedictory speech was a propeace speech. She also at one point worked selling gloves in a store and tried organizing people in the store into a union. I didn't get that kind of appreciation of her until there was a women's movement.
>
> Seeing women be active in the world in roles other than taking care of kids and being the homemaker was really exhilarating. For me, my peers, as mentors or at least friends, had at least as strong an influence in terms of feminist activism. But in terms of the values which we learn to live by, my mother (and my father) were very strong influences.[76]

But mothers' influence was rarely acknowledged. Booth recalled the 1965 SDS conference in Champaign-Urbana, where at a session on the "women's issue," participants shared personal backgrounds, including their motivations for activism. Most talked about family situations in which at least one parent gave them support. For the majority, it was fathers. No one talked about mothers.[77]

Others of the four Chicago friends felt mainly anger, and sometimes betrayal, at what they viewed as mothers' subordination to fathers and to men generally. "I really did not want to be like my mother," Kesselman admitted. "I did not think of her as an empowered person at all. And in my family she was really systematically diminished by my father who had all the brains and the political expertise; I wanted to be like him and discovered that nobody was going to let me do that. . . . There were strong women in the culture that we lived in but they were mainly seen as secondary in the life that mattered. The life of the mind."[78]

Naomi Weisstein, as the daughter of Mary Weisstein, her politically radical mother who gave up her career as a concert pianist to raise her family, made a vow: "I would never get married and . . . I would never have kids. I was sure it ruined her life." Weisstein's mother had gone to Julliard and studied with Aaron Copland; she was a brilliant pianist who combined her art with politics, performing at socialist and anarchist programs—the highlight of her life was accompanying Paul Robeson at one such event. But all her life, Weisstein's mother struggled against her husband's "male supremacy." Weisstein thought she was never going to be like her mother, "because she gave up." "She struggled all her life, but she stopped being. That was terrible as far as I was concerned." Weisstein believed "that she really hated the daughters," Weisstein and her sister, because they "had destroyed her career."[79]

But at the same time, Weisstein recognized her mother's contributions to their lives. She relished her mother's stories, especially about her own grandfather, "a Jewish Humphrey Bogart," the Menshivik from Russia who became an anarchist and union organizer and sat smoking and eating a ham sandwich on the shul steps in New York to show his contempt for religion. Weisstein tells of how this grandfather, a cabinet-maker, encountered anti-Semitism at his workplaces. "At one shop he once took a hand saw and held it in front of him. 'I hear some of you don't like Jews,' he said. 'Speak up . . .' He never had trouble there again." Her mother inherited that spirit, playing piano "like a militant angel come down from heaven to set things right in this world of injustice." When she died, the strains of Chopin's fiery "Revolutionary Etude" flooded Weisstein's head. Despite her mother's truncated career as a pianist, she did remake herself as a psychotherapist, dispensing a "decidedly unorthodox Freudianism." Weisstein remembers her standing instruction to her female patients: "Make him give you oral sex." "The legacy of resistance went from Grandpa, to Mary, to me."[80]

The women's movement provided the context for understanding mothers whose aspirations had been thwarted by the forces of postwar domesticity, even in leftist households. Kesselman had not understood the reason for her mother's departure from the Communist Party— "because people weren't nice to each other"—as a substantive political position until feminism enabled her to see that she was criticizing the party's authoritarianism. She did not understand her mother until feminism made her think "differently about the dynamics" of her family.[81]

Booth admired her mother's strong Jewish values and courage but not the limits of her domestic role. When her mother recommended that her daughter, then in high school, read Friedan's *Feminine Mystique*, which had strongly influenced her, Booth refused: "I didn't think of myself as a housewife," as her mother did. With the rise of the women's movement, however, Booth "came to understand the incredible strength and . . . real human beauty" that her mother had.[82]

Weisstein had a similar experience: "When feminism came along, I moved beyond my crude adolescent take instead to really appreciating [my mother] and thinking, my God, what a hard life, trying to continue her music when my father snored loudly whenever he heard it. What had seemed weakness on the part of mothers now became attributable to the inexorable workings of the patriarchy." At a memorial service for her mother, Weisstein declared her to have been a "true original" whose legacy, a model of "combativeness," she treasured. Despite the turmoil and conflict, her mother was her "inspiration," her "call to courage."[83]

Kesselman suggested that the characteristics validated by women's liberation, which included strength, intelligence, toughness, wit, and a kind of brazenness and boldness, might have been especially applicable to the proverbial "sharp-tongued, pushy," urban—read: Jewish— woman.[84] This might well have included mothers.

The legacy of the Holocaust exerted a significant, if silent, influence as well in shaping the attitudes of these radical feminists. "One of the things that influenced my politics in the 1960s was the lesson I drew from the Holocaust, which was the value of collective resistance," Weisstein declared in the group's discussion of this issue with me. "I'd always been a resister. But the idea . . . that you needed collective resistance to change the world and change the way things work, that occurred to me more after I started thinking about the Holocaust."[85]

Rothstein concurred. "I was affected in the way in which I understood the progressive forces, particularly in Germany, could not coalesce against the Nazis." Rothstein found that college friends on the left were in fact hostile to German Jews for not fighting back. It shocked her that such people "had no understanding really of what people went through and what they lost and really no sympathy." For years, she stopped talking to activist colleagues about her parents' experience. "It wasn't very safe."[86]

Awareness of the Holocaust was part of Booth's background as well. She saw the numbers written on the arm of her uncle Pinkus, and she thought not only about the terrors of the Holocaust but also about resistance. She felt "it was part of a long continuum of what . . . Jewish history was, a struggle for justice in the face of injustice."[87]

Kesselman did not tie the experience of the Holocaust to resistance and struggle, but nonetheless, her sense of herself as a Jew of eastern European heritage included awareness of seventeen family members who died in the concentration camps. After the war, her parents had a heightened sense of Jewish identity and sent Kesselman to a secular *yiddishkeit* shul.

In addition to the traditions, experiences, and attitudes of Jewish family and community, then, beliefs about the Holocaust played a role in shaping these women's notions about protest and collective action. A consciousness of oppression, the strong pull of social justice ideals derived from Jewish values, and a sense of themselves as outsiders, often alienated from the general culture, provided the Gang of Four with the ability to view women's condition critically and helped to galvanize their commitment to work for radical change. The women's movement provided insights that were crucial.[88] In so doing, it helped them move beyond the lessons of postwar female subordination to create new identities as empowered women.

"We Never Talked about It": Jews in the Feminist and New Left Movements

As Weisstein framed it in our group conversation, "even though our families were dissenting Jews, Jewish values permeated our lives." Yet this influence went unacknowledged. As Weisstein put it, "we *never* talked about it."[89]

Several reasons explain this silence. For example, Weisstein suggested that there was a tacit agreement to ignore the substantial presence of Jews in the New Left and women's liberation. Any undue attention might well have compromised the notion of universality. "Our holding back about our Jewish backgrounds related in part to a general approach to Jewishness that was widespread in the New Left," Weisstein said. "I had grown up in the hothouse of New York City Red Diaper Baby politics— for me this included participation in the Young Communist League and the Bronx High School of Science Forum—and when the New Left and then feminism began to emerge, we wanted to build a broader movement than those we had grown up in, and wanted to convey that our new movements were not just a repeat of the Old Left, which we identified, I think correctly, as disproportionately Jewish."[90]

Like Weisstein, Kesselman rejected "the creation of separate communities, the fierce defense of 'our kind' of people, blind loyalty to a group." She recalled, "I have a vivid memory of sitting in my parents' kitchen in my senior year in high school while my mother listened to the radio. Someone was reading the list of all the winners of merit scholarships in New York City. My mother was counting the number of Jews and cheering for each Jewish name. I found it deeply disturbing and in contradiction to what I thought we all believed in—the desire for all people to excel."[91] This "antipathy to tribalism," Kesselman suggested, represented a strong element in the politics shared by the Gang of Four and others who worked toward building a "larger and more diverse movement."[92] "Our identification with the outside world, in opposition to our parents' narrow (and self-protective, fearful) views," added Rothstein, "was rebellious and progressive, . . . a response against the broader society's divisions by ethnicity and religion. Why would we identify ourselves as Jews when we wanted to promote a vision of internationalism and inter-faith and interracial solidarity?"[93]

Despite the friends' rejection of the particularism they identified with ethnic identity and their silence about their own bonds as Jews, they suspected that Jewish women were highly represented among women's liberationists. "If you compare NOW and women's liberation," Rothstein observed, "you will see a much greater percentage of Jewish women in women's liberation. This is probably because they came out of the Left and from large urban centers. They also drew on a legacy of immigrant culture, where as outsiders, it was easy to be critical. Criticism was encouraged in Jewish culture. My mother used to say that there was no Jewish pope—no authority to dictate—and therefore everyone has her own relationship to God. Judaism encourages independent thinking. To be critical is not blasphemous but the basis of the religion."[94]

Booth agreed that Jewish women may have been even more disproportionately represented in the radical feminist movement than they were in liberal feminism. For Booth, strong moral, often religiously based values may have explained the presence of Jewish women in both branches of feminism, as it did for many Catholic feminists.

Nevertheless, as Weisstein pointed out, "the obvious Jewishness, both on the left and in women's liberation, was suppressed. We didn't talk about it. . . . It was so embarrassing to have so many Jews around, since Jews weren't the workers who built the garrisons." But, she added, "of course they were. . . . It was sort of a whiff of anti-Semitism. There was even a silent agreement that we didn't bring it up because it was counter to the universalist vision of that time. At least I was a little defensive about having so many Jews around."[95] As Weisstein noted, this defensiveness about Jewish origins was a product of the ideology of universalism that was characteristic of many New Left groups at the time, not just women's liberation.

Negative stereotypes about Jewish women permeated the Left and counterculture, making it even harder for radical women to identify as Jews. Weisstein recalled an incident when, while a doctoral student in Harvard's graduate psychology program, gurus Timothy Leary and Richard Alpert handed out magic mushrooms. Many students became delusional; Weisstein had a paranoid nightmare and hallucinated for a month. "We knew you would," Leary commented. "You're an uptight Jewish female who can't let herself go." Weisstein called them "sleazeballs."[96]

Others noted the Jewish presence in the feminist movement in negative ways. Booth recalled, "Amy and I were teaching in a high school with another friend, Robin Kaufman. Tobis and Booth were not Jewish-sounding names, but Kesselman and Kaufman were. The principal, who we think had been in the Greek Partisan army for the Nazis, always got us confused and treated us the same way. We all looked different but we were all Jewish. Finally we were all fired in different ways." While at the time they did not discuss the reasons for the dismissals, they suspected anti-Jewish prejudice. The principal was against almost everything they did.[97]

Stereotypes about Jews were manifold in the communities where the women worked and volunteered. None of the community people whom Rothstein worked with as organizer in the poor neighborhoods of uptown Chicago believed she was Jewish because she was not rich. The only Jews that residents knew were wealthy landlords.[98]

In addition to discrimination, negative stereotypes, and internal silencing, the difficult political climate for American Jews in the late 1960s played a part in minimizing radical activists' self-conscious identification as Jews. The first women's liberation groups formed a few months after the 1967 Arab-Israeli War. For most American Jews, Israel's military victory signified a source of deep pride, even among young Jews strongly identified with the antiwar and civil rights movements. But some progressive Jews condemned Israeli military actions.[99]

Kesselman did not speak out, but when she took a job at the Chicago Jewish Community Center's day-care center in the midst of the war, she felt she had to "lie about what [she] thought." She speculates now that had she identified more explicitly as a Jew, she might have used her Jewish identity more politically, taking on issues that troubled her within the Jewish world.[100]

Rothstein also cited the politics of the established Jewish community as a reason for avoiding Jewish identification. When she returned from her trip to North Vietnam in the summer of 1967, she had to earn back the money she borrowed by doing speaking engagements. Although she spoke in churches of every denomination, not one synagogue invited her. Acknowledging Jewishness would have made little difference, Rothstein believes, for she was unsure whether at that moment, there was a place for radicalism within the Jewish world. As the child of immigrants,

Rothstein had a further reason to avoid Jewish identification. People on the left "hated German Jews," she explained; they thought that German Jews should have fought back and resisted the Nazis. "So I just didn't really talk about it. It wasn't very safe."[101]

"All of these reasons for not speaking about [the fact] that we were Jewish when we were so Jewish!" Booth exclaimed at the "Women's Liberation" conference. But while the Jewish influence on their activism was not explicit, it definitely impacted these women's lives. Rothstein summed up her own experience this way: "It's become clear to me that [my Jewish background] is what largely propelled me into activism." Although Kesselman is still ambivalent about her own Jewish identity, she acknowledged that Jewishness might well have played a role in the women's friendship and in the movement. "The four of us shared . . . a belief in a broad and inclusive movement," she recalled at the conference. "What we appreciated in each other were things like a spirit of inquiry, a desire for intense conversation, and all the things the people have been identifying as characteristic of Jewish culture."[102]

West Side member Evi Goldfield concurs, suggesting that the large Jewish participation in the group might be explained by the "largely unconscious affinity for certain personalities to group together and understand one another."[103] Although this factor may have played a role in drawing the women together, their Jewish backgrounds remained under the radar for decades. For feminist friends who discussed almost every personal and political topic, this inarticulateness about a significant feature of their backgrounds remains striking.

The Gang of Four, CWLU Sisterhood, and Its Decline

The friends became an influential political cohort, "the spine behind the inception and first four years of CWLU," in Weisstein's words.[104] The CWLU was a political organization but had service projects such as clinics and co-ops to help women meet their needs, offering training through workshops and schools. The idea for the group came from a trip to North Vietnam that Rothstein had taken in late 1967 as part of a peace delegation in which representatives of the Vietnamese Women's Union explained how they were organized from the village to the provincial and national levels. Rothstein described the Vietnamese

Women's Union to the West Side Group, and it became the direct model for Chicago's socialist-feminist CWLU.[105]

As an "explicitly radical, anti-capitalist, feminist . . . organization committed to building an autonomous, multi-issue women's liberation movement," the CWLU was unusual among women's liberation groups because of its formalized structure, consisting of workgroups, a steering committee, and semiautonomous chapters.[106] While other organizations preferred a loose (or nonexistent) structure, a phenomenon that Jo Freeman labeled the "tyranny of structurelessness," the CWLU established provisions for regular elections, meetings, and communications, providing accountability through rotating steering-group membership, shared chairmanships, planning committees, citywide forums, and elected leadership.[107] Under Rothstein's direction, it developed leadership training for members, priding itself on its commitment to maximum involvement in decision making both among the chapters, which were devoted to consciousness-raising, and at the project level. In Rothstein's view, the CWLU's inclusionary structure demonstrated a vision of feminist pluralism that influenced organizational practice. The decentralized nature of the CWLU reflected a unique feminist structure.[108]

In a study of the seventeen socialist-feminist unions formed between 1969 and 1975, sociologist Karen Hansen found the CWLU more aligned with women's projects (e.g., abortion counseling, a rape crisis hotline, a women's graphic collective, the women's rock band) than with the socialist politics that characterized most socialist feminist unions.[109] For many years, the organization escaped the factionalism that beset most of these unions. In 1972, Rothstein conjectured that the lack of sectarianism resulted from the fact that although the CWLU was structurally innovative, it was not on the theoretical cutting edge: it was "never in the vanguard in terms of ideas, situations, or life-styles." As opposed to New York, no theoretical breakthroughs came from Chicago: "We didn't figure out very early about sexism, about violence toward women, about nuclear families, and so forth. But when these breakthroughs finally arrived in Chicago, they didn't appear in the form of ultimatums."[110] She added another reason the CWLU was not in the theoretical vanguard: "We existed in a very much more oppressive city with a very oppressive political and cultural milieu. We were also in an organizing culture which was strong and which trained many of us

Figure 1.1. Naomi Weisstein (second from left), with the Chicago Women's Liberation Rock Band, 1971. Courtesy Chicago Women's Liberation Rock Band and Virginia Blaisdell.

to outreach to others, to provide service and engagement and to build organization. It wasn't a city of writers and intellectuals but of activists and organizers."[111]

Nonetheless, the CWLU faced sectarian takeovers (from the Socialist Workers' Party, the Revolutionary Union, the Communist Workers' Party, the October League, and others). It disbanded in 1977 shortly after expelling a leftist sectarian group, surviving longer than any other socialist-feminist union, with the exception of the Baltimore Union.[112] According to Weisstein, "sectarian mayhem"—the "dogmatism, purification, and relentless obsession" with narrowing the CWLU

Figure 1.2. Heather Booth and her son at women's liberation
march, Chicago, May 1971. Photo by Jo Freeman.

to politically appropriate members—was a primary reason for the
organization's death.[113]

"Trashing"—the movement's denunciation or silencing of leaders as
elitist—affected the CWLU as it did other women's liberation organizations. Jo Freeman, whom Susan Brownmiller described as "the odd
woman out" among West Siders, found herself excluded from meetings
of the West Side Group early on.[114] Freeman left Chicago in 1968 and
wrote "The Tyranny of Structurelessness," "Trashing," and "The Bitch

Manifesto" about the problems of leadership in the movement.[115] Weisstein acknowledged that the "tyranny of structurelessness" was a brilliant insight, regretting the outcome of Freeman's experience in the West Side Group.

Weisstein herself suffered from the "trashing" that silenced so-called undemocratic feminists who moved into the limelight. She had come under attack from the Chicago Women's Liberation Rock Band because she had become its "mother, . . . its *de facto* leader." She was trashed when band members refused to stand up to a growing dogmatism about elitism. But the band died three months after Weisstein left the city. She explained her view of the reason: "we were not honest about the skills we needed to develop and because trashing had replaced compromise and generosity as the dominant political modus operandi of the radical women's movement."[116] At the time, however, committed to a "deeply utopian egalitarianism," Weisstein went along with the practice. "People didn't want to recognize that there were enormous differences in

Figure 1.3. Amy Kesselman at a demonstration in Chicago against street harassment, March 1970. Courtesy Amy Kesselman.

Figure 1.4. Vivian Rothstein (on the left) at a demonstration outside the Department of Health, Education, and Welfare, Washington D.C., November 1969. Photo by Jo Freeman.

individual talents, abilities, gifts. I spent years trying to appease other women in the movement, trying to be less powerful, so they wouldn't hate me."[117]

As coordinator of the CWLU, Rothstein was the target of criticism from different groups of feminists because of ideological issues. There was no specific targeting of Jewish women within the CWLU, but some women's liberationists ruminated that Jewish women may have been unequally affected by trashing in several cities because of their strong roles in the movement and their outspoken styles of participation and leadership.

Conflicts between the "politicos" and pro-women's arm of the women's liberation movement also took its toll on the friends. As the sectarian rifts within the women's movement and on the left grew more strident in the early 1970s, the group bemoaned the loss of community. According to Booth, the women's movement had moved away "from the sisterhood of the earliest years to increasing battles over the meaning of 'true feminism.' There was a harsher edge to the political conversations." More time was spent in meetings on discussions about the "correct position" and less on outreach and mobilization. The CWLU moved away from its early focus on "direct action, non-sectarianism, and a sense of loving sisterhood."[118]

Despite the disappointments of movement politics, including tensions among themselves, the Gang of Four was indelibly transformed by the Chicago women's movement. Movements needed to be "wild [and] anarchic," Weisstein commented; she would "do it all again." "We changed a lot of women's lives, just as feminism transformed [our lives] forever. Those who lived through those early years were transformed in the visionary ways you see in the early parts of . . . movements," such as the early Russian Revolution. In Weisstein's view (though not necessarily the others), she became the "passionate brilliant orator," Booth "the world's best activist," Rothstein "the world's best organizer," and Kesselman "the world's most brilliant theoretician." "What transformed us was a deeply resisting, deeply visionary organization and movement transformed by our righteous indignation, transformed by our compassion and hopes for the future, transformed finally by a group of women who, at a particular time in history and under particular social circumstances all acted much better than we ever thought we could."[119]

Rothstein spoke for the group when, in 1973, she wrote to Kesselman, "It is so hard—when we once felt we were making history and the lives of hundreds of people were dependent on our actions—to resolve ourselves to less significant and far less ambitious work. . . . Now that I don't feel I'm making history, I don't know exactly what to do with my life."[120]

After the CWLU

In Chicago, the Gang of Four worked together for only a few years; all left the CWLU before its 1977 collapse. After Kesselman came out as a lesbian, she felt isolated, with her three closest friends all married. She left Chicago in 1970 to live in a women's commune in San Francisco. After her departure, a "profound sense of loss" permeated the group. Kesselman felt she "had lost [her] political home" and never again felt as "personally and politically close with any group of friends."[121]

The women took different paths after Chicago, struggling to find their own ways. In their late twenties and early thirties, the women were uncertain about their identities and felt "easily judged, hurt, or abandoned by each other." [122] But twenty-five years later, as the Gang of Four wrote their essay together, they felt the connection they had experienced earlier and the exhilaration of their joint commitment to radical feminism. Each had gone on to make outstanding contributions to feminism and to social change efforts. Part of a group of women's liberationists who pioneered feminist research and teaching, Kesselman and Weisstein made their mark in women's studies, one of the most important offshoots of early radical feminism. Rothstein and Booth continued their activism as organizers.

After Chicago, Amy Kesselman helped to develop women's studies programs on the West Coast and received a master's degree in history from Portland State University. She taught women's studies at various colleges in the Portland, Oregon, area, then enrolled in a doctoral program in history at Cornell University, where she wrote her dissertation on women who worked in the Portland-area shipyards during World War II. Kesselman taught in the Women's Studies Program at the State University of New York from 1981 until her retirement in 2012. She is the author of *Fleeting Opportunities: Women Shipyard Workers in Portland and Vancouver during World War II and Reconversion* and a co-editor of several editions of *Women: Images and Realities: A Multicultural Anthology*, widely used in introductory women's studies courses. She is working on a book about women's activism in New Haven, Connecticut.

Naomi Weisstein left Chicago in 1973 for a position in the Psychology Department at the State University of Buffalo. By that time, an article that she published in 1968, "Kinder, Kirche, Kuche as Scientific Law: Psychology Constructs the Female," which criticized the field of psychology for failing to understand women's experiences, was widely circulating in the women's movement. In 1970, with Phyllis Chesler and others, she founded American Women in Psychology, which became an important division of the American Psychological Association. This group and her article, reprinted over forty-two times in six languages and the subject of a Festschrift on Weisstein in 1993, helped to establish the field of women in psychology. Weisstein published over sixty articles for leading scientific journals, including six in the highest-level journal *Science*. Her research highlighted the active role of the brain in making sense of visual input, interpreting what comes in. Throughout her career, she battled the sexism that she experienced in universities and the scientific establishment and expertly outed it to a larger public. Despite chronic fatigue syndrome, diabetes, and other illnesses that kept her bedridden for over thirty years, Weisstein remained involved in scholarship, criticizing what she saw as an increasingly conservative bent in the field even among feminist psychologists, until her death in 2015.[123]

After leaving Chicago for Denver in 1974, Vivian Rothstein worked with the American Friends Service Committee on its Middle East Peace Education Program and later with Planned Parenthood through the North Carolina Coalition for Choice. In 1982, she moved with her family to Los Angeles, where she was community liaison officer for the Santa Monica city government. From 1987 to 1997, she directed the Ocean Park Community Center, a nonprofit agency providing shelters and services to homeless adults and youths and battered women and their children. Rothstein became involved with and then led the Santa Monica Living Wage campaign, aimed at the city's low-wage hospitality industry. Working with the hotel workers' union, UNITE HERE, and the L.A. Alliance for a New Economy, she spent the next eighteen years organizing community allies to bring livable wages and health benefits to primarily female low-wage service workers in the region's tourism industry. In organizing, "you were at the back, helping people find their voice," said Rothstein. "It is a "holy profession."[124] Rothstein continued the interfaith work she had begun in the civil rights movement throughout her career, serving on the board of Clergy and Laity United for Economic Justice for many years. She was also engaged with the Progressive Jewish Alliance in Los Angeles (now called Bend the Arc).

Heather Booth describes her more than fifty years of activism with words that resonate with Rothstein's: "If you organize, you can change the world."[125] Booth remained in Chicago the longest. In 1973, she founded and became the president of the influential Midwest Academy, a grassroots, activist-organizer training school in Chicago, its mission to create an army of activists working for change on the local, state, and national levels. The Midwest Academy is a focus for Booth's efforts to "expand the space of democracy and civil participation" in society, but she has worked on many other fronts, managing political campaigns, including Carol Moseley Brown's 1992 Senate campaign, and serving as training director of the Democratic National Committee and director of the NAACP National Voter Fund. She was the lead consultant for the founding of the Campaign for Comprehensive Immigration Reform and was the director of the Health Care Campaign for the AFL-CIO. Booth also served as the founding director of Americans for Financial Reform, fighting to regulate the financial industry, and now consults with the Voter Participation Center, one of the largest voter-registration and get-out-the-vote organizations. Within the social change community, her influence is mythic. According to one colleague, at any progressive political event in Washington, D.C., where Booth has lived for several decades, it is easy to find someone of any age who would say, "I'm here because of Heather Booth. She taught me how to do this, she recruited me, she inspired me."[126]

Working with so many different political and cultural groups, Booth was surprised when a friend remarked to her that without naming it as such, so much of her world had been the Jewish social action world. Booth recalls that by the early 1970s, she had moved away from the Jewish community, not connecting it to her social justice organizing, but she reengaged a decade later, when as the deputy field director for the Mayor Washington Campaign in Chicago, she "saw anti-Semitism rear its head" in the city and reacted. She also began to connect with a Jewish feminist group that was then developing. By the early 1990s, Booth was becoming more directly involved with Jewish social justice work along with other political and activist involvements. With Leonard Fein and a few other Jewish social activists, she started Amos: The National Jewish Partnership for Social Justice, designed to move social justice to a more central role within the Jewish community. Amos was the prophet who had so deeply inspired her during her teenage years. In 2000, Booth became acting director of the organization. Though Amos closed in 2002, Booth has taken heart in the continuing flowering of social justice action work within the Jewish community; she and Rothstein are the two members of the group of friends to have worked directly with Jewish groups. In Booth's own life, the commitment she made in 1963 at Yad Vashem is still ongoing: "in the face of injustice, I would work for justice / tikkun olam."[127]

Marilyn Webb: Jewish Identity and the Widening Networks of Women's Liberation

Marilyn Salzman Webb, who had been involved in the civil rights and New Left movements, represents the wider group of Chicago radical feminists for whom religion and ethnicity were unimportant, unspoken dimensions of activism. Starting in Chicago, Webb went on to organize the Washington, D.C., women's liberation collective and founded the feminist journal *off our backs*.

Webb rightly deserves a place in the honor roll of radical feminist foremothers. Born in New York City to a lower-middle-class Jewish family, Webb graduated in 1964 from Brandeis University, where she had been a scholarship student, and went on to study educational psychology at the University of Chicago, receiving a master's degree in 1967. She started one of the first Chicago preschools for the children of poor women, which she directed for three years. At the same time, she directed a second preschool at Saul Alinsky's community organizing project, working with mothers on welfare. "I learned to be a woman from them," Webb said.[128] In Chicago, she joined SDS, the organization's new headquarters, and met SDS national leader Lee Webb, head of SDS's Vietnam Summer Project, whom she married. Webb's close ties to the New Left's male leadership mirrored those of Rothstein, Weisstein, and Booth, with whom she started an early women's liberation group that met briefly after the 1965 SDS Champaign-Urbana conference.

Webb organized several events that galvanized New Left women activists and that helped spawn a new women's movement. In January 1969, she attended the catastrophic counter-inaugural rally organized by the National Mobilization to End the War in Vietnam (Mobe) to protest Nixon's second-term swearing-in. Webb had been invited by Mobe to address the rally, but because she was identified with an SDS-friendly women's liberation perspective, Shulamith Firestone demanded that she speak on behalf of women advocating a clear break with the Left. Highlighting women's oppression within the capitalist system, Webb began her speech. Historian Ruth Rosen describes the moment: "Suddenly pandemonium broke out in front of the stage. Webb plunged on, denouncing a system that treated women as objects and property. To her horror, she watched as 'fist fights broke out. Men yelled things like

"Fuck her! Take her off the stage! Rape her in the back alley!"' . . . Shouts followed, like 'Take it off!'" "It was absolutely astonishing," Webb recalled, "and this was the Left."[129]

Firestone grabbed the mike. "'Let's start talking about where *we live, baby*," she shouted. "Because we women often have to wonder if you mean what you say about revolution or whether you just want more power for yourselves."[130] Men in the audience booed and yelled out obscenities; the atmosphere was frightening. Although Webb recalled some men in the audience trying to silence the hecklers, she was shocked that longtime antiwar activist Dave Dellinger was not one of them and in fact told her to "shut Shulie up." "If radical men can be so easily provoked into acting like rednecks," proclaimed Ellen Willis from New York, another Jewish-born women's liberationist, "what can we expect from others?"[131] "A football crowd would have been . . . less blatantly hostile to women," Firestone wryly observed.[132]

After the disastrous event, Webb and Firestone, with Ellen Willis and other women's liberationists, held a postmortem at Webb's D.C. apartment. The phone rang with a message from a female caller: "If you or anybody like you ever gives a speech like that again, we're going to beat the shit out of you. SDS has a line on women's liberation, and that is *the line*." Webb believed she recognized the voice of SDS colleague Cathy Wilkerson (later she learned that the caller was an imposter, a COINTELPRO agent trying to divide Left groups).[133] For Webb, though, it was "the last straw." The incident became the "catalyst where radical feminists left the male-dominated movement," according to Ruth Rosen.[134] It marked the second instance in which Shulamith Firestone intervened when left-wing men attempted to silence women. This time with Marilyn Webb, she was again part of a foundational moment of radical feminism.

Webb had come to Washington from Chicago with her husband, who joined the leftist Institute for Policy Studies. With other leftist women, mainly non-Jews, she founded D.C. Women's Liberation in 1967, one of the earliest and most active women's liberation groups, with dozens of discussion groups and project activities including an abortion-counseling service and an education program with classes held at the Institute for Policy Studies, suburban churches, and local college campuses. D.C. Women's Liberation also planned direct actions and the national meetings in Sandy Springs and Lake Villa.[135]

In 1970, Webb founded one of the first women's studies programs, at Goddard College in Vermont. That year she also started *off our backs*, a collectively produced women's liberation newsletter, published from 1970 to 2008, the longest-lasting radical feminist newsletter. But like numerous radical feminist leaders, Webb was "trashed," forced out of *off our backs* because of her journalistic expertise. "First it was 'You can't write at all; you have to help other people,'" she told author Susan Faludi. Then she was told that she could not accept public speaking engagements. "And then it was just 'Get out!'"[136]

It was ironic, in fact, that Webb was attacked for her leadership position within radical feminism, her expertise and confidence seen, perhaps, as a consequence of a privileged upbringing. But Webb came from a working-class background, the first in her family to go to college, and she recognized similar backgrounds among other Jewish feminist activists. Webb understood about class very early on, and it became the key element in her political beliefs. Her grandfather's family was German Jewish, and her mother's family was eastern European: "the eastern European family was seen as déclassé, and the German Jewish family was not." There were two other things that Webb recalled as relevant to her Jewishness: "One, when I was four, my grandfather on the German side took me to synagogue. He was an Orthodox Jew, although he probably was more Conservative than Orthodox. And I was four years old, and he made me sit by myself, up in the balcony, with the women. I can't tell you how terrifying that was for a four-year-old. I didn't even know anybody." The second thing was her grandfather's refusal to come to her wedding to Lee Webb. "I had married out of the religion; therefore, I was dead." Thus, from her father's family, she understood Judaism—"the temple-going Judaism"—to be very punitive.[137]

Webb's family provided lessons about gender as well. While men claimed status as pious and educated scholars, it was the women, such as her maternal grandmother, who ran a laundry, who were often the breadwinners. After the death of Webb's father, when she was a teenager, her mother supported the family. From her mother's immigrant family, she learned the strength of women.

Still, patriarchal attitudes dominated; she recalls her paternal grand-father's warning, "Women shouldn't go to college because you won't be able to find anybody to marry you. You'll be too educated." She believes that the only reason her family let her go to college was because she ended up going to the nonsectarian, Jewish-sponsored Brandeis University: "Jewish college is okay."[138] Even though her college choices were limited, Webb recognized that on both sides, her family held a strong belief in education as liberation. This belief, the understanding of class, and the importance of strong women to Jewish families became the Jewish values that shaped her.

For most of Webb's life, however, she did not explicitly recognize the contribution of these values to her development. Brandeis was not particularly Jewish for Webb either; she received a good education, appreciating radical professors such as Herbert Marcuse—and she loved the fact that Eleanor Roosevelt had once taught there—but, as she remembers, "I still did not identify as a Jew." Her years in SDS did little to foster that identity; if anything, it introduced her to dashing non-Jewish men; Lee Dunholm Webb III was the first of three non-Jewish husbands. In retrospect, however, as Webb told me, her choice of Lee Webb as a husband may have unconsciously had something to do with her Jewish background. "Part of it had to do with the Holocaust. I married the most goyish guy I could find, to have a child. . . . I did not want her to be a victim—or any child I had—of any Holocaust."[139]

Although Webb's identification with her Jewishness was never explicit, about fifteen years ago, she decided to trace her eastern European family roots and returned to her grandparents' shtetl in the Ukraine. There she visited a field where twenty-five thousand Jews were killed: "All put in this river basin, shot in the back, and there were no Jews left. Standing there, looking at this ravine and seeing if my family hadn't come here, there's where I would have been. And it was then that I understood that I could not get away from this."[140]

Webb believes that it was because of the Holocaust that her family distanced itself from Judaism: it was just "too painful." Webb, too, distanced herself from the religion, studying and practicing Buddhism for thirty years, but recently she has come to understand how much Judaism has influenced her culturally her whole life—not just the Holocaust but "the social justice values the culture has always transmitted, the trade unionism, civil rights, peace, fairness of opportunity, caring for others."[141]

Webb is a distinguished professor emerita of journalism at Illinois's Knox College, where she started an award-winning investigative-reporting program that drew inspiration from the muckraking tradition, and she is also the author of *The Good Death: The New American Search to Reshape the End of Life*, which was nominated for a Pulitzer Prize. Today she is writing about her ancestors' experiences. Webb recognizes the profound importance of Jewish history as a connecting link between the past and present and acknowledges that her eastern European family taught her about class and organizing. "They also taught me to value myself and look within my own life for answers that could speak to a larger community."[142] Like the four friends who met in Chicago decades ago, the memory of oppression and of the Jewish activists who fought against it is providing Webb with a potent touchstone with which to claim her Jewish identity.

* * *

While Jewishness did not rise to the forefront of the four Chicago feminists' consciousness at the time or of Webb's either, it would not be accurate to label most of the pioneers discussed in this chapter as "minimalist" or "non-Jewish Jews," in Deutscher's famous phrase. Several were explicitly aware of the ways in which Jewishness had shaped their views, and for others, the contributions of Jewish backgrounds and values lingered in their imaginations and memories, latent rather than powerfully present but nonetheless formative.

Notwithstanding the gender universalism of the women's movement, Jewishness did matter to these women's liberationists. But it was a different form of connection than that of Kesselman's secular parents, who deliberately "embraced their Jewish identity as a political act," or of others in that cohort who were mindful of Jewish identifications or in conscious denial of them. These women's liberationists were less concerned about the ramifications of Jewishness than their parents' generation were, and they embraced the commonalities they shared with their movement sisters and generally paid scarce attention to Jewish roots. It took decades before most of them confronted their relationships to Jewish life and heritage.

Nonetheless, the Jewish legacy that helped to spur these women's activism was a product of the universalism embedded in the Jewish credo, an ethos that regarded Jewish values as universal truths and positive social norms. It was not equivalent to a narrow particularism, which the women's liberationists regarded negatively, but reflected a concern for ethical values and consciousness of human commonalities. Interpreted in this way, Judaism can be seen as grounding a pluralist politics congruent with the emphases of 1960s social rebellions, in which Jews played a significant role. In the civil rights, antiwar, and consciousness-raising movements, Jewish participants projected the racial liberalism of colorblindness and empathy toward the oppressed, values that their families had taught them and that found roots in Jewish thought and experiences. Emphasizing inclusiveness rather than exclusion, these engagements may have reflected what Michael Walzer names a "peculiarly Jewish" "low-flying universalism," directly attuned to the political landscape, which aimed to transcend differences and parochial identities. For Walzer, "acknowledgement of the other derives from Jewish particularism": universalism was "the turning outward of a particularist perspective."[143]

While Jewish universalism was one of the major factors that facilitated a connection to radical feminism, it intersected with other triggers, particularly the radical feminist ideology of sisterhood. This stance became a powerful organizing tool, promoting cohesion and collective identity among liberationists. But however sincere the intent to diversify the movement, it had the unintended consequence of blurring "racial/ethnic" difference, according to sociologist Benita Roth, keeping feminists of different racial/ethnic backgrounds in distinct organizations.[144]

By seeking equality through universalism, women's liberationists avoided ethnoreligious differences as well. Later, in the "ethnic revival" that Matthew Frye Jacobson writes about, white ethnic feminists from different backgrounds began to articulate the ways in which "feminist activism was informed by an ethnic sensibility."[145] But very few Jewish women's liberationists joined their self-conscious reappraisal. The Jewish influence in their collectives lay below the surface, but it had nonetheless been a powerful motivator.

"Feminist Sexual Liberationists, Rootless Cosmopolitan Jews"

The New York City Movement

For Rosalyn Baxandall, the women's liberation movement was "love at first sight." Baxandall joined New York Radical Women (NYRW), the first women's liberation group in the city, the minute she heard about it. She began going to activities three times a week: consciousness-raising sessions, a study group, and guerrilla street theater. Baxandall said, "Feminism solved my life's puzzle: It showed me I wasn't a weirdo. I felt we activists had all sprung from Medusa's head and were truly sisters." For four years, Baxandall enjoyed the heady days of participating in a social movement with other rebellious women; she was a member of NYRW in its heyday, from 1967 to 1969, and then joined NYRW's most prominent offshoot, Redstockings. By the time Baxandall left Redstockings in 1971, she was burned out, tired of the "splits and backbiting," and concerned that liberal feminists had appropriated and muted radical women's social change activism.[1] But, despite the disappointments, Baxandall knew that she had participated in a historic moment.

The New York movement differed from many important women's liberation hubs, with more artists, more single and working-class women, and more women who had not been to college. Its greater heterodoxy in regard to age, class, and educational, marital, and work backgrounds created an exciting, often volatile mix. Ti-Grace Atkinson explained the appeal of the city for radical feminists such as Shulamith Firestone and herself: "You come to New York, and you're a weirdo, and you're so happy to be with all the other weirdos who don't think you're weird. . . . It's surprising, it's thrilling, it's like you've discovered your twin."[2] In New York, Jewish women were part of this varied, exciting group, open to experiments in ideas and practices and hoping to inaugurate, in Ruth Rosen's words, "a truly democratic, egalitarian, and participatory movement."[3]

Numerous Jewish women played major roles in developing radical feminism in the city. All worked alongside many other colleagues who emphasized universal goals, and most did not identify Jewishly. Nonetheless, their motivations and the ethical vision they brought to the movement were inflected by Jewish influences. In the exciting mix of ideas and actions that became women's liberation, Jewish values and perspectives played a significant role.

Jews' long association with subversive movements and their comfort with adversarial cultures made the Jewish presence within New York radical feminism of a piece with earlier intellectual and radical American movements. As had been the case for previous generations, social protest flourished in New York, providing safety for daring ideas and intellectual spaces in which experimenters could come together to formulate and disseminate them. Tolerant of diversity and with a secure and successful Jewish population, the city offered a perfect environment in which theories about a free womanhood percolated. As the communications hub of the nation, New York provided ready access to media, which were quick to recognize the news potential of the unfolding movement. The publishing industry's interest in new ideas further encouraged risk-taking. As Jeffrey Gurock argues in *Jews in Gotham*, New Yorkers "believed and acted on the faith that their city could be the incubator of great ideas and the center for transformative movements."[4]

The New York movement was distinctive among the nation's proliferating women's liberation groups because of the pioneering contributions of its radical feminist contingent. Probably the most important innovation was consciousness-raising, the process of sharing personal experience in a small group, which became the primary mode of understanding and theorizing about women's condition. Kathie Sarachild of Redstockings, who had learned the practice during her time in the civil rights movement in the South, coined the phrase.[5] The theoretical contributions of the New York women shaped emerging women's liberation dialogues. In 1970 alone, they published a series of groundbreaking books: Kate Millet's *Sexual Politics*, Germaine Greer's *The Female Eunuch*, Robin Morgan's anthology *Sisterhood Is Powerful*, and Shulamith Firestone's *The Dialectic of Sex*.

While Chicago's feminists were unable to escape the influence of New Left men, in Jo Freeman's view, New York's women's liberationists, many of them civil rights veterans, were "freer to experiment." Shulamith Firestone, who started three New York City women's liberation groups and who had participated in CORE in St. Louis, represented "radical feminism uncontaminated by left-wing rhetoric, something one didn't encounter much in those days," according to Freeman.[6] Baxandall describes the difference between Chicago and New York women's liberation as the difference between Heather Booth, who had been closely involved with SDS and was married to Paul Booth, its former vice president and national secretary, and Ellen Willis, who had no close ties to the New Left. While Baxandall exaggerated the extent of these differences, given that Booth and her Chicago friends created a feminist space apart from their male partners, she expressed the perspective of New York women's liberationists who believed that their comrades elsewhere, particularly in Chicago, were "practically speaking for their husbands' factions."[7] In turn, Chicago feminists criticized the New York comrades as "elitist intellectuals" who focused too much on theory. "They were in a bubble."[8] Chicago's strong labor and activist bent, contrasting with New York's writers and intellectuals, also shaped emerging women's liberation patterns.

Yet differences between "politicos" and "radical feminists" also roiled the New York movement. Divisions were so sharp, according to Susan Brownmiller, a member of New York Radical Women, that feminists outside the city came to describe the New York women's liberation movement as a "sea of barracudas." Socialist feminists and women-centered radical feminists clashed over whether capitalism alone or male supremacy in tandem with the class system should be the main target of attack. Even those who espoused the pro-woman line disagreed over structural, strategic, and ideological questions. Conflicts over the relative weight to be given to consciousness-raising versus action projects, elitism versus egalitarianism, and issues involving marriage, families, sexuality, and lesbian separatism all led to heated charges and countercharges. The intensity of feelings challenged the city's radical feminists to hone their arguments and sharpened their theoretical contributions to the movement. In Brownmiller's words, New York radical women "up[ped] the ante."[9]

Jewish Radical Feminists of New York

Combative and feisty, a "prima donna" who never liked to do any of the menial work involved in movement life, the brilliant, articulate Shulamith Firestone was a leader in the three New York City groups that she initiated: New York Radical Women, Redstockings, and New York Radical Feminists. Firestone had been barely twenty-two when she was told to "cool down" and prevented from bringing the women's resolution to the floor of the National Conference for New Politics in Chicago in 1967. After founding the New York groups, Firestone's influence on women's liberation became national in scope. She was "the firebrand," "the fireball," says writer Susan Faludi in her *New Yorker* profile of Firestone. To her friends, she was the "prime minister" of women's liberation.[10]

Firestone's writing helped to ground the early movement and articulate its place in feminist history. She was the author of several important essays—"Women and the Radical Movement," "The Jeannette Rankin Brigade: Woman Power?," and "The Women's Rights Movement in the U.S.: A New View"—and the founder and editor of the movement's unofficial newsletter, *Notes from the First Year* (1968), *Notes from the Second Year* (1970), and (with Anne Koedt) *Notes from the Third Year* (1971). These anthologies played a crucial role in transmitting new ideas to women's liberation groups throughout the country. At a time when scholarship on the historical roles of women in the U.S. was in its infancy, Firestone boldly reassessed the first-wave feminist movement led by Elizabeth Cady Stanton and Susan B. Anthony and their peers as a radical, rather than reformist, struggle, identifying second-wave women's liberationists as its heirs. Her best-selling 1970 book *The Dialectic of Sex* gave the movement one of its earliest treatises based on radical feminist gender theory. Her book was not an academic study but a "manifesto," a "fierce, funny, and outrageous exhortation to political change."[11]

Within a few years, however, Firestone retreated into a more private life as an artist and poet and turned her back on the movement. Feminists later learned that she suffered from crippling mental illness, probably schizophrenia, and had endured decades of difficult treatments that further isolated her from family and friends. "For a long time, our movement was haunted by the terrible absence of Shulamith Firestone," recounts Phyllis Chesler, comparing the demise of such a "shining and brilliant star" to that of Sylvia Plath a decade earlier—except that Firestone was very much alive. Historian Alice Echols asked how the trajectory of the women's liberation movement might have changed "had Firestone stuck around."[12] After Firestone died, alone and undetected for several days, in the summer of 2012, a grieving community of friends asked the same question. And they asked another: might Firestone's Jewishness have been an ingredient in her unique contribution to radical feminism? Firestone never explained the connection of her Jewish background to her feminist work. What was the nature of her connection to Judaism and to Jewishness? No one seemed to know.

The matter of Jewish identity also looms large in the case of Firestone's Redstockings collaborator Ellen Willis, who came from a nonobservant Jewish background. In her almost forty years as a cultural critic for the *New Yorker*, the *Village Voice*, and other periodicals, Willis wrote bold, passionate, cutting-edge essays on popular culture, feminism, sexuality, psychoanalysis, politics, war and peace, religion and Judaism. While Firestone remained silent on Jewish issues, Willis explicitly referenced her Jewish identity. Willis saw "identity politics"—in her words, the "collective rubric for the liberation movements of women, blacks, gays and other subordinate or marginal groups"—as leading to fragmentation, "comparative victimhood," and moral superiority. Yet she rejected its claims from the logic of her "own particular standpoint in the world" as a woman and Jew: "that is," she said, "I speak as a woman who does not represent 'women'—and as a Jew convinced that the fundamental bond among Jews is neither Zionism nor the 613 commandments but our historic commitment to the ever-unpopular position that the Messiah is yet to come." Her positive identity as both feminist and Jew was rooted in her stance as a radical, utopian universalist, attempting to "recreate a politics that emphasizes our common humanity."[13]

This chapter highlights two other prominent members of New York radical feminist groups: Redstockings member Alix Kates Shulman, author of *Memoirs of an Ex-Prom Queen* (1972), the best-selling "first" second-wave feminist novel; and Susan Brownmiller, author of *Against Our Will* (1975), the landmark "discovery" of rape as a social, sexual, and feminist issue, who was associated with New York Radical Women.

Along with Firestone and Willis, Shulman and Brownmiller etched out major principles of radical feminist theory in their groundbreaking works. The four women's powerful indictment of patriarchy ranged over women's life course: exploitative sexual double standards, rape and domestic violence, unequal relationships in love and marriage, the constraints of motherhood. Firestone's, Brownmiller's, and Shulman's books and Willis's *New Yorker* and *Village Voice* articles helped to put radical feminism on the national stage.

Shulman, a midwesterner like Firestone, and Brownmiller, from one of New York City's outer boroughs, did not consider their Jewish backgrounds important at the time of their participation in women's liberation, but later, in conversations with me, each reassessed her Jewishness as a factor in her feminist awakening. In a place where it seemed that "everyone was Jewish," transplants such as Shulman and Firestone felt free to develop their creative and political passions, unfettered by the strictures of Orthodoxy or Jewish tradition or by the marginality or anti-Semitism with which they had grown up. Willis, raised in the Bronx and Queens, and Brownmiller, from Brooklyn, were secular atheists who nonetheless carried with them a deep connection to Jewishness that helped frame their ideas. The four women's stories suggest that in New York's women's liberation community, as in Chicago, there was no single model for how Jewish-born radical feminists shaped their multiple identities. A brief account of the paradoxical Jewish background of Rosalyn Baxandall, a friend and associate of all of the women in the chapter, further complicates these heterodox patterns.

Of the group, only Willis seemed especially aware of the "out-of-proportion" involvement of Jewish women in women's liberation. But she observed that their numbers were not enough to dominate leadership positions in the movement throughout the country. Furthermore, she speculated that outside New York, there were probably fewer Jewish women participants. New York City, she well knew, was a very special case.

For Willis, New York was a "real and imagined city where feminist/sexual liberationists, rootless cosmopolitan Jews, not-nice girls/boys/others, loudmouth exiles of all colors are an integral and conspicuous part of the landscape." She believed that coming together in this "pariah community," they would create a feminist revolution inflected by the

Jewish cosmopolitan-exile experience.[14] In eastern Europe and Russia, Jewish "cosmopolitanism" had been associated with urbanity, tolerance, and universalism, but it was a mind-set that had put Jews in jeopardy. Throughout the nineteenth and much of the twentieth century, anti-cosmopolitan propaganda had been a major component of anti-Jewish campaigns. Even in small towns and cities of the U.S., Jewish cosmopolitanism was sometimes associated with a dangerous libertinism and elitism. In America's greatest city, however, Jewish radicals and feminists embraced the designation. Here they could call themselves citizens of the world.

The cultural-political perspectives of Jewish feminists interacted with the ideas of many other pioneering women's liberationists in the city, Jewish and non-Jewish, including Kathie Sarachild, Carol Hanisch, Irene Peslikis, Peggy Dobbins, Anne Koedt, Pat Mainardi, Robin Morgan, Ann Snitow, and Vivian Gornick. Acting within a communal context, innovative theory and practice emerged from group interaction.

Gornick did not participate in radical feminist organizations but is the author of an important *Village Voice* essay on the women's liberation movement and co-editor of an early and influential anthology, *Women in Sexist Society*. She has had a distinguished career as a memoirist and nonfiction writer and has written about Jewish literature. Morgan, founding member of New York Radical Women and key organizer of its protest against the Miss America Pageant in Atlantic City, was one of thirteen "politico" cofounders of the short-lived WITCH (Women's International Terrorist Conspiracy from Hell), an activist group known for its anticapitalist, antisexist street-theater protests, but then devoted most of her energies to writing and speaking as a radical feminist. Her anthology *Sisterhood Is Powerful* became an early manifesto of the movement. Morgan is the author of twenty books, including *Sisterhood Is Global* (1984) and *The Demon Lover: The Roots of Terrorism* (1989), which incorporates interviews with Palestinian women in the West Bank and Gaza. Ann Snitow, a founding member of New York Radical Feminists and co-editor of the 1998 anthology *The Feminist Memoir Project*, became a professor of gender studies. None of these women identified as a "Jewish" feminist activist or writer. Although they are not subjects of this chapter, each contributed through her writings to innovative feminist literature, helping to provide a broad understanding of the movement in which they were active participants and further understandings of Jewish women's contributions to radical feminism.[15] The list of New York's Jewish radical feminists could be expanded a great deal further.

Despite frictions among individuals and groups, the women highlighted in this chapter and other radical feminists in New York seized on the many opportunities for innovation that the city offered. Their movement was a revolutionary endeavor.

Shulamith Firestone: The "Prime Minister" of Women's Liberation

Historians and sociologists who have studied the rebirth of feminism in the 1960s posit complex motivations, including changing social expectations, limited opportunities, and an increasingly frustrated constituency of young, educated women. Carol Hanisch, a major participant in New York Radical Feminists, said, "The question of what made any of us a feminist is a rather silly one. All we had/have to do was look around, our own lives included. What leads us to activism is the real question, and that has to do with seeing/finding a way to fight back."[16] For Shulamith Firestone, who had attended a Jewish girls' seminary and become an art student and then a New Left activist in the late 1960s, the patriarchy in her family, her education, and male-dominated leftist politics brought her long-simmering anger to fever pitch and inspired her to find a way to fight back.

Firestone and Pam Allen (Chude Pamela Parker Allen), a former SNCC worker from San Francisco, started New York Radical Women in October 1967 shortly after Firestone left Chicago, having co-founded the West Side Group there. Allen heard about women's liberation from Sue Munaker, a member of West Side.[17] "That women would get together to talk about their lives without any males present was radical," says Allen. "It freaked people out."[18] New York Radical Women, whose membership included Kathie Sarachild, Robin Morgan, Carol Hanisch, Anne Koedt, Pat Mainardi, and Kate Millet, performed several major actions. The most famous, the 1968 demonstration against the Miss America Pageant, when several dozen feminists placed high-heeled shoes, bras and girdles, *Playboy* magazines, brooms, and curlers into a Freedom

Trash Can on the Atlantic City Boardwalk, attracted enormous publicity with its theatrical protest against patriarchy. Barely two years later, Firestone left NYRW and in February 1969, with Ellen Willis, formed Redstockings, an autonomous women's liberation group not associated with the broader Left. The immediate catalyst for their action had been the shocking contempt shown by New Left men for radical women at the D.C. counter-inaugural, yet the split between "politicos" and radical feminists within NYRW had been brewing for some time. Radical feminism "alone succeeds in pulling into focus the many troubled areas of the leftist analysis, providing for the first time a comprehensive revolutionary solution," Firestone wrote.[19] In contrast to NYRW and the nascent Chicago Women's Liberation Union, Redstockings was unabashedly in the radical feminist camp.[20] Coined by Firestone and Willis, the group's name was a combination of two traditions: the "bluestocking" label disparagingly pinned on first-wave feminists and "red" for revolution.

Although Redstockings continued for a few years before officially disbanding as a result of burnout and political conflict, within six months, Firestone became disaffected with the group's consciousness-raising focus. For Firestone, this was a missed opportunity to build a mass movement based on action. In February 1969, she started New York Radical Feminists (NYRF) with Ann Koedt. The first group it organized, West Village One, included writers Susan Brownmiller and (later) Alix Kates Shulman, both of whom had been involved in earlier radical women's groups.[21] But Firestone quit NYRF in spring 1970, after the group repudiated the "brigade"-based structure she had created.[22] For Firestone, who felt that "mob rule" was responsible for the debacle, the break coincided with the beginnings of a steep psychological decline that soon isolated her from the movement. Nonetheless, she had initiated three feminist groups in New York that might not have existed without her.[23] Each played a significant role in reorienting the national conversation about sexism.

Born in 1945, Shulamith Firestone was the eldest daughter of six siblings—three boys and three girls—and the only one born with the surname Feuerstein, which had been Anglicized by her paternal grandfather, then changed back, briefly, at the time of Shulamith's birth in Ottawa, Canada, the home of her maternal grandparents. Raised in

Kansas City and St. Louis, Shulie (the name everyone knew her by) studied at the Yavneh Teachers Seminary for women, which was affiliated with the all-male Telshe Yeshiva near Cleveland. She spent two years at Washington University and, an aspiring artist, became a student at the Art Institute of Chicago, graduating with a BFA in June 1967, shortly before her involvement in the women's movement began.

The fate of her eldest brother, Daniel, the firstborn, weighed heavily on Firestone.[24] Just a week under one year apart, they had grown up "almost like twins," celebrating their bar and bat mitzvahs the same week; in the Orthodox tradition, girls come of age at twelve and boys at thirteen. Danny had been sent to yeshiva but shocked his family by leaving it to study philosophy, later teaching at a college and eventually finding his way to a Zen Buddhist monastery in Rochester, New York. Their father, Sol Firestone, an assimilated Jew from Brooklyn who became Orthodox as a young adult, warned his son about leaving the faith, as he did all his children, telling daughter Tirzah that "leaving the Torah life is like a fish leaving water." Their mother, Kate Weiss Firestone, a Holocaust refugee, agreed: "You cannot leave your roots and expect to get away with it."[25] Her own brothers had been ordained as rabbis in eastern Europe, although they also had secular PhDs. The Firestone parents cut Danny off, giving him the "ostrich treatment."[26] They also cut off contact with Tirzah, when she took a non-Jewish husband.

In May 1974, Danny committed suicide by a gunshot wound to his heart; his body was found in a meadow in New Mexico, in front of a statue of Buddha. Although he had not spoken to Shulamith since high school, when she broke the Sabbath while their parents were away, the death of her brother shook her to the core. Danny's death contributed to her "own growing madness," she later revealed.[27]

How much Shulamith's declining mental health had been exacerbated by family events or the disappointments she experienced within the movement, her own particular psychology and genetic inheritance, or a combination of these factors is difficult to determine. But it is useful to turn to Tirzah Firestone's account of growing up in the Firestone household, as published in her memoir, *With Roots in Heaven*, as well as the reflections of sister Laya, who shared many movement experiences with Shulamith. Tirzah became a Renewal rabbi; Laya is a psychotherapist.

"Our parents raised us with an iron hand, rigid not only in religious doctrine but in methodology," Tirzah recalled. "This meant that, quite aside from living ritually observant lives, any personal choices outside of my parents' prescribed menu were minimal. My siblings and I grew up with an ever-present tension, an almost fanatical injunction to live 'correctly' as dictated by our parents and their dogmatic religious approach. In the end, the Jewish heritage we received was, sadly, not enriched by the intensity with which it was transmitted, but rather drained of its intrinsic joy and goodness."[28] The regimentation of this upbringing was not easy on the children. With Shulamith's intensity and quickness to anger, it left her as rebellious as Tirzah, who (like their elder brother) often thought of suicide. For Tirzah, the only recourse was to travel "as far away from Judaism and anything representing [her] parents' values as possible." The Firestone siblings, who lived within the Orthodox community, never had any non-Jewish friends. Tirzah was excited to leave it to "discover the world beyond Jewish walls, and to become part of it." So were Shulamith and Laya, who was two years younger. Tirzah, nine years Shulamith's junior, explored an alternative spiritual path in Israel, New Mexico, and Boulder, Colorado. "Can't you see how you are killing your mother?" her father asked Tirzah when she went off to explore a "higher consciousness."[29]

According to Laya, Shulamith had always been "much more than [her] parents knew how to handle." As a child, she asked endless questions about subjects that adults spoke about only in whispers, such as the Nazis and concentration camps. She brought home stray dogs, begging her parents to keep them. Once she organized a student visit to the Jewish Home for the Aged. Hearing a woman moaning in Yiddish, she tried to interview her. Had she been in the war? What did she see? What did she remember?[30] Shulamith gravitated to people in underdog situations, Laya remembers. "She felt she wanted to raise them up. She was seeing real things because she had blinders pulled off. . . . She perceived suffering in a way that few people did. She would walk right into the fire."[31]

Shulamith was always questioning, particularly about God and Jewishness. The rabbis at yeshiva could not handle her. "She had such vibrancy," says Laya. "She was so animated, and she had such a great sense of self-reflection." She was extreme, brilliant, fierce. "No one else had that fire." She was driven to find out all the secrets that were covered up—for example, why family members refused to talk about her uncle Ernest, her mother's brother, who defied his father's wishes and became a doctor instead of following him into the rabbinate. Years later, he took his own life, nearly a decade before his nephew, Shulamith's brother, also suffering the psychological costs of rebellion, committed suicide. The Holocaust was another secret that Shulamith probed relentlessly. She devoured everything she could about it, Laya remembers. At the age of twelve, she wrote to Etta Shiber, author of *Paris Underground*, a book about Shiber's work in the Resistance, and was delighted when the author wrote back. Unflinching in her examination of what lay beyond the world her parents had circumscribed, Shulamith became Laya's "portal to the rest of the world."[32]

Shulamith's intensity and stubbornness pitted her directly against her father, who "threw his rage at Shulie." Their younger brother Ezra, who with brother Nechemia remained strictly Orthodox, felt that "he wouldn't bend, and she wouldn't bend. They were both very brilliant and very, very opinionated." Kate Firestone provided little support for her daughters, holding a "completely passive view of femininity," according to Tirzah. Yet, despite the fact that Shulie and her father were often at loggerheads, it was Sol's death in 1981 that sent her into psychosis, in Tirzah's view. "She lost that ballast he somehow provided."[33]

When *The Dialectic of Sex* came out, Firestone's parents faced a challenge from their eldest daughter far greater than her childhood bluntness, for the book embraced a truly radical idea: the annihilation of the nuclear family. Kate Firestone (who may never have read the book) boasted to her community that her daughter's work was being read around the world and had been adopted for use in college classrooms. Her husband was not pleased by her notoriety. Tirzah remarked, "My father publicly howled in laughter at Shulamith's outrageous views, declaring her manifesto to be the joke book of the century. I don't think he ever realized just how much his own rigid, patriarchal style had served to shape his daughter's politics."[34]

Firestone had written *The Dialectic of Sex* in a white heat, finishing it in six months. Baxandall recognizes that some of its ideas grew out of the consciousness-raising discussions and readings that took place in New York Radical Women.[35] Firestone was then only twenty-five and, with the help of Ellen Willis, who introduced her to a publisher, on her way to national fame, although the polarizing book also led to vilification, which took a heavy toll on her. The book boldly takes on Marx and Freud for their neglect of gender as a system based on unequal power relations. For Firestone, the theorist closest to the truth was Simone de Beauvoir, but she believed that even her existentialist heroine missed the mark by failing to see that women's "Otherness" was founded in biology—from sex itself—women's childbearing and child-rearing roles.[36]

Reviewing the book in the *New York Times*, John Leonard complimented its author for her "sharp and often brilliant mind" but took umbrage at some of Firestone's "preposterous" assertions about gender and masculinity.[37] Her call to free women from the "tyranny of their biology" through technologically managed reproduction and to replace the nuclear family with nontraditional households attracted widespread condemnation.[38] Even Firestone's radical friends were shocked by some of her beliefs. *The Dialectic of Sex* became what Ann Snitow called feminism's most famous "demon text," "demonized, apologized for, endlessly quoted out of context." Snitow explained that it was patriarchy that Firestone wanted to smash, not mothers.[39] In the decades since *The Dialectic of Sex* appeared, several of Firestone's proposals have come to pass, including technologically assisted reproduction, but at the time, people many considered Firestone an outrageous provocateur, a destroyer of the family. Susan Brownmiller suggests that the mixed reviews were a "crushing defeat" for Firestone, leading her to lose her "emotional equilibrium and her sense of herself in the world."[40]

Firestone's treatise called for "not just the elimination of male *privilege* but of the sex *distinction* itself: genital differences between human beings would no longer matter culturally."[41] In her utopian society, procreative sex would be abolished along with the biological family and heterosexual love relationships, which she saw as a "holocaust" for women because they were founded on "unequal *power*." Firestone urged the overthrow of marriage and monogamy, which she saw as chains on women's autonomy. Freedom would arise only after women seized control of reproduction, including their own fertility and "all the social institutions of childbearing and childrearing."[42]

Firestone was among the few radical feminists who saw a path to revolutionary gender and social relations in "cybernetic socialism," including such advances as in vitro fertilization and surrogate mothering, then barely on the horizon.[43] While her ideas seemed like science fiction to many people, Firestone believed they could eradicate the power imbalances that subordinated women. A successful revolution "against all aspects of the biological family" would bring on nothing less than a "Messianic Age." The alternative was "our own suicide, . . . the creation of a hell on earth."[44]

Firestone underscored the suffering of children under patriarchy as well. Drawing on her own experience, she presented childhood as a time of economic dependence, shame, and restraint. Children were "repressed at every waking minute"; *childhood is hell.*" As an alternative, Firestone proposed ten-person nonrelated households composed of children and adults, with limited ten-year contracts. Children would no longer be minors under the control of parents but would have full rights of their own. If the child did not like the household into which she had arbitrarily been born, she would be helped to transfer out. "Down with childhood," Firestone declared, and down with "oppressive "femininity," "power psychology, sexual repression, . . . family chauvinism."[45]

Firestone's polemic encompassed the history of feminism, art, culture, ecology, and more; there was little in the history of civilization she left untouched. Her chapter on race was one of her most controversial, attracting the ire of critics who saw it as reductive to assert that racism was rooted in patriarchy and the family while ignoring the historical conditions of slavery, race-specific oppression, and poverty. "*Racism is a sexual phenomenon, . . . sexism extended,*" Firestone declared. Her focus was on the strategic parallels between black people and women: "If racism was expungeable, why not sexism?"[46]

Firestone drew on the lessons of the civil rights movement to advocate radical changes in gender relations.[47] For later black feminist critics, her grand assertions misfired. They believed that, in her intense desire to illuminate the pitfalls of the nuclear family, Firestone had turned a blind eye to the centrality of familial support to black women and ignored black women's own resistance to the worst aspects of machismo.[48] While Firestone's rambling account of racism had its defenders, its reception presaged later conflicts among feminists.[49]

Firestone was disappointed that the book did not propel her into the front ranks of American thinkers; she had wanted to become the American Beauvoir. According to Kate Millet, whose influential treatise *Sexual Politics* came out a few months prior to *The Dialectic of Sex*, it was "the malice of the critics, the 'talk show' hosts, anti-Semitism, the residual mess of anticommunism" that "destroyed" and "overwhelmed" Firestone—"burned her alive, consumed her."[50] Other friends surmised that the shy young woman deliberately stepped back before the avalanche of publicity to focus on her art and poetry.

Firestone was equally devastated by her expulsion from New York Radical Feminists; "it was like she'd been rejected by her family," commented a friend.[51] Firestone virtually disappeared from the women's movement. A few years later, Brownmiller encountered a "pathetic little waif" near the New York Public Library. "Shulie?" asked Brownmiller, "not altogether believing" what she was seeing. "Shulie, is that you? It's Susan." Firestone responded, "Look at me—this is what you did to me."[52] Firestone wrote only one other book, *Airless Spaces*, a fictionalized account of her psychiatric hospitalizations and psychotropic treatments, illuminating both mental illness and poverty.[53]

Because of Firestone's writing and the women's liberation groups she initiated, her legacy endured, but as her sister Laya put it, she left behind a "mystery as her essence."[54] Only after her death did the issue of her Judaism emerge as potentially vital to understanding her. Heather Booth raised the question in an email to Shulie's List, a listserv created to share thoughts about Firestone and the movement after the shock of Firestone's passing in 2012. Booth told the three dozen women on the list that she had been alerted to the significance of Jewish identity to the movement by the NYU conference and my own work, commenting that no one had addressed Firestone's Jewishness as a factor in her life.[55]

Anne Forer Pyne, a friend of Firestone in the early years of women's liberation, recalled a dozen or so remarks that led her to believe that Jewishness was indeed a fundamental influence on Firestone. In Pyne's view, "first last and always, Judaism was central to Shulie, . . . the main part of her identity."[56]

Some friends wondered whether growing up in an unsparingly rigid and "fundamentalist" Orthodox Jewish background might have pushed Firestone to rebellious activism. Several recalled Shulie's views about the Orthodox prayer "Thank God for not making me a woman." Peggy Dobbins remembered Shulie saying that her brother repeated these words three times, striking his chest each time.[57] Pyne thought that the prayer made Shulie believe that Judaism was a religion "that had no use for women at all, and that men were everything, only men counted."[58] The prayer offended Firestone tremendously, recalled Marilyn Webb, and was likely to have been "a strong starting point for her feminism."[59]

Firestone had gone to Israel in the summer of 1968, staying for several months. This trip and her experience visiting Israeli kibbutzim played a large part in her thinking about gender. In *The Dialectic of Sex*, she talks about the limited success of the kibbutz: it was "no radical experiment" in socialist equality, yet it had achieved a "spectacular" weakening of the "division of labor, the nuclear family, sex repression, etc."[60] Rosalyn Baxandall recalled that she asked Firestone if she had gotten "more religious" after her trip to Israel, as some people believed, but Firestone denied it, cutting off further discussion. And there was "nothing religious" around her apartment, Baxandall observed.[61] The only specific comment Firestone made about her trip to Israel, Pyne recalled, was that she got a suntan there and turned "tangerine." "She was very happy about it."[62]

Roxanne Dunbar-Ortiz recalled sharing a table with Firestone at the Socialist Scholars Conference in 2002, during the Second Intifada. Firestone brought up the Israeli occupation and pronounced herself "pro-Palestinian"; she did not share her family's Zionist, anti-Palestinian views.[63] Dunbar-Ortiz believes Firestone separated "her strong and positive Jewish identity and the state of Israel's politics." But when Pyne told Firestone that she had not been raised to identify with Israel, Firestone was "shocked" and quoted Hillel to the effect that if she were "not for the Jews, who will be?" In Firestone's eyes, Pyne was not a "good Jew." Pyne felt that Shulie's outlook was clear: "For her being Jewish and Israel were one and the same."[64] Firestone's reported identification with Israel and her belief in the humanity of Palestinians were not necessarily contradictory, reflecting a stance taken by many women's liberationists and Jewish feminists.

Whatever Firestone's views on Israel, growing up in an Orthodox Jewish home was clearly formative to her ideas about sex roles and family life. She incorporated both positive and negative aspects of her religious background into her relentless critique of patriarchy. Alix Kates Shulman believes that it was the religious discrimination against Firestone that presaged her feminism. In Shulman's view, Firestone's not being able to attend "real" yeshiva because she was a girl was the "heartbreak" of her life."[65]

Of course, other influences were also in play, including the rampart sexism that Firestone experienced at the National Conference for New Politics and the Nixon counter-inaugural rally and the antifemale attitude of the Art Institute of Chicago, which put her through a grueling examination, recorded in a notorious 1967 film, remade in later years by Elizabeth Subrin. The collective anger of young women at the "limits of liberalism," which Firestone expressed elegantly in her "new view" of the "Women's Rights Movement in the U.S.," became the seeds of the revolt she helped lead.[66] "She was energized by righteous rage," comments Shulman. "More than anyone I've known, she was able to harness negative emotions . . . and turn them into the kind of rage needed to fuel a revolutionary movement."[67]

Firestone's Judaism was much less public than her feminism was. Although it escaped the scrutiny of friends because Firestone held her Jewish identity privately, her colleagues did recognize her unusual background. "She was the first Orthodox Jew I ever met in the radical movement," Amy Kesselman told me.[68] Firestone herself was shocked when she learned that there was another Orthodox Jew among the New York radical feminists. Of course, while Firestone had been raised in that tradition, she had left Orthodoxy far behind at the time of women's liberation.

At least one prominent Jewish feminist recalls that Firestone did attend meetings of the then-emerging Jewish counterculture in the early 1970s. Arlene Agus, co-founder in 1971 of Ezrat Nashim, the first American religious Jewish feminist organization, remembers Firestone at several Jewish conferences and counterculture retreats, including those at Weiss' Farm in Long Branch, New Jersey, beginning in 1973. By then, Firestone had left the radical feminist groups she had launched. She was also connected in some ways to Jewish friends; she had gone to elementary school with at least one of the retreat participants. She did not exactly "fit in," Agus recalls, but she was brilliant. What Agus remembers most was Firestone's razor-sharp anger, directed at social inequalities and, on this occasion, at the Jewish establishment.[69]

Firestone might have given a clue about the significance of Jewishness to her activism when in the late 1980s, after decades of being known to her artist friends and movement colleagues as Shulie, she insisted that henceforth they address her by her more formal, and also more clearly Jewish, name Shulamith, as Heather Booth recalled to the friends.[70] Another clue involved a talk at a university that Firestone had been invited to give in the 1980s about her days in the feminist movement. Needing the fee, she accepted, but onstage, she realized that the subject "bored her to exasperation," as a friend to whom she told the story recalled. So she began talking about Jewish mysticism, which then interested her a great deal but which baffled the audience. Firestone was "gently escorted off the stage."[71] Firestone had told Brownmiller in their chance encounter a decade earlier that she was researching Rosicrucian images (related to a late medieval secret mystical sect), which corresponds with an interest in kabbalah, a mystical tradition within Judaism.[72]

When Laya went to Shulamith's apartment after her death, she found her sister's Book of Psalms, the pages very frayed, "taped together multiple times because of overuse and annotated in her handwriting with which to say for which conditions and how many times to say them." "I'm sure she did a lot of prayer, a lot of saying Psalms," Laya said, perhaps using the prayers to slip into mystical states. "I think she did not really want to live in this world as it is." Shulamith had long been drawn to "a very deep strain of Judaism, the messianic," which, Laya said, "we're always looking for when the world is finally perfected and balanced. This world that we live in is not."[73] In *The Dialectic of Sex*, she talked about the ultimate triumph of a gender-free polis as the "Messianic Age." For this reason, Firestone looked toward the prophetic tradition to call out the wrongs she saw around her. "I think very much that Judaism was extremely deep for her," said Laya. "It never left her."[74]

Ellen Willis: "Next Year in Jerusalem"

Ellen Willis's struggles with her Jewishness emerge on the record, removing the guesswork that Firestone's changing beliefs require. Willis was born in 1941, the daughter of a policeman and a housewife. Until she was ten, she lived in a solidly Jewish Bronx neighborhood; then the family moved to a lower-middle-class Irish Catholic community in Queens. "Growing up in the friendly atmosphere of New York City," she wrote in an article in the *Village Voice* in 1974, "I always felt—at least on a conscious, day-to-day level—relatively secure in my Jewishness. I regarded it, when I regarded it at all, as a positive part of my identity as an iconoclastic intellectual: it implied a complex and ironic adversary relationship with American society."[75]

Willis's class background and her Jewish identity, embedded in a deeper pluralism and budding intellectualism, became important factors in her developing worldview.[76] Also important was the fact that she was a "red-diaper baby," the daughter of former Communist Party members. "From an early age being a political rebel was something that was in my world and not off the wall," Willis recalled. "I didn't have to come to . . . some sudden conversion that maybe there was a reason to criticize the mainstream of society."[77]

Willis graduated from Barnard College in 1962 and spent a year doing graduate work at the University of California at Berkeley. Back in New York, she became involved with the Free University of New York, a radical alternative school deeply immersed in the new counterculture. Robert Christgau, whom she met at the school, introduced her to "pop art" and, in her words, "got me started about thinking about rock and roll as a serious cultural issue."[78] Willis's first music piece, an article about Bob Dylan, appeared in *Commentary* in 1968 and drew the attention of *New Yorker* editor William Shawn, who hired her as the magazine's first pop-music critic. For Willis, rock was a "metaphor for world events, and criticism [was] a way of drawing out its poetic subtexts."[79] She became an "accomplished . . . female rock writer in an era when there were precious few women in the profession at all." Her articles, praised as "a tour de force of journalism," also acted as a "barometer of second wave feminism."[80]

Just as Willis expressed the "Zeitgeist of her age" in her music criticism, so did her reportage of the women's liberationists communicate the movement's message to a large public audience. Willis saw feminism as "the most dynamic cultural radical movement in modern history. . . . In one generation," she wrote, feminism "transformed the cultural and political landscape; its imprint is everywhere in American life."[81]

Willis's path to radical feminism differed from that of many of her peers. Though she had "all the Jewish-leftist tropisms" and "marched for integration and against the bomb," she did not feel welcome in the civil rights or leftist movements and was not an active participant. In 1968, after reading Firestone's *Notes from the First Year*, she went to her first women's meeting with the women behind *Notes*, finding none of the "prickly suspicious aloofness" she experienced at other political meetings. The key activity of consciousness-raising—sharing personal experience, then "generalization, analysis" and ideally action related to the analysis—led Willis to feel "the exhilaration of finding out it's not just me."[82] She attended the January 1969 counter-inaugural rally in Washington, when radical men heckled Marilyn Webb and Shulamith Firestone. The fiasco caused Willis to rethink her position about women's role on the left. "A genuine alliance with male radicals will not be possible until sexism sickens them as much as racism," she concluded, turning away from collaboration toward a "separate movement." The New York women at the counter-inaugural concurred, deciding to form an "action group based on a militantly independent radical feminist consciousness."[83]

Willis and Firestone started Redstockings two months later. Willis was in her late twenties, older than most members, and a *New Yorker* author. Although later she commented that her status as a writer privileged her within a movement that rejected hierarchy and elitism, she served as a "unique bridge" between two 1960s subcultures, radical feminism and pop culture, shaping and disseminating the ideas of both movements and providing a unique perspective on feminism's place in the countercultural revolution.[84]

Willis envisaged Redstockings as a "very militant, very public group" committed to action as well as to consciousness-raising.[85] In March 1969, just a month after the group's founding, Redstockings joined these two modalities to bring attention to an issue then relegated to secrecy and silence: the experience of abortion. Inventing the radical technique of the speak-out, Redstockings staged a public hearing at Judson Memorial Church in Greenwich Village, where a dozen women told a crowd of several hundred about their own abortions. The effect was electric, sending shock waves through the community and the nation and helping to lead a groundswell of action against illegal abortion, one that culminated a few years later in *Roe v. Wade*. This first speak-out, organized by Firestone, Irene Peslikis, and others, inspired similar events elsewhere, including in France, where a number of prominent women, including Simone de Beauvoir (Willis's heroine as well as Firestone's), risked imprisonment by publicly declaring, "I have had an abortion."[86]

In addition to the public speak-out, Redstockings popularized the technique of consciousness-raising, and its writings—confessional essays, poems, and manifestos, including the influential "Redstockings Manifesto"—radicalized many women. Its core slogan, "the personal is political" proved to be a powerful change agent throughout the world.[87]

Willis's role as one of the radical feminists' premier activists and theorists survived the breakup of Redstockings, and she channeled her energies into other feminist arenas, consistently advocating for sexual freedom. For Willis, this meant "access to safe and legal abortions, the right to sexual pleasure, . . . the break between reproduction and motherhood" (here she echoed Firestone), and the encouragement of alternative family forms. Sexual expression and pleasure were the keys.[88]

In the 1980s, Willis led the so-called pro-sex radical feminists in their heated challenge to the antipornography movement. Countering the arguments of Andrea Dworkin, Catharine MacKinnon, and others that "sexual liberation is a male supremacist plot," Willis proclaimed that sexual liberation was the keystone of broader social and cultural change.[89] She saw freedom as a broadly cultural goal that included the pleasure principle as a central component. Unlike many feminists but similarly to Firestone, Willis was deeply influenced by Freud; she also appreciated William Reich, who was more positive about all forms of sexuality. In fact, she was writing a book on psychoanalysis and politics at the time of her death in 2006.

Willis brought her sharp analytical skills and her penchant for debate to Jewish issues as well as feminist and broadly political ones. Secular, perennially skeptical, and often directly challenging Jewish practices, Willis nonetheless proclaimed herself a Jew, publicly and often. In a series of powerful writings about Jewish issues over some thirty years, she explored the meaning of Jewish experience to liberals and radical leftists. Like everything else about her, Willis's Jewish identity was up front, quirky, unique.

Willis's earliest writing on Judaism, and one of the most extraordinary pieces in her entire body of work, was the three-part, twenty-thousand-word article "Next Year in Jerusalem," which she wrote for *Rolling Stone* in 1977, about her struggle with her younger brother's conversion to Orthodoxy.[90] The article had an immediate impact and is read and admired today; writer and former *Gawker* co-editor Emily Gould calls it "maybe the best personal essay" she has ever read.[91] Willis had gone to Jerusalem in October 1976 to meet her brother, Michael, nine years younger, where he was studying at the yeshiva Aish HaTorah, an ultra-Orthodox religious sect that espoused, in Michael's words, "613 commandments, . . . Puritanism, . . . political conservatism, . . . [a] Jews-first philosophy." Michael, then twenty-four, had stopped in Israel the year before on his way home from seven months in Asia. Disillusioned with the situation in Cambodia and Vietnam and facing uncertain prospects in the U.S., the highly intellectual, reserved young man became engrossed in his Jewish studies. In a seven-page letter to Ellen, he explained his attraction to the religion. Ellen, who felt an "almost mystical identification" with her brother, considering him what she "might have become" had she been a man, was shocked, filled with "a kind of primal dread" at Michael's adoption of "Judaism in its most extreme, absolutist form. . . . The Torah's laws . . . must be obeyed in every detail." This was the kind of Judaism that the Firestone daughters had tried to escape. "In my universe," Willis wrote, "intelligent, sensible people who had grown up in secular homes in the second half of the 20th century did not embrace biblical fundamentalism. . . . How could anyone familiar with the work of a certain Viennese Jew possibly believe in God the Father?"[92]

Michael's letter in response, debunking evolution and attempting to explain the truth of Torah, impressed Ellen with its logic but faltered on the woman question. In Ellen's words, "Orthodox Judaism enshrined as divine law a male supremacist ideology I had been struggling against, in one way or another, all my life. It was a patriarchal religion that decreed separate functions of the sexes—man to learn, administer religious law and exercise public authority: woman to sanctify the home. For Mike to accept it would be (*face it!*) a betrayal."[93]

Although her brother conceded that Judaism gave men "the better deal" from a secular viewpoint, he argued that women had religious advantages: "fewer commandments to perform, fewer opportunities to sin, and by having children could approach God more easily." Ellen was not persuaded: "I couldn't believe in the Jewish God. He had been invented by men seeking a rationale for their privileges."[94] She had explained her position in an earlier letter to Michael, couching her rejection of religious patriarchy in her own ideas about God: "The idea that one group of people has the right let alone the religious obligation to dominate another, that the sexes' functions are rigidly separate . . . & above all that God is male—this to me is just such blatant arrogance!" It was "alien" to her "whole feeling of what God is."[95]

Mike's arguments on a trip home at Thanksgiving failed to convince her or her parents. But her parents' objections differed from Ellen's intellectual approach. Mrs. Willis considered herself "in some sense religious, she believed in God, even believed that the Torah might be God-given. But she couldn't see that God required us to observe all those regulations. Wasn't it enough to be a good person? Characteristically, she focused on practical concerns. Was Mike happy? Would religion give him what he badly needed—something satisfying to do with his life?" Ellen's father, the son of an Orthodox rabbi, was a rationalist whose hero was Clarence Darrow, the supreme evolutionist; yet he was tolerant of all religions and prepared to understand his son's conversion. Willis's parents visited Michael in Jerusalem, relinquishing their objections when they found him happier than he had ever been. Ellen, however, saw Michael's enthusiasm as a "manic façade." Nonetheless, Michael asked questions she could not answer. "How did I explain the creation of the world? How did I explain the strange history of the Jews—their unremitting persecution and unlikely survival, their conspicuous role in world affairs? How did I explain the Torah itself?"[96]

Willis admitted that as a "radical, . . . a leftist and feminist activist," she had "struggled perpetually with doubts." But even that tendency was a Jewish one: "I was aware of the link between my skepticism and my Jewishness. It was, after all, the Jew who was the perennial doubter, the archetypal outsider, longing for redemption while dismissing the claims of would-be redeemers as so much snake oil." Her skepticism made her realize that she could be wrong: "Since I could not prove Judaism was false, I had to admit that it could be true." This thought threw her into a deepening panic and made her understand that she had to muster the

courage to confront Michael's challenge. Otherwise she would be rejecting Judaism "simply because [she] did not care to accept it," rather than
because of honest intellectual principles; she felt she had no alternative but to imagine herself as observant. Her friends, who thought that
Michael's brand of religion was "eccentric fanaticism," "found it hard to
believe that someone so sensible and intelligent could be wondering if
she ought to become an orthodox Jew."[97]

There was only one possible resolution for Willis's doubts; she had
to go to Israel: "confront my terror at its source—to put myself in my
brother's place and see if I reached the same conclusions." While she
could not attend Aish HaTorah, a male-only yeshiva for *ba'al teshuvas*
(delinquent Jews who have "returned"), she held close conversations
with Michael, his teachers, their wives (*rebbetzin*), and other women. At
the *rebbetzin*'s classes for women, Ellen encountered Jewish ethics and
began to realize "how Jewish [her] feelings were."[98]

Although Willis was an outsider, because she was Jewish, she was
"also family," accepted as part of the Orthodox community. The ecstasy
that Willis had previously experienced on LSD now came to her as a
religious impulse. "Whatever holiness was," she wrote, "the city breathed
it." Having gleaned from talks with her brother that Judaism was a
plausible intellectual possibility, Ellen's living in Jerusalem conveyed
that "Judaism was a plausible way of life": "And that realization slid
relentlessly into the next: that it was plausible even for me." The study
of Torah suddenly seemed "no more inherently compulsive than [her]
own search for the precise adjective, or the care with which feminists
analyzed the minutiae of sexual relationships." She began to question
her "hyperurban, freelance existence": "Did I really have my priorities
straight?" Questioning her secular life led her to imagine her life as an
observant Jew. But she would not be a traditional Jewish mother; she
would work outside the home. She convinced herself that the religion
permitted these options. "Even within the bounds of Judaism I could be
a feminist of sorts, crusading for reforms like equal education, perhaps
contesting the biased halachic interpretations of male rabbis. And my
experience would put me in a unique position to reach women like me
and bring them back."[99]

Though it was difficult to accept that Orthodox Jewish women might
be content with their female identity, even their sexuality, there it was:

The big lie of male supremacy is that women are less than fully human; the basic task of feminism is to expose that lie and fight it on every level. Yet for all my feminist militance I was, it seemed, secretly afraid that the lie was true—that my humanity was hopelessly at odds with my ineluctably female sexuality—while the rebbetzin, staunch apostle of traditional femininity, did not appear to doubt for a moment that she could be both a woman and a serious person. . . . I was too much the product of Western libertarian values to travel the rebbetzin's route to self-acceptance, and so far I had not succeeded in finding my own.[100]

Willis thought that she would capitulate to the belief that was beginning to form: "that it was all true, that I was only resisting because I couldn't stand the pain of admitting how wrong I was." If she did not make plans to return to the U.S. right away, she might end up staying in Israel. In the end, she resisted her attraction to Jerusalem and Aish HaTorah, feeling that while "it was one thing to consider the abstract possibility that women's role in Judaism was not inherently oppressive," it was "another to live in a culture that made [her] feel oppressed."[101]

Willis prepared to leave Israel, knowing that "at least for the present," she would "not become an Orthodox Jew": "My decision had involved no epiphany, no cathartic moment of truth; my doubts remained and perhaps always would." She was leaving based on her intuition that she would be happiest in the secular world, where rock music was readily available and where feminists fought for their liberation. But she was keenly aware that she and her brother were at that moment a study in "contrasting male and female sensibilities"; Michael had reached his decision to become ba'al teshuva on the basis of logic and reason, while she, the most cerebral of her feminist friends, had relied on emotion.[102]

Beneath Willis's turmoil lay a characteristic willfulness that she also identified as a factor in her leave-taking. "As I kissed my brother goodbye," she recounted, "I still did not know whether my refusal to believe was healthy self-assertion or stubborn egotism; the Jews, the Bible tells us, are a stiff-necked people." However much she fought her attraction to the Orthodox Jewish life, her final "refusal to believe" attached her to Jewish peoplehood even as she rejected a geographical, spiritual connection. She returned home with her skepticism—and her Jewish identity—intact, resuming her secular life. Her brother—her "male mirror image"—became a rabbi; he has served in that capacity for more than forty years, heading Aish HaTorah in South Africa.[103]

Willis continued to struggle with the issue of Jewish belonging. "What did peoplehood entail, where did it lead?" she asked in "Radical Jews Caught in the Middle," a piece she wrote for the *Village Voice* in 1981.[104] In articles about anti-Semitism, anti-Zionism, and Jewish politics, she left earlier doubts behind, but her trademark skepticism emerged as she considered new paths in Jewish politics and age-old questions regarding the Jewish condition. Central to these writings was the sense of "oppression and marginality as defining facts of Jewish existence."[105] While she did not explicitly analogize the connection between her struggles against antidemocratic institutions, including patriarchy, and her framing of the "Jewish question," the common dimensions of these problems emerged. Alix Kates Shulman, Willis's longtime friend, explained that while Willis wrote about being a Jew, she found "complete commonality among anti-woman, anti-Jew, anti-black, anti-everybody." They were all "aspects of the same thing."[106]

Willis came to understand anti-Semitism personally as well as intellectually. Although she had grown up as a New Yorker comfortable with her Jewish identity, after the 1967 Six-Day War, she experienced "a loss of innocence," feeling vulnerable as a Jew for the first time. With most of her leftist friends unconcerned "if Israel went under," she felt more alone than when she lived in "overwhelmingly WASP environments" in Colorado and upstate New York. "I feel—a word I try not to use lightly these days—oppressed," she wrote in the *Village Voice* in 1974.[107]

Five years later, in the article "The Myth of the Powerful Jew," Willis sought to provide a psychoanalytic explanation for the "dark impulses" that made anti-Semitism a growing social force but one that her colleagues were reluctant to recognize. For Willis, anti-Semitism was a "systemic and pervasive pathology," endemic among the American ruling class and with a powerful impact on international politics.[108] Now she took on the radical Left, the Jewish Left, and mainstream America for downplaying its continuing existence.

In Willis's view, anti-Semitism was at its core a "deeply irrational" force, a "chronic social disease that exists mainly under the surface." "The psychology of anti-Semitism, the way it functions in society, and the nature of the threat to the Jews are in certain respects unique. . . .

Jews are simultaneously perceived as insiders and outsiders, capitalists and communists, upholders of high ethical and intellectual standards and shrewd purveyors of poisonous subversive ideas. The common theme of these disparate perceptions is that Jews have enormous power, whether to defend established authority or to undermine it. It is this double-edged myth of Jewish power that has made Jews such a useful all-purpose scapegoat for social discontent."[109] The contradictory combination of success and vulnerability made Jews emotional symbols of strength when they were in fact powerless: "To kill a gnat," said Willis, "imagining it's an elephant, is to feel powerful indeed." The danger was ever present, though often less from "overt anti-Semitic malice than from impersonal, institutional anti-Jewish bias."[110] Yet the accusation persisted that anti-Semitism was "unreal," simply "paranoia" on the part of Jews. For Willis, this was "gaslighting" at its worst, making the situation even more troubling.[111]

Willis partly blamed Jews for their predicament. Because "anti-Semitism feeds on human misery, on social inequality" and Jews had persistently served as "the lightning rod for the rage of the oppressed," if they identified with power and relied on the protection of the powerful, they merely "set themselves up" for harms.[112] Even though she saw Jews "as far to the left of non-Jews in comparable economic and social circumstances," she deplored class bias and racism among them.[113] Defending American power—and refusing to confront social ills—would never make American Jews (or Israel) safe; it would only isolate them from minorities and increase the possibility that they would be scapegoated.[114]

Covering the first national conference of the progressive New Jewish Agenda (NJA) for the *Village Voice* in 1981, Willis addressed the Left's anti-Jewish bias, which was based on the "false assumption that anti-Semitism is no longer a threat." "The left has been as anti-Semitic as the rest of society; therefore we need a self-conscious Jewish left that will fight our oppression instead of perpetuating it."[115] But she was skeptical that a separate organization of progressive Jews was the answer. "Why not just carry a commitment to *Tikun Olam* into the general left?" she asked. She referred to "an organization that would join forces with the larger left while challenging it to respond to a distinctive Jewish voice."[116]

Willis found the NJA conference exciting, with 650 people in attendance and hundreds more turned away, but she was put off by the kosher food, the observance of Shabbat, and a general sense "that Jewish identity must be rooted in the religious tradition and/or some other particularist culture[al] Zionism, Yiddish, Bundism, organized Jewish communal life."[117] Her reservations sprang from her feelings about her own Jewish identity: nonreligious, not even Jewish counterculturalist.

> My sense of Jewishness has less to do with any form of cultural separatism than with the Diaspora Jew's historical role as critical outsider, living on the margins of dominant cultures, thus in a position to combine familiarity with skepticism. For me the question of what Judaism (or Jewish tradition) says about how we should behave politically is important not as a direct guide to action, but as a clue to what the Jewish condition is about. When I think about formulating a Jewish politics I think about questions like, what does the messianic vision of liberation mean, in secular terms? Why have the Jews been hated for 3000 years—and yet survived? Why have the Jews—a tiny minority, after all—played such a central role in social crises? What is the relation between anti-Semitism and oppression in general?[118]

Although Willis wanted to find some way to work with NJA, she was disheartened that the unity statement that the conference produced implicitly dismissed her own definition of the Jewish problem as oppression and marginality for being too "negative," too focused on "enemies," rather than "ethics." This was a "false duality." "Every Jew faces the question of how to respond to our enemies: we can try (futilely) to fit in, make ourselves invisible, placate the powerful, or we can embrace the opportunity our outsider status offers and become radical social critics. What was the commitment to transform one's oppression into a weapon against oppressors if not a positive ethical stance?"[119] Willis believed that the refusal to take anti-Semitism seriously skewed the Left's perception of the Israeli crisis.[120] In 1974, she wrote that she considered the "hardline anti-Zionist position that the Jewish state is illegitimate and should be abolished" to be "objectively anti-Semitic" because the demise of Israel would "result in the death or dispersal of a great many Jews and encourage an active resurgence of anti-Semitism."[121]

Years later, writing as a "quintessential Diaspora Jew," she maintained that Israel was a haven for Jews against the threat of anti-Semitism. While Israel's misuses of power had to be condemned, she denounced the Left's "villainization of Israel." She continued to champion the Jewish state as a bulwark against anti-Semitism, although she criticized its policies and supported Palestinian rights. In "Why I'm Not for Peace" (2002), Willis ridiculed the idea that "getting tough and imposing an Israeli-Palestinian settlement" was a "route to safety" in the Middle East. Islamic fundamentalists did not want a settlement, she noted, but only to have Israel "go away." Their ideology would wreak havoc not only for Israel but for Palestinians as well.[122] In an influential article the next year, "Is There Still a Jewish Question? Why I'm an Anti-Anti-Zionist," she wrote that the "runaway inflation of Israel's villainy aligns with ingrained cultural fantasies about the iniquity and power of Jews." The "traditional pariah status of Jews" had been replicated by a "Jewish pariah state," and "the anti-Jewish temperature [was] rising." The Left's anti-Zionism made it complicit in the fact that Israel had become the "wild card of world politics and the lightning rod of political crisis."[123] Willis published "Why I'm Not for Peace" in *Radical Society* and her piece about her "anti-anti-Zionism" in Tony Kushner and Alisa Solomon's collection *Wrestling with Zion: Progressive Jewish-American Responses to the Israeli-Palestinian Conflict*. She published similar articles in left-wing journals such as the *Nation*. Though always a progressive voice, on this hot-button issue, she was a dissenting one.

Willis's engagement with Jewish issues reflected her strong Jewish identity coupled with her "Sagittarian compulsion to aim straight at the cosmic bull's-eye," as she described her spiritual crisis over her brother's Orthodoxy. "The blessing and curse of being a Jew," she said, quoting Rabbi Noach, was the "misplaced searching for God. Every Jew is a neurotic."[124] Yet her Jewishness was only one of several identities she inhabited over her lifetime, existing alongside her vibrant feminism. Sometimes these parts of her identity came close to merger, as when she told friends that perhaps she would join a Jewish feminist consciousness-raising group. There is no evidence that she did that, but she remarked to Letty Cottin Pogrebin in 1981 that her "group had just finished doing C-R [consciousness-raising] on anti-Semitism."[125] Years earlier, she had written to her brother that she had been reading "all kinds of stuff about Zionism and anti-Zionism" and was again feeling that she would "like to start a Jewish consciousness-raising group": "I think it would fill in a lot of gaps in my personal political analysis."[126]

While Willis did not foreground Judaism in her lifestyle or affiliations, like Firestone, she had a sibling who did. Both Michael Willis and Firestone's younger brothers embraced ultra-Orthodoxy. Although Laya Firestone Seghi did not affiliate with any denomination, she remained deeply rooted in Jewish tradition, while Rabbi Tirzah Firestone founded Congregation Nevei Kodesh, a Jewish Renewal community in Boulder, Colorado. Willis, from a red-diaper background, and Firestone, from a deeply Orthodox one, both struggled with yet maintained ties to Jewishness. Willis did so as a secular Jew, explicit in her public affiliations; Firestone, while not openly proclaiming her spirituality, was unable to completely shake off her heritage. Willis fought anti-Semitism and anti-Zionism along with patriarchal repression in its multiple forms; Firestone championed a complete break with authoritarian, sexist behavior but did not speak out on anti-Jewish prejudice. Yet each was influenced by a drive for personal freedom that sprang at least in part from a connection to their Jewish heritage. While there was no common core to their Jewish beliefs, the rebel from an Orthodox background and the woman who resisted the attraction to the Orthodox life that she encountered in Jerusalem shared an impulse toward open expression and unfettered individuality that motivated their theories and actions.

Alix Kates Shulman: "Radical Feminism . . . Wasn't about Religion"

Although significant to Firestone's and Willis's personal identities, Jewishness did not matter at all to the collective identity of the feminist organizations they started. This point is brought home by a story told to me by writer Alix Kates Shulman, Redstockings collaborator and friend to both women. Shulman was an early member of Redstockings; after the group collapsed in 1971, she joined New York Radical Feminists' West Village Brigade Number One, and after leaving that organization, she became a founding member of first one and later a second group, both unnamed, that had the ambitious hope of reviving women's liberation.

Figure 2.1. Alix Kates Shulman at the 1968 Miss America protest, Atlantic City. Courtesy Alix Kates Shulman.

The first, founded in about 1975 ("Redstockings Plus," Shulman jokingly calls it, since it included four early Redstockings members), met for years at Rosalyn Baxandall's apartment. The membership changed, but the final group into which it eventually morphed was stable, meeting weekly until the mid-1980s and then less frequently for another decade. "I was intimate with many of these women," said Shulman. "They were like my family." Yet she was uncertain of their religious backgrounds. They talked about everything related to their lives as women, but not until the late 1970s or early 1980s did her group get around to talking about religion. Except for Ellen Willis, who was "outspokenly Jewish," said Shulman, "I didn't know who in the group was Jewish, who was Catholic, who was Protestant until we did that consciousness-raising on religion. I was ignorant about it until then."[127]

Back in Redstockings, everyone knew that Firestone and Willis were Jewish, but Shulman did not know about the other members and sometimes guessed wrong. In her later groups, Shulman learned that Ann Snitow, among others, was Jewish; she thought (incorrectly) that Rosalyn Baxandall was "one-quarter" Jewish; and Karen Durbin, whom she had assumed was Jewish, was actually raised Catholic, as was Brett Harvey. "This came as a complete surprise to me," said Shulman. The point was that religion "wasn't a big deal to [the women] at all. It wasn't important. . . . Radical feminism was about relations between the sexes, it wasn't about religion."[128] Shulman acknowledged that the representation of Jews in women's liberation was "disproportionate in terms of the general population." But class had more currency than religion, and friendships "crossed" backgrounds. At my Women's Liberation/Jewish Identity conference, Shulman speculated that this differed from the Chicago Gang of Four, each of whom knew the others were Jewish but did not talk about it. "We didn't know or care."[129]

Rosalyn Baxandall offered another explanation for the women's lack of Jewish self-consciousness and group awareness. Baxandall feels that while they knew about the Catholic backgrounds of some members because they had rebelled against Catholicism and talked about it, Jewish members were not rebelling against Judaism since it had been less important in their upbringings, and consequently they did not discuss it.[130]

The nonessential, and subjective, nature of Jewish identity among radical New York feminists is suggested by Baxandall's own life story. Her sister Julie verifies that Rosalyn Fraad Baxandall was the daughter of a father and a mother who were both "100% Jewish." Both parents were militant atheists and communists. Her father, a distinguished pediatrician who taught and practiced at Albert Einstein Hospital, came to appreciate the Jewish legacy to politics and culture. He told Rosalyn that the family should never deny its Jewish identity for fear of "Nazism." Pride in militant activism, and its association with Jewishness, became "almost like a badge of solidarity" to the Fraads.[131]

Despite these views and the family's atheism, which Rosalyn Baxandall shared, she would intermittently say that she was Jewish. Her son, Phineas, told me that he thought he was Jewish until he was twelve years old, wondering whether he was supposed to have a bar mitzvah. His mother told him that they "weren't really Jewish": "just half-jokingly that we lived in New York City and most of our friends were Jewish." He believes that his mother's refusal to give him a "straight answer" about being Jewish was not about disliking Judaism or Jews, since she believed that "Judaism was probably one of the least bad religions—because Jews had been oppressed for so long." Yet she could never satisfactorily explain to Phineas "why she wasn't Jewish." His mother embraced Judaism to a greater extent later in life, "if only because so many of her Jewish friends drifted toward greater religious identity," but she also mobilized against "Israeli Zionism" regarding the Palestinian situation.[132]

At the time of Baxandall's death in 2015, she was writing a book about her maternal great-uncle, Meyer London, a socialist, who had been the first Russian Jewish immigrant in Congress and of whom she was quite proud.[133] But most of her feminist friends did not consider Baxandall Jewish or recognize her occasional Jewish self-identification. For Baxandall, as for many other radical feminists, Jewish New Yorkers who identified as nonreligious or antireligious, Jewish identity seemed irrelevant in general and sometimes oppositional to their politics, yet it could exert cultural or philosophical appeal. In light of the fact that her two sisters identified positively and consistently as Jews and that Baxandall did not "come out" as Jewish even to her son, her ambivalence and inconsistency may have been extreme, but the voluntary association she placed on her identity characterized a large number of urban radicals such as herself.

Shulman views her own obliviousness to Jewishness within Redstockings as related to her New York identity as an "atheist in a cosmopolitan world" as much as to the group's universalist orientation and disregard of religion. She described how she felt moving to the city in the early 1950s: "so comfortably lost in my Jewishness that I can take it for granted." Shulman considered Jewishness as only one of "several self-defining tags, from radical feminist to author of sexually explicit novels to political activist." Only after a disturbing incident in the small island community in southern Maine where she spent some forty summers as the only Jew did Shulman come to sport Jewish identity there "like a red banner." "After decades of my Jewish identity being obscured in the blur of Jews around me," she wrote in 2003, "I suddenly felt as if I were outlined in felt-tipped pen: Jew." Singled out in Maine by a local missionary as a target for conversion, she seemed to herself "more the Jew than ever," always to wonder "how I am perceived and never [to] feel as if I quite belong."[134] In this personal way, Shulman came to understand Ellen Willis's insight about the psychological roots of Jewish oppression and her belief that Jews were doomed to feel "permanently insecure."[135]

Shulman had grown up in a comfortable and "completely assimilated" midwestern family. Her parents and their siblings became "proud happy atheists," who felt they were leaving behind the superstition and irrationality of their own parents, immigrants from eastern Europe who had settled in the Cleveland area in the 1890s. After her grandparents' death, they never had another seder. "We were completely secular," Shulman reported. Yet her family never denied its Jewishness. Shulman's parents were "Roosevelt activists": her father a lawyer and her mother a "Jewish activist," three-time president of the Federation of Jewish Women of Greater Cleveland after she left a Works Progress Administration job as designer of history projects. The highlight of Shulman's youth was attending a convention of Jewish organizations with her mother in Atlantic City. Her mother's work had more to do with "anti-anti-Semitism" than with Judaism per se, but the dinner-table conversations about "the politics of the thing" were vivid and exciting.[136]

Both parents had been subject to anti-Semitism, and there was "plenty of anti-Semitism" in Shulman's midwestern childhood. Her parents wanted her "to know that [she] was a Jew and not to say, no I'm not."[137] The identification became difficult for Shulman when she wound up in a high school that was "half Jewish and half not and everything was segregated," including the all-important social clubs. Even the high school's staircases were segregated—"there was the Jewish staircase and there was the Gentile staircase"—and the after-school "milkshake hangouts" were not shared by Jews and Gentiles.[138]

Despite this background, Judaism did not become meaningful to Shulman until she went to New York in 1953 to study philosophy in graduate school at Columbia University. There she discovered a subculture of Jewish intellectuals, which, although they were all male, led to a "romance with Judaism." The works she was reading were written by male authors, except for the occasional female; Shulman was particularly excited to encounter Hannah Arendt because she was Jewish.[139] "I got really interested in all these different kinds of Jews there were," especially those who created culture. "If somebody's Jewish, I may feel a certain commonality."[140]

Shulman enjoyed graduate school, but her male colleagues' disdain for the women students stung. "As soon as we spoke, everything stopped. No one listened to us. They waited until we were done and then they went back to discussing what they had been discussing before we spoke. I wasn't enraged because that wasn't an acceptable attitude for a young woman. But I was burning inside. It was a slow burn."[141]

Shulman married and had two children. In 1967, she went to her first woman's meeting. In her graduate classes, she had never heard girls or young women talk "like people of the world." Immediately she "understood for the first time that things did not have to be the way they were, that they could be changed": "A lot of us felt that way, and that's how the movement started. It was a thrilling thing to be alive and to be there at that moment."[142]

The women were excited to include the thirty-five-year-old Shulman, for she embodied the challenge they hoped to address: freeing the wife and mother from her chains. She started going to meetings every night, at first surreptitiously. As her relationship with her husband began to change, Shulman drew up a marriage agreement, dividing chores and pleasures down the line, fifty-fifty, which she published in a small feminist magazine in 1970. Shulman had no idea that its main principle, that "a woman and man should share equally the responsibility for their household and children in every way, from the insidiously unacknowledged tasks of daily life to the pleasures of guiding a young human to maturity," would cause such uproar. Reprinted in the debut issue of *Ms.*, in *Redbook* (attracting two thousand letters), *Life*, a Harvard textbook on contract law, and other anthologies, it drew scorn from Norman Mailer, who famously mocked Shulman by declaring that he never would be married to a woman like her—*he* would never help his wife with the dishes! In 2005, thirty-five years after the still-controversial piece's first appearance, author Caitlin Flanagan attacked it in the *Atlantic* and a subsequent book.[143]

Shulman participated in many of New York radical feminism's iconic moments: the 1968 Miss America Pageant protest; Redstockings' 1969 abortion speak-out; a 1970 "Ogle-In" on Wall Street, in which women whistled at and shouted out catcalls to men; and the massive march down Fifth Avenue on August 26 of that year to celebrate the fiftieth anniversary of women's suffrage.[144] Shulman was also present at the 1969 sit-in at the *Ladies' Home Journal*, when feminist journalists took over the magazine's editorial offices to demand fair coverage for women.[145]

In addition to these actions, Shulman's novels, short stories, memoirs, and essays testified to the growing relevance of second-wave feminism to women's lives. Her novel *Memoirs of an Ex-Prom Queen* (1972) sold over one million copies in paperback. Though it had some autobiographical elements, Shulman explains that she was not trying to represent herself but rather "a certain white, middle-class, Midwestern suburban girl of that era, subject to all the forces of sexism that had yet to be articulated in fiction."[146] She was more concerned about examining the invisible social forces that molded women's lives than in portraying individual and family psychologies. Jewish identity is rarely expressed in the novel in an explicit fashion. Shulman admitted that she was "far more interested in middle class white female experience than in a more narrowly ethnic one."[147]

Shulman's second novel, *Burning Questions*, published in 1978, told the story of Zane IndiAnna, a radical feminist teaching a course in "revolutionary women" at the New School. Shulman considered the book, presented as a first-person memoir, as a historical novel. Echoing one of Shulman's favorite themes, in the preface of this roman à clef, Shulman's narrator quotes the real memoir of revolutionary socialist Angelica Balabanoff: "the experience of the individual in relation to historic events does not belong to oneself alone."[148] Like many innovative works of feminist novelists, this novel's vision of radical social change attracted the ire of mainstream critics. The *New York Times* reviewer wrote that the novel would "set back the cause of women fifty years," a disparagement that the newly organized Feminist Writers' Guild protested.[149]

Another of Shulman's successful writing projects, her biography of Emma Goldman, like herself an atheist Jewish feminist intellectual, came just after she joined the women's movement. Given an opportunity to write a biography for a new Women of America series, Shulman chose Goldman, most of whose works were then out of print. "Emma was my education," Shulman said; "she connected me with a radical world."[150] Goldman's conflicts over the problem of individualism, dissent, minority voice, authority, hierarchy, and her great issues—"the relation between the sexes, the organization of society, and most profoundly, the connection between the two"—paralleled Shulman's own, and Goldman's life immediately gave Shulman a context in which to understand the unfolding women's liberation movement. From Goldman, she learned that "an idea, a cause, a movement could give meaning to a life," a lesson she was beginning to draw from her own life and came to inspire several of her novels.[151] Another parallel lay in their attitudes toward Judaism, which each discarded as a formal identity but remained connected to in characteristically Jewish ways. An atheist, Goldman never criticized Judaism as harshly as she did Christianity, and she considered Jews to be "the mainstay" of "every revolutionary endeavor." Her oratory often contained biblical references, and her radical style was rooted in the prophetic tradition.[152]

Like Goldman, Shulman never defined herself as a Jewish radical activist, preferring to see herself as a participant in a larger social and cultural struggle. What was a "great joy" to her about Redstockings was that "it was secular" and that the women "were all equal in that movement." To the question of what the relationship was between the women's liberation movement and Jewish identity, she responded, "In my experience, the answer was none."[153]

Also like Goldman, Shulman's relationship to Judaism evinces some paradoxes. While believing that Jewishness had little impact on women's liberation, Shulman disclosed points of significant personal contact with Jewishness: her mother's work for Jewish groups; the "Jewish and Gentile" staircases in high school; her "romance" with Judaism in graduate school; encounters with anti-Semitism. The explanation may lie in her rejection of the particularism of ethnicity and religion, which Shulman envisions as narrow and confining. These views characterized the early phase of radical feminism. Redstockings declared the unity of all women, dismissing merely situational differences. Its manifesto proclaimed, "Women are an oppressed class. . . . We . . . repudiate all economic, racial, educational, or status privileges that divide us from other women."[154] By not noticing the presence of Jewishness in the movement, Shulman and other Redstockings women avoided addressing ethnic and religious differences that seemed unimportant. With the exception of Ellen Willis, the Jewish women of Redstockings did not reflect on how their Jewish backgrounds might have influenced their feminism.

Yet beneath the surface of the movement's universalism lay specific forces that helped propel each liberationist into her activism. In years to come, the changing role of race and ethnicity in radical feminism made greater room for acknowledging distinctive heritages, though religion generally remained an outlier. As radical feminists moved on to other stages of their lives, they came to embrace aspects of these identities. "The older I get, the more I feel and celebrate my Jewish identity and aspects of Jewish culture," Shulman told the Women's Liberation and Jewish Identity Conference.[155] She is now co-editing the documentary anthology *Writing the Women's Movement* for the Library of America. As a participant in the movement whose writings contributed enormously to its popular appeal, Shulman is well qualified for the task, but she feels a sense of urgency about finishing it. To guide her, she draws on the famous saying of Rabbi Tarfon (from the *Pirkei Avot*, the "Ethics of the Sages"): "You are not required to complete the task, but neither are you free to abandon it."[156] This ancient Jewish wisdom is her advice to young writers and, by extension, to feminists of the contemporary generation.

Susan Brownmiller: "The Heritage Is Still with Me"

Born in 1935, three years after Alix Kates Shulman, Susan Brownmiller (née Warhaftig) grew up in a densely Jewish section of Flatbush, in Brooklyn. Like Shulman's, her family was "just plain-old Roosevelt Democrats," her father a Macy's salesman, her mother a secretary at the Empire State Building. Brownmiller's childhood Jewishness was strong, tied into the Holocaust and the hopes for a Jewish homeland. She remembers being very happy when the state of Israel was declared.[157]

Brownmiller went to a Jewish camp in Pennsylvania for several years and also to Hebrew school at the East Midwood Jewish Center, where she studied Hebrew and Jewish history—biblical history, Palestine's history, eastern European history, and all the holidays—two afternoons a week. "There was a lot to cover," she recalled, "and it all got sort of mishmashed in my brain except for one thread: a helluva lot of people over the centuries seemed to want to harm the Jewish people."[158] The experience was formative in many ways. Caught up in the fervor of Israel's formation, teachers and fellow students became enthusiastic Zionists, talking about immigrating to Israel to work the land. "The idea was thrilling," Brownmiller thought. "I wanted to be part of this brave, new movement. I wanted to help. I went to the Ocean Avenue synagogue on Saturday morning and chanted the prayers."[159]

In what Brownmiller calls a typical mocking Jewish manner, one of her aunts took to calling her "the Rebbetzin."[160] "What's a 'rebbetzin'?" Brownmiller asked her mother, "thinking it must mean a serious, dedicated, intelligent person." But her mother only laughed. "A *rebbetzin* is a rabbi's wife," she informed her daughter. "What a deflating blow to my ego and ambitions! A rabbi was a revered personage; a rabbi's wife served cake and tea and preened in his reflected glory. My instinctive feminism (no lessons needed) could not be reconciled with this severe limitation on my life's path. The sly mockery had its effect. So much for Judaism, so much for religion—I became an atheist, a secularist, and never looked back."[161] Brownmiller went on to Cornell on scholarship. Her Jewish commitment was muted there, although she did attend some Hillel events, singing the songs she knew from camp and Hebrew school. Seeing the joy on her face, the rabbi encouraged her to join the group. Despite her pronounced atheism, she suspects that her connection to Judaism operated on a subconscious level.

Brownmiller remained at Cornell for two and a half years, then returned to New York to try for a theatrical career and did some off-Broadway roles. Acting, she remembers, was more acceptable than writing or politics (she had majored in government at Cornell), both of which required what was then seen as a masculine type of ambition.[162] The transformation in her life came from participating in the civil rights movement—first up north, picketing Woolworth's in 1960 for its discrimination toward blacks, and then in the South, where she joined SNCC's Mississippi Freedom Summer Project in Meridian in 1964. Another transformation came when her friend Jan Goodman, who had gone to Mississippi with her, heard from Carol Hanisch, a leader in New York Radical Women, that a group was meeting to talk about women's liberation. Brownmiller was then a full-time news writer at ABC and a staff writer for the *Village Voice*. She went to the meeting, and her life

Figure 2.2. Susan Brownmiller at Women Against Pornography march, New York City, October 1979. Photo by Janie Eisenberg.

changed. "This was always in my heart," she observed; "I was always a feminist."[163]

In March 1970, while working as a freelance writer, Brownmiller coordinated the sit-in at the *Ladies' Home Journal*, which protested its sexist treatment of women. Women from Redstockings, New York Radical Feminists (including West Village-One, Brownmiller's consciousness-raising group), and some female journalists participated in the successful occupation.[164] The following January, Brownmiller instigated a "speak-out" on rape with New York Radical Feminists, followed in April by the New York Radical Feminist Conference on Rape. These events led her to undertake serious research and analysis on the subject, and her breakthrough book *Against Our Will* was published four years later to critical praise and great public attention. In 1975, *Time* magazine named Brownmiller one of its twelve "Women of the Year." The book is credited with stimulating awareness of rape as a pervasive aspect of patriarchal culture by which men dominate women; in Brownmiller's words, rape is "nothing more or less than a conscious process of intimidation by which *all men* keep *all women* in a state of fear." The book was translated into twenty languages, and the New York Public Library considers *Against Our Will* one of one hundred "Books of the Century."[165]

In Brownmiller's contribution to the Jewish Women's Archive's project on feminism, she comments that somewhere in *Against Our Will*, she mentions "quietly" that she is "Jewish from Brooklyn." But, she continues, "I have never stressed my Jewish heritage in my writing. Yet the heritage is still with me, and I can argue that my chosen path—to fight against physical harm, specifically the terror of violence against women—had its origins in what I had learned in Hebrew School about the pogroms and the Holocaust."[166] This remarkable acknowledgment, coming more than thirty years after Brownmiller's book, echoes the reflections of some of the Chicago Gang of Four and Marilyn Webb's views, as they retrospectively considered the motivations for their feminist activism. Brownmiller's assertion is particularly revelatory as it connects two kinds of violent oppression, the rape of women and the killing of Jews, which she had not explicitly discussed in her book.

Brownmiller went on to write other works—*Femininity* in 1984, the novel *Waverly Place* in 1987, and *Seeing Vietnam: Encounters of the Road and Heart* in 1994—before penning the social history of the radical feminist movement in which she had been such a significant participant, as both writer and activist. Her 1999 work *In Our Time: Memoir of a Revolution* was based on interviews with more than two hundred activists, quite a number of whom were Jewish. Yet Brownmiller did not ask any questions about possible connections between their women's liberation commitments and their Jewish identities, and there is no discussion of this matter in the book. The index has no entry for "Jewish" either. But a quotation from Sheila Cronan, a Catholic member of Redstockings, contains a revealing mention of Jewishness. Cronan remarks, "A lot of the Jewish women had grown up in radical families and had gone to expensive colleges where they'd been involved with radical groups. They were used to speaking out and being listened to at least to some extent. We didn't have that confidence. We felt that the Jewish women thought the Catholic women were intellectually inferior or kind of stupid because we didn't speak their political language."[167] Brownmiller describes a "triumvirate of working-class Catholics" in Redstockings. In addition to Cronan, there were Barbara Mehrhof and Pam Kearon, who felt like "outsiders" in the group. Mehrhof believed that Firestone,

Figure 2.3. Robin Morgan, Susan Brownmiller, and Gloria Steinem at Women Against Pornography march, New York City, October 1979. Photo by Bettye Lane. Courtesy of the Schlesinger Library, Radcliffe Institute, Harvard University.

Willis, and Kathie Sarachild (who may have been perceived as Jewish) formed a leadership clique, disregarding everyone else's ideas. The Catholic "triumvirate" began to meet separately on another evening, calling themselves the Class Workshop; Linda Feldman, a Jewish Redstockings member, joined them.[168] According to Baxandall, there were almost no WASPs in New York's radical feminist movement at the time.[169]

Although in Shulman's view, the Jewish women did not acknowledge connections among themselves, to the Catholic women, Jewish women's family and class backgrounds and leadership styles stood out.

* * *

Surrounded by so many other Jews in the city, Jewish radical feminists of New York did not experience marginality as Jews, which might have provided common bonds, and they did not share religious upbringings or rebellions against them, as did Catholic women. It was race, not religion or ethnicity, that occupied the foreground of the Jewish feminists' concerns about difference. Pioneering Jewish-born New York radical feminist Robin Morgan described to me the identity politics of the moment, particularly among those who had participated in the civil rights movement. "It was, 'Oh, my God, we're white.' 'I've looked in the mirror this morning and I was still white. Oh, Christ, what am I going to do?'" These women emphasized doing "good work . . . , political work. . . . Jewishness was . . . second." Still, Morgan said that a certain aspect of "Jewish culture" might have been present, creating "a warmth in the early CR groups that was very caring, very huggy, . . . potluck dinners . . . in people's homes."[170] Along with less admired elitist tendencies that some non-Jewish radical feminists noted among Jewish colleagues, this kind of familial connection and intimacy, under the radar as Jewish inflected, may have been characteristic of the pioneering New York radical feminists.

At the time historians of radical feminism wrote their books, the question of a Jewish connection to radical feminism did not seem relevant to them, as it had not to movement participants. But the experiences of Firestone, Willis, Shulman, and Brownmiller demonstrate that the currents of ethnic identity embedded in the experiences of the women's liberationists ran deep, even when submerged. Unique to each woman, the conundrums of Jewishness suggest a wide range of responses that interacted with feminist consciousness in distinct and varied ways. Despite shared elements, there was no common Jewish core that united their experiences.

Shulamith Firestone needed to break with Orthodoxy. In rebellion against patriarchy, whether the religion of her childhood or the undemocratic attitudes of New Left men, Firestone went on to disrupt normative ideas about gender, waging a vehement battle against sexist institutions. In the early years of radical feminism, she did not openly embrace her Jewish heritage, but the very fierceness of her attack suggests that the inequities she found in the religion signaled to her a painful betrayal of its core values, as did the radical men's perversion of communal, socialist ideals.

Ellen Willis, who had the most comfortable relationship to her Jewish background, simply extrapolated from her particular, New York–based secular, progressive, red-diaper-baby Jewish milieu. As a "conscious Jew," Willis recognized the historicity of Jewish identity, both the importance of situational context and the shared consciousness that tied generations of Jews to each other. Despite encountering anti-Jewish bias or occasions when Jews turned their back on their own liberal heritage, Willis was comfortable with the tradition, locating in her own skepticism and sense of herself as "critical outsider" the heritage of all Diaspora Jews. Her continuous, explicit, and deeply felt comments about Jewish life and Israel and her self-identification as a left-wing Jew and feminist were an anomaly among radical feminists.

Alix Kates Shulman had to uncover the meaning of a largely assimilated Jewish experience. She found no congruence between the concerns of radical feminism and the religious/ethnic backgrounds of its leaders. Denying these connections did not mean that she lacked appreciation for their significance in the lives of others. But in New York, where so many intellectuals and radicals were Jewish, a Jewish presence among the "downtown" feminists was hardly remarkable. For Shulman, it was only self-identified Jews such as Willis who stood out.

Susan Brownmiller, who grew up in a liberal Jewish home, belatedly connected her interest in rape and sexual battery to Jews' devastating historical experience of violence. Brownmiller eschewed Jewish religious customs and practice, but she did not cut herself off from Jewish identification. Only in hindsight did she understand the salience of her Jewish upbringing to her own feminist journey and perhaps those of the many other Jewish radical feminists whose movement activities she chronicled but whose Jewish backgrounds she did not interrogate. In recent years, she has become fiercely pro-Israel.[171]

Through rebellion, denial, assimilation, or connection, each of these women experienced Jewishness in a radically different way. Each became a major part of radical feminism's New York Jewish story, finding innovative ways to express and demand freedom—the centerpiece of the Jewish narrative—even if, as in Firestone's case, it meant breaking with key elements of that tradition, such as the nuclear family. Each hoped to "recreate a politics that emphasizes our common humanity," as Willis wrote of her own standpoint as a "woman . . . and as a Jew." Their identities diverged, but together they provide a snapshot of the ways in which ethnic and religious influences, feminist and class consciousness, and immersion in the exciting possibilities of a rapidly changing cultural moment combined to make history. "We were . . . poised on the trembling edge of a transformation," Baxandall explained.[172]

"Conscious Radicals"

The Jewish Story of Boston's Bread and Roses

On Mother's Day, May 11, 1969, after several months of preliminary meetings at the Massachusetts Institute of Technology (MIT) in Cambridge, six hundred women gathered at Emmanuel College, a small Catholic women's college across the river in Boston, to discuss forming a new kind of women's liberation organization. With workshops on dozens of political topics, karate demonstrations, movies, and more, the conference was "electric," as Meredith Tax wrote, but there was no clear mandate of how to proceed to organize a citywide women's group to fight against male supremacy, incorporating socialist principles but focusing squarely on the liberation of women.[1]

Cell 16, a radical feminist group led by Roxanne Dunbar, co-organizer of the Emmanuel conference, had organized the previous year in Boston, its program calling for "radical women to dissociate themselves from male-oriented, male-dominated radical organizations and join together in Women's Liberation groups."[2] The group considered itself part of a "female liberation" movement, aiming not only for the "equality of women in society but the liberation of the female principle in order to change the very structure of society."[3] Socialist feminists questioned Cell 16's separatist program, which Tax thought encouraged feminists to "leave their husbands and children and live celibate lives in feminist collectives." "We were interested in building a mass movement, not joining a cell," Tax elaborated.[4] Dunbar herself was extremely charismatic. "It was meeting her that turned me into a feminist instantly," Linda Gordon recalled. Unlike Cell 16 adherents, Tax and Gordon retained their connections to the New Left and began to imagine a different kind of women's liberation organization.[5]

Tax wanted a structure that could become the kernel of a "radical, mass, autonomous women's liberation movement." For Gordon, with whom Tax had worked in a draft-resistance organization in London, the "key word was 'autonomous,' not independent or separate," a description that marked a distinctive feminist mission but also the organization's initial formation within the larger New Left.[6]

Tax and Gordon formed a small political collective of socialist feminists in Boston, with Jean Tepperman and Fran Ansley, who had been involved in local SDS groups and the draft resistance movement. The group placed a notice for an open meeting in the *Old Mole*, the local New Left paper, and the weekly countercultural paper the *Boston Phoenix*. The women hoped such a meeting would spin off additional collectives to study the oppression of women and develop action responses.[7]

The gathering took place in June and was followed by regular Friday meetings of fifty to seventy women throughout the summer. By September, the group coalesced into a citywide organization, Bread and Roses, named after a women's labor song from a strike in Lawrence, Massachusetts, in 1912: "Hearts starve as well as bodies / Give us bread but give us roses!" The name reflected the founders' belief that liberation required material improvements but also a more holistic quality of life, as well as the turn to women's past to provide models for current action.[8]

By early 1970, two dozen collectives had been formed, usually on the basis of friendships and neighborhoods.[9] Tax and Gordon's initial group stayed together and included nine women in addition to themselves: Fran Ansley, Jean Tepperman, Trude Bennett, Michele Clark, Marya Levenson, Grey Osterud, Sara Syer Eisenstein, Marsha Buttman, and Judy Ullman. They became Collective #1. Collective #2 was formed at about the same time, largely by close friends of members of #1. The women wanted to keep the collectives small enough to give everyone a turn to speak.[10]

Bread and Roses became one of the most influential women's liberation groups in the country. It was the first declared socialist women's liberation organization, preceding the organization of the Chicago Women's Liberation Union by one month.[11] With upward of two hundred to three hundred regular members, Bread and Roses established an organizational structure based on biweekly mass meetings in combination with weekly meetings of the smaller collectives. The mass meetings and small groups informed each other, actualizing the theory that "the personal is political" by working out the political meanings of private experience through consciousness-raising, studying women's historical experiences, and political organizing. Bread and Roses also developed "project" or "work" groups, based on particular interests. Members participated in demonstrations and protests around a variety of issues, such as reproductive rights, workers' rights, equal employment, racism, sexism in family roles, and violence against women.[12]

The organization viewed its purpose as bringing together "socialism and feminism, women and the revolution," in theory and practice. Its main tenets were the "fight again male supremacy as it exists in all institutions, and in its structural basis, the bourgeois family," and the overthrow of capitalism to create a socialist society—"one free of all forms of exploitation, racism, imperialism, and male supremacy."[13] Anti-imperialist and antiracist as well as feminist, Bread and Roses had the goal of working for the liberation of all oppressed groups, not only women. The group was also "anti-reformist," refusing to ally with "institutions of power." The focus was on direct action—protests, demonstrations, making demands from "outside."[14]

Unlike Marxist discussion groups, Bread and Roses groups did not begin by reading. Through consciousness-raising—the exploration of private experience as a lever to understand such oppressive social institutions as families, schools, mass media, politics, and sex and gender roles—they believed that they would find their way to enlightenment and action. The groups "started with the evidence at hand of women's lives in the 1950s and 1960s," as Gordon points out. "Encounters that once seemed routine or idiosyncratic were reinterpreted as socially constructed patterns." While African Americans always understood their own oppression, women needed to unlearn the "false consciousness" they experienced as a consequence of their femaleness.[15]

The organization was particularly concerned with outreach to poor, working-class, and minority women, aiming to correct the "white" focus of education and population policies. Tax articulated these beliefs in an early pamphlet: "We cannot talk of sisterhood without realizing that the objective position in society of most of us is different from that of welfare mothers, or the black maids of our white others and of women in 3rd world countries. Sisterhood means not *saying* that their fight is our fight, but *making* it our fight."[16]

While Bread and Roses prided itself on the breadth of its politics—liberal and progressive, "communist, feminist, anarchist, in lots of varieties and combinations"—it recognized the disadvantages of diverse goals and loose structure. One problem involved translating the energy and trust developed in the small groups to the larger whole. How to navigate New Left politics, while developing a philosophy and strategies as a radical women's movement, posed another challenge. Bread and Roses had been inspired by New Left ideas, including those about women's workplace oppression under capitalism, but most members did not believe that forming caucuses within existing male institutions was a viable strategy. In Marya Levenson's words, it was not just a "similar-but-worse condition shared by men."[17]

The organization attempted to dodge the split between "politicos" and "radical feminists" in the new women's liberation movement in Chicago, New York, and elsewhere. As an autonomous organization, it hoped to work on its own as part of the overall New Left in Boston.[18] But autonomy did not come easily. In a memo a few months after the group formed, Jean Tepperman of Collective #1 warned about following the lead of male comrades and turning Bread and Roses "into the lady's auxiliary of SDS." The organization needed to build a strong and "organic" women's liberation movement that incorporated socialism and internationalism, she reiterated, but on its own terms. They would need to be "conscious radicals," Tax asserted.[19]

As in other women's liberation groups, the personal grounded the political, as the excitement of building a women's movement launched passionate friendships. "Much of the energy that had heretofore gone into sexual relationships and especially couples was now being directed towards women friends and the women's community in general," Bread and Roses member Ann Hunter Popkin put it. "Even women who remained in traditional heterosexual couples report 'getting high' from the energy level." Popkin observed that in talking about themselves as "sisters," members borrowed a family metaphor from the black movement, which used the terms "sister" and "brother" to show solidarity. Even as Bread and Roses members focused on how to eradicate oppressions of the nuclear family, they sought the "intensity, the closeness, the permanence and reliability" of an ideal family form. "Thinking of other

Figure 3.1. Bread and Roses women at antiwar rally, Soldiers' Field, Boston, May 8, 1970. Photo by Jeff Albertson, Department of Special Collections and University Archives, W. E. B. Du Bois Library, University of Massachusetts, Amherst.

women as sisters in the family sense carried with it the desire for an unbreakable bond, 'forever.'"[20]

Yet within two years, Bread and Roses had collapsed, in part because of the difficulties of establishing a strategic vision, organizational structure, and leadership capacity that could move its goals forward. "Bread and Roses never wrote down what it stood for; consequently it attracted many women who weren't socialists," said Tax. "All we came up with was a laundry list of demands coupled with a utopian vision."[21] There was no formal communications system or regular newsletter (though Bread and Roses irregularly published a xeroxed one, called *Hysteria*) and no elected or appointed leaders. As elsewhere in the new movement, the women feared elitism.[22] "We were terrified of power," Tax said. "Power meant oppression, . . . acting like bosses or fathers and being hated."[23] Rejecting "star-tripping," Bread and Roses chose a different model: when the organizers of an antiwar march asked for a speaker, it sent three women, all wearing masks.[24]

Figure 3.2. Bread and Roses members, wearing masks, at a Boston anti-war rally, May 8, 1970. Photo by Jeff Albertson, Department of Special Collections and University Archives, W. E. B. Du Bois Library, University of Massachusetts, Amherst.

In a memo written to movement colleagues, Tax offered another reason for Bread and Roses' collapse: its "non-struggle politics." With conflicts turned into "personal differences" or "glossed over with a phoney frosting of sisterhood," she charged the group with "failure to struggle for ideological leadership" of the women's movement. She believed the lack of political clarity crippled the organization's ability to create a mass movement.[25]

Linda Gordon identified different issues. She considered Bread and Roses' meetings to be orderly, "following Robert's Rules to a fault." However, this resulted in overly long gatherings, difficult for working women with jobs and/or children. And while "radical egalitarianism" worked well for the small groups, "letting everyone have a turn" and other anti-hierarchical principles diminished the large organization's effectiveness. Gordon also cited the fact that highly educated, confident women spoke a lot ("maybe too much"), with their contributions carrying disproportionate weight. The result was a growing resentment of these "heavies" and a failure to focus on internal development of leaders.[26] But overall, Gordon evaluated Bread and Roses' pluralistic approach positively. With individual groups free to start and operate their own projects without having to get approval from the larger organization or meet any ideological test, it "let a thousand flowers bloom," an orientation that brought in new members and spawned innovative and often long-lasting social action projects.[27]

Bread and Roses' demise is dated either as January 1971, after an informal set of meetings (dubbed "crumbs and petals") could not reconcile differences, or early March, when 150 activists from local women's groups, led by Bread and Roses members, took over a Harvard building at 888 Memorial Drive to demand the creation of a women's center and low-cost housing for area residents. After the women held the building for ten days, Harvard capitulated, buying a house for the movement, an important recognition of the "power of militant collective action," in Gordon's view. The following year, the women's coalition opened what became the longest running women's center in the U.S. at the site, offering resources relating to sexuality, lesbian lives, violence toward women, employment and education, and other issues.[28] Some Bread and Roses projects developed into independent organizations, including the Boston Area Rape Crisis Center and 9 to 5, a grassroots women's office workers' collective. In 1972, women from Bread and Roses established the Women's School, offering classes on such subjects as writing, art, auto mechanics, self-defense, lesbianism, capitalism, black history, and Native American women. Members worked for abortion reform, did draft counseling, and supported the Black Panthers. They also pioneered one of the first battered women's shelters in the U.S.[29]

Figure 3.3. Boston-area feminists take over a Harvard building, March 1971, demanding a Women's Center and low-income housing for the community. Photo by Marie Gamache.

Many of these projects had lasting influence, as did the basic process of consciousness-raising that lay at the core of the group's mission. Several collectives lasted longer than did the larger organization. In these ways, Bread and Roses served as a model for other women's liberation groups. The conference at Emmanuel College that spawned the organization had another major consequence: the formation of a women's health collective that created the groundbreaking book *Our Bodies, Ourselves*. Several of the collective's founders were members of the first Bread and Roses groups; the work of the health collective is ongoing.

Although none of the works that discuss Bread and Roses or the Boston Women's Health Book Collective mention the Jewish background of members, Jewishness is a significant part of the history of both groups. This omission is not surprising since Jewish issues were never a central focus—and usually were no focus at all—of either organization. Yet my evaluation of the extensive survey of Bread and Roses members done by Ann Popkin, who wrote a 1978 dissertation on the organization, suggests that perhaps half or more of her seventy-five interviewees were Jewish, though most grew up in secular homes and did not practice any religion.[30]

Numbers alone do not reveal the full story. As in Chicago and New York, Jewish radical feminists in Boston's Bread and Roses did not identify themselves as Jews, nor did its collectives examine issues regarding Jewishness, or ethnicity and religion specifically, focusing instead on more universal problems of sexism and patriarchy, particularly as they related to race and class. They sought ways to repair sharp divisions among gays and straights, "politicos" and radical feminists, and the failure to attract many women of color or working-class women disappointed them. Sociologist Winifred Breines, a former Bread and Roses member, writes that members' "theory was more interracial and racially sensitive than was their practice."[31] Neither Jewish identity nor Judaism as a religion made the cut of important issues.

But there may be differences between Bread and Roses members and radical liberationists in Chicago and New York. Consciousness-raising in some Bread and Roses collectives included mentions of Jewish parents or other aspects of ethnic and religious backgrounds, even though these remarks did not become focal points of discussions. Yiddish backgrounds, seders, the Holocaust, Anne Frank, and parents' radical affiliations were brought up as collective members shared ideas in consciousness-raising discussions. More unusual were public mentions, such as Jean Tepperman's feminist poem "Witch," circulated in movement literature, which included a line about "frizzy" hair that "looks Jewish."[32] Members did not take special note of these conversations or readings. In discussions with me, several registered their surprise at the numbers of Jewish women among them.

Yet my interviews with approximately two dozen members of Bread and Roses Collective #1 and the Boston Women's Health Book Collective, as well as other Bread and Roses members, reveal that at the time of their involvement in radical feminism, Jewishness was a relevant factor in individual women's lives.[33] In their childhoods and young adulthood, these women had encountered a variety of experiences and associations with Jewishness that shaped their identities. These factors included Jewish religion or spirituality, Jewish ethics, the influence of the Holocaust, anti-Semitism, the experience of marginality, radical Jewish politics, family backgrounds of immigration, and cultural or "lifestyle" Judaism. While the women saw themselves as part of a broader movement on the left devoted to fighting sexism and creating new models of change, links to a Jewish past helped frame their adaptation to the possibilities of the moment. As elsewhere in the women's movement, Jewishness may have been more of a latent rather than explicit factor, but it was present. Despite the women's universalist goals, Jewishness was an important lever for feminist activism.

In ensuing years, a number of Bread and Roses women developed deeper Jewish connections. Several became leaders in Jewish peace organizations; others chose religious or spiritual paths, attending services and becoming involved in synagogue life. Some women remained secular but Jewish identified; a few had always been religious minded. Most of the women struggled with issues regarding the Israeli-Palestinian conflict, a subject that was deeply emotional as well as political for them. Later in life as before, the spectrum of Jewish identifications ranged widely.

A Profile of Bread and Roses

The women of Bread and Roses were white, middle class, college educated, usually in their twenties, and mostly single and childless. Studies
of Bread and Roses by doctoral candidates Kristine Rosenthal and Ann
Popkin in 1972 and 1978, respectively, provide a demographic portrait
of the group. From direct interviews and questionnaires, Rosenthal and
Popkin ascertained the women's high level of educational achievement
and their considerable political engagement. Of the 150 women polled
by Rosenthal, 83 percent had college degrees, and half had done graduate work; 27 percent had received master's degrees, and one-fourth were
currently enrolled as students. Almost 80 percent came from large East
Coast urban areas, predominantly New York City and its suburbs. Popkin notes that 80 percent of members came from middle- or upper-
middle-class families. Over three-quarters had at least one parent
working as a professional, compared to less than one-third in the general population. The proportion of Bread and Roses women with mothers who worked as professionals or in the technical sector was more
than four times that of women in the general population.[34]

According to Popkin, the women's class and educational backgrounds
prepared them with verbal and analytic skills, while their activism prior
to involvement in the women's movement helped to shape their expectations and behavioral styles. Most of the women surveyed were in college during the 1960s. Thus, they came of age in a period of emerging
social protest involving civil rights, the war in Vietnam, and student
activism. Fifty-two percent had been politically involved in high school
in these causes. In college, they showed a preference for politics over
any other kind of student activity. A sense of "the movement" and a
developing "new left" culture provided a social context for their political
associations. These findings correlate with those of social scientists who
found that Jews (and Catholics) were more likely to become involved in
1960s activism than were youth from other backgrounds.[35]

Popkin suggested another reason for these women's attraction to the
social protest movements of the 1960s: the liberal or progressive political orientation of their parents engendered expectations of social equality that clashed with the realities of the world they encountered as they
came of age, including both the harshness of poverty and racism within

the U.S. and the bitterly fought Vietnam War. Parents' political attitudes were relevant to daughters' activism. While there were very few red-diaper babies (7 percent were children of communists, and another 11 percent were offspring of socialists), Popkin finds a "strikingly high" number of parents had "left of center" political attitudes: about one-third were left-liberal/progressives or liberal Democrats, and another 15 percent were described as Democrats. While these attitudes may have seeded their daughters' political views, in college and after, as they drifted to the left of their parents' values, their views often led to family dissention and personal frustration.[36]

Prior to creating or joining Bread and Roses, then, these aspiring feminists had been engaged in a wide variety of political experiences. They had the skills to engage in political debate and the motivations to search for meaningful political involvement and modes of personal and social change. Their education, class, and family backgrounds encouraged them to "think politically," as Rebecca Klatch says of the young rebels of both the Left and Right whom she interviewed for her book on 1960s youth politics.[37] The characteristics noted by Popkin, Rosenthal, and Klatch apply especially well to the Jewish women of Bread and Roses. Their experiences help us understand how the historical moment intersected with personal lives, including Jewish influences, so as to create a new and dynamic women's liberation organization.

According to Popkin, although all Bread and Roses collectives were theoretically equal, the collectives that formed early usually had the most prominence, because they contained a disproportionate number of leaders. The numbering of the collectives reflected their prestige, "with collective number one being the most prestigious."[38] This collective, the focus of this chapter, included some of Bread and Roses' founders and recognized leaders (Meredith Tax, Linda Gordon, and Marya Levenson were frequently named by survey respondents as movement "heavies"). It also included a high proportion of Jewish women: eight out of eleven collective members were Jewish, a fact unremarked by most of them. For this analysis, I construct the Jewish themes in the life stories of five members of the collective. A final Jewish story in the chapter belongs to Diane Balser, Bread and Roses' sole staff member and member of Collective #2, who worked closely with all the collectives. In these stories, Jewish roots and background emerge as significant factors in the motivations and styles of radical feminist activism. Narratives relating to the Jewish women of the Boston Women's Health Book Collective, which developed from Bread and Roses, will be told in chapter 4.

Meredith Tax and Linda Gordon: "Smart" Jewish Women, the Left, and Feminist Community

Meredith Tax and Linda Gordon were outliers to the early women's liberation movement with regard to the geography of their childhoods: Tax was from the Midwest, and Gordon was from the Far West, not the urban meccas of the Northeast or mid-Atlantic states. The women came from different Jewish and class backgrounds. Growing up in an upwardly mobile, nonpolitical Jewish family that enjoyed a suburban lifestyle in Milwaukee, Tax was exposed to organized Jewish life at Reform synagogue, where she absorbed positive ethical messages about Judaism. These contrasted with the contempt for women she discovered within the tradition, along with a sense of anxiety about her Jewishness. As an activist, writer, and lifelong organizer drawn to socialism and feminism, she put this childhood legacy and the influences of the social movements of her adult years to practical purpose, contributing to feminist literature and political life in myriad ways.

Gordon came from a lower-middle-class family of political radicals; her exposure to Jewishness came from the secular, Yiddish traditions of immigrant radicalism. She shared with Tax an upbringing in which the anxiety of being Jewish was prominent, although in Gordon's case, this was folded mostly into the threats her family experienced as communists in the age of McCarthyism. Early on, both learned that smart girls in bourgeois society faced an unpredictable future. Combining activism and writing, they blazed a path for women's liberation, with particular attention to the oppressions of racial and ethnic minorities.

* * *

After Meredith Tax had spent four years in London, where she was active in the antiwar movement, she went to Boston in 1967 and helped initiate Bread and Roses. Tax left Boston for Chicago after a few years and participated in the Chicago Women's Liberation Union before eventually going to New York, where she also played a role in women's liberation.

She believes that the Jewish presence in Bread and Roses was the most significant of all the feminist groups she worked with, but aside from occasional references, it was a subject that no one dwelled on. "We were interested in the things that united us," Tax recalled, and especially "why so much separation," "why there were no black women."[39]

Tax's Jewishness was central to her identity. Born in 1942, she grew up in Wisconsin, first in a small town and then in Milwaukee, and then she moved to Whitefish Bay, a suburb that had been restricted until shortly before the Taxes moved there. "We weren't the first Jews on the block," said Tax, "but there weren't a lot of them."[40] Jewishness was ever present in her childhood home and among her extended family, but it was ingrained with a fearful and secretive defensiveness. Her immigrant grandparents had come to the U.S. to save the family from "pogroms and starvation." Her parents, a successful physician father and a homemaker mother, gave their children the benefits of a suburban lifestyle with "good (i.e., white) schools": "We should be grateful, keep our heads down, and not ask questions."[41]

This attitude especially affected Tax's mother, who had grown up in a small country town where her family members were the only Jews. Her father had served in the Medical Corps during World War II, enlisting twice "because he wanted to defeat Hitler."[42] Although his unit liberated one of the concentration camps in Germany, Tax discovered this experience only after his death, since he refused to discuss it. The Holocaust was a forbidden subject for her mother as well. When, at age ten, Meredith found a box of old photos of a foreign-looking family, including four boys with shaved heads, her mother avoided all her questions as to their identity. On another occasion, she remembers her mother turning off a TV newsreel showing the liberation of Auschwitz, telling her, "I can't stand to look at those people."[43]

Tax connected her mother's high anxiety level with being Jewish. "She was always afraid people would know. When we kids talked too loud in a public place, she would say, 'Shh, you sound like Chicago Jews,' or, if we were really loud, 'Shh, you sound like [a] New York Jew.'"[44] Her mother lived her life in fear, even refusing to let her daughter get her ears pierced "because the Nazis would rip them off."[45] Tax learned quickly that "to be a Jew in the heart of the Midwest is to be part of an obvious and conscious minority, the object of curiosity or attack."[46]

Despite the uncommunicativeness of Tax's parents, she discovered that Hitler had succeeded in "killing Grandma's whole family." "How could such a thing happen?" she asked herself. "Could it happen again? Could it happen in Milwaukee?" She was not reassured by the Nazi paraphernalia on display in war-souvenir stores that she passed on her way to the main library in Milwaukee—medals, uniforms, swords, and swastikas—frightening symbols to a young child that remain power-fully etched in her memory.[47]

Other incidents added to Tax's sense of Jews as a threatened minor-ity. There was the history teacher who told the class, "Say what you want about Hitler, he built good roads." In the Bavarian Inn, a suburban retreat where Tax attended Sweet Sixteen parties, there was the sign hung until after World War II that read, "No dogs or Jews allowed." And there was the social segregation between Jews and non-Jewish youth, which left Tax feeling socially isolated: "You dated Jewish boys or you didn't date." By the time she was a junior, her social reference group "was not mainly Jewish but a little group of smart girls and misfits, and whatever boys came with them. Some of us were Jewish, some were not."[48]

Yet there was a more positive side of Judaism, which Tax encoun-tered at weekly Shabbat services at the local Reform synagogue, where her father's sister and brother-in-law were pillars of the congregation and where Tax was later confirmed. It was at this synagogue that she "absorbed the culture of ethical Judaism, based on Hillel's principle that which is hateful to you do not unto others, and the precept that what God required . . . was to do justly, love mercy and walk humbly": "I did my best to live by those ideas and still do."[49]

But the contradictions between these precepts and some practices of Milwaukee's Jewish community troubled Tax. In 1955, when she was thirteen, she wondered why congregants in her temple did not organize to support the civil rights movement. When her family moved from Milwaukee to the suburbs that same year, Tax fought bitterly with her parents, accusing them of furthering segregation. She went through a brief religious period in high school but lost interest in religion, never to regain it, finding the intellectual and emotional offerings of Reform Judaism unfulfilling.

Tax was warned repeatedly against being too smart. "At first, I couldn't understand what they were so worried about," Tax recalled, "because I thought it was good to be smart. 'Not for girls,' they said. I asked my mother, 'Is it true nobody will want to marry me just because I'm smart?' 'Nobody Jewish,' she said." Tax's relatives joined the chorus, saying she was "too smart for a girl": "Nobody would ever marry me. If only my brother had my brains, and I had his eyelashes." When later, she began to study Jewish history, Tax learned that "contempt for women runs like a dark thread through Jewish tradition—like the traditions of other religions," but at the time, she only knew that her ambitions, and her intelligence, were deemed unfeminine and inappropriate.[50]

For Tax, attitudes toward Jews and women—"especially smart women"—ran together. The "contradictions in [her] life as a Jewish girl" led her to become a feminist "before there was a women's movement and before [she] even knew the word." But everyone just laughed at her ideas about gender equality, and so, finishing high school, she chose a college where women and Jews would be more accepted.[51] Tax selected Brandeis University over Harvard: "not to explore my Jewishness but to free myself from having it hanging around my neck all the time; was it possible that if Jews were in the majority I would be seen not as Jew but as a person?" She also thought she could be "a smart girl" at Brandeis; her "weirdness" would be tolerated.[52]

Tax enjoyed Brandeis, especially being immersed in aspects of Jewish culture and having friends "who were sophisticated, secular Jews from New York," but "being a smart girl was still kind of risky," given the sexism of the times and the fact that Tax was never appropriately deferential.[53] Tax had to grapple with the "commonly held idea that education for women should be regarded as a prelude to marriage. A palpable gloom settled over the smart girls of the senior class, who were going to have to kill the years waiting for Mr. Right either by continuing in school or becoming a secretary for some guy very like their male classmates." These attitudes became "background to [her] ideas about Jewish identity."[54]

On a Fulbright scholarship to London after Brandeis, Tax embarked on graduate work in English literature, but by 1967, a sense of political urgency interrupted her studies. News of the civil war in Nigeria, the Six-Day War in Israel, and the Vietnam War saturated the daily front pages, as did troubling reports of race riots in U.S. cities. Tax quit her thesis work and became a full-time political activist. It would be the end of her "brilliant career." "I had formed myself in opposition to the suburban world I came from, but as an artsy bohemian, not a political radical. These self-definitions became obsolete overnight."[55]

Returning to the U.S. from London, Tax became immersed in the women's movement in Boston. After it formed, Collective #1 of Bread and Roses met at her house. "What we want is to make politics more human, more in touch with reality, and more responsive to the mass," she wrote in a letter "to the Boston movement," reflecting the group's belief in the overriding political importance of their work. "We must . . . think of ourselves as carriers of ideas which have transformed us and will transform the world."[56]

Tax found her calling in the movement. "I never knew who I was until the women's movement," she said. "Without it, I had no community, no place I felt at home."[57] She began to write, penning a four-part essay, "Women and Her Mind: The Story of Daily Life," which was published as a pamphlet by the New England Press in 1970. *Notes from the Second Year* published the first two sections in 1970, and the 1972 anthology *Female Liberation* included the other two sections. Examining the loss of ego and the stifling of intelligence due to women's socialization and objectification, "Women and Her Mind" sold 150,000 copies and is considered to be a founding document of women's liberation.[58] Shortly after writing this piece, Tax began researching the story of union women, hoping to find a more usable past for women radicals than the suffrage movement, which seemed to her too compromised by its class dimensions and politics.[59]

Tax married Jon Schwartz in 1968. In 1972, the couple moved to Chicago to become part of a Maoist group and start a new revolutionary party; Tax dropped her aspirations for an academic career. She worked in two factories, went to China during the Cultural Revolution, and spent a year and a half as a nurse's aide. In constant struggle with the leadership of the Maoist group, she was kicked out of it in 1975 for being a feminist and criticizing leadership. When her daughter was one year old, her husband left. She moved to New York a year later to start over.[60]

In New York, she finished *The Rising of the Women: Feminist Solidarity and Class Conflict, 1880–1917*, a historical account of cross-class alliances between American working-class and middle-class women.[61]

Tax went on to write two acclaimed historical novels about working-class Jewish radical women, *Rivington Street* (1982) and *Union Square* (1988).[62] Tax never specifically looked for Jewish women in these works—"they were just there," she said—but as her research deepened, she recognized that the connection of her personal history to these stories was more complicated. "I was constructing an alternative family for myself where the people wouldn't be afraid."[63]

In addition to writing, Tax continued her political activism on behalf of women. She was the founding co-chair of the Committee for Abortion Rights and Against Sterilization Abuse (CARASA), formed in 1977, which helped start the Reproductive Rights National Network.[64] In 1986, Tax and Grace Paley initiated and became co-chairs of the PEN American Center Women's Committee. Later, Tax became founding chair of International PEN's Women Writers' Committee. From 1994 to 2004, she was founding president of Women's WORLD, a global free-speech and mutual-aid network for women writers that fought gender-based censorship.

Tax has also been involved in Jewish issues. At Women's WORLD, she began a project to draw attention to the work of Israeli and Palestinian feminist peacemakers. As the "president of a global feminist organization and as an American Jew," she spoke out against Israel's occupation policies, especially involving Palestinian women. Tax served on the advisory committee of Brit Tzedek v'Shalom / Jewish Alliance for Peace and Justice, which advocated for a two-state solution.[65]

Through Tax's participation in the free expression, women's, and human rights movements, she developed a concern about women and Islam, writing about threats to women because of Muslim fundamentalism and other ideologies that fuse religious dogma and politics. She is the chair of the international advisory group of the Centre for Secular Space, which sees its mission as strengthening secular voices, opposing fundamentalism, and promoting universality in human rights, and has written *Double Bind: The Muslim Right, the Anglo-American Left, and Universal Human Rights* and, most recently, *A Road Unforeseen: Women Fight the Islamic State*.[66] Tax makes it clear that her enemy is all fundamentalisms, whether Jewish, Christian, Hindu, or Muslim. She hopes to bring attention to the plight of women subject to abuse anywhere around the globe.

Although Tax carries on her battles from a theoretical space that she calls secular, she continues to be guided by the ethical principles she learned at Temple Emanu-El B'ne Jeshurun in Milwaukee: "That which is hateful to you, do not do to your neighbor." She quotes Rabbi Hillel, "That is the whole Torah; the rest is commentary."[67] She brings her Jewish values and her concern for peace in the Middle East together with her stance as a global feminist, organizing and writing to protest injustices and to create change. As a Jew, she identifies as a "proud citizen of the Diaspora": "comfortable almost anywhere and able to meet and work with all different kinds of people without hiding my Jewishness." She believes that there is no solution to the problem of Jews "except as part of the solution to the problems of everyone else."[68] Nor does she think it possible to isolate the problems of women from those of the rest of society. The struggles that she engaged with in the heady days of Bread and Roses continue.

* * *

Linda Gordon grew up in a "very Jewish home" in a geographic location where Jews were a distinct minority and where her family's class and political radicalism further isolated her, and she experienced some of the same issues of alienation that troubled Tax.

Gordon was born in Chicago, where she spent the first five years of her life; her family lived above her grandparents in a tenement. Both her parents were immigrants whose first language was Yiddish, which Gordon's mother spoke to her own parents. Gordon studied Yiddish for a year at an Arbeiterring shul (her grandfather was an Arbeiterring member), managing it well enough to be able to converse with her grandmother, who cared for her while her mother, a nursery school teacher, worked.

Gordon's maternal grandfather in Chicago was a leader in his synagogue, which he attended every day. He liked to conduct theological discussions at large dinners and seders, and Gordon remembers him provoking discussion by saying, "Let's suppose there is no God, then what?" For Gordon, "intense Jewishness combined with agnosticism" characterized both sides of her family: "the two were never contradictory to me."[69]

Gordon's father conveyed other aspects of a Jewish worldview. Raised in a shtetl part of the time by a widowed mother, he vividly remembered non-Jews' view of Jews as effeminized, but this was an identity that he honored: he became very antiwar and disliked the macho male style, viewing gender equality as a Jewish value. Gordon's father and his older brother left Europe to come to the United States before the Nazis took power, but another brother was sent to Dachau. All of her father's relatives were killed in the Holocaust. The experience left Gordon's father deeply committed to antiracism and antinationalism, which he understood as core Jewish values.

After Chicago, the family moved south, where Gordon's father worked for the United Service Organizations (USO). Trained as a social worker, he became a political radical and Communist Party member. Called before the House Un-American Activities Committee (HUAC), he was an unfriendly witness, with the repercussion that he was unemployed for a year and half, during which time the Gordons lived with relatives. The family then moved to Portland, Oregon, where Gordon's father found work at a Jewish community center. Gordon remembers FBI agents knocking on their door more than once; her father rehearsed her on how to respond if they came when she was home alone. Out in the backyard barbecue, he burned radical leaflets. How "wonderfully ironic," Gordon said, "burning dissident material in the iconic symbol of American life, the barbecue." Experiencing McCarthyism intensified the insecurities that Jewish communities such as Portland felt in the wake of the Holocaust. For Gordon, it created "intense, if possibly subconscious feelings of vulnerability."[70] But it also accustomed her to being a dissenter.

Portland had very few Jews, and Gordon's status as a religious minority influenced her development as well. She was usually "the only black-haired" girl in her class, the one with olive skin, and the only student whose home had no Christmas tree. Her father drove across town twice a week to the only bakery in town that sold rye bread. As one of the only Jews in her working-class neighborhood and in her high school, where many of the poorer students called themselves "greasers," Gordon stood apart from her peers, as much for her smartness and ambitiousness as for her ethnicity.

At Swarthmore, the elite liberal school where Gordon went to college, she continued to feel different, more because of class reasons than Jewishness. Her family's lower-middle-class circumstances contrasted with those of many students who came from wealthier homes. In freshman year, she was placed with a roommate who was also Jewish and who had had a nose job. This was the first time Gordon had learned of such a procedure, which to her signified upper-class status. While there were many other Jews at Swarthmore, almost all came from upper-middle-class backgrounds and were better prepared. After college, Gordon went on to study for a Ph.D. in history at Yale; her dissertation was on the origins of the Ukrainian Cossacks. In London, where she was completing her studies, she became involved in New Left antiwar activities, which she continued when she moved to Boston and became involved in the new women's movement.

Gordon suggests that by varying degrees, Jews may have been different from other New Left participants because of their history of insecurity and their sense of being marginal to American self-identity. Other relevant factors may have been their propensity to challenge authority, their familiarity with left-wing ideas, and perhaps a sense of "superiority, at least intellectually" (the other side of "insecurity").[71] She believes that Jewish women's background on the left contributed to feminists' analytical categories—for example, the notion of structural as well as attitudinal sexism. Further, the Jewish experience of marginality provided insights that enabled radical feminists to pierce "taken-for-granted" truisms. And Jewish women challenged authority, which helped promote the movement, although this stance was never unique to Jewish women. In Gordon's mistaken impression, Collective #1 had few Jews in relation to non-Jews, speaking to the fact that Jewishness, even if casually mentioned by collective members, was not a significant marker of identity.

Two other factors deserve attention. First, Gordon suggests that the influences in her own background may have made her immune to the kinds of guilt, "even self-flagellation," that became widespread in the women's movement, particularly in regard to racism. "I just didn't think I had much to feel guilty about."[72] She remains uncertain about whether this might have been a reaction related to Jewishness or to class factors, but the possibility bears reflection.

Second, looking back from a perspective of some forty years, Gordon wonders whether the attack on the "heavies" of Bread and Roses, a variant of the assault on leadership throughout the women's liberation movement, may have had something to do with Jewishness, since the "heavies" were disproportionately Jewish. "It was a group of exceptionally articulate women . . . who loved talking and always had something to say, . . . who frequently sounded very sure of themselves, often quite unjustifiably so." Gordon believes that the "confident articulateness" of these women made it more difficult for others to speak up at large meetings and acknowledges that she and others were insensitive to the need to encourage their participation. But resentment against the "heavies" squelched leadership and weakened the movement. "Was there anti-Semitism in that agenda?" Gordon asked. "Was there a Jewish style . . . that offended others, a non-upper-middle-class style?" In raising these questions, Gordon thought back to her non-college-educated, nonprofessional mother, a "pushy, articulate, and dominating" woman, frustrated that she had no opportunity to use her innate talents.[73]

Whatever the challenges of the women's movement, it provided nurturance, knowledge, and the opportunity for profound emotional and intellectual growth. "It seems impossible that adults have ever learned so much as in fact we did then," Gordon said. "We taught each other sexual politics, emotional politics, the politics of the family, the politics of the SDS meeting."[74] "It's different for women," said Gordon, echoing Tax, "because the women's movement gave us such a sense of community."[75]

For Gordon's younger brother, Lee, like the brothers of several other women's liberation pioneers, Jewishness directly served as a fulcrum for community, identity, and politics. Gordon's parents sent Lee to Israel for his junior year in high school in the early 1970s. Lee came back a Zionist, but his politics turned leftward when he returned to Israel to volunteer during the 1973 war and was placed in a socialist kibbutz. After college and graduate school in the U.S., Lee and a Palestinian cofounder started Hand in Hand, a network of bilingual and bicultural schools in Israel, serving both Arab and Israeli children. In creating these integrated schools, Lee hoped to build cooperating communities around them, bringing together peoples long in conflict and providing models of coexistence and equality. Lee remained in Israel for twenty years, even after his wife, a therapist, was murdered in her clinic by a deranged former patient. Today he continues his pioneering work with Hand to Hand from the United States; the schools and the communities of support that have grown up around them continue to prosper. Linda Gordon journeyed to Israel frequently to visit her brother and his family, both before and after his wife's tragic murder. She shares his politics and understands the depth of his feelings about Israel. She remarked, "We Jews do feel differently [about the Israel question]. We do feel that what Israel does is of particular concern to us. We cannot completely separate ourselves from it. We are connected to Israel, and we cannot deny that. We cannot honestly say, 'Well, Jews are one thing, and Israel is another.' It's a very painful, difficult situation."[76]

Gordon went through a period in which her Jewish identity did not seem very important, but it later became more significant. The women's movement and her teaching and scholarship about women of diverse backgrounds have remained vital to her. She taught for many years at the University of Wisconsin, Madison and, since 1998, has been at New York University, where she is a professor of the humanities and professor of history. Her books have won many awards. Her first book was *Woman's Body, Woman's Right: A Social History of Birth Control in America* (1976). In 1988, she published *Heroes of Their Own Lives: The History and Politics of Family Violence*, a study of how the U.S. has dealt with family violence. Gordon then wrote *Pitied but Not Entitled: Single Mothers and the History of Welfare* (1994), focusing on black and white women on welfare. Changing direction, Gordon turned to narrative as a way of bringing large-scale historical developments to life, authoring *The Great Arizona Orphan Abduction*, the story of a vigilante action against Mexican Americans, in 1999; a biography of photographer Dorothea Lange, *Dorothea Lange: A Life beyond Limits* (2009); and, with Gary Okihiro, *Impounded: Dorothea Lange and Japanese Americans in World War II* (2006). She also co-authored a book about the history of U.S. women's movements.Her most recent book is a study of the Ku Klux Klan in the 1920s.[77] Gordon's focus on African American, Mexican American, and working-class subjects points to a framework based on a broad multiculturalism that is sensitive to the experience of minorities, women, and gender. In this way, her childhood experiences and her early understandings of social class, ethnicity, race, and religion have had significant input into the bold work of her mature years.

Marya Levenson, Michele Clark, Grey Osterud: Culturally Jewish, with Religious Overtones

The religious traditions of Judaism experienced by Marya Levenson, Michele Clark, and Grey Osterud of Collective #1 reflect a broad spectrum, from the wealthy, alienating Reform congregation of Levenson's childhood to the more traditional Conservatism in which Clark was raised to the ideals of Reconstructionist Judaism that inspired Osterud. Secular and cultural Jewish life, including Jewish camp, schools, and youth groups, and encounters with the Holocaust and anti-Semitism also left their mark on the women's development. Each woman came to the social movements of the 1960s and then to feminism driven by different motives, encouraged by their friendships and networks. But the religious, cultural, and secular dimensions of Jewishness and Judaism played a role in stimulating their political energies and ideas.

* * *

Marya Levenson grew up in West Hartford, Connecticut, where her maternal grandparents founded a Conservative synagogue. Her mother, Ann Heilpern Randall, moved away from Judaism and started a school for the arts in Hartford. Her father, Wilbur Rosenberg, an advertising executive, changed his name to Randall because of anti-Semitism in that business. Later in his life, he followed Marya's brother, who had become Orthodox, and her sister in reclaiming the family surname.

In the eighth grade, Levenson attended school at a West Hartford Reform synagogue; with the curriculum focused on comparative religion, she learned about Mormonism and Christianity as well as her own tradition. When Levenson said she did not think she believed in God, the senior rabbi did not reassure her, nor did his habit of gifting his confirmation students with a framed eight-and-a-half-by-eleven-inch photograph of himself. Neither was she happy with the congregation, which seemed to care more about what people wore and how well-off they were than the sermons and prayers. She quit the synagogue and did not go further in her Jewish education. A more positive connection to Judaism came through the Jewish summer camp she attended in the Catskills, run by her aunt and uncle.

Levenson began Bennington College, in Vermont, and for her junior and senior years transferred to Brandeis, where she became deeply involved in politics, including the incipient antiwar movement. Unlike Meredith Tax, who also graduated from Brandeis in 1964, Levenson had little interest in secular Jewish culture at Brandeis or elsewhere. She married upon graduation and had a child soon after. During this time, she began organizing welfare mothers in Boston, helping to create Mothers for Adequate Welfare, or MAW, which connected with SDS's work on ERAP (Economic and Research Action Project). She also became involved with SDS's antiwar and civil rights activities.

In 1967, Levenson attended the National Conference for New Politics in Chicago with Nancy Hawley, an event that left them both wanting to spread the word about women's liberation. Hawley and Levenson joined in organizing the first meetings of Boston and Cambridge women, which was to become Bread and Roses. Within a few months, they co-authored a memo urging Bread and Roses, "act on our own complex rage against our own forms of oppression as women" rather than as "white and middle-class women," urging poor and minority women to organize and take action. "None of us got turned on to the women's movement through a leaflet," Hawley and Levenson wrote. Before they could make demands on other women to join the revolution, they had to model risk-taking behavior on their own.[78]

While in Bread and Roses, Levenson began studying education at Boston University. She remained an activist outside the classroom, helping to found the Boston Teachers Center and Madison Park High School, and became one of the first women elected to the Executive Committee of the Boston Teachers Union. Levenson encountered several negative comments about Jews from some members of the Irish-dominated teachers union. Especially disturbing was the time her son came home from kindergarten and told her an anti-Semitic "joke" he had heard at school. The incident led her to recall her mother's comment to her when she was in high school, which had made no sense at the time. When she told her mother, "I'm not Jewish because I don't believe in the Jewish religion," her mother replied, "You may not think you're Jewish, but as long as people perceive you as Jewish, you will be."

Living and working in Boston in the 1970s, Levenson acknowledged her mother's perceptiveness but determined to affirm her Jewish identity in a positive way. She now felt, "we could interact with Judaism in a way that could reflect our values."[79] Along with friends in the commune in which she lived who celebrated Passover as a holiday of freedom, she began to have seders and wrote her own Haggadah. Although she divorced her first husband, she kept his name because, unlike her father, who had changed his, she felt that a Jewish last name was a helpful marker of Jewish identity.

Levenson became principal of Newton North High School in Massachusetts, then superintendent of schools in North Colonie in upstate New York and a member of the Executive Council of the New York State Council of School Superintendents. For a number of years, she participated in a women's group in the Albany area whose members (all Jewish) talked about what it meant to them to be Jewish women. So different from the invisibility of Jewishness in Bread and Roses twenty years earlier, these sessions were a further turning point, helping Levenson to integrate Judaism into her life. Today, she often lights candles on Shabbat, but she sees herself as "culturally Jewish," by which she means a focus on inquiry and the social justice values she learned growing up that she believes are central to Jewish tradition. When she returned to Brandeis in 2003 to chair its Education Program, Levenson imagined that her grandmother and mother would take pride in knowing that she had found a unique way to integrate her passion for education with the values of Jewish life.

Like the other members of Collective #1, Levenson viewed the women's movement as universal, dedicated to the goal of a promoting an inclusive sisterhood. "Religion was particularist, and it was going to fade away."[80] In retrospect, Levenson acknowledges that her Jewish identity played a role in motivating her to question injustice and become a leader in Bread and Roses—and, subsequently, in her work in educational policy and practice.

* * *

Michele Clark distinguishes her background from that of most of her Jewish friends in Collective #1, noting that she came from an observant "Conservadox" home, not the "lefty" homes that she believes characterized the others. Her parents kept kosher, did not go shopping on Saturday, attended synagogue, and observed all the Jewish holidays. Clark was born in 1945 on the Lower East Side, where her grandfather had a kosher butcher store and delicatessen (the now iconic "Shmulke Bernstein's"), and the family moved to Jackson Heights, Queens, when she was four. She believes that her family's narrative represented the American dream of success and material progress, though it minimized what was pushed aside: "the old values of the *mitzvoth*, moderation, and community obligation" that typified the crowded urban neighborhoods they left.[81] Her parents were not "socialists or Zionists or Bundists" or politically active at all. They were solid Democrats who were grateful to their country, and their politics consisting of one question only: "Is it good for the Jews or bad for the Jews?"[82]

Clark went to synagogue as a young girl, and at the age of thirteen had a bat mitzvah (though on Friday night rather than Saturday morning and without reading from the Torah, which girls were still not allowed to do). She continued on to Hebrew high school and participated in United Synagogue Youth, the Conservative movement's youth group, attending national youth conventions and becoming "very involved in everything Jewish." At the time, her life goal was to go to Israel. There she would feel at home—less "tormented" in her daily life than in the States.[83]

Clark's torment grew out of her concern with the Holocaust. One of her Hebrew teachers, a refugee, told her preteen students about the horrors of the Shoah in vivid detail, "skin made into lampshades and all," and that there was no safety: "they came for the observant Jew and the Jews who tried to hide in assimilation." "Whatever her motives," said Clark, "she passed the torch to me, a top student. I became obsessed with The War. I dreaded and long[ed] to read about it, think about it, hear about it."[84] Clark read about the Holocaust from books in the public library stacks, and at home, she read from the War World II volume in *The Jewish Encyclopedia*, trying not to be afraid and feeling ashamed when she did. On Friday nights, when her parents went to synagogue, she would look at the book and then close it, repeating the process many times. When she confessed her obsession to her parents, they sent her to an elderly child psychiatrist. When she refused to go back, her parents hid the book; Clark found the hiding place and continued to read about the Holocaust in secret.

By Clark's teen years, the effect of the Holocaust on her had receded, and she became a self-described "beatnik" and activist, critical of her family's material aspirations. She wanted to be "part of a community which placed its ethical values first," much as she thought her grandparents had done; she no longer wanted to attend family seders or cousins' bar and bat mitzvahs. By the time she began City College, she felt "done with everything Jewish."[85] Though she studied Hebrew because she loved the language and read a lot of I. B. Singer, she had little connection to Judaism. She became more deeply committed to radical politics—civil rights, SDS, and the student and antiwar movements. After the collapse of her marriage to a filmmaker, she found her way to Boston and became involved in the women's movement, joining friends who formed the consciousness-raising group that eventually became Collective #1. At this time in her life, New Left politics and the women's movement offered a more visionary outlet for political and even spiritual change than Judaism did.

Clark's relationship to Jewishness remained complicated. Most fundamental was the fact that because she did not want to be like her parents, she felt that she did not want to be Jewish. Yet she believed that she was more aware of her Jewish identity than most other Jewish members of her collective were, and she shared her feelings about Jewish issues with another collective member who she believed was also Jewish identified. While she was a strong advocate for Bread and Roses' multiclass, multiracial framework, she implicitly linked her own sense of social justice to Jewish values. As a Jew, she said, "you have to fight for the freedom of others": "I never understood how anyone could not deduce a progressive message from being Jewish." But she recognized that Jews on the left were always interested in "every culture in the world" except their own.[86]

In 1974, Clark joined the Women's Mental Health Collective, a small group that had spun off from the Boston Women's Health Book Collective.[87] Becoming interested in psychology, especially women and psychology, she moved to Vermont with her second husband and developed a career in mental health counseling. For twenty-five years, Clark did nothing to claim her Jewishness. However, she often found herself yearning for Shabbat and the Hebrew language she loved. "My longing to be more Jewish would become acute," said Clark, but she and her husband—who assumed the couple were united in "agnostic, multicultural humanism"—saw her desire as an "atavism, a family weakness," "something to get over, something to squash."[88] Eventually Clark started a Jewish women's study group that supported her as she made her way back to Judaism, and she is a regular member of the small synagogue in her community. Today she writes a blog, *Rivington at Essex*, about the Lower East Side in the 1940s and 1950s, centered on her grandfather's kosher butcher store. Writing about her experiences in the Jewish feminist journal *Bridges*, she said, "I was a Jewish child, and then I became an adult humanist, political activist. . . . Every word of Hebrew brings me intense pleasure. . . . I have stopped running."[89]

* * *

Grey (Nancy) Osterud was not born a Jew but has identified as one for most of her life, formally converting to Judaism in 1979. Osterud has been able to imbue her leftist politics with a guiding vision of Jewish radicalism that is "non-Zionist, pacifist, socialist, and feminist." In contrast to most Collective #1 members, Osterud combined her politics with an active religiosity, from childhood days in her native Seattle to participating in the Havurah / Jewish Renewal movement in the Boston area. Today she is affiliated with both a *havurah* (informal Jewish fellowship community) and a Conservative synagogue.

Born in 1948, Osterud grew up in the midst of the Jewish Left in Seattle. Her father came from a Norwegian American, Minnesotan family of atheists and socialists. Her mother's mother, an orphan, was of immigrant stock, and her lineage was unclear, though she may have been Jewish. Osterud's mother was raised by her father and grandparents and was treated as a perpetual outsider, although by the time she got to college, she identified with her Jewish roommates.

After the marriage of Osterud's parents, both scientists, they moved to Seattle. Her father's department at the University of Washington housed a good number of Jewish refugee scientists and others who, like Osterud's father, had refused to sign a loyalty oath stating that they had never been members of the Communist Party. The families of the thirteen nonsigners at the university, all Jewish except Osterud's father, were ostracized by everyone else—Grey herself was banned from nursery school and the local Girl Scout troop. They became a tight-knit community and educated their children in the values of an ethical Judaism that welcomed prayer but not the concept of Jews as a "chosen people." They started what would now be called a *havurah* for their community; by the time Osterud was in high school, the group affiliated with Reconstructionism, which they thought was a good fit with their beliefs, and founded a Reconstructionist synagogue. The Osteruds participated in both ventures. Nobody worried about whether Grey was halachically Jewish (i.e., according to body of biblical Jewish law), so she grew up identifying as a religious Jew, which is how she saw herself when she went east to go to Radcliffe College (the affiliate of the all-male Harvard) in 1966. But to some college colleagues, she was a "dubious Jew," not being understood to be Jewish by people who did not know her and not being welcomed by the campus Jewish community.[90]

Osterud became deeply involved in SDS at Harvard, working on antiwar and anti-imperialist issues and living in SDS's Northeast regional headquarters with Jean Tepperman and others. At that time, she became very close to her boyfriend's grandmother Nima Adlerblum, a founder of Hadassah, whose vision of a progressive, feminist Judaism—a Judaism dedicated to the reformation of the world but without the structure of organized religion or "any shred of particularism"—had a lasting influence on her.[91]

In addition to Bread and Roses, Osterud participated in other women's movement activities. She spent the summer of 1970 in Seattle, organizing the Anna Louise Strong Brigade (a federation of women's groups) and a regional women's conference in Eugene, Oregon. In 1972–1973, she helped establish the Bay Area Women's Union in Berkeley, California. In 1975, while attending graduate school at Brown University, she was active in the Socialist Feminist Caucus of Women of Brown United.

Osterud's background growing up in an unconventional leftist Jewish community was important in her women's movement activism. "I never felt that we had to adopt others' philosophies, e.g., Maoism," she said. In both the Jewish alternative world in which she had been raised and in radical feminism, she felt "enriched and validated by historical continuity: [the] sense of being part of an international left and

American socialist movement [and the] sense of belonging to a people who have recited these prayers for centuries." But as "a marginalized woman," she felt about Judaism much the same as she did about the Left: "it was worth struggling for full and equal participation and, if that seemed impossible to achieve within existing institutional structures, we could create our own alternatives within the tradition that would help facilitate change."[92]

After Osterud completed her Ph.D. in American civilization at Brown, her activism took a new turn. Like other women's liberationists who became academics, she hoped to create institutional structures and historical narratives that could bring about new understandings and real social change. The author of several works about rural women and farming communities, she was a member of the editorial collective of *Gender & History* and became its North American editor. Today she works as an editor on books dealing with women's studies, international human rights, and violence and conflict resolution. The sense of continuity she has felt in Judaism helped sustain her professional and community work. "Jewish communal life still nurtures my orientation toward repairing and transforming the world," Osterud said.[93] She has helped her *havurah* create a prayer book with gender-sensitive language and participates in other reforms designed to give women an equal place in Judaism.

Osterud developed a strong Jewish identity by dint of her upbringing, her adoption of Jewish ethical and religious practices, and her conversion to Judaism. Perhaps because she had to claim her Jewishness, even at the time of her early activities within the women's movement, it served as a conscious rather than latent guide for her activism.

Diane Balser: Neither a "Minimalist" or "Maximalist" Jew, Just "Jewish Identified"

Diane Balser participated in antiwar and civil rights activities before joining Bread and Roses Collective #2; she had been part of the organizing committee for the very first conference at Emmanuel College. As the sole staff member of Bread and Roses, she was deeply involved in its varied activities and represented the organization in antiwar protests and general protests of the Left.

Balser describes herself as one of the few members of Bread and Roses with an overt relationship to religion. Today she is a practicing Jew, working to build a feminist presence at her synagogue, and is deeply committed to Jewish issues, having served as Boston co-chair, national vice president, and CEO / executive director of Brit Tzedek v'Shalom / Jewish Alliance for Justice and Peace, an organization that was dedicated to achieving a negotiated settlement to the Israeli-Palestinian conflict. She has been actively involved in women's politics as well, serving as founder and executive director of the Women's Statewide Legislative Network of Massachusetts, and is a longtime teacher of women's studies who codirected the Women's, Gender, and Sexuality Studies Program at Boston University.[94]

Balser's connections to the religious and secular worlds and to the dual aspects of her own identity have sometimes caused conflict. Born in 1943 in Washington Heights, New York, Balser went to Hebrew school and was the first in her family to have a bat mitzvah, which she considers to have been a radical act at that time. Her parents, schoolteachers with some ties to the Left, were religious, Conservative Jews who kept kosher. That strong, religious-identified background bolstered Balser's identification with Judaism throughout her life, even as she struggled to bring her Jewish identity in consonance with her work as a secular social justice advocate.

Balser's neighborhood and family had a large contingent of Holocaust survivors, though many had been lost in the Shoah. What she calls the "grief-stricken" resonance of the Holocaust was a prominent factor in her identity as a Jew. She identified, too, with her Orthodox, eastern European grandparents and the strong Jewish women of her family. To Balser, they were "very oppressed women but extremely powerful women, some of whom saved their families from destruction in Europe."[95] Like her grandmother, who had supported the 1909 garment workers' strike, several became union and political organizers. Other role models were Emma Goldman, who her mother bragged came from her own home town of Rochester, New York, and Bess Meyerson, the first Jewish Miss America, whom Balser's mother held up to her as an example of a young woman from a working-class background who used her platform to talk about racism and anti-Semitism. Because of these heroines, Balser knew that "Jewish women held the 'big picture' of things" and that her "scope in life was expected to be large and important." She wrote her first protest letter as a young teen when she felt Meyerson was discriminated against on the TV show *I've Got a Secret* because she was "dark and a much smarter woman" than the blond panelist. Balser's mother insisted that, given the Holocaust and the family's Orthodox background, it was imperative that her daughter "stay Jewish." Balser considered this a "gutsy political act." Her parents encouraged her to be smart and outspoken, advice that she saw as in definite conflict with the "white Protestant ideals of femininity at the time."[96] Despite her Jewish role models, the disparity between these standards and the feminine norm caused her emotional conflict.

Balser was an activist at an early age, becoming involved in peace activities as an adolescent. She had been sent to a progressive, socially aware summer camp when she was fourteen; Robby and Michael Meeropol, sons of Julius and Ethel Rosenberg, were fellow campers. But as much as her experience at camp was a "profound, changing" experience for her, so, too, was going to synagogue. "I did both, and you can do both," she told the audience at the "Women's Liberation and Jewish Identity" conference.

After Balser received her B.A. from the University of Rochester in 1964, she went to Chicago for a master's degree in teaching and history. She was influenced there by Marilyn Webb and especially Heather Booth and attended the fall 1967 National Conference for New Politics, which stimulated one of the first feminist rebellions against the sexism of male SDS members. When the conference passed a resolution condemning Zionism as racism, Balser worked to help eliminate it. It was the first time that she felt a conflict between her social justice activism and her Jewish identity.

Bread and Roses became pivotal in Balser's life. The organization was "tension-ridden" but "so damn exciting"; she would not trade "the some five-thousand-odd discussions [they] had, from whether you should cut your hair to whether you should go to jail," for "anything in the world." The movement caused an "explosion" everywhere: "We changed our lives, and we changed the lives of women throughout the world." For Balser, the movement overlapped with her Jewish femaleness and desire for basic social change to such a degree that she said, "sometimes I cannot tell them apart." Nonetheless, coming into the women's movement "with a very secular, Jewish face and identity" while maintaining a "religious, Jewish connection" was difficult, although in retrospect, "being in both worlds was also a tremendous strength."[97]

Balser recognizes that the movement was initiated and led by "very powerful, outspoken and gutsy women," many of whom were "very very Jewish," though at the time, she said, "none of us talked about how many of us were Jewish." "We didn't see the intersectionality." Nor did they even think of *themselves* as Jewish. Even for someone with as strong a Jewish identity as Balser had, being Jewish did not define "who you were" as a feminist. "The sole place Jewish identity emerged was when babies were named after Rosa Luxemburg and Emma Goldman, the only Jewish names we were proud of."[98]

For a while, Balser retreated from her Jewishness; her brother, Henry, in contrast, had gone from civil rights activism to becoming a Conservative rabbi. Perhaps the most difficult part of her lapse from Judaism was "calling up and talking to her mother." On one occasion during the civil rights movement, Balser had gone south with three Jewish women, Carol Cohen McEldowney, Judy Schwartz, and Nancy Miriam Hawley (along with Hawley's one-year-old daughter), to meet with women's groups. They had several frightening experiences, including being stopped by state troopers in Mississippi. But the most daunting was going into a telephone booth to call her mother to tell her she "could not come home for seder." Nancy Hawley had to hold her hand. "It was the first year of my life that I didn't have a seder with my family."[99]

Balser reconnected with her Jewishness later in the 1970s, holding seders in the women's collective where she lived. A number of incidents involving Israel and Jewish politics caused her to speak out: once when some women in the collective attempted to put up a poster of a Palestinian woman suicide bomber; and again when the Red Bookstore in Cambridge refused to display an anthology published by a Chicago Jewish collective named Chutzpah, which included writing by Balser's sister, Ruth, and brother, Henry. When Golda Meir's speech at Brandeis in June 1973 was disrupted by picketers holding signs that said, "Gramma, how many babies did you kill today?" Balser protested. Her family adored Golda Meir—and, further, "this was *Brandeis*," where Balser was then enrolled as a Ph.D. student in sociology. Regardless of her disagreement with the Israeli prime minister's policies, Balser saw the placards as "anti-Semitic and as misogynistic attacks on a Jewish woman." "I was ready, finally, to formulate a response from my broader identity."[100]

By the early 1980s, as growing numbers of feminists began to assert themselves more positively as Jews, sometimes in response to anti-Semitism, Balser found a way to bring together the two parts of her identity. She attended the UN World Conference on Women in Nairobi in 1985 on behalf of the New Jewish Agenda and continued working with the Israeli Women's Network, with which she connected in Nairobi and at the fourth UN World Conference on Women in Beijing a decade later. "I could be a feminist in the global sense and retain my strong ties to being a Jew," she said. "At the same time, I could have a place in the Jewish world as a feminist."[101] Balser later became the executive director of Brit Tzedek v'Shalom / Jewish Alliance for Justice and Peace, pursuing a two-state solution to the Israel-Palestinian conflict. Taking a stand that she felt was deeply principled allowed her to "embrace more of [her] Jewishness." Women struggling with these issues "began to find each other, to feel less alone."[102]

In 2003, Balser decided to reaffirm her bat mitzvah, this time reading from the Torah, which she had been prohibited from doing in 1956, surrounded by feminist friends and family. She also began to wear a Jewish star. "It tells the world that I identify as an unassimilated Jew," she said, "and its visibility links me to yellow stars, to my roots of having been born during the Holocaust. And at shul, until sexism ends, I wear a yarmulke."[103]

As Balser works to create a "feminist presence in shul," teaches about sexism, global feminisms, and intersectionality ("racism, class, homophobia, disability, age, etc.") at her university, and fights the battle for social justice in Jewish-oriented and other political groups, she finds a merger between the concerns of "particularism and universalism" more possible today than in the first years of radical feminism. But, she said, "how we stand up for ourselves as Jewish women, for all women, and how we use our strength and power to fight for social justice in the present" is a continuing challenge. It is one she hopes to meet neither as "a minimalist or maximalist Jew but, rather, [as] a Jewish-identified Jew."[104]

* * *

Even though women's liberationists in Bread and Roses never explicitly considered Jewishness as one of the factors in their class or gender analysis, the narratives in this chapter reveal that values and experiences associated with Jewish life significantly influenced their activism. First, almost all of the women interviewed came from homes where parents shared leftist views, whether socialist, communist, or other kinds of radicalism, or where forms of liberalism associated with "FDR Democrats" were espoused. The importance of parents' political views in the socialization of 1960s activist leaders shows that youth leaders were more likely to share the political proclivities of their involved parents than to rebel against them. Having politically active parents is considered "above and beyond other influences" in stimulating children to engage in political protest and movement activities.[105] This was clearly the case with most women discussed in this chapter, who felt guided by their parents' views. Fathers' and mothers' political choices, in combination with generational experiences, became formative elements in their own politics.

An influential survey of 1960s youth activists by political scientists Margaret and Richard Braungart ascertained that for some SDS leaders, "a strong Jewish element infused their political backgrounds." For these interviewees, parents' political attitudes—whether leftist or liberal—were signifiers of Jewishness, with the youth referring to parents as "Jewish leftists" or "Jewish liberals." Several interviewees added the qualifier that their parents' major concern was their "Jewishness, not their politics."[106] Bread and Roses women similarly associated their parents' political attitudes with Jewishness, tending to regard parents' politics as informed by Jewish-based ethical and moral values. However, the parents of some of the leading members of the collective, such as Tax and Levenson, were not political at all. Tax's ethical values and political choices came more in opposition to those of her parents than because of their influence.

Like some of the SDS leaders in the Braungarts' survey who cited the influence of Jewish grandparents (e.g., Menshevik radicals or Holocaust victims), Bread and Roses women also mentioned the influences of grandparents, aunts, and uncles. Levenson's grandparents founded a synagogue, and a summer camp started by an aunt and uncle initiated her into Jewish traditions. Clark's grandparents and aunts and uncles, all of whom participated in the family's Lower East Side kosher butcher shop and their local community, served as beacons of civic action. Balser referenced her grandmother as a role model. The close family friends with whom Osterud grew up in Seattle helped to shape her life-long political values. This community became Osterud's Jewish "family" and her moral compass.

For most of the Bread and Roses women whom I interviewed, the Holocaust played a central role in shaping identity. Born during or shortly after World War II, this cohort grew up in the shadow of the Holocaust. Several had relatives who perished in the tragedy; some had family members, neighbors, or teachers who were survivors; others encountered stories about the Shoah at school and in their reading or in movies. Clark became so obsessed with the Holocaust after hearing terrifying stories from her Hebrew-school teacher that her parents sent her to a psychiatrist. Her negative exposure mirrored the experience of Tax, whose mother hushed up any questions about the Holocaust and whose father, a soldier who liberated the camps, also cast a veil of silence around it. Balser's family treated the subject more openly, and she grew up hearing stories of women who helped their families and communities survive the Shoah. For Balser, the Holocaust and the strong women she associated with it provided a positive pathway to being Jewish. Even for those who had more adverse experiences, the Holocaust functioned as a signpost of identity that had carried significant meaning.

Direct experience with or awareness of anti-Semitism contributed to these women's liberationists' Jewish identity. The sense that Jews were a beleaguered people might have created fear—as it did for Tax, who had to pass store windows with Nazi regalia on sale on her way to the library, but it also gave her a sense of Jews as a people apart, with a unique history and a difficult present. Bread and Roses women spoke of anti-Semitism and its connection to other prejudices. For Gordon, anti-Semitism was linked to political repression—specifically, McCarthyism—which afflicted her family during the 1950s. Osterud grew up amid an alternative community of Jewish family friends who also suffered from McCarthyism. Later, as a college student and SDS activist whose Jewishness was not readily apparent, Osterud became aware of anti-Semitism on the left. Tax experienced McCarthyism

indirectly, with her family worrying if the Army-McCarthy hearings—
and also the execution of the Rosenbergs—were "bad for the Jews."[107]

A distinct sense of marginality contributed to these women's intellectual development and social activism. Growing up in cities with small
Jewish populations intensified feelings of insecurity and exclusion.
Grappling with this sense of vulnerability, Gordon compensated by
working harder than her classmates, but as Tax acknowledged, being a
"smart girl" carried its own fears and penalties and seemed inseparable
from Jewishness. Even though these women ought to have been insiders, because of their own achievements or, in some cases, their family's status, they considered themselves outsiders. Judy Ullman, another
member of Collective #1, suggested that Jews' sense of themselves as
outliers may have contributed to their strong motivation to help others:
"When you're fighting for someone else, you don't have to look at yourself and the ways in which you've been marginalized." In this way, they
could escape "some form of shame," Ullman said, but she noted importantly that Jews could marginalize themselves. She considers herself an
"outsider" even among Jews.[108]

A final factor in the mix of influences that shaped several of these
women's Jewishness was an early, formal connection to the religious
aspects of Judaism. Coming from Conservative, synagogue-going families, Balser and Clark were bat mitzvahed, an uncommon practice for
girls in the 1950s. Levenson studied briefly at a Reform synagogue, and
Tax went to services regularly at her Reform temple. Osterud was affiliated with a Reconstructionist one. Balser and Clark gave up the religious
component of their identities in the early years of the women's movement but later embraced spiritual aspects of Judaism. Like Osterud,
they are deeply committed to their synagogues today. Levenson's religious commitment is more personal. Though always Jewish identified,
Tax is a passionate secularist but remains guided by the prophetic teachings of the Torah.

These findings about the religious and cultural influences on Bread
and Roses women coincide with the conclusions of scholars who have
studied the connections between Judaism and the protest movements
of the 1960s. In addition to the Braungarts, Rebecca Klatch explored
motivations of New Left and New Right youth protesters in the 1960s.
Interviewing thirty-six SDS leaders, including seventeen women, she

discovered that about half of the Jewish subjects were raised in Reform synagogues, where they attended services and, if male, were bar mitzvahed; the other half had no religious background—some had parents who were "devout in their renunciation of religion." Yet despite the religious skepticism of these parents and the fact that many of their activist children also rejected religion (as did others who were raised in religious, even Orthodox, homes), Klatch found that "virtually all identified *culturally* with Judaism." Many told Klatch that the values they learned as Jews significantly impacted their politics. Klatch concludes that "religion and religious values were important factors that shaped [activists'] political consciousness, . . . giving them an ethical framework for their developing beliefs."[109]

Direct encounters with anti-Semitism were important, too, because they created in these SDSers the experience of being social outcasts, which they could analogize to the role of movement activist, outside the mainstream. Anti-Semitism enhanced Jewish SDSers' ability to understand racial bigotry; the perception and experience of anti-Semitism correlated with the commitment to fight racism. These factors came into play in the descriptions that Bread and Roses women gave of their childhood and early adulthoods. Klatch emphasizes, however, that the most salient factor in the SDSers' political development was their parents' roles in transmitting values. She notes that her respondents came from atypical homes with politically aware parents who were engaged and involved in the world and who encouraged their sons and daughters to be vocal and active.[110] While Klatch's pattern applies to her SDS sample, it is the case for only half the Bread and Roses women interviewed in this chapter; parents of the remaining half were more religious, or if culturally Jewish, they were less politically identified and active.

The narratives of the Jewish women in Boston's pioneering second-wave women's liberation group Bread and Roses help us understand the complexity of identity construction among Jewish radical feminist activists not only in the 1960s and 1970s but also over the entire life course. Identity emerges as fluctuating and mutable, although bounded by core elements concerning Jewish culture and religion that collapsed and expanded over time in relation to political and social opportunities and responsibilities, the changing sociohistorical landscape, and significant life events and transition points.

In the late 1960s and early 1970s, the political task at hand for these Boston feminists was building a radical, socialist-based, autonomous women's movement, separate from the male-dominated Left with which many of the women had been closely associated. They hoped to devise a groundbreaking theory that would collapse the stranglehold of sexism, capitalism, and imperialism on the lives of women and their families. Though the organization utilized familiar social and political networks to build its core base as it embarked on this task, with the consequence that many of the women came from similar backgrounds, a key goal was to include individuals from other social classes and races.

The particular, middle-class entitlements of the Bread and Roses organizers, including their Jewishness, were obstacles to be overcome as they sought to create a compelling revolutionary strategy and philosophy. Not until much later did the Jewish members of this group recognize the links between the Jewish-based factors in their experiences, such as anti-Semitism and marginality, and some of the other "isms" they wanted to eliminate.

At this historical moment, moreover, there was no Jewish feminist movement to challenge patriarchy within Judaism itself or in Jewish communal life. Even at those times when the Boston Jewish women's liberationists did acknowledge their Jewishness, they had to confront a sex-and-gender system within Judaism that disturbed them far more than it did their brothers, several of whom, such as those of Balser, Gordon, and Levenson, found a place for themselves within Jewish communities here and abroad. Whether male siblings were constructing alternative models of a more democratic Judaism or establishing themselves within traditional Jewish spaces, they found it easier to connect to Jewish life.

In years to come, in response to events in these women's own lives and the new possibilities offered by a feminist-based Judaism or by innovative, progressive, secular movements dealing with Jewish issues, some of them, and others from Bread and Roses, found a range of opportunities to engage those Jewish aspects of their identities that had helped to form their political attitudes and propelled them forward in search of women's liberation.

Our Bodies and Our Jewish Selves

The Boston Women's Health Book Collective

On May 11, 1969, Nancy Miriam Hawley stood in front of a small group of women at Emmanuel College, leading a workshop titled "Women and Their Bodies" at Boston's first Female Liberation Conference, which she had organized with Roxanne Dunbar of Cell 16. Like Hawley, who had recently given birth to her second child, a number of women at the workshop who had been involved in the New Left and the new women's movement were having babies. "Birth control and children were prominent issues for us," Hawley recalled.[1]

The session caught fire when Hawley recounted a remark made by the obstetrician who had delivered her daughter a few weeks earlier: "He said that he was going to sew me up real tight so there would be more sexual pleasure for my husband."[2] Outraged participants told of their own experiences with demeaning and sexist doctors. The group quickly came to realize that they should continue to meet to share information, including a list of doctors whom the women felt they could trust.

As the summer passed, the list kept growing smaller, with negative information about so-called trusted doctors continually surfacing. The women began to develop their own reports on topics about women's health. Calling themselves the "Doctors' Group," they began meeting in each other's homes to prepare a course on the subject.[3] "At the time, there wasn't a single text written by women about women's health and sexuality," said Hawley. "We weren't encouraged to ask questions, but to depend on the so-called experts. Not having a say in our own healthcare frustrated and angered us. We didn't have the information we needed, so we decided to find it on our own."[4] In the fall, they put together a twelve-session course on women's health issues, held at a lounge at the Massachusetts Institute of Technology (MIT). On the basis of what they had learned in the course and because requests came in from women's groups, they reworked their ideas into a 193-page stapled newsprint booklet, called *Women and Their Bodies: A Course*, which was published by the New England Free Press.[5]

The women published a revised copy of the booklet in 1971 through the auspices of the nonprofit New England Free Press. Rejecting the alienating third-person pronoun "their," they called the new booklet *Our Bodies, Ourselves*, putting themselves at the center of the project.[6] Like the new title, the introduction emphasized the collective nature of the endeavor to build a new movement based on women's gaining control of their own bodies. This newsprint edition of *Our Bodies, Ourselves* made feminist and publishing history, with 250,000 copies of the booklet sold largely by word of mouth and through a substantial network of alternative bookstores.[7]

In 1972, the group of a dozen women formally incorporated and became the founders of the Boston Women's Health Book Collective (BWHBC).[8] The collective published its first commercial edition with Simon and Schuster the following year. The volume provided a strong basis for empowering readers through new knowledge and strategies for self-help; subsequent editions provided additional materials and reflected changing foci. The seven sections in the revised 1984 edition— "Taking Care of Ourselves," "Relationships and Sexuality," "Controlling Our Fertility," "Childbearing," "Women Growing Older," "Some Common and Uncommon Health and Medical Problems," "Women and the Medical System"—were less medically oriented than in the 1973 book: "more focused on what we as women can do for ourselves and for one another."[9] All royalties earned went to sustain the organization's modest payroll for work on the book and for grants for feminist projects.

In 1976, by which time *Our Bodies, Ourselves* had sold an astonishing two and half million copies, it was named as one of the ten all-time best books for young people. It remained on the *New York Times* bestseller list for almost three years. In Europe, the book became one of the first books to become a best-seller in translation from English. By 2010, over four and a half million copies had been sold, printed in more than twenty-five languages.[10] Now in its ninth edition, the book is widely recognized as the bible of the women's health movement. "We didn't set out to transform the global conversation about women's health," said Nancy Miriam Hawley, "but that's what we had a part in doing."[11]

Like other women's liberationists in Chicago, New York, and Boston, most of the founders who produced *Our Bodies, Ourselves* had participated in civil rights, student, peace, and welfare rights groups before they came to the women's movement. As they began to inform themselves about the patriarchal culture that constrained women from making informed medical choices, the common cultural history wrought by their advanced education and their immersion in the civil rights and New Left movements deepened their consciousness of the impact of gender inequality on their lives. Being on the "cutting edge politically," as founder Wendy Sanford put it, led them to place issues of women's health within a larger, systemic critique of capitalism and sexism.[12] The collective aimed to promote social programs that would "reduce people's need for expensive medical interventions and work for deeper social changes which will help eliminate poverty and racism."[13]

The collective believed that giving women access to information about their own bodies would allow them to make choices about health care and diminish the medical establishment's stronghold over women's lives. A key instrument of this revolution would be readers organizing CR groups, as the BWHBC did itself, around issues in the book. By the time of the publication of the 1984 edition, the founders group had been meeting together once a week for twelve years.[14] Its feminist values included eschewing the traditional male-dominated organizational model, often derived from establishment practices such as Robert's Rules of Order, and inventing its own governance, work, and financial management standards.[15] In its structure and methods as well as its mission, the BWHBC was a radical endeavor.

Although the BWHBC operated out of Boston, with strong ties to the Boston women's movement and the Boston Left, it quickly exerted national influence. The relative lack of tension between "politicos" and radical feminists in Boston nurtured the collaborative spirit of the group. Several members were involved in Bread and Roses; others participated in different feminist consciousness-raising groups or in varied New Left projects. The development of collective authorship as the group's means of evoking feminist change benefited from the unusual connection between personal consciousness-raising and political organizing in that city.[16]

The BWHBC became a fulcrum for the burgeoning women's health movement, providing a model of consciousness-raising and consumer advocacy that questioned traditional, male-dominated medical practices. Working with women's health groups throughout the country, it fought for the legalization of abortion and helped the 1975 launch of the National Women's Health Network as the "action arm" of the women's health movement, hoping to influence policy in Washington, D.C.

While most radical feminist groups from the late 1960s and early 1970s have long since disappeared, the BWHBC not only has survived but has grown in outreach and coverage. The book has been adapted throughout the world, with teams of women in at least twenty-five countries selecting and editing the material according to local needs. In 2011, *Our Bodies, Ourselves* celebrated its fortieth anniversary with a new edition of the book and a symposium that included representatives of its partner organizations from Armenia, Bulgaria, India, Israel (representing Jewish and Palestinian communities), Japan, Moldova, Nepal, the Netherlands, Puerto Rico, Senegal, Serbia, Tanzania, and Turkey.[17]

One of the factors that distinguished the BWHBC from other women's liberation collectives was that except for three of the original founders, all members were wives and mothers. Several knew each other from children's or mothers' groups or connections forged by their husbands' work or schooling. Wilma (later Vilunya) Diskin knew Hawley from a mothers' group. Her husband was an MIT colleague of Hawley's husband, as were the husbands of Pamela Berger, Ruth Bell, and Jane Pincus. Pincus joined the summer group because she knew Hawley from their children's playgroup and Diskin from a tots swimming class. Wendy Sanford and Esther Rome's husbands were in architectural school together. Paula Doress-Worters gave birth to her second child shortly after the Emmanuel conference. Joan Ditzion, wife of a medical resident at the Peter Bent Brigham Hospital, had her first child several years later, as did Rome. In addition to these nine women, the founders group included Judy Norsigian, twenty-three, the youngest member, and childbirth educator Norma Swenson, forty, who came on board in the fall of 1971. Norsigian, not yet a mother, and Swenson, who had older children, gave more time to the collective's work, including travel, interviews, and collaborating with other organizations. They became the public face of the BWHBC.

Scholars who have written about the BWHBC note that its original membership was highly educated, predominantly middle class, and white, factors that promoted cohesion but also sameness. Although the founding group's racial composition is seen as significant, its Jewishness remained invisible.[18] Yet of the twelve original founders, eight were Jewish (the total number includes one founder who moved to Canada and left the collective after the first year).[19]

The Jewish stories of the founders of the BWHBC must be viewed as constituents of a larger portrait of Jewish and feminist identities that shaped the social change movements of the late twentieth century. In historian David Hollinger's view, understanding the Jewish-related characteristics of "dispersionist" groups such as the BWHBC is also key to a much broader conception of American Jewish history, one that goes beyond a focus on Jewish-identified "communalist" groups whose connection to Jewish life is explicit.[20]

This chapter tells the Jewish stories of six Jewish founders of the BWHBC and three non-Jewish founders, whom the group's Jewishness also influenced.[21] Despite racial and class privileges, as Jews, these members inherited specific values and outlooks of a minority culture, which had repercussions for the BWHBC's organizational life. The legacy of Judaism, which included pride and critical thought as well as marginality, contributed to the content and approach of *Our Bodies, Ourselves*, encouraging innovation, antiauthoritarianism, and self-help. These factors combined with the perspectives and heritages of non-Jewish founders, which played an important role as well in shaping the BWHBC.

The narratives of the Jewish founders follow the pattern of Jewish women in liberation groups already discussed in Chicago, New York, and Boston, which developed consciousness-raising and action agendas pertaining to women as a universal group, with issues relating to ethnicity and religion rarely surfacing. Despite these groups' considerable proportions of Jewish women, Jewishness was not a topic of discussion. Yet it was meaningful in the women's personal lives, serving as a backdrop for social activism, intellectual concerns, ethical values, and community building.

Figure 4.1. The founders of the Boston Women's Health Book Collective. Back row: Jane Pincus, Vilunya Diskin, Joan Ditzion, Esther Rome, Paula Doress-Worters, Wendy Sanford. Front row: Norma Swenson, Pamela Berger, Ruth Bell Alexander, Miriam Hawley, Judy Norsigian. Photo by Phyllis Ewen.

In women's liberation groups in these cities, members' varied Jewish backgrounds included red-diaper and secular influences, religious and traditional components, connections to the Holocaust and anti-Semitism, and experiences of marginality. All of these factors shaped the coming of age of the Jewish founding members of the BWHBC as well. But the collective was the only one of the organizations discussed thus far that included an observant Jew, another who had gone to an Orthodox day school, and a third woman who had been a child survivor of the Holocaust. The presence of Judaism as a religious faith, largely because of the observant member, established a tone of respect for religion at a moment in time when feminists of different faiths often viewed religion solely as patriarchal and oppressive. Other BWHBC founders were influenced by the social justice concerns of a more secular Judaism. Both cultural and religious Judaism formed the background to the group's Jewish influences.

Because of the longevity of the BWHBC, it became central to its members' lives in an unusual way. Several members described the collective as an extended family that shared leisure time, holidays (especially Passover seders), and life-cycle events as well as professional and political work.[22] The close integration of members' daily lives and social concerns created a spirited community environment as well as a safe space for topics related to personal identity and growth. Though not a part of the collective's project, Jewishness was important to individual members, and issues regarding anti-Semitism were frankly discussed when they emerged. But it took several years for the fact of the group's large number of Jewish members to surface. Various members recall the "eureka" moment at a meeting in the early 1970s when together they realized that more than three-quarters of the group were Jewish.

The connection to parenting is another factor related to the collective's Jewish identity. Issues of female health, sexuality, childbirth, and reproduction were at the forefront of the collective's concerns, but because of the women's own experiences as mothers, support of parenting became a goal as well. In contrast, most members of the initial women's liberation collectives were younger and single. Bread and Roses, for example, included day care and other parental supports in its laundry list of issues, but these concerns were not central.

The BWHBC formed a parenting study group, which created a second book, *Ourselves and Our Children*, published by Random House in 1978. The book disseminated the notion that good parenting was vital to feminism, women, children's well-being, and society at large. Even after the parenting group dissolved, the issue remained among the spectrum of BHBCW concerns. Some members connected this focus to the influence of the family values by which they had been raised.

Members point with pride to the fact that the BWHBC became a multigenerational community, with three and even four generations of families involved in Passover seders and other celebrations. Children, parents, and sometimes grandparents and grandchildren, as well as friends of family members, became part of the amplified *Our Body, Ourselves* group. This intergenerational community spoke to the women's ongoing commitment to each other and to their families' well-being, extending beyond casual get-togethers to lifelong support. The seders also expanded to include significant others, children, close friends, and colleagues, until it became a large communal gathering for an important segment of the women's health movement in Greater Boston.[23]

The family aspect of the collective helps us to understand the ways in which the whiteness of the organization's first decades was also a product of its Jewishness. In the preface to the 1973 *Our Bodies, Ourselves*, the founders identified themselves as "middle class . . . [with] at least some college education, . . . some [with] professional degrees," and although they did not specify race, they were definitively white as well.[24] The fact of Jewish identity, unmarked by outsiders and, at least for several years, unacknowledged even by the founders themselves, created additional familiarity that enhanced group solidarity.

Yet the close ties between founders created unintended problems. In scholar Kathy Davis's view, the collective's "mythical narrative," composed of "origin story, heroic tale, and family saga," unwittingly prevented newcomers from joining the group on equal terms.[25] Davis contends that because of the founders' failure to confront the differences that separated them from newer staff, they ignored the "institutionalized, heterosexist, and racialized" power structures that operated even within feminist organizations. Conflicts between women of color and white women founders played out as racial issues. Davis notes that similar problems plagued other feminist groups originated by largely white, middle-class women, who, in spite of attempts to diversify, inhabited layers of privilege difficult for latecomers to penetrate.[26]

BWHBC founders attempted to mitigate power differentials in varied ways. Starting with the earliest editions of the book, they gave drafts of chapters in progress to readers from different backgrounds, seeking feedback regarding exclusions or insensitivities. They had multiple relationships with women of color who were working colleagues across the U.S. and abroad. Collective members also participated in a variety of antiracist workshops.

But while the founders hired women of color to perform many of the paid staff tasks since founders had jobs, careers, or family interests in between book productions, they did not invite new staff members into the group's inner circle of personal intimacy and confidentiality or make them co-authors of *Our Bodies, Ourselves* or members of the BWHBC. According to founder Norma Swenson, the gap between the founders' shared experiences and newcomers' sensibilities was not easily bridged. "We genuinely wanted to diversify our working teams in the office, [but] they inevitably felt excluded, because in fact they were, by virtue of their social class backgrounds as well as their races. The totality of the social distance between most of them and most of us was very wide, even if we did have progressive politics . . . and even if the everyday atmosphere was always cordial and collegial."[27]

Founders acknowledged that the problem was one of structural racism. "Like many groups initially formed by white women," Jane Pincus admitted, the group had to struggle against the "internalized presumption that middle-class white women are representative of all women and thus have the right to define women's health issues and set priorities."[28]

The collective continually expanded the book's content coverage to include more representative voices and added women of color to the board and advisory groups as well as staff. By the 1990s, the organization was no longer a collective with its original ethos of voluntarism but a group of founders with paid staff. Nevertheless tensions between the founders and some newer staff led the staff to unionize, and in 1997, several black and Latina staff members brought a discrimination complaint against the collective, which was dismissed by the Massachusetts Commission Against Discrimination in 2003.[29] The conflict led the BWHBC to become a more formal organization with a more empowered staff and a community board of directors, with less direct involvement of most original founders.[30] To mark the difference between the original structure and the new one and to reconcile the group's name with that of its famous product, the community board changed the group's working title from the Boston Women's Health Book Collective to Our Bodies Ourselves (OBOS).

Outside the U.S., the collective held its central authority loosely, deferring to the experience of local translators and adapters.[31] OBOS's efforts promoted grassroots health activism throughout the United States, Africa, Asia, Latin America, and Europe. By developing innovative ways for global "translators" to adapt the book to local needs and experiences and expanding input from diverse readers and staff for the domestic volumes, the collective transformed the racial homogeneity of the original founders' group into a more broadly based co-authorship.[32] By the book's eighth edition in 2005, the organization enlisted Latina medical anthropologist Zobeida Bonilla to serve as "tone and voice editor," assuring that more heterogeneous voices were represented in the volume.

Other significant differences also emerged among the founders group and between founders and readers, especially during the BWHBC's early years. At one point in the mid-1970s, questions involving the parenting subgroup threatened group harmony. The selection of the chapter title on lesbianism caused division. The resolution of these issues required intense discussions about the development of materials, the role of readers, and the inclusion of diverse perspectives.[33] How to nurture more collaborative modes of knowledge gathering and dissemination remained a challenge, but the founders' commitment to each other and their mission-driven work, as well as to working out differences, solidified relationships.

The narratives presented in this chapter complicate the issue of diversity within the OBOS by pointing to the impact of experiences with race, ethnicity, sexuality, and parenting that stem from Jewish backgrounds. There was no uniformity in the founders' Jewish experience. Esther Rome was a practicing, observant Jew throughout her life. Paula Doress-Worters and Vilunya Diskin were influenced by religious factors in childhood, although they identified more secularly in adulthood. Nancy Miriam Hawley, a red-diaper baby who turned to the study of kabbalah in the 1970s, came to meld secular and spiritual values over the course of her life. Joan Ditzion and Jane Pincus remained secular, although elements of their Jewish backgrounds informed their work as well. Rather than being based on ethnoreligious sameness, the bonds created by Jewish background developed from respecting Jewish and other differences among collective members. There was no common repertoire of Jewishness to draw on, as there were shared female experiences.

Nonetheless, for all the Jewish women I interviewed, Jewish background was important as a motivator for personal activism. Being Jewish fostered attitudes that heightened social responsibility. It helped shape political values, bringing the women to the social movements of the 1960s and the women's health and parenting movements that emerged at the end of the decade. Despite the diversity of Jewish pathways, Jewish heritage cemented community among the founders group, including the non-Jewish founders, providing a basis for heterogeneity and innovation. The outsider perspective of Jewish life and its characteristic mode of questioning also predisposed collective members to think differently and creatively.

Taken together, the Jewish-themed stories of the OBOS create a kaleidoscopic portrait of Jewishness and feminist health activism in the late twentieth century. While Jewishness was not a precipitating factor in the mix of circumstances that led the founders to create the initial collective, it did matter a great deal.

Esther Rome, Paula Doress-Worters, Vilunya Diskin: Spiritual Progressives

Esther Rome, Paula Doress-Worters, and Vilunya Diskin shared a deep commitment to empowering women as actors in their own lives through the power of knowledge. Rome was an observant Jew all her life. Doress-Worters attended an Orthodox Hebrew day school in a working-class community in Massachusetts, and Diskin, a child survivor of the Holocaust, was exposed to Orthodox religion in early childhood. Doress-Worters and Diskin identified social activism with secular imperatives stemming from the civil rights and women's movements.

* * *

Esther Rome was a key figure in the work of OBOS before her death from breast cancer in 1995. Rome co-authored all editions of *Our Bodies, Ourselves* and served on the board and staff of the collective. Focusing on such topics as menstruation, food, nutrition, sexually transmitted diseases, breast implants, and body and self-image, she had a comfort with her own body that assured that she took a leading role in the group's innovative explorations of sexuality and reproduction.[34]

In turn, the collective changed Rome's life. When she went to the Emmanuel College conference and then participated in giving the "Women's Health" informal course at MIT, she was a young married woman, with a B.A. from Brandeis, where she majored in art, and a master's in teaching from Harvard. She taught art for one year in an intermediate school in the suburbs but found it to be a trying experience.

She had no idea that her life would take a completely different turn after the fall of 1969.

The youngest of four, Esther Seidman Rome was born in 1945 and grew up in Plainfield, Connecticut, a small town where hers was the only Jewish family.[35] Aided by the Jewish Agricultural Society, which relocated eastern European Jewish immigrants to rural areas in the Northeast, Esther's paternal grandfather, who had emigrated from the Ukraine, settled his family in Plainfield, where he became a shopkeeper. His son, Leo, met his wife, Rose, at the dedication of the one-room shul that their fathers had started in a nearby village. Esther's maternal grandparents had emigrated from eastern Europe and also became farmers. Esther's brother, Aaron, remembers their grandmother Bessie Seidman telling the children a story about the Cossacks who slashed every feather bed in town because they believed that Jews hid their money there. Esther was close to this grandmother and brought her children to hear these same stories after her grandmother retired from her business and moved to Florida and later western Massachusetts.

Esther's father was a devout Jew who taught himself many of the Hebrew prayers. He davened (prayed) three times a day and, with his wife, kept a strictly kosher home. Shabbat dinners every Friday night included Torah readings, with all the children taking turns reading and discussing the portions. The family was ideologically Orthodox, if not Orthodox in practice, because Leo Seidman kept his variety store open on Saturday. The children were tutored by Orthodox teachers and later studied at a Hebrew school in the nearest city. The Seidman family was gender neutral with regard to Jewish observance as it was in other respects; Esther's mother taught her sons as well as daughters domestic skills such as embroidery and baking.

Because Esther was Jewishly isolated growing up, she chose Brandeis University for her undergraduate work so that she could be with other Jewish students. During college, she met Nathan Rome, and they married in 1967, a year after graduation. Rome came from a learned European Zionist family. In the 1930s, his grandfather Salman Schocken started a publishing company in Berlin that moved first to Palestine and then to New York after the Nazis shut it down. Schocken Books made its place in literary history by publishing the works of such Jewish authors as Martin Buber, Franz Kafka, Franz Rosensweig, and S. Y. Agnon. Esther's relationship with her mother-in-law, Chavah Rome, the wife of artist Theodore Herzl Rome, lent a new dimension to her Jewish identity. She learned to bake Chavah's special challah.

When Esther Rome saw a notice for the women's liberation conference at Emmanuel College in June 1969, she was new to political movements, a young wife with a degree in art but no clear direction in her life. She quickly found meaning in the explorations conducted by the free-flowing group that formed to study women's bodies and the foibles of the medical system. Wendy Sanford recalled, "We met every week for over a decade and every month after that in a circle of personal sharing and political work which transformed each of us. For Esther, there was a sense of coming out of a childhood of relative isolation into a circle of women that gradually moved into the heart of our lives. After a month or so, Esther said, looking around at us, 'This group is the best thing that ever happened to me.'"[36] Self-educated in the female body and its anatomy, and with artistic skills, Rome played the major role in preparing the book's anatomy chapter and supervising graphic artists. More than that, "it was her vision," said Paula Doress-Worters, that *Our Bodies, Ourselves* should offer a view of women's bodies from their own perspective, "viewing the outside first, and then moving inward."[37]

Rome was a "supremely practical feminist," added Sanford. "She started from the experience of her own body and sexuality, and developed original, commonsense strategies to improve health." Her answer to the problem of women being raised to be ignorant and ashamed of their bodies was "to have a look." She "matter-of-factly demonstrated a cervical examination to us, and her demonstration was photographed for an early edition of the book." Rome was as creative as she was pragmatic. When the others first met her, Sanford recalled, she was completing a pair of camping pants "with a zipper that ran all the way from front to back, so that a woman could pee freely in the woods."[38] Her husband, Nathan, called the pants "liberators."[39]

Rome's imagination made her especially important to the collective, as did her willingness to take on difficult issues and confront powerful medical and corporate interests. For the collective's traveling exhibit, she embroidered anatomically correct vulva and pubic hair on a Raggedy Ann doll and gave the doll a mirror and flashlight. She developed critiques of agribusiness and the beauty and cosmetics industry and sought to combat anorexia and bulimia. To provide an alternative to useless inserts in tampon packages, she developed a red-ink menstruation brochure. Arguing for stricter guidelines on tampon labeling to prevent toxic shock syndrome, she served as consumer representative on the American Society for Testing and Materials' Tampons Task Force. In the 1990s, she joined a working group at the U.S. Food and Drug Administration to foster better research and information on toxic shock syndrome. At the time of her death, Rome had just completed a co-authored book, *Sacrificing Ourselves for Love: Why Women Compromise Health and Self-Esteem, and How to Stop*, about the health risks in women's lives, including sexually transmitted diseases, domestic violence, rape, body image, and breast implants.[40] Rome's gift to the collective, said Sanford, was a "politics free of ideology . . . thoroughly embodied in the practical."[41]

But while Rome's work as a health advocate was progressive in every way, in her life outside this realm, she was a supremely traditional woman. OBOS was an "extended family," her older son, Judah, remarks, enjoying many events together and looking out for each other, yet for the most part, Rome separated her work life from her family life. "When she was home, she was just my mother, committed to being Jewish and to having a Jewish house," he recalled. "We kept kosher at home. We always had Shabbat. Every Friday night, we lit candles, and we had dinner together as a family. We didn't go out, even in high school. If there was a party or something, it didn't matter."[42] His mother was always excited for the Jewish holidays, loving the traditional meals and cooking that went along with them, and she was passionate about the rituals, fasting on Yom Kippur, changing all the dishes for Passover, boiling all the glass bowls. Scrubbing the countertop on Passover was not good enough, her husband, Nathan, remembers; she demanded that he make a separate piece of plastic laminate to cover it.[43] When Rome was very ill, with only a few months to live, she was simultaneously concerned with completing her book, preparing her house for Passover, and planting her garden for the next year. When a friend asked if she could help clean Rome's house, Rome told her to use a toothpick to make sure there was no *chametz* (leavened foods) lurking in the cooktops. "This was a quality of commitment that marked every aspect of her life," said

Doress-Worters. "She would have made a wonderful old woman. . . . She knew the lore that for many of us was lost with our mothers and grandmothers. She knew everything about plants. She knew traditional women's crafts, and laws and rituals of the Jewish people."[44]

For Judah and his brother, Micah, being Jewish was "just part of everyday life," how Rome structured and ran the family. But they were equally comfortable with their mother's public profile as a women's health advocate dealing with cutting-edge topics regarding sexuality and reproductive rights. "I knew the word 'vagina'" by the first grade, said Judah. "Doesn't everyone?" While it might seem contradictory to "take on the very traditional role of making chicken soup and cleaning the house for Passover and, at the next minute, be testifying for the FDA on tampon absorbency," Judah remarked, "they were just both parts of her identity."[45] There was no conflict. "Esther asked me once did I think her old-fashioned," remembered Doress-Worters. "I did not."[46]

Because of Rome's strong family values and her Judaism, Judah does not believe his mother should be called a "radical." She was not a militant, Sanford agreed; the Romes were "solidly married, deeply religious, really safe."[47] But neither was she a strict traditionalist. Esther Rome's open engagement with sexuality was not typical of observant Jewish feminists, for whom modesty remained a Jewish commandment. Her brand of Judaism was less Orthodox or Conservative than individualistic and self-defined. Observing the Sabbath, she would not attend OBOS events on Friday nights or Saturdays. She did not attend seders hosted by other collective members if they were not kosher for Passover. In order to participate in an OBOS retreat that had to be held during Passover, Rome brought all the food.

Rome's ardent dedication to her work and colleagues, her family, and her Judaism was to her a practical means of engaging fully in the world. Her determination may have stemmed from the fact that as a minority in the non-Jewish community in which she was raised, she had to defend her principles and lifestyle, acknowledging her difference from others in positive ways. Religion and reason, work and family, became continuums rather than irreconcilable dualities. This hybridity drew on the comfort she derived from core religious beliefs and the feminist commitment she brought to her work with the collective.

OBOS founders cite Rome's Judaism as a primary reason for the group's acknowledgment of ethnic and religious identities.

* * *

At the NYU "Women's Liberation and Jewish Identity" conference, Paula Doress-Worters remarked that her background was also unusual, because most members of OBOS came from secular and/or socialist backgrounds, and she came from a religiously observant one. Doress-Worters moved away from traditional observance, "feeling more inspired by the spirit rather than the letter of the Jewish law."[48] Doress-Worters rejected the confining elements of the Orthodox Judaism in which she was raised but became active in Reconstructionist Judaism later in her life. She acknowledges that early religious teachings had an impact on her lifelong commitment to social justice.

Doress-Worters attended the first workshop of "Women and Control of Our Bodies" at Emmanuel College in 1969 and was involved in research leading to the first OBOS courses and *Our Bodies, Ourselves* editions through 1998. Her major contributions included writings on postpartum women in relationships with men, and women growing older. She co-authored *Ourselves Growing Older* (1986) and *The New Ourselves Growing Older: Women Aging with Knowledge and Power* (1994) with Diana Laskin Siegal and was a co-author of the 1978 *Ourselves and Our Children*. In the 1980s, she co-authored with Wendy Sanford a series of articles opposing the radical Right's attempt to censor *Our Bodies, Ourselves*.

Paula Brown Doress-Worters grew up in working-class Roxbury, Massachusetts, where "at least 85 percent of the neighborhood" seemed Jewish. Her parents, immigrants from Poland, came to the U.S. separately in the 1920s and met in the West End of Boston, an area of first settlement for many immigrant Jews. Shortly after Paula's birth in 1938 and a few months after Kristallnacht, her mother's sister and her husband fled Austria; they lived with Paula's family in their Boston apartment for twenty years and became role models for Paula and her brother. Paula learned Yiddish as well as English as a toddler. Her uncle, who told stories about being among the first groups of Jewish men to be rounded up in Vienna, was an inspiration to Paula, a hero who used just the right mixture of "nerve, chutzpah, and quick thinking" to enable his freedom.[49] Several cousins who had been in refugee camps after the war stayed with the family for shorter periods. Doress-Worters observed, "growing up with personified models of refugees from the Holocaust and the language of the people, my ancestral people, was a very powerful effect on my Jewish identity." The loss of family members in the Holocaust motivated her to be socially active and taught her also that "silence was acquiescence."[50]

The family's religious observance was quite traditional. Doress-Worters's devout father prayed with tefillin every morning and, despite his lack of formal training, often led weekday evening services at shul; her mother was well educated in Hebrew and knew and taught the daily prayers to her children. Doress-Worters's father worked in a grocery store, then in a war defense plant; her mother had her own children's clothing store. Along with many other Jews who left Roxbury, the family moved to a better neighborhood in Dorchester, but the children's store closed because its customer base moved. Doress-Worters's mother returned to the factory work of her earlier years. Her father was affected by the decline of mom-and-pop stores but eventually found work in another grocery store.

From the second through seventh grades, Doress-Worters's parents sent her and her brother to Maimonides, an Orthodox day school in Roxbury started by the charismatic Rabbi Joseph Soloveichik. Doress-Worters received a firm grounding in Jewish learning there but often felt like a "fifth wheel," taunted by classmates, whom she called the "religion police," for such offenses as her mother's keeping her store open on the Sabbath. She convinced her parents to let her return to public school for junior high. Jewish identity remained important to her, and Doress-Worters fondly recalls her parents' Passover seders and Rosh Hashanah gatherings with Jewish teens around the community wall at Dorchester's Franklin Field.

Doress-Worters was conscious of the changing face of her neighborhood, which became more African American and lower income. On her way to high school, she would see "the black kids getting on the public bus" that she took. "The conductors didn't treat them as nicely as the white students. They would yell at them or be critical of them." It made Doress-Worters think of the Holocaust and "the way Jews were at first, just isolated and humiliated": "By the time I got to college," she recalled, "I was really convinced that race was the big central problem in our society."[51] This belief created empathy for outsider groups and helped propel her activism.

Without funds to attend a four-year college, Doress-Worters completed a two-year business program at Bentley School of Accounting. After two years of office work with some night classes, she transferred to Suffolk University, a commuter school with a diverse student body primarily of white ethnics from Boston neighborhoods and western Massachusetts. After college, she worked for a peace group, then was a community organizer in Dorchester. While other college graduates were going south to participate in civil rights actions, Doress-Worters thought that "as someone who grew up in Roxbury and Dorchester and saw the neighborhood change," she could make a contribution locally. She became the sole staff member at the Washington Street Action Center, immersing herself in the community's culture and hoping to contribute to the welfare rights movement. The program was initiated by ERAP (the Economic Research and Action Project), an offshoot of SDS.

Doress-Worters married Irv Doress, a sociologist, and after the birth of their first child, moved to Arlington, where they both worked on fair-housing campaigns and other civil rights projects. Doress-Worters also joined a woman's consciousness-raising group. When a young woman remarked to her that she had gone to Boston "to be in the women's movement," Doress-Worters realized that Boston was developing a national reputation as a center of the growing movement.[52]

Doress-Worters pointed out one difference between Boston's two women's liberation groups at the time. Cell 16, also known as Female Liberation, was the first women's group in the city. Drawing on young women in their early to midtwenties, it focused on consciousness-raising, self-defense, and advocacy of separatism from men. Bread and Roses attracted a slightly older group, young women in their mid- to late twenties and a few, like Doress-Worters, in their early thirties. Most were socialist feminists, closely aligned with the New Left.

But there was another difference. One former Female Liberation member told Doress-Worters that while her group attracted non-Jews, the Jews went to Bread and Roses.[53] Doress-Worters agreed and added, "the majority of women in the [OBOS] group were Jewish, but we weren't talking about being Jewish because we were much more focused on gender equality and learning about our bodies." Yet she was aware of the Jewish members of her various women's groups: the consciousness-raising group, which was more diverse; Bread and Roses; and the Boston Women's Health Book Collective. In Bread and Roses, she was "drawn to Jewish women from New York who just were so out there about being Jewish. Not that they were talking about being Jewish but they weren't self-conscious about being perceived as too aggressive or too loud." To Doress-Worters, these Jewish women demonstrated a confidence and pride different from the attitudes of Jewish women such as herself who had grown up in Irish- and WASP-dominated Boston. Given their political backgrounds, they seemed "entitled to have a platform to somehow effect social change. And they just seemed very capable and strong and just very good role models."[54] Rather than the negative connotations of Jewish women's assertiveness internalized by others, for Doress-Worters, Jewish women's stereotypical traits reflected more positive characteristics. And as opposed to many Jewish women in women's liberation groups who declared that they had been unaware of members' religious/ethnic backgrounds, Doress-Worters was well aware of Jewish women's voices and presence. Boston is a very ethnically conscience city, she noted, and at college, she was often asked, "What are you?"—meaning what ethnic group: "as if that were the core of our being."[55]

After three decades, Doress-Worters retired from women's health work and came to the Women's Studies Research Center at Brandeis University to explore the legacy of suffragist Ernestine Rose, a nineteenth-century pioneer women's rights advocate neglected by historians, perhaps because of her identities "as an immigrant, an atheist, and a Jew."[56] Doress-Worters has published a two-volume collection of Rose's speeches and letters and established an Ernestine Rose Cemetery Society to restore Rose's burial site. In 2012, she traveled to Poland with her daughter to present a paper on Rose at the twentieth anniversary of the Women's Studies Program at Lodz and to visit the city of Rose's birth in nearby Piotrków and her parents' birthplaces in the Ukraine.

Like Ernestine Rose, Doress-Worters sees herself as a committed feminist social activist but also as a "radical Jew." "In the civil rights and feminist movements, we identified as universalists," Doress-Worters noted."[57] Yet although OBOS never explicitly recognized the influence of Jewish social justice values, she believes that it enabled members to act in the tradition that she calls radical Jewishness. "While we may have universal aspirations in terms of wanting to come up with interventions [and] social actions that will benefit society as a whole, we come to these goals with our own individual particularities," Doress-Worters said.[58] As for many other women's liberationists, Jewish particularity, reflected in the ethical values and political actions of Jewish culture, was the other side of universality.

* * *

As a child survivor of the Holocaust, Vilunya Diskin has a unique profile within the collective. Exposed to Jewish observance early in her life, she strayed from it in later childhood and her adult years, rekindling her spiritual connections decades later. At OBOS, Diskin (known as Wilma until she changed her name) focused on international women's issues. She has traveled extensively to promote women's health abroad, particularly in Mexico and India.[59] Diskin also created and managed Vilunya FolkArt, a shop and gallery of indigenous art, and is involved with various textile projects.

Diskin was born in the small town of Przemyślany, Poland, in 1942. Her family had been prosperous; her grandfather owned a textile mill, her mother was a lawyer, and her father was a chemist. With the exception of Vilunya, her entire family perished at the hands of the Nazis. In addition to an older brother, she had a twin sister who died either at birth or as an infant; she does not know the details. Diskin was saved because her parents made arrangements with their Catholic maid to hide her in her village. After the Soviets liberated the town of Lvov two years later, the woman brought Diskin to Rabbi Israel Leiter, and his wife, Esther. The Leiters joined the partisans, attempting to save Jewish children. They took Diskin into their home, where she lived as the Leiters' daughter for a few years; they had lost one of their daughters during the war.

The Leiters were warned that the authorities were about to arrest them and fled Lvov. Diskin remembers their escape to Czechoslovakia and then to Hamburg, Germany, where they spent two years waiting for a boat to America. In 1948, they finally arrived in New York. Her memories of that time focus on the family's Shabbat dinners, which included other refugees, with prayers, candles, food, a beautiful table, and the singing of *zmirot* (Jewish hymns) after dinner. "I felt the joy and longing in their singing," she recalled. "I was a witness to a profound example of survivors integrating their excruciating losses, as these wounded people, who had lived the imaginable, found the capacity to create a haven of warmth, love, and safety for their children. I felt cherished and enveloped in that love. It formed the emotional core of Judaism for me."[60]

Following the policy of the Hebrew Immigrant Aid Society to place refugee orphans with American families, a Jewish family in Los Angeles adopted Diskin. She described them as conventional, middle-class liberals who felt terrible about the Holocaust and "wanted to help the kids." She enjoyed a normal, happy childhood with them, but in retrospect, she realized that she experienced a "cultural chasm" in moving from a European, Orthodox household to an American, Conservative one. In the Leiters' home, "God was the life force": "All our actions, thoughts, and desires were focused on obeying biblical rules and regulations because this was the ethical code for living a worthwhile life." At her adoptive family's home, "God was a once-a-week and holiday presence." Friday nights were different: "there was no joyous singing, no lingering over prayers, no emotional attachment to God." Religion was now "a series of rituals to perform" rather than a "joyous emotional" experience.[61]

Although Diskin went to services with her family and for some years attended Jewish summer camp, if she identified as Jewish, it was only "lightly so." Being Jewish did not "figure much in [her] consciousness." Authentic Judaism meant the Leiters' religious enthusiasm, not the secular liberalism of Los Angeles Jews. Nonetheless, Diskin was able to develop a sense of moral purpose that fit her assimilated upbringing. Fundamental Jewish values led her first to the civil rights and antiwar movements and then to women's liberation and the Boston Women's Health Book Collective. As Diskin explained, "I began to transfer my visceral feelings of connection to God to a cultural identification with Judaism, which later morphed into activism and politics. I began to feel that being Jewish didn't necessarily mean a belief in God, but it did mean living according to the prescribed code of Jewish ethics. Being

Jewish meant making a commitment to recognize discrimination, and prejudice, to fight against it, and to be vigilant in fighting against another Holocaust. In the American context, this meant organization and advocating for equal rights and opportunities for all."[62]

As a student at the University of California at Berkeley and then UCLA, from which Diskin graduated in 1963, she became active in the civil rights movement: "as did every other Jewish person in my crowd." She "identified with Blacks and felt that [the two groups] shared a common history because Jews had been slaves in Egypt. Blacks were treated as less than human in the American South: Jews had been treated with suspicion and prejudice throughout Europe culminating in the Holocaust. Standing in solidarity with the civil rights movement felt familiar, the right place to be." Participation in civil rights was integral to Jewish values and to Jewish peoplehood. "It never surprised me when Jewish people were at the forefront of social justice."[63]

Diskin shared her passion for social justice with Martin Diskin, the son of Russian-immigrant Jews, whom she described as a "progressive, intellectual, culturally identified but non-practicing Jew." Both studied the anthropology of Latin American societies, moving to Mexico shortly after their marriage to do field research. All their friends were non-Jewish Mexicans. Working with indigenous peoples, their Judaism never surfaced. "We never even celebrated the Jewish holidays." Back in the U.S., where Martin had taken a position on the anthropology faculty at MIT and Vilunya gave birth to her first child, she tried to re-create the "warm Jewish presence" she had imprinted from childhood but still felt great loss.[64]

In Cambridge, Diskin's friend Jane Pincus, whom she knew from a childbirth class, told her, "We're going to a women's liberation meeting." Diskin asked, "Liberation? From what?" The two women joined a consciousness-raising group that became one of Bread and Roses' first collectives and were core members of the group that formed OBOS. The collective shaped the course of Diskin's work life and contributed to her personal growth over many decades.

"We got to be such good friends," Diskin remarked. "We got to be family. We worked together. And our families became friends." They went to each other's parties, weddings, bar and bat mitzvahs, seders. Because of this familiarity and because Jewishness had played such a meaningful role in several of the women's lives, "being Jewish was very comfortable in the group." Collective members discussed their own Jewish identities when relevant, but they did not dwell on them. When difficult subjects such as the Holocaust and anti-Semitism arose, these issues were discussed openly. Diskin remembers a non-Jewish member describing how she felt when her family made anti-Semitic remarks and, on another occasion, the woman responding to Diskin's diatribe against "terrible atrocities committed in the name of Jesus" by reminding Diskin that "Jesus was a good guy." "I'm ranting about all the people in his name who don't act like Jesus at all," she responded. "*Our Bodies, Ourselves* was a safe environment where you could really discuss anything," Diskin commented. "We had lots of heavy-duty discussions. But at the end of the day, we would get through whatever it was that we got into because of the enormous trust and love and affection [that] was there—and respect."[65]

Diskin's Jewish identity grew deeper over time. For many years, she felt that her Jewish journey had taken her down two parallel paths: the intense, emotional connection to Judaism, which she identified with the Leiters, and the secular identification developed in her American household. While she mourned the loss of the religious longing and joy she experienced with the Leiters, she rejected their God-centered theology that seemed irrational to her after the horrors of the Holocaust. Eventually Diskin understood that there were "many examples of good behavior in terrible circumstances" and that she could hold two opposing truths. The two paths now seemed interwoven, "like a *khallah*," she said, rather than contradictory.[66]

Today she has come "full circle." She participates in a Reconstructionist Jewish synagogue, studying Hebrew and the Bible. "When I hear the Hebrew prayers," she said, "I feel a bond to the generations of Jews who came before me," even though as a child of the Holocaust, she never knew her family of origin. For this reason, her bond to the Jewish collectivity may have become even stronger. And she is fully engaged in teaching her grandchildren "Jewish values: the importance of education, critical thinking, compassion for those different and poorer than ourselves and to act in the world to leave it a better place."[67] Prayer and ritual along with activism and social consciousness have emerged as joint touchstones of her Jewish identity.

The Boston Women's Health Book Collective and Diskin's Judaism have served as the two parallel paths of her life. The critical thinking and social action that *Our Bodies, Ourselves* generated, leading to concrete improvements in millions of women's lives throughout the world, stand as enduring testimony to the power of goodness and the force of ethical action amid the complex and often terrifying conditions of human existence. Diskin's participation in, first, the Jewish-inflected community of the Boston Women's Health Book Collective and, later, its multicultural, global one has been one expression of her Jewishness. At the same time, the collective affected that Jewishness through its core values and achievements. Carrying those values with her, Diskin has at last found a home in the synagogue she chose because of its commitment to gender equality, feminism, and social action. With many mixed families, it is a diverse and pluralistic Jewish community. Being a part of two special communities—the synagogue and the OBOS collective, both dedicated to the pursuit of social and ethical imperatives—Diskin considers herself fortunate. "*L'dor v'dor*," she said—from generation to generation. "Let us maintain and add to the traditions we all share."[68]

Nancy Miriam Hawley, Joan Ditzion, Jane Pincus: Political Radicalism and Jewish Family Values

As daughters of political radicals, Nancy Miriam Hawley and Joan Ditzion shared a red-diaper background. Their parents' beliefs helped shape their political convictions and, together with their exposure to youth and student movements during college, brought them to the New Left and antiwar movements. Jane Pincus's family background did not orient her to activism, but she became involved in antiwar politics and feminism.

* * *

Nancy Hawley co-wrote several *Our Bodies, Ourselves* chapters, serving on the collective's board for many years. She has been a clinical social worker, group therapist, and organizational consultant. Like several of the collective's founder-authors, Hawley re-created her Jewish identity over her life course. She began with a connection to Jewish traditions that led to political radicalism. Later she commenced a course of study that took her to kabbalah, Jewish renewal, mysticism, and Buddhism. As she was turning fifty in the early 1990s, she changed her name from Nancy to Miriam, a mark of the bond she felt with one of the Jewish tradition's most iconic heroines.

Hawley came to political radicalism through the New Left and to the women's movement through her experiences as a mother and radical. She gave birth to her first child in 1966 and, shortly after, became part of a consciousness-raising group in Cambridge, Massachusetts, most of whose members had young children. She was already a member of SDS when in the fall of 1968, she got a call from Marilyn Webb urging her to go to Lake Villa, outside Chicago, where SDS women planned a November gathering to discuss women's issues. Unlike other attendees who were disturbed by the rancorous proceedings, Hawley came away euphoric. Having heard Shulamith Firestone pronounce pregnancy "barbaric" and call for the replacement of biological means of reproduction with artificial ones, she intuitively understood that the movement needed her pro-motherhood voice.[69] She began meeting with several SDS women to consider "what it was like to be a woman within the Left."[70] From these beginnings came the Emmanuel College conference, at which Hawley offered the auspicious workshop on "women and their bodies."

Hawley grew up in a minimalist Jewish family, the daughter of parents who had what she calls a German Jewish and Russian-Polish Jewish "mixed marriage." Her mother was raised in the small town of Sweetwater, Tennessee, where they were the only Jewish family; her grandfather, because he looked the part, played Santa Claus at the town's Presbyterian church. Hawley's father was a first-generation Jew from a poor family on New York's Lower East Side. Two stories about her paternal grandfather, a barber, became family lore. One was that he got permission from the rabbi to work on Saturday to support his six children. The second was that he trimmed Trotsky's beard when Trotsky was in New York.

When Hawley's mother went to New York at age thirteen, she was eager to learn Hebrew. Her devout Christian friends in the South had prayed for her salvation by Jesus Christ, and now she saw the opportunity to learn a tradition of her own. But she dropped out after being placed in a Hebrew class with six-year-olds. That was the end of her

Jewish learning. She would have nothing to do with Jewish life, becoming an atheist. Hawley's father had also moved away from Judaism, though Hawley believes that while outwardly he gave up the trappings of the tradition in which he had been raised, privately he remained a spiritual person. When he died, she said, "I decided to say Kaddish for him . . . every night, knowing that he would appreciate it, and that was a spiritual connection between us that was unspoken."[71]

Later in childhood, Hawley and her family moved from the Upper West Side to suburban Westchester County, where they were among the only Jewish families. In her new community, she felt she had to keep her Jewishness hidden, though apparently her family's ethnicity was known. On one Rosh Hashanah, when Hawley went to school, a classmate berated her for being there on a High Holiday. "I felt mortified, . . . really furious at my parents that they didn't keep me home," she recalled.[72]

Hawley was a red-diaper baby whose parents, especially her mother, were involved in the Communist Party in the 1940s and early 1950s and active in the defense of Julius and Ethel Rosenberg. "Social justice was the family's religion," she noted. "I grew up singing songs of Woody Guthrie, Pete Seeger, the Weavers, and Odetta."[73] But as the child of political radicals, Hawley felt "equally hidden," unable to speak about her family's politics. Although she was visible by being smart and athletic, she felt "shut off" from her real identity. Hawley's sense of alienation and her anger at her parents mirrors the experiences of many Jewish teenagers from left-wing families during the McCarthy period. Jewishness and radicalism were a difficult combination, particularly for those in communities that welcomed neither left-wing politics nor Jewish culture.

Hawley was the first person in her family to go to college. Looking for a "political home," she aptly chose the University of Michigan and was there for the birth of SDS on its campus in fall 1960, when she entered the school. "It was very, very fulfilling," she recalled. "I found that I could be out as a radical political person. Judaism was not an issue. That went underground completely at that point."[74] She felt a tinge of anxiety, though, when midway through college, she married Andy Hawley, a non-Jewish SDS activist who at one point had roomed with Tom Hayden, an SDS founder, but her parents and paternal grandparents readily accepted her husband and the marriage. All her mother wanted was for her to complete her degree.

In the "hot center" of radical activity at college, Hawley graduated with a degree and social and political connections. After the Lake Villa conference, she played a key role in developing and spreading ideas about an autonomous women's movement, participating in her Cambridge consciousness-raising group and Bread and Roses, and co-organizing the Emmanuel College conference and the women's health course that followed. Hawley also coordinated the first *Women and Their Bodies* newsprint publication.

"The women of the Collective are my family," Hawley said.[75] Wendy Sanford remembers the collective meeting in Hawley's living room, as Hawley sang Hanukkah songs to members' children. In the early 1970s, now divorced, Hawley met Jeffrey McIntyre, the son of a Methodist minister and a serious student of Buddhism; she and McIntyre married in 1978. His influence helped her to acknowledge the spiritual and religious interests that had lain dormant for years. In the early years of the women's movement, religion was still regarded by many leftists as "the opiate of the masses," Hawley remarked.[76] But through her husband's religion-centeredness, the influence of Esther Rome's practices, and the bonds that the collective's Jewish women and children shared, Hawley began a journey to rediscover her Jewish heritage. She was guided by an impressive group: Yuval, an Israeli teacher of kabbalah; Zalman Schacter-Shalomi, the charismatic leader of the new Jewish Renewal movement; and Thich Nhat Hanh, Vietnamese Zen Buddhist teacher and noted peace activist. From these teachers, Hawley created her own eclectic mix of Jewish-Buddhist practice, eventually joining B'nai Or, the Jewish Renewal movement synagogue in Boston. With Rabbi Schacter, she created a "Budda-Mitzah" (rather than bar mitzvah) for her son.

In 1991, shortly before Hawley's forty-ninth birthday, she decided to change her given name to Miriam, admiring the leadership qualities of the biblical heroine. She created a naming ceremony for herself, with her guests sharing a *mikveh* (ritual bath) with her in a New Hampshire lake. She asked her parents to speak on why they had not given her a more Jewish name. "It wasn't in the tradition then," her mother replied.[77]

Hawley's journey into Judaism continues. While sometimes she feels "like a misfit in terms of not being a religious Jew," she is buoyed by her children's interest in their heritage, despite the fact that their assimilated upbringing repeated her own. She helped her granddaughter create a bat mitzvah ceremony and is proud of the fact that one young grandson started to learn Yiddish. Like Diskin, Hawley noted that "the traditions go on" and that it is "totally thrilling." With four generations now attending OBOS's seders, Hawley remarked on the empowering aspect of reclaiming the tradition of Judaism: "the same way we had reclaimed our bodies."[78]

* * *

Joan Ditzion, co-author of all nine editions of *Our Bodies, Ourselves* as well as *Ourselves and Our Children* and *Our Bodies, Ourselves: Menopause*, comes from a secular, socialist background. In addition to writing for OBOS, she helped edit the publications and was the collective's principal art designer. Ditzion's work with the collective inspired her to go to social work school, and she became a geriatric social worker, focusing on aging, older adults and family caregiving.

Ditzion emphasized the ways in which Jewish family values meshed with the collective's perspective on parenting. Raising children is all-important work, she said, and parenting—if chosen—"should not be the turf of the right wing." OBOS claimed a "feminist perspective to family values" and a parallel goal for women to control of their bodies and reproductive rights, which connected to Ditzion's upbringing.[79]

Born in 1943, Ditzion grew up in a close, extended family with a strong, cultural Jewish identity. The family did not go to synagogue, but they celebrated Jewish holidays. Because of her father's stories about his boyhood, anti-Semitism became a "palpable theme" in Ditzion's childhood. Ditzion's father, a first-generation American, grew up in the Bronx in an immigrant, Yiddish-speaking home and had to navigate his way through a neighborhood where gangs of young toughs made the life of a young Jewish boy (the "Yid," as he was called) difficult. Ditzion grew up in a Protestant area of the Bronx, and as one of the few Jewish children in school to stay home on Jewish holidays, she also had to deal with difference early on. When she saw young girls wearing pretty organdy dresses for their communions at the neighborhood church, she absorbed that standard of beauty as her ideal. "It wasn't like, 'I'm proud to be Jewish,'" she commented, even though today she declares her pride in her Jewish identity and heritage.[80]

Although Ditzion's immediate community "didn't feel Jewish at all," her family was the "core center" where she always felt a strong sense of her Jewishness. At her paternal grandparents' house in the Bronx, she would watch her grandmother make Shabbat. In addition to her father's Orthodox old-school parents, she was influenced by her maternal grandparents, born in America and much more assimilated than her father's family. Her maternal grandmother had supported the suffrage movement and shared the work of a ready-to-wear store that she and her husband owned. This grandmother and her aunts provided Ditzion with "vital, strong" female Jewish role models. Ditzion said, "Feminism was a logical thing; it wasn't a rebellious thing ever. It was just an outgrowth of my roots." Nonetheless, although her brother was bar mitzvahed as a matter of course (he became a Jewish communal executive), a bat mitzvah for her was not discussed. The men in the family were "great, good men," not really sexist, but the women "kept things going." Ditzion was aware of women's contributions, despite the "1950s mentality," but it was not until the women's movement that she adopted a "women-centered" worldview.[81]

The progressive, social justice values of Ditzion's parents were crucial ingredients in the social consciousness she formed at an early age. Her father, a high school math teacher and department chair, and her mother, a guidance counselor who worked primarily with African American students, were members of the teachers' union, linked to the Communist Party. Growing up, Ditzion was unaware of this affiliation, learning of it only in the early 1970s. When friends of theirs lost their teaching jobs because of McCarthyism, she attributed their distress to the fact that they were all members of the union. Ditzion remembers the shock of the Army-McCarthy hearings, which she watched on television with her parents when she was in the fifth grade. McCarthyism on the negative side and the struggle for civil rights on the positive were formative ingredients in what she called her "social justice upbringing."[82]

Recollections of the harassment that the Ditzions' teacher friends experienced during the McCarthy years led them to go west to support their daughter, who had to appear before Max Rafferty, the superinten-dent of education in Berkeley, California, and sign what they suspected was a loyalty oath in order to receive her teaching certificate. Joan had gone to the University of California at Berkeley for her master's degree in art education after graduating from City College in 1963. She ran smack into the middle of the Free Speech Movement and was arrested at one protest, spending one day in jail—hence the parental visit, which Joan found moving, if unnecessary.

Ditzion did get her certification and returned east after a year of teaching at Berkeley High School. In 1967, she married Bruce Ditzion, then an intern at Brigham's Hospital in Boston and later a medical resi-dent at the National Institute of Health in Bethesda, where Joan taught art in an experimental junior high school humanities program. In January 1969, she attended the anti-Nixon inauguration protest in the nation's capital. She has a keen memory of hearing women from Bos-ton's Bread and Roses speak out against male chauvinism: "We are not going to be making coffee and taking notes. We want full participation in this political process, and we want to end gender inequities."[83]

The Boston women made a great impression on Ditzion, and when the couple returned to that city in the summer of 1969, she started a consciousness-raising group with a friend from Berkeley. At about that time, she saw an ad in the *Old Mole*, the New Left underground news-paper published in Cambridge, for a course on "know your bodies." Ditzion enrolled and became hooked by the importance of the mate-rial and the revolutionary self-help consciousness-raising tool that the women were inventing. "It was such a breakthrough to begin to own and affirm a women's point of view of our bodies, reproduction, and female sexuality," she recalled. "I was excited to hear a range of first-hand accounts of childbirth experiences and learn about the pioneering work of the natural children and breastfeeding movement. My mother's childbirth account was 'I was in the hospital, anesthetized, and then the doctor brought you to me!' "[84]

With feminism in the air, the work of *Our Bodies, Ourselves* "just spoke to" Ditzion, she said. "It touched me at the core like no other social change movement. It was one of the most transforming moments in my life."[85] Although several OBOS founders had young children when she joined the group, she was the first to become pregnant while

Figure 4.2. The OBOS founders gathered around Joan Ditzion, pregnant, mid-1970s. Photo by Elizabeth Cole.

collaborating on the Simon and Schuster edition of the book. Ditzion stayed home with her two children, working part-time but spending much time with OBOS.

At the time, not all radical activists sympathized with the desire to have and raise children. Jane Pincus recalls a banner that hung from a neighbor's flat, "Down with the Nuclear Family," which she felt represented a significant feeling within women's liberation. OBOS stood for more equal gender and parenting roles as well as for empowering women's knowledge and practice of health. It validated parenthood and gave great support to Pincus and other mothers. Reproductive rights were central to the perspective of OBOS, but within that context, "choosing parenting is a terrific option, maternity is a terrific option," Ditzion said. To hold this view "within the context of the women's movement" was unusual and important.[86]

Ditzion appreciates the compatibility of her choices with the collective's work plan and its ideology, which she attributes in good part to her own strong family values—Jewish family values, she said. She asserted that family values must not be ceded to right-wing moralists and pointed to OBOS's continuing support for birth control, abortion rights, and open sexual expression, as well as maternity, paternity, and parental choices. To Ditzion, the large Jewish representation in the collective contributed to this stance and created a "core bond, a Jewish bond."[87] In her view, OBOS expressed traditional Jewish family values, but in a modern, radical, way.

* * *

Jane Pincus came from a secular background like Hawley's and Ditzion's and was a participant in several of the social movements of the 1960s. Active in antiracist work in CORE (the Congress for Racial Equality) and the NAACP (the National Association for the Advancement of Colored People), she protested the war in Vietnam. Pincus became involved in women's liberation through Bread and Roses and attended the Emmanuel College workshop on women and their bodies. She was a mainstay of OBOS, writing the chapter on pregnancy for the first publication and co-editing several editions of the book with Wendy Sanford.

Born in 1937, Pincus grew up in a small town in upstate New York and then in White Plains, in a household that did not practice "anything at all."[88] Her mother wanted the children to enjoy the trappings of Christmas, so they had a tree every year. They did not observe the High Holidays, and Pincus's only connection to a synagogue was the dancing lessons she took at a nearby Reform temple. Pincus was not aware of the Holocaust growing up or of its effect on any member of her family. Spending much of her childhood in the country, without any Jewish friends at school and no Jewish family traditions, she had no feeling for Judaism or Jewish culture. The exception was Passover, when her extended family gathered at her grandparents' house. Her grandfather was Orthodox, though her grandmother was a spiritualist with no connection to Judaism.

Later in life, Pincus learned from her mother that her father would have loved to have been a cantor; he was a deeply religious man, according to her mother, and loved to sing. But, deeply affected by the Depression and fearful of not being able to support his family, he became a businessman. Pincus was never aware of these Jewish yearnings. She was also surprised to learn as an adult of the family's push toward assimilation. Her father, born Pesach Katz, went to school as Percy Katz but changed his name to Paul when he was teased as "Pussy Cat." After being "persecuted" in various ways in the 1930s for being Jewish, both he and his brother went through another name change. On Pincus's birth certificate, her father is listed as Paul Wolfe Kates.[89]

Without any Jewish education or role models, Jewishness was not an important theme in Pincus's life, but there were times when it resonated. Going to Pembroke College, the women's affiliate of Brown University, in the 1950s was one of those experiences, since the institution segregated its dormitories by religion, housing Jews with Jews, Catholics with Catholics. Many religious discussions ensued, which Pincus approached as a pantheist. "I believed in nature," she said. "Just a belief in the allness and wonder of things. I had no religious language or background training whatever." Other students criticized her for not "carrying the Jewish burden."[90]

At college, Jane met Ed Pincus. Coincidentally, her father had known Ed's father, whom he called "Pinkie," in the textile business. Ed's family observed the High Holidays, and Ed had been bar mitzvahed; but neither Ed nor his family considered themselves religious. Ed and Jane married in 1960 and moved to Massachusetts, where Ed was a graduate student in philosophy at Harvard (he became a noted documentary filmmaker) and Jane briefly taught art in junior high school, then French at Wellesley High School. One night she watched Alain Resnais's "immensely strong and upsetting" film *Night and Fog*, about the Holocaust. "I went to school the following day with my whole worldview transformed, into disbelief, deep sorrow and outrage, and that was my true initiation into learning about the Jewish past."[91]

Although the Pincuses did not keep a Jewish household, observe the holidays, or provide their two children with a Jewish education, some Jewish sensibilities emerged. "I'm very Jewish in my awareness of who is Jewish and who isn't," Pincus said. "However unreligously we live, being Jewish is (pretty much always) somewhere in the background, popping out or more subtly coming forth at sometimes surprising times."[92]

Both the Pincuses were involved in political work in the mid- and late 1960s, protesting the Vietnam War through marches, sit-ins, and draft counseling. Everybody Jane knew was resisting, many of them Jewish, but nobody thought of themselves as Jews, just activists demanding an end to the war. In 1965, pregnant with her daughter, she met Vilunya Diskin, and they became close friends. Learning about Diskin's background as a child survivor, Pincus began reading books about the Holocaust and creating paintings in relation to what had happened. The two friends joined one of the first consciousness-raising groups in Cambridge that grew loosely out of SDS affiliations; the group met weekly for several years and became one of the Bread and Roses collectives.

With Diskin, Pincus attended the Emmanuel College conference, her newborn son at her breast. She met with the group throughout the fall, helping to plan and give the first course in November 1969 and working with others to put together the first women-centered publication on women's bodies. This was her work group, as distinct from the personal consciousness-raising group, which soon disbanded. As OBOS founders came to know each other, their bonds deepened, and members began to share not only their work but the stories and events of their lives. Pincus thinks that the ratio of Jews to non-Jews among the founders, about three to one, created an unusual environment where Jewishness stood out and led to a consideration of Jewish aspects of social justice that may have led non-Jewish members to be "ultrasensitive" to Jewish issues, but in a positive, shared, and open way. Jewishness was simply accepted, yet it existed alongside other traditions, such as Judy Norsigian's strong Armenian perspective and Wendy Sanford's Quaker one. For Pincus, Esther Rome's presence in the group as an observant, progressive Jewish feminist who seamlessly combined tradition and innovation mattered deeply.

OBOS began to have seders in the mid-1970s, when the women realized how many members were Jewish and that the non-Jewish members were interested in the Passover freedom holiday as well. One year, Ed Pincus filmed the collective's seder, with Jane chopping nuts and apples to make *charoset*. Jane is talking about how much she misses Jewish traditions in her own life. Being part of OBOS enriched her with these connections to Jewishness and because of the collective's support of parenting and family life, which Pincus, like Ditzion, associated with Jewish values.

Pincus's commitment to the mission of the collective in fostering the empowerment of women and the well-being of their families was total. As writer, artist, editor, and board member and in many other capacities, she made a lasting contribution to OBOS, even though for several decades she had to commute to Boston from her home on the top of a mountain hideaway in central Vermont, where she and her husband moved with their children in 1975.

The Pincuses were the only Jewish people in their small town, and they sometimes experienced anti-Semitic comments. Soon after they moved to Vermont, Jane noticed that "there was a closet in the bathroom; inside, right next to it, an enclosed, empty space just big enough for one person." From the start, she thought of it as "the best place to hide in when 'they' came for" the couple. She discovered subsequently that separately, she and her husband had considered it a hiding place— "just a thought, at the back of our minds."[93]

The reason the family fled to Vermont adds a bizarre chapter to the story of Pincus's Jewish journey. Although her father and uncle changed their name to avoid anti-Semitism and successfully assimilate, Ed and Jane Pincus, graduates of a prestigious Ivy League university and engaged in successful careers, had little reason to worry about prejudice against Jews. But in the early 1970s, Dennis Sweeney, a former associate and student of Ed's who had become disgruntled and mentally unstable, threatened them, their young children, and congressman Allard Lowenstein, accusing them of being part of an international Jewish conspiracy.[94] The Pincuses fled to an inaccessible part of Vermont to escape him. Congressman Lowenstein was not so lucky. In 1980, Sweeney went to Lowenstein's Manhattan office and shot and killed him. Sweeney was found not guilty by reason of insanity and was committed to a hospital for the criminally insane.

This atypical story of murder—along with Pincus's latent feelings of anti-Jewish danger and threat—belies the sense of security that men and women of Pincus's generation enjoyed as mainly assimilated American Jews. However unusual, it demonstrates the inalienability of identity that has been a fact of life for Jews over many generations.

Wendy Sanford, Norma Swenson, Judy Norsigian: "One Pure WASP, One Pure Ethnic, and One Complete Mongrel"

The three non-Jewish original founders of OBOS offer insights into the way in which ethnic and religious identity became part of the group's life over several decades. Their stories differ, but as Norma Swenson described them—"one pure WASP, one pure ethnic, and one complete

mongrel"—these women shared an appreciation for the Jewish component of their colleagues' backgrounds and the way it shaped individuals
as well as the collective life of the community.[95]

* * *

Wendy Sanford joined the collective through Esther Rome. Their husbands were at architectural school together, and she and Esther had
been "couple friends." Going to Rome's for Shabbat dinner was the first
time she had ever encountered Jewish observance. "I didn't know Judaism," Sanford said. "I had so little political and social consciousness, I
barely knew I was a WASP at that time. My parents were anti-Semitic,
anti-Catholic, anti-, you know, you name it."[96]

Sanford grew up in Princeton, New Jersey, part of the upper middle
class, and went to a private girls' Episcopal boarding school in Maryland,
a "WASPY school with lots of debutantes." Despite her parents' osten-
sible refinement, they told "fairy jokes, black jokes, Jewish jokes" that
made her uncomfortable.[97] One of Sanford's high school boyfriends was
Jewish, but his family had changed their name; when her grandmother
learned who she was dating, she would have none of it.

Sanford graduated from Radcliffe College in 1967, marrying soon
after and not expecting to work. Wives in her social set "volunteered,
gardened, played tennis and golf, decorated their homes—and got pregnant."[98] After Sanford gave birth to her son, she suffered from significant
postpartum depression, a condition that was not diagnosed and that she
did not understand. A transformative moment came when Esther Rome
took her to a lecture on sexuality by the women's health group that was
teaching a course on women's bodies at an MIT lounge. Sanford learned
that her depression was a "real phenomenon," with a name and "physical and societal causes," and that other new mothers suffered from it.
She felt an immediate "glimmer of elation, as if someone had lifted the
flap of a heavy tarp that had settled on [her]"; she "jumped into teaching the 'Bodies' course, into women's health activism, with the energy
of one sprung from a trap."[99] Sanford stayed with the group to help give
the course again and began to speak to audiences of women about their
bodies, even though at first she had to practice words such as "mastur-
bation" and "clitoris" in front of a mirror so she could say them without blushing. After a lifetime of private-school education that had set

her apart, she loved "standing on this common ground." "Feminism had opened a third eye in my head," she recalled. "I noticed the politics of everything." Sanford helped prepare the mimeographed manuscript that was to become OBOS's first book. "We were stumbling into, marching into, our life's work," she said.[100]

Her marriage did not survive the dramatic changes in her life. After a while, she came out as a lesbian. The collective, supportive throughout these changes, became her new family. "All but three were Jewish," Sanford noted. "I was the only blonde in the group," "a naive, sheltered, WASP." She was also the only lesbian, though she ruefully noted that many people assumed that all the collective members were lesbians. "Why else would you question traditional relationships?"[101]

The collective's life included Shabbat dinners at Rome's, where Judaism was a "deep, spiritual observance"; Hanukkah at Hawley's or Rome's; and feminist seders. Sanford also recalls the many bar mitzvahs and bat mitzvahs of children. She loved services "with all the kids running around and making noise that didn't bother anyone," very different from the Episcopalian ones she grew up with, where the kids "listened to the minister and then left."[102] Sanford conjured up the atmosphere at the Romes' Shabbat dinners: the "candles and the Sabbath prayers, . . . the challah and the roast chicken." She described Hawley's house at Hanukkah time. Ten women and varied children were gathered around her in her bedroom, singing the dreidel song; Diskin signaled for Sanford to sit and whispered that she would "catch on." She searched for the rhythm, clapping awkwardly.[103]

Although Sanford did feel "very strange," somewhat "on the outside," she said, "They made perfect room for me because the Jewish holidays are incredibly inclusive. They just included me."[104] At that moment, Sanford realized that these women "might be the ones" with whom she "was going to grow old."[105] It was a great joke among the group when Sanford began to learn Yiddish. Her first word came from Pincus. "This is my *schmatta*," Pincus said, and Sanford said, "What's that?"[106] Just as Sanford had to practice sexually explicit language, now she had to practice Yiddish terms as well.

Reflecting on the Jewish aspect of the collective, Sanford observed, "We were kind of a holistic, family-oriented group, so it makes sense that people's Judaism would also be something that people brought in the door with them."[107] She believes that because the collective was less ideological than many feminist groups were, its family orientation to sexuality and reproduction stood out. "You have eleven people who've known each other since they were very young mothers, or pre-mothers, who have shared births, deaths, divorces, marriages, remarriages, bat mitzvahs, bar mitzvahs, illness, and then husbands' illnesses and deaths, and then my coming out—we went through [all] that. We met once a week for a long, long time. You do become a family, particularly if you're talking about family issues like sexuality and relationships and birth." Shaped by the familial nature of founders' lives and the intimacy among members, the collective's family values were rooted in a "community orientation."[108] They were part of a fabric of connections and inclusivity, not confined within the traditional nuclear family.

That the focus was on bodies and family-related matters meant that potentially divisive issues such as class and race were not always addressed. One of the first times that the collective had to face issues of race internally, rather than in regard to public outreach, concerned the complaint of women-of-color staff members that the founders had not shared power with them. Sanford, who chaired the collective's board at the time, saw the problem as a product of the older generation of founders becoming "used to being the good guys," while in fact they were "running everything." She noted that in spite of collaborating with the Combahee River Collective, the National Black Women's Health Project, and other women of color, the founders' group remained narrowly constituted and lacked awareness about their decision-making privilege. In the face of "unintentional," "historical," structural racism, the issue became racialized.[109]

Sanford also observed that Israel was not often discussed in the collective, no doubt in unspoken recognition of members' strongly held but disparate views about the topic. The avoidance of this subject suggests the highly controversial nature of the issues regarding Israel and the Palestinians. OBOS's reticence on the topic shielded the group from internal divisions. The politicized nature of the issue also strayed from the core OBOS mission.

Sanford became a "strong" Quaker and in 1999 had a Quaker wedding with her partner of twenty years, Polly Attwood, in which collective members participated. She finds her branch of Quakerism to be very accepting of different religious pathways, but she has done work in her meeting to review the kinds of supersessionism—often veering into anti-Judaism and anti-Semitism—that distorts Christian values. Sanford admitted that she does not know if she would have taken leadership in her community around these issues if she "hadn't spent thirty-five, forty years in the Boston Women's Health Book Collective."[110] At the same time, Sanford's leadership regarding issues of diversity with regard to race and sexuality contributed to melding OBOS's sensibility and cementing its achievements.

* * *

According to Norma Swenson, she and Judy Norsigian are correctly included as the tenth and eleventh of OBOS's founders, but she asserted that the original core group was really eight, all of whom were Jewish. Sanford became the ninth member a bit later. Everyone has a different chronology, Swenson laughed. But her own chart of origins (including her description of the founders as a "pure WASP," a "pure ethnic," a "complete mongrel—and the rest were Jews!") was telling. The first two are Sanford and Norsigian; Swenson herself is the "mongrel."

Swenson recognized the collective's Jewishness from the beginning and has thought about it frequently over the years because of the "enormous influence of Jews and Jewishness and Judaism" on her own life.[111] The daughter of a Roman Catholic mother of Polish origin and a Christian Science father with a Spanish heritage, Swenson (born Norma Meras) learned about Judaism from high school friends and came to respect its traditions. Swenson spent her early years in Exeter, New Hampshire, already something of an outlier because of her parents' mixed marriage.

After the Meras family moved to Boston, Norma became best friends with her neighbor, Diana Laskin Siegal, with whom she walked to the Girls' Latin School, now the Boston Latin Academy, every day for five years.[112] Getting to know Siegal's family and learning about Jewish culture and tradition was an important by-product of those years. The girls' parents became friends, and the families frequently had meals together; there Swenson learned about and participated in Jewish rituals. By that time, she was finished with her mother's organized religion and her father's agnosticism.

Swenson's first exposure to Jewish life may have been to the devastation wrought by the Holocaust. A teenager when World War II ended, she remembers the horrific newsreels of the concentration camps and the photographs and stories she saw in *Life* magazine when she babysat in neighbor's homes. The Holocaust was the final proof to her of the horrible things "done in the name of people who called themselves Christians. That was the end."[113] With Siegal's family, she also experienced the emotional moment when Israel became a state. Siegal's mother was a member of Hadassah, which had been very involved in advocating for statehood, and Laskin herself was part of a Labor Zionist youth group, with a fantasy of going off to Israel to live on a kibbutz. When she heard that Brandeis University, which had opened the same year that Israel received independence, was offering modern Hebrew, Laskin applied and was accepted, graduating with its first class. Swenson was a frequent visitor to campus, dating friends of Laskin (one of whom later became her partner after both their first spouses passed away) and appreciating its culture. "I took on a Jewish worldview through these experiences," Swenson said.[114]

Swenson graduated from Tufts, married and started a family, and became active in the maternity-care and childbirth reform movement. She served as president of the International Childbirth Education Association. That work connected her to OBOS, and in 1971, she and Judy Norsigian joined the founders. More than sixteen years older than Norsigian, Swenson considers herself to be of a different generation than most of the original members, yet she was only five years older than Jane Pincus and Paula Doress-Worters. She shared the women's passion to create means that would allow women to learn about and control their own health and sexuality. In some ways, she viewed her own lifestyle and attitudes as less conventional than that of her younger peers in the collective.

For Swenson, Jewishness has been a definite ingredient in the mix of beliefs and lifestyles of the group. She speculated, "Those of us who were not Jewish were so comfortable in our own identities that it did not matter to us to borrow or take on the Jewish identity (for shorthand) that we did take on." "We took it on at several different levels," she said, participating in Jewish holidays and life-cycle celebrations and respecting the rituals and the meanings behind them.[115]

A second level of appreciation for Jewishness in the collective related to the ways in which the women challenged patriarchy in the organization of information and the provision of health and medical care. Swenson defined the "style of challenging and questioning, the principle of disagreeing in order to come to a better understanding," as "a combination of Jewish and feminist style." It "informed everything that everybody did. In some ways a unique ethos emerged from all that which was a large part Jewish, but not exclusively Jewish." In the collective, the "non-Jewish activists learned from the Jews how to do this, . . . how to organize, . . . how to demand accountability." One example of what Swenson called "Jewishness, for lack of a better term," highlights not only questioning and organizing but a kind of "dogged scholarship that refused to give up," which was reflected in Rome's work on toxic shock syndrome. "Nobody else had done what she did," said Swenson. Her work "belongs in the Smithsonian": "She was a Jewish scholar in my eyes."[116]

For Swenson, the Jewish input into the OBOS collective had major consequences. She concluded, "The presence of a majority raised in awareness of their Jewish heritage, regardless of how observant they may have been, had a profound—and yes, a defining—influence on our work as well as our personal growth and development, individually but also within our social group."[117]

Swenson has written about Jewish themes herself. In a decade-long writers' group with OBOS founders Wendy Sanford and Paula Doress-Worters, as well as Mary Fillmore and Hilary Salk, both of whom focus on Holocaust-related fiction, Swenson has penned several short stories based on historical research that centers on the Jews of Prague. In "Prague Weekend: A Political Memoir," the narrator visits the old Jewish ghetto in the city, visiting the famed New Old Synagogue and the Jewish cemetery, trying to understand why Prague was "once a very special place for Jews," asking why their numbers continue to dwindle there.[118] In "The Last Passover [1939]," Swenson writes about a woman who buys a beautiful set of china for her family's seder but learns from her husband that the Germans have closed down the city's matzo factories and may be hunting Jews. They will have to flee the city, relinquishing both the dishes and their celebration of Jewish freedom, the seder.[119]

In the act of imagining the devastation that affected Prague's Jews in these stories, Swenson has paid the ultimate tribute to the Jewish influences on her life and work. She jokingly calls herself a "wannabe Jew," but, more importantly, her writing shows that Jewish life and history can serve as sources of inspiration and meaning to those who were not born Jewish. She considers herself to be a knowledgeable "Jewish-identified woman," well tutored by her OBOS colleagues and the women of her writing group.[120]

As Swenson looks back on her years with OBOS, she highlights the collaboration between Jews and others in the collective and the ways in which various religions and cultures interacted. Jewish members married non-Jews, and vice versa, and Protestant, Jewish, and other traditions merged in ways that prompted innovation and imagination. Swenson's contributions, like those of Sanford and Norsigian, were enormous, expanding the repertoire of activism and learning. The collective was more than an organization, said Swenson. "We had created a sisterhood."[121]

* * *

The daughter of Armenian parents, Judy Norsigian was raised in Watertown, Massachusetts, one of the largest centers of Armenian life in the U.S. Norsigian's Armenian heritage shaped her worldview and her lifelong civic engagement and activism. "When you come from a background where there is an Armenian genocide or a Jewish Holocaust," she remarked, "you can't but understand there is deep inhumanity. . . . When you have this consciousness, then you are more likely to relate to the social injustices around you. They are not . . . invisible because you have already been tuned into this world." Norsigian sees equivalence between her own early awareness of the Armenian genocide and her Jewish friends' consciousness of the Holocaust. In both cases, she said, "you just inhale the fact that only people . . . in large numbers can change things."[122] The imperative to demand social justice and to organize collectively for change was an essential part of both groups' makeup.

Norsigian noted that, because of similar values, Armenians and Jews often marry. Her own marriage to Boston native Irv Zola, distinguished professor of sociology at Brandeis University and an internationally regarded leader in the area of disability rights, fits a well-trod path. Until his death in 1994, Norsigian and Zola were among Boston's best-known activist couples, each of them social justice pioneers, working together on many pursuits. Neither was religiously oriented. Norsigian was an agnostic because of her father, who held forth regularly about the evils of two particular institutions: the Catholic Church and the field of psychiatry. Zola was very "Jewishly un-Jewish" in the sense of rejecting most religious rituals, yet he considered himself culturally Jewish. The couple's daughter was raised with both cultural Jewish and Armenian values.

Unlike Swenson, Norsigian did not know much about Jewish history and culture growing up. There were only a few Jewish students at Watertown High School, and although she knew them, they seemed "nervous" about talking about themselves as Jews because of anti-Semitism. Her first major exposure to Jewish secular values was during high school, as a member of NEYO (National Ethical Youth Organization), and she often played her cello for the Ethical Culture Society in Boston, most of whose members were Jewish. By the time she graduated from Radcliffe College in 1970 and had started to become involved in social activism, Norsigian had met many more young Jewish men and women, and members of the rural commune she joined in 1970 were Jewish as well. Over the years, she said, she has been aware that Jews have filled the majority of leadership roles in social justice pursuits.

After Norsigian had lived communally for more than a year, through friends she heard about the women's group that was developing a new book about women's health. Barely twenty-three but knowing even then that she very much wanted children, Norsigian was drawn to these savvy activists, most of whom were mothers. She joined the group in the fall of 1971, planning to contribute a chapter on nutrition. She stayed for nearly forty-five years, serving as an author and editor for each of the nine editions, becoming the lynchpin of the founding board as staff, director, and the group's primary spokesperson. She served as its executive director from 2001 through 2014.

Norsigian believes that the Jewish aspect of collective life was always in the air: "we did talk about it."[123] After the collective had met weekly for several years, she remembers the first time that they went around the room and counted the number of Jews. Members may have done a silent individual count, but this was the first time that the women as a group recognized the large number of Jewish women in the collective.

Norsigian agrees with other collective members about the importance of Jewish holidays in creating group cohesiveness. She sees them as "community-building" events, which provided "added glue" to shared beliefs about feminism and the crucial importance of the new women's health movement.[124] Commonly held values about social justice and the legacies of prejudice and discrimination experienced by many of the women's families were also important in building and nurturing community. Norsigian agrees with Swenson that one of the great strengths of the collective was that, while Jewishness was an element in shared bonds, it was never exclusive or definitional; the closest relationships among women of the collective were not necessarily those between its Jewish members.

Norsigian acknowledged that as in any long-lived organization, there have been personal conflicts, power struggles, and moments when one or another member may have felt injured or betrayed. But the underlying passion for the work, the group's mission, and its common bonds kept the group united, vibrant, and strong. She, too, noted that the collective afforded a safe place to talk about anti-Semitism, an issue that several members had found difficult to address.

In spite of differences among members, the group understood that in crucial ways, they "were all alike." Norsigian used Esther Rome as an example. Deeply observant and coming from a traditional background, Rome was nonetheless "on the cutting edge of building a feminist movement."[125] Though unique in the group because of her religious commitments, she was a role model for all of them.

Norsigian also reflected on the importance of racial issues in the collective's history, which became far more divisive than ethnicity or religion. "We're a group of white women who always have [had] white privilege of varying degrees," Norsigian acknowledged. These privileges acted as a barrier for some of the women of color who joined the staff after the founders had been together for several decades. For Norsigian, the important question about race was what white feminists did with the privilege they enjoyed. "Do I speak up, speak out about injustice when I see it? Do I say something as a bystander when I see racist acts? Do I take my white privilege and just go my merry way. or do I do something about that racism?"[126] She believes that the collective's commitment to diversity remains embedded in its very nature, a product of the group's core values, its unique ethnic and religious makeup, and its willingness to develop new forms of outreach at home and abroad. Norsigian's Armenian heritage, her profound commitment to social justice, and her enduring role as OBOS director played a major part in building the collective.

* * *

The stories of Norsigian, Swenson, and Sanford demonstrate that Jewishness was a vital element of collective life for the non-Jewish founders as well as the Jewish ones, adding to the cohesiveness of the group's social life and reinforcing their shared bonds. Beyond the sociality that Jewishness provided, the non-Jewish founders appreciated elements of Jewish tradition that they saw reflected in their colleagues' heritage: social justice ideals, tolerance, a commitment to fight prejudice, deep inquisitiveness, and critical thinking. Esther Rome's key role in the group's political and written work, combined with her outward religious observance, connected non-Jewish and Jewish members with Jewishness, fostering a respect for religious values that was unusual in the women's movement and leftist groups more broadly.

As the biographies of the Jewish founders make evident, most of them did not see themselves as Jewish activists or explicitly identify themselves Jewishly, yet their motivations for activism and the ethical vision they brought to the women's health movement were deeply affected by Jewish influences, which their non-Jewish colleagues recognized and respected. Bound together by a shared mission to empower women by providing up-to-date knowledge of their own bodies, the founders identified themselves as "white, middle-class, educated"; only later did Jewishness come to be acknowledged and counted as an aspect of identity, but it had been embedded from the beginning in the group's mission and its membership profile. As with other women's liberationists, several of the Jewish founders recognized themselves as "not quite white," even though whiteness was the identity people on the outside consistently applied to them.

The stories of the founders show that the impulse to social justice included a variety of Jewish stimuli: the political legacies of left-wing parents, strong female role models, the prophetic imperatives within religious Judaism, the tragedies of the Holocaust, a reaction against anti-Semitism. Beyond the commitment to social justice, which motivated founders to develop a new approach to empowering women, Jewish influence was manifest in the group's social networks, the shared passion for knowledge, the assertiveness members demonstrated in pursuing their goals, and the values of diversity and antiracism that several of the women attributed to the particularities of their heritage.

The experience and inheritance of marginality, shared by many of the Jewish women's families, if not themselves, may also have encouraged collective members' penchant for original thinking. In addition to the positive effects of outsider skepticism, the ability to strike out for new ground—to turn "sacred text on its head"—was influential, aptly describing the process by which untutored young mothers first took apart the medical culture that patronized them and proceeded to offer new perspectives and questions—the "engines of creativity."[127] The founders of OBOS created one of the women's liberation movement's most enduring treatises, one that, like key texts of the Jewish tradition, derives its vitality from continuing discussion and revision.

The ongoing connection between women's health movement activism, the social nature of the group's enduring bonds, and perhaps a growing spiritual aspect to the group's core mission solidified members' commitment to one another and their common work. In the article "Taking Our Maternal Bodies Back," a discussion of the first twenty years of OBOS, Robbie Pfeufer Kahn draws on theologian Carol Christ's distinction between what she calls a "social quest" ("women's struggle to gain respect, equality, and freedom in society") and a "spiritual quest" (the recognition of being grounded in "powers of forces of being larger than the self"). Kahn suggests that even as the book focused on knowledge strategies designed to reform society, the various editions of *Our Bodies Ourselves* increasingly became grounded in a larger spiritual reality.[128] Although Kahn does not refer to religion or to Judaism as a factor in the book's evolution, Jewish rituals bolstered group unity. Holiday celebrations, traditions, and values associated with non-Jewish founders' heritages enhanced cohesion as well. Spiritual connections between the body, community, and nature may also have resonated with the non-Western women who were becoming a growing part of the book's audience.

As we have seen, Jewishness within OBOS was diverse, ensuring that non-Jewish members' traditions blended easily with majority members' sociality and culture. There was no core Judaism, no indispensable beliefs or practice, common to the Jewish members. Founders came from many geographic, cultural, and religious backgrounds: from small towns where Jews were scarce minorities to urban centers where they were plentiful; from secular Yiddishkeit backgrounds steeped in Jewish radical traditions to deeply observant ones. While the Holocaust lingered in the women's consciousness, its valence differed among collective members, standing foremost in the life of the child-survivor of the Shoah's horrors and more distant for those who had grown up in assimilated households.

Because of the collective members' different backgrounds, they oriented themselves in a variety of ways to Jewish ethnicity and to Judaism. These orientations changed over the life course; for many, connections to Jewishness and Judaism deepened. For example, red-diaper baby Nancy Hawley, now Miriam, joined the Jewish Renewal movement; Paula Doress-Worters led a major effort to bring Jewish foremother Ernestine Rose into the annals of women's history and returned to her ancestors' Polish homeland to integrate her own historical roots into her life; Vilunya Diskin became an enthusiastic participant in a Reconstructionist synagogue and a student of Hebrew and the Bible. Once an understated, if implicit, component of these women's identities, Jewishness became inscribed in more salient ways as they matured.

Identifying as women's health activists interested in creating empowered, feminist health communities, these women did not self-consciously apply the hyphenated title "American-Jewish feminist" to themselves. The Jewish women of OBOS were not part of the self-conscious "ethnic revival" in post-civil-rights America that Matthew Frye Jacobson describes.[129] We may consider them "postethnic," maybe even "post-Judaic," to use David Hollinger's and Shaul Magid's terms, since they were animated not by the particular concerns of their ethnic or religious group but, as the expanding authorship and readership of *Our Bodies, Ourselves* makes clear, by a respect and appreciation for transethnic, transnational, multiracial communities of women.[130]

The collective's profile as white, middle class, and generally privileged was far more important to staff, board, affiliates, and the scholars who have written about the group than Jewishness was. Likewise, the problems that troubled the staff members of color concerned the collective's class and racial composition, not Jewish commonalities. But the charge of middle-class privilege leveled at OBOS, as at many other white-majority feminist groups, did have an effect on the group's Jewish identity. "To define ourselves as a Jewish collective" when "it just was not cool in the women's movement" would have been problematic, Joan Ditzion recognized. Jewish identity seemed too narrow and particular, especially to people outside the collective, and it did not reflect OBOS's mission or its expanding constituencies. Nevertheless, Ditzion joins her OBOS colleagues in her belief that Jewishness was a relevant factor in the development of *Our Bodies, Ourselves* and the group's health advocacy. Jewish identity in relation to the collective was something Ditzion "felt proud of," she commented, "and it was open."[131]

While the Jewish OBOS members acknowledged the significance of Jewish identity to the collective, Jewishness as such never constituted the examined center of the group's shared life. Rather, it was integrated into its empowerment mission and the social space of the collective, largely because that space became a "family" space over time, in the sense that collective members saw each other as family and that they included their own family members in community holidays and celebrations. Jewishness provided an important link in the chain of connections, even though it was not an intentional one. In that sense, the Jewish women of OBOS occupied a postethnic space in which their common ethnicity was one of several important factors that brought them together and shaped their lives.

PART II

"Feminism Enabled Me to Be a Jew"

Identified Jewish Feminists

5

"We Are Well Educated Jewishly . . . and We Are Going to Press You"

Jewish Feminists Challenge Religious Patriarchy

In February 1973, nearly five hundred excited Jewish women packed the ballroom of the Hotel McAlpin on the corner of Broadway and Thirty-Fourth Street in New York's Herald Square. Built in 1912, the once-glorious McAlpin, the largest hotel in the world at the time, had even boasted two gender-specific floors, where women could reserve a room on the women-only floor and bypass the lobby, checking in directly at their own floor. In 1973, however, when women need not conduct their business fearing for their safety and modesty, the hundreds of delegates to the first National Conference of Jewish Women proudly proclaimed their presence at the hotel for three days of women-only meetings. Within a few years, the McAlpin, still dignified if significantly down at the heels, was converted to rental apartments. The 1973 Jewish women's conference, along with a follow-up conference the next year, to which Jewish men were invited (but only to select sessions), marked one of the last but among the most historic events it ever hosted.

For many of the feminists who attended and who had not been particularly Jewish identified, the 1973 conference became a major "portal into Judaism," recalled Blu Greenberg, who gave the keynote address. For more Jewishly identified women, it deepened a resolve to bring together the Jewish and feminist aspects of their lives. For Greenberg herself, an observant, Orthodox Jew, the conference was a pivotal experience that changed the course of her life.[1] In addition to other milestones of the early 1970s, it served as a trigger for events throughout the decade and into the next that transformed the lives of the Jewish and feminist communities.

In addition to Greenberg's well-received address, a talk given by Judith Plaskow (Goldenberg), a young woman who was finishing her doctorate in theology at Yale, electrified the delegates at the McAlpin with a statement that articulated the core beliefs of the new Jewish feminist movement. "The identity of the Jewish woman," Plaskow began, "lies somewhere in the conflict between being a woman and being a Jew and in the necessity of combining the two in as yet unknown ways. . . . We are here because a secular movement for the liberation of women has made it imperative that we raise certain Jewish issues now, because we will not let ourselves be defined as Jewish women in ways in which we cannot allow ourselves to be defined as women."[2]

So did Plaskow publicly mark the moment by which Jewish women declared, inspired by secular feminism's powerful attack against patriarchy, that Jewish women had now to recognize themselves explicitly as Jews and carry on the fight against sexism within Jewish religion and community life. That struggle had begun a few years earlier and was already dividing newly declared "Jewish feminists" into secular feminist and religious feminist camps, although for the moment, at the 1973 and 1974 conferences, the split between the two groups did not seem irresoluble. The momentum was toward building a collective entity that could unify Jewish women, supporting their efforts to come out as Jews within the feminist movement and creating a new activist force within the Jewish community.

Jewish women's liberationists had been reluctant to assert a Jewish dimension to their feminism or to bring the issue of gender equality to the Jewish community, because in the women's movement, "gender trumped all other aspects of identity."[3] But a growing feminist consciousness led some of them to become painfully aware of the inequities that women experienced in Jewish law, culture, and religion. Before they could reconcile issues of Jewish identity with their feminism, however, those with strong links to Jewish tradition would have to confront the problems of women's position within religious life, an issue largely ignored by secular Jewish feminists.

The first group to publicly challenge sexism within Jewish religion was Ezrat Nashim, a women's study group founded in New York City in September 1971. The group was part of the independent youth-organized New York Havurah, organized two years earlier in an effort to create alternative, lay-led Judaic practices. Literally meaning "help for women," "Ezrat Nashim" also referred to an area of the ancient temple in Jerusalem that was reserved for women. While the name thus connoted separation of the sexes, the collective saw its mission as promoting women's religious equality through integration and equal access. Ezrat Nashim's ten members made headline news six months later when they interrupted the annual convention of the Conservative movement's Rabbinical Assembly to demand full equality for women.

Ezrat Nashim provided the flame that ignited the movement for gender equality within Jewish religious life. Historian Paula Hyman, then a graduate student in Columbia University's history department, where she had organized a women's caucus, was a key member, as was Martha Ackelsberg, who with Dina Rosenfeld had organized the group. Deeply influenced by the wider women's movement, each found ways to channel the impulses of radical feminism into Judaism. Judith Plaskow, who joined Ezra Nashim a few years later, became the first Jewish feminist theologian, helping to guide the religious direction of the Jewish feminist movement. For Plaskow, "becoming a self in the feminist community" extended organically to feminist theology, "the process of becoming selves in religious communities."[4] Other women broke barriers to full religious participation by becoming rabbis and cantors.

In addition to Martha Ackelsberg, Judith Plaskow, and Blu Greenberg, this chapter profiles Arlene Agus, an Orthodox member of Ezrat Nashim, and feminist rabbis Laura Geller and Rebecca Alpert, from the Reform and Reconstructionist communities, respectively. The stories of these women, all of whom were present at the 1973 conference, point to the varied paths that feminist Jews pioneered in the Jewish women's movement. Several of the women became part of the Jewish feminist group B'not Esh (Daughters of Fire), founded in 1981. Although B'not Esh meets only once a year, it has played a distinctive role in the creation of a meaningful feminist Judaism, broadening beliefs and building community.

Although there was never a strict divide between religious and secular Jewish feminists, those who were dedicated to communal and political change faced different challenges than did women whose primary identities were based in religion. Seeking to find a place for themselves within the radical feminist movement and the male-dominated Jewish Left, the women whom I call secularists rejected the gendered inequities of mainstream Jewish life. But they did not address religion per se, which many Christians and Jews considered to be a primary—and irredeemable—source of oppression.

The work of self-described "post-Christian" radical feminist theologian Mary Daly, author of the 1968 volume *The Church and the Second Sex*, convinced many Christian women's liberationists that they needed to separate from a hopelessly patriarchal church and create their own religious practices. Daly's 1973 *Beyond God the Father: Toward a Philosophy of Women's Liberation* further influenced feminist spiritual seekers.[5] Others found spiritual alternatives in Goddess religions or turned to Eastern religions such as Buddhism.

But religiously inclined Jewish feminists did not wish to follow radical feminist spiritual practices or secular mandates. As Hyman observed, they felt that they could not turn their backs on the Jewish past. "Jewishness was a fundamental aspect of their identity," transcending the constraints that traditional Judaism placed on them because of their gender. "They could not define themselves solely through their feminist ideology and affiliations."[6]

The efforts of these women to meld feminist ideas with their Jewish identities entailed considerable struggle, involving conflicts with the Jewish community, families, friends, feminist colleagues, or their own inherited beliefs about gender and Judaism. On the basis of interviews conducted in the late 1970s with a dozen women from Ezrat Nashim and other early Jewish feminist groups, sociologist Steven Cohen discerned numerous tensions between Jewish feminists' religious and gender identities. Although all the women were committed to dual belief systems, Cohen found few in the group who navigated between them without difficulty. Without consciously doing so, they created strategies to deal with potential discord. Cohen named these measures "conflict denial," holding that the two belief systems were compatible; "withdrawal," participating in only one of the communities; "moderation," muting criticism of both ideologies and communities; and "avoidance," refusing to act on irreconcilable differences. He suggests that by using such strategies, religious Jewish feminists avoided an otherwise-inevitable collision between dissonant beliefs.[7] In my own interviews with several of these women decades later, I found similar, varying approaches to conflicts between Judaism and feminism. For most of the women, the struggle to integrate the multiple aspects of their identities has been a lifelong effort.

The stories of Martha Ackelsberg, Arlene Agus, Judith Plaskow, Laura Geller, Rebecca Alpert, and Blu Greenberg suggest the formative effect of feminist beliefs on Jewish women's religious liberation and the struggle to meld feminism with Jewish tradition. All participated in Jewish women's religious groups that helped channel the desire for greater gender equality in new directions, facilitating the coming to consciousness of wide numbers of Jewish women. These pioneers helped to stimulate the Jewish feminist movement that began in the 1970s and continues today. Their stories stand in for dozens of other pioneering Jewish religious feminists, representing a spectrum of religious pathways.

The connection between these women's religious awakenings and their nascent feminism was organic and powerful. From childhood on, they were knowledgeable about Judaism though often sensitive to its gender-based exclusions. As young adults, experiences with the sexism of male colleagues and the realization that they had adjusted their own expectations to those of male partners triggered realizations of their own subordinate status. Several joined feminist consciousness-raising and action groups that provided fuel for knowledge and rebellion. Personal encounters with women's liberationists encouraged them to identify as feminists and to develop their own protests against patriarchy. Questioning Jewish texts and traditions, they began to apply feminist principles to Jewish laws and observances.

The women's struggles to come to terms with the feminist and Jewish aspects of their identities may have differed from those of women's liberationists and secular Jewish feminists, but they were no less intense and fraught. Many lived their lives as social activists and offered deep critiques of their own tradition, despite their own attachment to Jewish religion and community. Although some in this group might describe themselves as liberal feminists, they were radicals in their religious dissent and innovations.

Whatever the tensions Jewish religious feminists felt, they received considerably less opprobrium than feminists such as Shulamith Firestone or even Betty Friedan, whose work many in the Jewish community found threatening. The religious feminists, strongly attached to

Judaism despite their critiques of it, were treated as "the loyal opposition," as Susan Dworkin wrote in an article in *Moment* in 1975.[8] But they found that despite their strong links to the community and its general tolerance of their rebellion, changes in social attitudes and religious practices were not easy to effect.

Notwithstanding the staying power of tradition and the forceful opposition to gender equality, religious Jewish feminists have achieved many of their goals. In the past four decades, they have been responsible for new rituals, liturgies, texts, art, and music that have revitalized religious practice. They have brought egalitarian language into prayer books and liturgy and introduced new notions of God and Torah based on feminist perspectives. As rabbis, cantors, religious scholars, and community leaders, they participate in all aspects of Jewish life. They have constructed new models of education for girls and women, while challenging the typical hierarchical base of rabbinical service and relationships.

Though gaps in the agenda of religious Jewish feminists remain, the changes of the past decades have been remarkable.[9] These transformations have affected secular women and their male colleagues as well, providing a basis for a fuller identity.

Martha Ackelsberg: "The Spiritual Is Also Political"

Martha Ackelsberg graduated from Radcliffe College in 1968. Although she followed the traditional scenario laid out for even the nation's most brilliant young women, marrying immediately, within two years, Ackelsberg was involved in the feminist movement and simultaneously with a new *havurah* in New York, a combination that upended any semblance of domestic traditionalism and thrust her into the leadership of the embryonic Jewish religious feminist movement.

Ackelsberg grew up in Bloomfield, New Jersey, the daughter of Jewish parents who were deeply involved in synagogue life. Politically aware progressives, Oscar and Sylvia Ackelsberg never fit into their suburban community. They had been Zionists in college (he at City, she at Hunter) who intended to make aliyah to Israel; Martha's mother majored in psychology in order to develop the expertise to run a kibbutz children's home in Israel. But the outbreak of World War II foiled the couple's plans. When the Ackelsbergs married and became parents, they moved out of New York to raise their children, not to the land of Zion but across the river in New Jersey. Yet the political ideals of Zionism continued to shape their worldview. Martha and her sister were raised with a Zionist affirmation of Jewish peoplehood, and she believes that both her sister's and her own lifelong romance with collective life springs from this inheritance.

More important than the suburban Judaism of Ackelsberg's synagogue were the many summers she spent at Camp Ramah in the Poconos, affiliated with the Conservative movement, where she was inspired by innovative programs and vibrant religious practices. She was an excellent Hebrew-school student, although aware that boys and girls were treated differently there. Her bat mitzvah took place on a Friday night, while the boys she had been schooled with were called to Torah on Saturday morning for the more "authentic" service. While boys could go on to study and practice Judaism, for most purposes, the girls' religious lives were over. Ackelsberg recognized the inequalities but did not start to think seriously about them until college.

Ackelsberg's feelings about gender inequalities remained inchoate. When in the June following her college graduation, she married a Harvard graduate who was in medical school in New York, she admits to being confused. When a friend asked her, "How are you spending the summer?" she had no answer. "I felt like I had become my mother. I was reading magazines; I wasn't even reading books. . . . It was my two months of being a 1950s housewife. It was awful."[10]

The situation improved when Ackelsberg started graduate school in political science at Princeton and joined a women's consciousness-raising group composed of the girlfriends and young wives of medical students. But the women were still doing the cooking and housework and spent a lot of their time waiting for their "husbands to come home." Never knowing exactly what plans they could make, they began to come to a realization: "We didn't need to . . . continue just sitting here talking about our lives. We need to do something. . . . Enough!"[11]

Ironically, it was through the women's husbands that they found a purpose. A few of the men were involved with the Health Policy Advisory Center, or Health/PAC, a group trying to reform health-care bureaucracies to establish greater equity in the health-care system.

Ackelsberg and several women from her consciousness-raising group began to meet with women working with Health/PAC, and in 1970, at about the same that the Boston Women's Health Book Collective formed, they started the New York Women's Health Collective (also known as the New York Women's Health and Abortion Project).[12] Ackelsberg was a passionate participant in the collective, engaging with key issues of the new women's liberation movement and honing her skills as activist and change agent.

Like the Boston Women's Health Book Collective, the New York women's group offered classes on women and their bodies. Taught in a dorm at New York University and in a housing project on the Upper West Side, the classes drew on the growing knowledge of self-taught collective members. Ackelsberg gave lectures on the anatomy and physiology of women's bodies, especially menstruation and reproduction, using as resources the pamphlets she got from Kotex and Modess boxes and an obstetric text that her husband gave her. "I didn't know from nothing," she recalled.[13] The New York Women's Health Collective also held teach-ins on women's health and picketed meetings of obstetrics-gynecology physicians, demanding that they speak up in favor of abortion.[14] Because of impending abortion legislation in New York State, women's liberationists devoted great attention to this issue. The bold stance of the group and its grassroots tactics left its mark on Ackelsberg's ideas about social justice and feminism.

With Ackelsberg's graduate cohort at Princeton, she was involved in a community that also "raised hell," trying to eradicate rules that had little purpose. "Things were changing all over the place. Nobody was willing to accept the idea that because this is the way we've always done it, this is the way we should do it." Rather, they looked at the situation in its context, asking, "Does this make sense? If it doesn't, let's change it."[15]

Ackelsberg was getting inspiration from the new women's liberation anthologies, such as Robin Morgan's *Sisterhood Is Powerful* and Vivian Gornick and Barbara Moran's *Women in Sexist Society*. "Everybody was devouring these things as they came out," Ackelsberg remembered; "it was just beginning, it was amazing."[16] But there was a disconnect between what she was learning in graduate school and the messages she received from feminist writers and antiwar agitations she participated in. Though her dissertation work focused on anarchist collectivism in Spain, it took her a long while to see the connections between her scholarship and the radical communities of which she was a part.

In 1970, Ackelsberg joined the New York Havurah, founded the previous year, which engaged in similar rethinking and direct action as her other two communities did; each reinforced and cross-fertilized the others. A small, informal, lay-led prayer and study group, the New York Havurah stood between the spiritually oriented Havurat Shalom (Fellowship of peace) in Somerville, Massachusetts, and the politically minded Fabrangen (Bringing together in joy) in Washington, D.C. New York members wanted to create a community where "the people you prayed with were the people you studied with, were the people you did politics with." They shared dinners, held study sessions, went on monthly retreats, and participated in antiwar demonstrations. A "do-it-yourself" cooperative mentality was in the air. "You saw things that weren't working, and so you made something that would," Ackelsberg noted.[17] According to anthropologist Riv-Ellen Prell, the Havurah movement was a way in which young Jews articulated a new form of Judaism by refashioning "the nature of Jewish organizations in light of the aesthetics of the American counterculture."[18]

Within a year, Ackelsberg and a few friends added a study group on women and Judaism to the group's informal classes, which were held in addition to the regular Thursday-night meetings, Saturday-morning prayer sessions, and monthly retreats. The impetus for the new study group had been a feminist "click" moment for Dina Rosenfeld and Ackelsberg, who had been present at Shabbat morning services when, in a discussion of the meaning of prayer, a male member of the *havurah* attempted to explain the emotional content of an uplifting spiritual experience as comparable to ejaculation—a spiritual climax compared to a physical one. The analogy shocked Ackelsberg: where was she in his description?[19] Gathering a group of eight women, most from outside the *havurah*, Ackelsberg and Rosenfeld organized a weekly text study class to find the answer. Among those who came to share their wisdom with the group, and who subsequently became members, were Judith Hauptman, then a student at the Jewish Theological Seminary, and Judith Plaskow, studying feminist theology at Yale, who joined the group in 1974.

A second "click" moment for Ackelsberg came after the women's study group had been meeting for about a year. In the fall of 1971, men of Havurat Shalom and the New York group met in Boston to discuss the future of the Havurah movement. Since this was a meeting of friends, they explained, no women were invited. Feeling the sting of exclusion again, members of the New York women's study group journeyed to Boston to meet with the women at Havurat Shalom to consider women's place within Judaism and the problem of sexism in the Havurah movement.

The joint meeting clarified the need for gender equality within the movement and established priorities for change. While Ackelsberg and some others urged further study, a larger group wanted to add activism to consciousness-raising. Their arguments convinced the New York women. With the intention of going public, they named themselves Ezrat Nashim—literally "help for women" but also an area of the ancient Jerusalem temple reserved for women. In addition to Ackelsberg and Rosenfeld, the group included Paula Hyman, Arlene Agus, Leora Fishman, Elizabeth Koltun, Maureen McLeod, Deborah Weissman, and Betty Braun.[20]

Hoping to attend the annual conference of Conservative rabbis, which met every March in the Catskills, Ezrat Nashim sent a letter to Rabbinical Assembly leaders requesting a spot on the program, but they were told that the agenda had been set. "This being the sixties," Ackelsberg recalled, "we said the hell with that," and the group decided to go anyway. Photocopying articles on women in Judaism and typing up a one-page "Jewish Women Call for Change," they contacted the New York newspapers to tell them of their upcoming protest. Then the "ten schlemiels" of Ezrat Nashim got in two cars and drove upstate to the Concord Hotel in Kiamesha Lake with their packets of materials.[21]

The "storming" of the Rabbinical Assembly took place the next day. Although the women had no formal place on the agenda, the assembly gave them a room, and they were able to meet with over one hundred rabbis. Ezrat Nashim held a countersession on the morning of March 1, 1972, to publicly air their demands. Along with a few curious men, some 130 women attended, most of them rabbis' wives. "What took you so long?" asked one *rebbetzin*. Among the demands that Ezrat Nashim made were that women should be granted membership in synagogues, be counted in the minyan and considered as bound to fulfill all mitz-voth equally with men, be allowed full participation in religious obser-vances, be recognized as witnesses before the law, be allowed to initiate divorce, and be permitted and encouraged to attend rabbinical and cantorial schools.[22]

Ezrat Nashim did not anticipate that its well-mannered protest would unleash a torrent of media interest and public enthusiasm. The *New York Post* covered the Concord event, and the *New York Times* ran a feature story about the young feminists. Requests for speakers poured in. Eager young women who wanted to join the collective besieged the group. Ezrat Nashim women helped to start similar groups, but after the fall of 1972, when they admitted a few new affiliates, they closed the collective to new members. Hoping to maintain the intimacy that had spawned their initial understandings, they returned to study and dis-cussion, modifying their activist path but continuing to meet through the 1970s. While text study played a major role, group meetings increas-ingly focused on consciousness-raising involving the vexed issues that challenged women's liberationists as well: relationships, images and rep-resentations, gender-based authority and power.[23]

The seeds of a new direction for Jewish feminism had been planted. Secular and religious women would work together on the first national Jewish women's conferences and the founding of the Jewish Femi-nist Organization in 1974, but the clarity of the religious women's goals enabled them to prioritize their issues. The Reform movement ordained its first woman rabbi, Sally Priesand, in 1972; two years later, the Reconstructionists ordained Sandy Eisenberg Sasso. Although the Conservative movement debated female ordination for over a decade before ordaining Amy Eilberg as its first woman rabbi in 1985, within a few years after the Ezrat Nashim protest, its Rabbinical Assembly voted to permit women to be counted in a minyan. Many congrega-tions throughout the country allowed women nearly equal participa-tion in other rituals. As Ackelsberg wrote in the 1976 anthology *The Jewish Woman: New Perspectives*, a revised edition of a special 1973 issue of *Response* magazine, both edited by Ezrat Nashim member Eliza-beth Koltun, "the Jewish women's movement seems to have arrived."[24] Ackelsberg voiced the hope that new "rituals, myths, halachot [laws], or other educational materials" encouraged by the work of these new

Figure 5.1. Ordination of Amy Eilberg, first female Conservative rabbi, 1985. Courtesy Jewish Theological Seminary. Photo by Joyce Culver.

religious feminists would create a "position of true equality for women in Jewish life."[25]

Within a few years, Ackelsberg, along with Judith Plaskow and several other Jewish feminist pioneers, began to reconsider equal access as the major objective of religious change. The right to participate in religious life as fully as Jewish men remained important, but they believed that the next stage of Jewish feminism should focus on "what a Judaism that takes women's experience seriously would look like," in Ackelsberg's words.[26] Reconfiguring Judaism from a feminist perspective—that is, creating new liturgies, rituals, and other texts and practices that could express women's special beliefs and experiences—became central to Jewish feminists' attempt to define and shape a women-centered spirituality.

Ackelsberg left New York in 1972, when she moved to western Massachusetts to take a job teaching political science at Smith College. She continued to promote community building among Jewish feminists, and in 1981, with Plaskow and a dozen other women, she established B'not Esh, a collective of religiously committed Jewish feminists who come together annually at a retreat center in Cornwall-on-Hudson, New York, to focus on consciousness-raising and activism among religious

Jewish feminists. Individually, B'not Esh members "felt the pain of being feminist and Jewish in a Jewish community which does not fully recognize or appreciate the experience of modern women," in Ackelsberg's words. Together they hoped to meld "the personal and the communal, the emotional and the intellectual, spirituality, politics, and community," creating safe spaces for religious experimentation and social activism. The women recognized that it was necessary to develop new modes of religious expression but also to confront social and structural issues that impeded gender equality, such as inequalities in Jewish education and issues of family life and child care. "The spiritual is also political," Ackelsberg wrote in 1986. "Politics is the work we do to make the world safe for our spirituality," she told me several decades later.[27]

Despite resistance from traditionalists who feared that the changes advocated by Jewish feminists would destroy Jewish religion and even the Jewish family, the movement begun by Ezrat Nashim proceeded remarkably well. A great part of its success can be attributed to the fact that Jewish feminist leaders were deeply rooted in the Jewish world. Rather than break away from it, they sought equal access to its institutions and practices, resembling the moderate approach of liberal feminists, although in fact they upended these institutions, reshaping their content and approach.

The focus on the community rather than the individual was a factor in the ability of religious Jewish feminists to accomplish their goals. The collective nature of their undertakings fit well with the structure of Jewish prayer: the minyan, the religious community formed by any ten male adults.[28] Jewish women pushed to alter this exclusive preserve to include women, while also creating all-female forms of worship—including Rosh Chodesh and *tefillah* (prayer) groups—that drew strength and identity from women's collective experiences. Feminists pressed for change at the grassroots level as well as the institutional and national levels.[29]

Today Ackelsberg is concerned that the Jewish feminist agenda move beyond the concerns of the Jewish community, as traditionally defined, to include broader social issues such as sexual harassment and racial and class inequality, which have expanded from local and national women's liberation issues into the global arena. Just as the women's liberation movement guided Ackelsberg as she took its insights to her *havurah* and Ezrat Nashim, she calls on this heritage to help her and colleagues shape the next stage of Jewish feminism.

Arlene Agus: "I Think We Created a Revolution"

Arlene Agus was one of three Brooklyn College graduates to join Ezrat Nashim. Although historians usually identify Ezrat Nashim women as coming from a Conservative Jewish background, Agus is proudly Orthodox and asserts that close to half of group members had also grown up Orthodox. One of the first group came from a Reform background.[30]

Born in Brooklyn into a family that traced its lineage to the tenth and eleventh centuries as direct descendants of Rashi, the notable Talmudic scholar, Agus attended the Yeshiva of Flatbush, thanks to her father's liberal attitude about girls' education. Like most Ezrat Nashim members, she was knowledgeable about Judaism but chafed under the limitations imposed on religious study for women.

Agus had an epiphany about Judaism's patriarchal attitudes early in her life. She was only six when she took her first feminist action, walking up to the bimah (synagogue platform) during the Shabbat service to confront the rabbi at her Borough Park synagogue for choosing her male cousin, who could not carry a tune, rather than her, to lead the congregation in the closing song.[31] Her second protest came when she led a rebellion at her yeshiva against the withdrawal of Talmud study from the girls. Although she did not win that battle, like Martha Ackelsberg, she had learned that the promise of equality for Jewish boys and girls was a chimera.

Agus loved Judaism from the very beginning and, because of her family history, felt a personal duty to become a part of the transmission of knowledge and tradition. Yet despite her day-school education, she felt ignorant about the role of women in Jewish history and in its guiding texts. "I didn't know whether a woman was obligated to *bensch* [bless] or to pray. . . . These things should have been obvious in a yeshiva," and it was "astonishing" that they were not.[32] When she joined Ezrat Nashim, it was with the passionate conviction that women needed access to all aspects of Judaic education and practice. "When we first started realizing that we could trust our intuition," she said, "we started allowing our rage to be legitimate, because we felt that it came from legitimate Jewish guts and was grounded in all the right Jewish values."[33]

Despite Agus's devotion to Jewish religious life, she was uneasy about limiting her world to its confines. Many of the teachers at her yeshiva were Holocaust survivors, and that, too, imposed a sense of limits that she found oppressive. As a college student, she sought a wider canvas, choosing Celtic studies as her major: "I needed to breathe the air of the rest of the world."[34] Celtic studies took her to Wales and Ireland, whose music she loved. Agus went on to do graduate work in music therapy and began her professional life in the field of special education.

Yet Agus's background and interests pulled her back into the Jewish world. In college, she headed the Brooklyn chapter of Student Struggle for Soviet Jewry; as the movement gained headway, she took a job with the Greater New York Conference on Soviet Jewry. For Agus, freeing Soviet Jews was a bridge issue that united Jews not only with one another but also with non-Jews, giving her the sense of working on a Jewish issue that had appeal to a broader community; she stayed for a decade. In later years, she has worked almost exclusively within the Jewish community.[35]

Agus is credited with the 1971 rediscovery of Rosh Chodesh, the ancient Jewish women's holiday marking the New Month, and popularizing it as a key aspect of a new women-centered Jewish spirituality. Rosh Chodesh groups developed throughout the United States, connecting women with older female traditions and becoming vehicles for new women-centered, spiritual explorations. A few years later, Agus created the first Jewish women's *kolel* (community-funded Talmud study). In 1982, she staged the first successful action to free an *agunah* (chained wife, whose husband refused to grant her a Jewish divorce). Agus also designed a women's prayer shawl, or *tallit*, co-founded the first all-women's *tefillot* (prayer quorums), and has composed egalitarian ceremonies for births, bar and bat mitzvahs, and weddings and commitment ceremonies, as well as *tkhines* (women's petitionary prayers). With these innovations, Agus helped to carve a pathway to feminist religious life that went beyond Ezrat Nashim's initial goal of equal access, to innovate gender-specific modes of spirituality that empowered women by expressing their unique perspectives and values.

Agus considers herself a "temperate feminist" committed to "communal unity," but like other Jewish feminists who challenged traditional religious mores, she was seen as a "radical fanatic" by some family and friends. Agus responded to criticisms by emphasizing the traditional within the radical. She stresses that Jewish feminists have been inspired by the same values that motivated biblical Jewish heroines, "tradition, family, continuity," and emphasizes that Jewish feminists acted in "deliberately measured" ways in their traditional communities.[36]

Agus argues that Judaism is inherently feminist but that this aspect could flourish only after the secular Left and women's liberation provided a context for egalitarianism. Look at the Jewish prayer book, or the Bible, she says, both of which begin with the one and go to the many. She views feminism as starting with the "I," not the individual person but "I" as "women" or "community," seeking wholeness and authenticity. Feminism is not one story, Argus observes, but a composite of many. She considers Jewish feminism as a collective, empowered by its communal aspects.[37]

This philosophy permitted both Agus and Ackelsberg to envision Jewish feminism within a wider context of religious revitalization. Because of the clarity of their goals, their knowledge and strategic flexibility, these and other members of Ezrat Nashim have left an indelible imprint on Jewish life.

Judith Plaskow: "Feminism as a Process of Radical Transformation"

No one has been more important to the feminist reconfiguring of Jewish texts than Judith Plaskow. Her articles and books, especially the groundbreaking 1990 work *Standing Again at Sinai: Judaism from a Feminist Perspective*, have been widely influential. Plaskow came to feminism as a theologian, focusing on belief and thought rather than actions and deeds, the emphasis of most of her Jewish feminist colleagues.[38] From childhood on, Plaskow had inquired about "the meaning of human existence, whether there was a God, who God was and how there could be evil in the world."[39] Because at that time there was no program in which she could study theology in a Jewish context, she majored in Protestant theology at Yale in the late 1960s and did her first work in that area. But

Judaism compelled her, and as Jewish feminism was developing in the 1970s, she began her lifelong encounter with Jewish theology envisioned from a feminist perspective.

Plaskow's route to Jewish feminism paralleled that of the founders of Ezrat Nashim. She kept abreast of the group's early actions through Martha Ackelsberg, whom she met at a conference in 1970, and soon joined the collective. The two became partners after both divorced their husbands in the early 1980s, celebrating their commitment ceremony in 1986.[40] Sharing a deep commitment to religious Jewish feminism, separately and together they have played major roles in shaping new women-centered Jewish rituals, liturgies, and theology.

Born in Brooklyn in 1947, Plaskow grew up with a positive sense of Jewish identity. When she was young, the family moved to West Hempstead, a Long Island suburb with a substantial Jewish minority. Plaskow felt comfortable in the community, yet she was aware of not being part of the dominant culture.[41] Although her parents were not observant Jews, Plaskow was drawn to Judaic study. Her father, Jerome, an accountant, and her mother, Vivian, who became a schoolteacher when Plaskow and her sister were in grade school, joined the local Reform synagogue, as much for social as religious reasons. Plaskow went to Sunday school there, the only student voluntarily continuing through twelfth grade, but found it "a complete waste of time."[42]

Yet Plaskow feels that she was "born a theologian." She wanted to become a rabbi, a more familiar occupation but one reserved for men only. The Holocaust played a formative role in shaping her ideas about Judaism; she became "obsessed" with the Shoah after one of her Sunday-school teachers, who had been an army colonel during the war and was involved with the liberation of the camps, told her about it.[43] The victimization of the Jews, the nature of evil, and the moral responsibility to respond to tyranny were seared into her consciousness at a young age. But while the Holocaust and "Jews as victims" were central to her Jewishness, it was "never the whole" of her Jewish identity.[44] Judaism for Plaskow also meant Sabbath and holiday observance: "the stories of my ancestors, the words of the prophets calling us to justice and social engagement."[45]

The prophetic message that Plaskow took from the Jewish tradition was supplemented by the social concerns demonstrated by her parents.

Plaskow's mother was a progressive who flirted with socialism in college and developed a radical analysis of social problems. Her father was less political than his wife, but his indignation over southern resistance to desegregation, particularly at the time of the Little Rock school crisis, when Plaskow was ten, became a defining moment for her.[46] Plaskow began participating in civil rights demonstrations during high school. In 1963, she went with members of her temple to the March on Washington for Jobs and Freedom, hearing Martin Luther King, Jr., deliver his "I Have a Dream" speech at the foot of the Lincoln Memorial. As a student at Clark University, where she enrolled the following year, Plaskow was part of the Worcester Student Movement for civil rights, a group that worked with the black community in that city running after-school programs, painting houses, and helping out in other ways.[47] Plaskow said that because of her perspective as a Jew, she "was always very aware of being a member of the minority and seeing things that other people didn't see."[48] This position as outsider/insider stimulated her concerns about racial and religious justice.

A feeling for feminism came more slowly. When Plaskow's mother, who "went nuts" about Betty Friedan's *The Feminine Mystique*, recommended the book to her teenage daughter, Plaskow would not read it, just because her mother wanted her to. She often thought about how her life would have been different had she listened earlier to her mother. In college, Plaskow was not ready to hear the feminist message, finding the one student who tried to get people to talk about women's issues "a pain in the ass."[49]

After graduating from Clark in 1968, Plaskow began a Ph.D. program at the Yale Divinity School. Yale did not admit women to its undergraduate program until the following year; Plaskow remarked that Yale prepared itself for the education of women "by putting full-length mirrors in the bathroom and hiring a gynecologist for the medical center."[50] This response led women in the graduate school to consider their own situation, calling a meeting to discuss "how it was that [women had] been at Yale for eighty years and no one had noticed."[51] The group named itself the Yale Women's Alliance, meeting regularly to explore the ways in which they had been socialized as girls, always considered "too smart," told they were not "properly feminine" and "weren't going to get husbands." What had seemed like Plaskow's individual experience she now understood as part of society's structural constraints. "We all had the same narrative," she said. "It was like seeing the world with new eyes."[52] It was at the Women's Alliance that Plaskow met Carol Christ, a graduate theology student a year above her, beginning a lifelong friendship when they discovered a common interest in applying feminist ideas to theology.[53] As for Ackelsberg, who also attended a formerly all-male Ivy League university, a graduate students' women community became a crucible for new ideas about women's second-class status. "In the fall of 1969," said Plaskow, "I became a feminist."[54]

The Yale Women's Alliance combined consciousness-raising with activism. The group took action against Mory's Tavern, a private club near Yale that was open only to men and where law firms customarily interviewed male students. Another consequence of the group's activities was that the graduate students joined with law school women to plan a conference to be keynoted by Naomi Weisstein, the pioneer feminist from the Chicago Women's Liberation Union, already well known as an innovative feminist psychologist.

Weisstein's talk at Yale in February 1970 became another turning point for Plaskow. Speaking about what it was like to be a female graduate student at Harvard, "with the men smoking their pipes in classes and the pretentiousness," Weisstein enthralled her audience. Plaskow recalled, "every single word she said described our experience at Yale: the condescension with which we were treated" and the preference given to male graduate students. Weisstein addressed how women shut the door on their own expectations: "Women want to be lawyers and doctors and ministers and end up lawyers' wives and doctors' wives and ministers' wives." For Plaskow, who had married Robert Goldenberg, a graduate of the Conservative Jewish Theological Seminary, eight months earlier, the critique was personal. "I had wanted to be a rabbi as a girl, and I married a rabbi," she said. Dissatisfied with her own Reform upbringing, especially after a trip to Israel the summer after the Six-Day War, she admired her husband's greater religiosity. After her marriage, she began keeping kosher and going to Shabbat services with him. "I moved into his world," she reflected.[55]

The revelation Plaskow experienced on hearing Weisstein's words provided a sudden understanding of her choices. This was "the minute of utter conversion," Plaskow recalled. She began to connect her own history as a girl who was "too smart" with an understanding of women's socialization.[56] Although she had been prepared for Weisstein's remarks because of the consciousness-raising work that her women's group had been doing, nonetheless, she was "totally blown away": "I went home and cried all night that I wasted my life; I was 22."[57]

Weisstein's central theme was not the plight of female graduate students but that women had to come together in community to create change. "You can't do it alone"—"change in social structure requires a social movement."[58] Plaskow took this insight into her engagement with feminist theology. She had determined to write a feminist dissertation—perhaps the second in religious studies in the U.S.—but on the subject of Protestant theology, since she was in a Christian-dominated institution that paid no attention to Jewish experience. But as she set out to become a feminist academic, she was also undergoing a simultaneous, "more difficult, process of awakening as a feminist Jew."[59]

One critical moment involved Shabbat services at Yale, where Plaskow was relegated to the back of the chapel, since the Orthodox service, the only one at Yale, segregated women from men. Plaskow said, "I decided I was never going to go to a service where I wasn't counted." Feeling excluded as a participant in Jewish prayer and Jewish life, she chose the topic "Can a Woman Be a Jew?" when the Yale Hillel rabbi asked her to address the group.[60] As for Ackelsberg and Agus, the experience of exclusion became a powerful motivator for rebellion against tradition.

At a meeting of religious women in Grailville, in Loveland, Ohio, Plaskow joined with Christian theologians to explore women's liberation as a religious experience. Doing so might allow them to capture the significance of feminist community, as Weisstein had urged, but in a religious setting. At Plaskow's suggestion, the women focused on the story of Eve and Lilith as a paradigm for sisterhood. When Eve and Lilith join together, Plaskow imagined, "theology, the world, and God must change."[61]

Plaskow published her first theological essay, "The Coming of Lilith," about this story. Written as a midrash (interpretative text), it reflected her attempt to use traditional Jewish modes of expression, though she did this in a "semiunconscious" way. The essay provides an important explanation of sisterhood as feminist experience. "I make my decision for self-transformation in the context of a community whose support is ongoing," Plaskow wrote. "The continuing process of questioning, growth, and change remains collective. Thus, not only is my decision reinforced, but my energies for change are pooled with the group's energies." Plaskow found the feminist mode of collaborative questioning and transformative community to parallel religious experience, pointing to commonalities in the use of rituals and symbols, token heretics and infidels, the language of "sisters."[62]

For the theologians meeting in their own small women's group, the myth of Lilith embodied the central theme of sisterhood as community. According to rabbinic legend, Lilith, demon of the night, was Adam's first wife. Created equal to him, she finds she cannot live with him and flies away. In the women's version, Eve sees Lilith when she attempts to return and discovers a woman in her own image. Eve swings herself over the wall to encounter Lilith. "'Who are you?' they asked each other. 'What is your story?' And they sat and spoke together, of the past and then of the future. They talked for many hours, not once, but many times. They taught each other many things, and told each other stories, and laughed together, and cried, over and over, till the bond of sisterhood grew between them. . . . And God and Adam were expectant and afraid the day Even and Lilith returned to the garden, bursting with possibilities, ready to rebuild it together."[63] Plaskow summed up: "Lilith by herself is in exile and can do nothing. The real heroine of our story is sisterhood, and sisterhood is powerful."[64]

Powerful as communities of sisters might be, they were not always unitary. A profound division, which Plaskow acknowledged in her address at the Hotel McAlpin conference in 1973, entailed the basic conflict between "being a woman and being a Jew." Although it was possible to belong to many different communities—as Plaskow herself said, "we identify as Jews, as women, as Americans, as students, as human beings"—at that time, she said, "Only one can be our organizing center. Only one community can be the 'rosetta stone' through which we view and interpret and give room to others."[65]

Early in Plaskow's own marriage, her husband had remarked that the couple seemed "intermarried," since to him, Judaism was primary, while to her, feminism took center stage.[66] But later, Plaskow refused the dichotomous choices that had seemed inevitable in her McAlpin speech. Throughout the 1970s, even though she experienced a "conflicted" relationship to Judaism and a disconnection between her academic life and her life as a Jewish feminist, she struggled to create a more integrated feminist Judaism.[67]

Plaskow found a supportive community of feminist scholars in the American Academy of Religion, which emphasized the ways that women express their own religiosity within patriarchal settings. Plaskow took a different approach, arguing that the "realities of women's subordination and exclusion" within Judaism were more significant than whether they had carved a niche within the tradition.[68] Her contribution was to develop a systematic critique of the tradition, not just to focus on particular texts and laws. In finding a voice for these views, she credited Jewish feminists. "My most important experiences with God have come through this community," she acknowledged, and it was to this community and its "struggle to create a Judaism that includes all Jews" that she felt most responsible.[69]

Plaskow's major work, *Standing Again at Sinai*, published in 1990, presented a new women-centered perspective on the subjects of Torah, God, and Israel. The book boldly applied the theories and methods of feminist scholarship to Jewish theology. By interweaving the tools of women's history, midrash, and ritual, Plaskow offered a systematic route to instill women's experience into the Torah, where there had been only silence. She also provided a critique of the problematic aspects of halacha (Jewish law), proposing a wide-ranging transformation in the legal obligations that rendered women invisible, objects rather than subjects. Plaskow addressed the subject of "Israel" as "Jewish community" as well, arguing that the idea of the Jewish people required openness and the acceptance of diversity, "whether the context is Israel, Diaspora Jewish communities, or the feminist movement." It was "the sum of all pieces," rather than one part speaking for the whole—whether "male Ashkenazi Jewish Israelis for all Israelis, elite male Jews for all Jews, middle-class white feminists for women . . ."[70]

Plaskow's reconceptualization of metaphors for God was another of the book's striking contributions. Rather than the image of God as "dominating Other" in a system of "hierarchical dualisms," Plaskow invoked a "Jewish feminist God-language" in "nonhierarchical relation." God was thus linked to a "new vision of community" that envisaged "divine power not as something above and over us but in and around."

God was a "lover and friend" rather than commander.[71] Affirming multiple images for God, Plaskow's vision of the deity stressed mutuality and interaction.

Plaskow hoped that a new feminist spirituality could transform the larger society as well as Jewish religion, for God was "present in connection, in the web of relation with a wider world." Rejecting the standard contrast between faith and politics, she believed that feminist Jews could show about all people that "our religious lives change the way we live, and our political commitments shape our spirituality." The "egalitarian communities" she envisaged could "draw the circle of community ever wider and wider," leading to a profound social transformation.[72]

B'not Esh, the spirituality collective that Plaskow started with Martha Ackelsberg and other Jewish feminists in 1981, helped to enable the feminist synthesis she desired. Even within this group, which Plaskow described as her "lifeline," conflict could not be avoided. "We were all looking for a group where we could be whole," Plaskow told me, "not a Jew to the feminists and a feminist to the Jews. We were so excited that we were finally going to be with a group of people who were all like us. And of course, we weren't. We spent the first Shabbat morning sitting in the hall crying because we couldn't agree what to do."[73]

The profound differences about the nature of feminist Judaism that appeared during the first B'not Esh retreat made the women feel "even more isolated," but within a few years, they learned that their religious dissimilarities, as well as those regarding "sexuality, class, Jewish ethnic identity and personal history," might serve as sources of group strength.[74] The modality for using differences to empower rather than limit was to allow the members to take turns in groups to create their own liturgy, with others present to "try on things" that might challenge their own boundaries. By not seeking a common denominator, they found ways to innovate feminist liturgies, some of which proved quite "radical," while still holding onto tradition.[75] Plaskow hoped that the "community of vision and struggle" that she discerned at B'not Esh could help effect "the transformation of the wider Jewish community."[76]

Plaskow's project of understanding and expressing the multiple aspects of her identity remains ongoing. The problem of Jewish victimization has been a key element for her, resonating with her thinking about gender-role constraints within Judaism and anti-Judaism within

Christian feminism. Coming to awareness of the problem of Christian anti-Judaism in the late 1970s, she reacted to the "deep shock of realizing that the bonds of sisterhood provided no protection against the mindless reiteration and reinforcement of a host of unequal power relations." For her, this was a "profound failure of the feminist ethic," a blow to her early conviction that "the women's revolution had the power to change the fabric of the world in which we live."[77]

After Israel's invasion of Lebanon in 1982, Plaskow turned a more self-reflective eye on issues of power dynamics between oppressors and the oppressed. Seeing herself "from both sides of the marginalized/marginalizer divide," she sought ways of understanding the "privilege of being an outsider—and being able to see the world in a certain way because you were an outsider."[78] In works such as "Jewish Anti-Paganism" and "Dealing with the Hard Stuff," she probed how Jews themselves could construct multiple "others."[79] "To be oppressed does not protect one from being an oppressor," she wrote in "Anti-Semitism: The Unacknowledged Racism." "To be a Jew and not a Nazi . . . guarantees nothing about who the Jew will be when s/he comes to power."[80]

Sexuality within Judaism became a key frame of interest for Plaskow as well, emerging in her theological works in the 1990s as she gave attention to ideas about the place of gay, lesbian, bisexual, and transgender persons in religious thought and communities. While she viewed the subordination of sexual minorities to be core ingredients in Jewish tradition, she believes that feminist Judaism can refashion these elements in ways that transform oppression and give increasing voice to diversity.

Plaskow appreciates the tremendous changes that religious Jewish feminists have wrought in her lifetime, allowing women to gain access to leadership roles across all denominations but also developing a women-centered spirituality, a fuller Torah that reflects feminism and egalitarianism. She alternates between believing that "everything has changed and [that] nothing has changed," noting the lack of "historical" and "communal memory" as feminist issues important to her generation wax and wane. Looking back on her own work and that of her Jewish feminist community, she also worries that perhaps too much of Jewish feminist work has been "navel gazing," set apart from concrete

Figure 5.2. The first meeting of B'not Esh, 1981. Courtesy of Martha Ackelsberg.

concerns such as those addressed by such secular groups s Jews for Racial and Economic Justice. Like Ackelsberg and Agus, she feels that communities of Jewish women must address broad social and political issues such as sexual abuse and poverty. "It's almost like we haven't figured out how our work as Jewish feminists illuminates that other world," she admitted.[81]

As Plaskow has helped to create a transformative feminist Judaism, she has constantly transformed her own life. Central to her development, and that of the new directions in feminist Judaism that has accompanied it, has been the framework provided by women's liberationists such as Naomi Weisstein and others, the "outsider/insider" perspective inherited from her youth, and her continually evolving, intersectional stance as a white woman, Jew, feminist scholar, and feminist theologian. A vital element, too, has been the force of community in her life, which she has both written about and lived through her involvement in several academic groups and especially with B'not Esh. She and Martha Ackelsberg are fond of quoting Margaret Mead's words: "Never doubt that a small group of thoughtful, committed citizens can change the world. Indeed, it is the only thing that ever has."[82]

Rabbis Laura Geller and Rebecca Alpert: "Spiritual Daughters" of Feminism

Women who broke the barriers to full participation as rabbinical leaders took a different path to religious change. But not all the early women rabbis adopted a feminist agenda. Laura Geller, the third woman to be ordained in the Reform movement, and Rebecca Alpert, the third woman ordained as a Reconstructionist rabbi, publicly identified as feminists. A central dimension of their rabbinates was the transformation of gender inequalities in Jewish tradition. They became a vital part of the revolution against sexism that stirred the women of Ezrat Nashim and so many other women in their generation.

* * *

For Laura Geller, the convergence between feminism and Judaism was clear. She taught feminist pioneer Betty Friedan that "the essence of Judaism . . . was not just holy words, . . . but it is action, deeds in society," a lesson Friedan acknowledged publicly. In 1979, three years after Geller's ordination, she called Friedan for advice about whether women rabbis ought to attend the Central Conference of American Rabbis in Phoenix, since Arizona had refused to ratify the Equal Rights Amendment. The conference leaders did not see the ERA as "a matter of Jewish 'survival,'" despite their support of women's rights. Should the women rabbis join feminists who were boycotting Arizona or their fellow rabbis planning to attend the convention? "Go to the conference," Friedan told Geller, "but invite me to speak." Friedan went, using her visit to Phoenix to join the women rabbis' "outraged protest."[83] In her speech, Friedan thanked her "spiritual daughters (some of whom are in the room)," for teaching her that it is "profoundly Jewish" to take "actions, not words, to break through barriers that keep [women] from participating."[84]

Born in 1950, Geller grew up in Brookline, Massachusetts, moving to New York as a teenager. Influenced by her Reform synagogue in Massachusetts and her studies of Christian ethics at Brown University, Geller became fascinated by questions of Jewish identity and ethics. How was theology connected to morality? From where did the Jewish sense of justice emanate? While at Brown, she participated in civil rights work with the Southern Christian Leadership Conference (SCLC), headed by

Martin Luther King, Jr.. On one occasion, she drove to Memphis with a group of mostly male SCLC workers. Geller was overwhelmed, feeling that she did not belong. When a young African American colleague noticed her discomfort and elicited the reason why, he told her, "go back and do your organizing in your own community."[85] To move forward, she would first have to define that community.

During a lengthy sit-in in Providence during the Passover holiday over fair housing, Geller came to understand how Jewish ethics could be the source of an authentic activism that sprang from her heritage. Because she could not eat *chametz* (leavened products), Geller had to give up the food shared by her group. She had an epiphany: both the sit-in and her abstinence were ways of being spiritually Jewish. She recalled a discussion she had heard at temple as a girl, in which members spoke of strategies to sell houses to African Americans and avoid redlining. This was what it meant to be Jewish—to be an activist concerned with the rights of others. Geller never forgot that the first message regarding social justice came at a synagogue.

Later, describing "the Torah of our lives," she explained that the Torah portion on Yom Kippur, the Jewish High Holiday, "begins with us standing together in community, a community that includes each one of us. . . . Our personal stories become the story of community, of responsibility to other people who need our help. Our stories are linked to the larger Jewish story of *tikkun olam*, the challenge to repair what is broken in the world."[86] Incorporating her social values and religious faith, her community would be that of the Jewish people.

Geller applied to rabbinical school after graduating from Brown in 1971 and was accepted by the Reform movement. The sole woman in her class of fifty men at Hebrew Union College, she felt merely a "symbolic" presence to her teachers, especially during her first year of classes in Jerusalem. But the women's study group that Geller formed with the wives of male students became a community that helped her glean insights from Jewish teachings relevant to women. The group created a Shabbat service for themselves, experiencing a "stunning" moment at the end of the year when each of them was able to hold the Torah for the first time. Another defining occasion came during Geller's second year of rabbinic study in New York, when her instructor told her class that there were no times in a Jew's life without a special blessing. Thinking of the many moments of women's life cycle unmarked by blessings, she recognized the incompleteness of Jewish tradition. "How to make women's experiences *Jewish* experiences" became a guiding objective of her rabbinical career. The ordination of women had brought Judaism "to the edge of an important religious revolution," she wrote in an essay for Susannah Heschel's 1983 anthology *On Being a Jewish Feminist*. "I pray we have the faith to push it over the edge."[87]

Ordained in 1976, Geller served for fourteen years as Hillel director at the University of Southern California, founding a Jewish women's faculty group and a Jewish women's research group, where both men and women presented new work in Jewish women's studies. One semester, Betty Friedan, in residence at USC as a university professor, offered thoughts about Jewish women and feminism as part of a Hillel-initiated interdisciplinary think tank.[88] In 1982, Hillel sponsored an influential national feminist conference, "Illuminating the Unwritten Scroll: Women's Spirituality and Jewish Tradition." From 1990 to 1994, Geller served as executive director of the Pacific Southwest Region of the American Jewish Congress, where she created the AJCongress Feminist Center, which became a model for Jewish feminist projects throughout the country.[89]

"I'm grateful I wasn't the first [ordained rabbi]," Geller said. "I came into the rabbinate already a strong feminist, and it might have been more difficult for somebody as outspoken and engaged [as I was] to have been the first. It was easier that someone else had opened the door."[90]

In 1994, Geller's integration of her feminist and Jewish passions took on new dimensions when she was appointed senior rabbi at Temple Emanuel in Beverly Hills, the first woman congregational rabbi on the West Coast and one of the first to become senior rabbi at a major metropolitan synagogue. At Temple Emanuel, where Geller served for twenty-two years, and in positions of national rabbinic leadership, she became a spokesperson for the greater inclusion of women into Jewish liturgy and practice, fulfilling the mission she set for herself decades before. She said, "When women became rabbis, everything changed because we brought the Torah of *our* experience to our rabbinates. So liturgy changed, prayer changed, theology changed, scholarship changed, everything changed—including the structures of institutions."[91]

* * *

In the late 1970s, Laura Geller teamed with another pioneering feminist rabbi, Rebecca Trachtenberg Alpert, whom she met at the 1973 McAlpin conference, to form the Women's Rabbinic Alliance. The alliance met in New York, Philadelphia, and New Jersey through 1983, with fifteen to twenty rotating members, about the number of women who had been ordained by that time.[92] Like Geller, Alpert was born in Brooklyn in 1950, and she was ordained the same year as Geller. Although the two women took different paths as rabbis, each pioneered new ways of integrating Jewish spiritual life and feminist practice.

Like Geller, Alpert grew up in the Reform tradition, but her parents were not synagogue goers or connected with Judaism in any way. Her father believed that religion was mere superstition, and her mother saw it as too expensive, feeling that working-class people such as the Trachtenbergs were not welcome in synagogues. As a child in Brooklyn, however, where Jews were everywhere, Alpert felt that she absorbed the "essence of Judaism," a basic, profound Jewishness.[93] Her comfort with this core identity formed the basis of her personalized spirituality.

Even as a child, Alpert felt that she could talk to God. Surprisingly, it was a religious-minded fifth-grade African American teacher who reinforced her Jewish identity: "You should be religious," the teacher told her, inspiring Alpert to ask her parents to send her to Hebrew school, where she excelled.[94] Although Alpert later became alienated from Reform observance, she participated in the Reform youth movement through high school and enjoyed services, which she considered "holy."[95] Alpert knew even then that she wanted to be a rabbi. What she did not understand was "what most people knew for a fact: there had never been a woman ordained to the rabbinate."[96]

Second-wave feminism helped tear down the barriers and made this possible. In Alpert's junior year of Barnard College, which she spent in Jerusalem, news of the explosive excitement of the new women's liberation movement encouraged her to apply to rabbinical school. "I heard from friends back home about their sit-ins at the *Ladies' Home Journal* and protests in the street for sexual liberation as the women's movement hit our campus with a vengeance. I read an article in *Newsweek* about rabbinical student Sally Priesand, in which she said she knew she had to be better than all her male colleagues to attain her goal if she were to be ordained. It was obvious to me then that the only reason she . . . would be ordained was because of the publicity the women's movement created."[97]

The *New York Times* noted Alpert's unusual career choice in a story about Barnard's 1971 graduating class. "The cherub-faced daughter of a furrier" was planning to "take on one of the most male-dominated fields of them all: She wants to be a rabbi."[98] Alpert chose Reconstructionism, attracted to its focus on Jewish peoplehood and culture. She and a classmate became the second and third women to matriculate at the Reconstructionist Rabbinical College (RRC) in Philadelphia, where she met and married fellow student Joel Alpert, with whom she had two children. She completed a doctorate in American Jewish religious history at Temple University while at the RRC.

Alpert spent her years at rabbinical college "speaking publicly wherever [she] could about the history of women's inequalities in Jewish religious life and responding to quips like 'what should we call your husband' and 'I've never danced with a rabbi before.'" Her feminism emerged in her academic research on the history of women in the rabbinate, the network of women rabbis that she organized with Geller, and the articles about women in Judaism that she wrote for *Lilith*, the *Reconstructionist, Response*, and other periodicals. Alpert thought that "being a rabbi would change the world." To her, it was a "feminist act," "defying an entire history." Yet she discovered that she was an "outlier." Only Laura Geller and a few other colleagues saw the rabbinate, as she put it, "as a feminist project or made connections to the secular world of Jewish feminists, got involved in the incipient Jewish Feminist Organization . . . or even joined in solidarity with our counterparts in Conservative and Havurah Judaism who were fighting for the rights we had already attained or took for granted—to stand on the bimah, count in a minyan, act as a witness, create new life cycle ceremonies, wear a tallit, lead prayer services in mixed company." To most women rabbis of her generation, "being a rabbi was all about, well, being a rabbi. 'Jewish woman' was not an identity that interested them."[99]

There was little help from secular Jewish feminists, since most thought that, as Alpert recalled, "women rabbis had no special role to play in the movement, including the women who invited me to lead one of the famous secular Jewish feminist seders in NY and then not so politely did not allow me to lead it. The anti-hierarchical nature of the movement meant that someone who arrogated to herself the role of 'leader' was not going to be welcome." Alpert had to accept the idea that the secular world of Jewish feminism and the world of the feminist rabbinate "did not neatly come together."[100]

After graduating from the RRC, Alpert worked as part-time pulpit rabbi at several synagogues, taught Jewish studies at Rutgers University, and took a staff position at the RRC before becoming associate dean there, serving until 1987. She credits her time in this post and her involvement in Jewish feminist consciousness-raising groups in the early 1980s with her coming out as a lesbian, which she did in 1986, after divorcing her husband, although they remained friendly. It was an important professional decision. "In coming to terms with being a lesbian rabbi, I found my voice." Of course," she added, "I also lost my job and would have to take that voice elsewhere for it to be heard."[101]

Leaving the "cocoon of progressive Jewish life," Alpert went on to a career as professor of religion at Temple University and director of Temple's Women's Studies Program.[102] She writes about Judaism, race, and sport, the subject of *Out of Left Field: Jews and Black Baseball* and *Religion and Sports: An Introduction and Case Studies*, and about Judaism and sexuality. She is the author of *Like Bread on the Seder Plate: Jewish Lesbians and the Transformation of Tradition* and, with Rabbis Sue Elwell and Shirley Idelson, editor of the anthology *Lesbian Rabbis: The First Generation*.[103]

Today Alpert considers herself to be a rabbi "on the side," counseling and performing life-cycle ceremonies for Jews who choose not to affiliate.[104] Her status as a rabbi/teacher gives her a platform from which to speak out about issues in the secular world that matter to her: reproductive choice, marriage equality, immigration rights, racial justice, and the Israel-Palestine conflict. "I have never regretted for one minute my decision to find my feminist home in the rabbinate," said Alpert, "and I hope I have used the power I have gained from my position as a good feminist should—*with* people, and not *over* them, to construct a more just and peaceful world." She observed that while she may be a "minimalist rabbi," she is not a "minimalist Jew." Rather, she considers herself a committed, lesbian, feminist, "maximalist" Jew, deeply immersed in the dialogues of contemporary Jewish life.[105]

Blu Greenberg: "Feminism Has Been a Way Into Judaism, and Not Out of It"

The story of Blu Greenberg, creator of the Jewish Orthodox Feminist Alliance (JOFA), attests to the varieties of religious experience undergone by feminist activists. At the NYU "Women's Liberation and Jewish Identity" conference, Greenberg spoke of the transformative events in her life wrought by the feminist movement and her admiration for the work of women's liberationists. For Greenberg, attending the conference "felt something . . . akin to the excitement of a person traveling to a rock-star concert." She was thrilled to hear from her "heroes"—Susan Brownmiller, the women from *Our Bodies, Ourselves*, the Chicago Gang of Four, and others. At the conference, Greenberg realized how much her "own activism, primarily as an Orthodox Jewish feminist has been influenced by, nurtured by, and connected to the wider feminist movement." These were the women who changed the world, "building something out of nothing."[106]

Blu Greenberg was born in 1936 into the modern Orthodox, Zionist Genauer family in Seattle, Washington. She defines herself as a "maximalist Jew" from an early age. Jews were a minority in Seattle—"a minority of a minority"—but the message she received from her aunts, uncles, and cousins was that to be a minority as a Jew was a "blessing and privilege, not a burden." Growing up in wartime, near a navy base, she remembers her father going to shul every Friday night and bringing home for Shabbat soldiers who had a furlough. Observing rituals, studying Torah, performing mitzvoth: "the whole package was central to our lives." Her parents were community leaders—her mother president of the religious Zionist Women's Organization and her father a rabbi, businessman, and Talmud scholar—who influenced her Jewish education.[107]

Yet Greenberg also experienced a sense of vulnerability. To be a minority outside her community meant encountering anti-Semitism. She could not ride her bike in certain areas: "I encountered Jesus Christ as [the] one who killed him." This "duality of pride and of vulnerability" made her both "appreciative and protective." Later, when feminists attacked the Torah and patriarchal Judaism, she felt discomfort: "Torah was my life, and the rabbis were my heroes." Even when she began to criticize patriarchy and rabbinic law herself, she felt an "internal tension" born of her love of the religion and her need to defend it against enemies.[108]

The duality that Greenberg experienced as a feminist Jew also came from her parents' different worldviews. Her father loved Judaism deeply. Gentle and kind, a peacemaker by nature, he could not stand disapproval. Her mother also loved Judaism, but as part of her passion for truth and social justice, she loved criticism. "Right was right and fair was fair. Tell it like it is and don't talk on any edges." Greenberg grew up with a father who would "brook no criticism and a mother who would take no prisoners." For the rest of her life, she shuttled back and forth between the "critical love for [her] faith and community and the need for truth and justice," for speaking out.[109]

The family moved to Long Island when Blu was ten; she attended the Hebrew Institute of Long Island and Central Yeshiva High School for Girls, getting a bachelor's degree from Brooklyn College and a degree in religious education from Yeshiva University's Teachers Institute. She received a master's degree in Jewish history from Yeshiva University and another master's in clinical psychology from City University. Blu married Irving (Yitz) Greenberg in 1958; they had five children in six years. Her husband, a modern Orthodox rabbi, became the chaplain at Brandeis University, then Harvard, before getting a Ph.D. He taught at Yeshiva University and then founded the Jewish Studies Program at City College of the City University of New York. He also served as president and co-founder of the National Jewish Center for Learning and Leadership (CLAL).

Blu Greenberg was living in her "Orthodox cocoon, rebbetzin of a large modern Orthodox synagogue, lecturer at a local college, and mother of a young family of five."[110] She saw the obligations of Jewish men to pray three times a day and wear a *kippah* as "burdens" that she was happy not to deal with.[111] Greenberg credits her husband with pushing her to be open to feminism; he became a feminist a decade before she did, encouraging her to read Friedan's *The Feminine Mystique* in 1963. "It was a white-hot idea and very just," she said. "But it wasn't about me, and it wasn't about my life and my mother's life."[112]

So it was "from the sidelines" that Greenberg watched feminism in the 1960s, identifying with social justice issues, particularly rape and domestic violence. But she put it "at a distance."[113] She did not declare herself a feminist until the first National Conference of Jewish Women. Arlene Agus and Toby Brandriss, Ezrat Nashim members and conference organizers, asked her to give a keynote speech, seeing her as a potential leader in the quest for Jewish women's religious rights. Greenberg felt she did not merit the invitation; she had not known about Ezrat Nashim and was satisfied with her own life as a *rebbetzin*. "Family, children, men, rabbis, these were my loves, my longings, my heroes." In her community, feminism was not a respectable term. Yet she agreed to give the speech.[114]

In researching sources for the speech, Greenberg came to grips with the painful reality that the tradition she loved placed women in subordinate roles. Once she began to view Jewish women's roles in religion from a feminist perspective, the fact of inequality loomed large, especially concerning the *agunah*. But Greenberg also faulted feminism's disconnect from the family—as well as "from the class of men in general." Her talk at the conference emerged as a "critique of both Judaism and feminism, as well as a discussion of how the two could be informed and enriched by each other."[115] She believed that half the audience gave her a standing ovation, while the rest resented her upholding traditional family values and her critique of feminism. She viewed these women as "orthodox" feminists, who saw their movement as a "religion—sacrosanct, untouchable, inviolable." They were part of the "radical fringe."[116]

The morning after giving the speech, Greenberg had a life-changing experience. Sitting alone at the back of the Feminist Torah service, she found it "totally discombobulating" to hear Arlene Agus read from the Torah. "My ears were popping and my eyes were bulging. . . . It was mind-blowing. To see women doing things that I thought women *couldn't* do—that was amazing, mind-boggling, exhilarating, frightening, challenging, upsetting." When two women came to get her to take part in *hagbah* (lifting of the Torah), she was shocked but went with them to the bimah. "It was the first time I had ever held a Torah. I had studied it practically all my life, . . . but until then I had never actually looked upon an open Torah scroll."[117]

The Jewish feminist conference became a "watershed experience" for Greenberg. The "cutting edge, sophisticated" event was Greenberg's first personal encounter with "women's initiative and power," introducing her to "the value of cohorts."[118] Greenberg soon came to embrace feminism, understanding that "all new movements have to be radical at first."[119] The path was not smooth, and sometimes she "switched gears from one moment to the next." As she became less anxious about feminism, she had to confront many people in the Orthodox community "who were tightening up and closing off." She recognized that much of the resistance was "political as well as religious," and she vowed that though she would never abandon tradition, neither would she "yield the new value of women's equality even though it may conflict with Jewish tradition. To do so, would be to affirm the principle of a hierarchy of male and female," which she no longer saw as "axiom of Judaism."[120]

In contrast to utopian movements such as socialism or communism, in which Jews gave up their roots when they became politicized, Greenberg said that feminism was "a way into Judaism and not out of it." At the McAlpin conference, she saw women who had never opened a Jewish text sit and study together in preparation for Shabbat.[121] Jewish women estranged from or ignorant of Jewish tradition were able to recover and claim their Jewish identities, remarkably as religious women. In the face of the prediction that feminism would erode Judaism, the opposite was true. Women came to their Jewishness "through the portals of feminism."[122]

The McAlpin conference remained a powerful motivator for Greenberg, shaping her work over the next decades as she incorporated feminism into her religious practice and writing. Most importantly, she learned that "you could critique the tradition and the earth didn't swallow you up."[123] In 1975, together with Rabbi Isaac Trainin, she invited Betty Friedan to join a New York Jewish Federation task force, Jewish Women in a Changing Society. The task force held conferences on the *agunot*, the Jewish family, infertility, and other topics.[124] In 1981, Greenberg published *On Women and Judaism: The View from Tradition*, essays on Jewish women and liturgy, ritual, divorce, and abortion, in which she framed feminist challenges to Jewish tradition and family life, seeking measures of reconciliation.[125] The book was controversial among feminists and Orthodox Jews but influenced new ways of thinking.

Later in the 1980s, Greenberg acknowledged that becoming an activist had enriched her life in ways she could never have imagined, strengthening her marriage and family life, extending her community, connecting her "more deeply to the Jewish people than anything [she] might have studied in a text or read in a history book." She experienced new bonds, those "we feel to each other as we give our time and energy to a cause, the sense of community and of rootedness to the Jewish people." As a Jewish feminist, she sought transformations "not merely about religious tradition, or rights and responsibilities, or the details of canon law. At it its heart, it is about the overarching matters of justice and ethics." Feminism strengthens Judaism, she averred, "because feminism is about justice, and incorporating a new measure of justice brings Judaism up to its own best level.[126]

One direction for Greenberg's activism became the desire to replicate the feminist collective experience that she had witnessed at the McAlpin conference within the Orthodox community. Eventually, this led her to organize the First and Second International Feminist Conferences on Feminism and Orthodoxy in 1997 and 1998 and to found the Jewish Orthodox Feminist Alliance (JOFA); Greenberg was its first president. JOFA has become a force for change within Orthodoxy, fulfilling Greenberg's hope that feminism and Orthodox religion could be mutually reinforcing.[127] With chapters across the U.S. and approximately six thousand members, JOFA uses consciousness-raising and study to build community and advance social change around gender issues in the Orthodox world.

Greenberg was the first in the Orthodox community to try to move Jewish feminism outward. But she bemoans the slow pace of these efforts. While Orthodoxy is arguing about divorce, whether women can be ordained, and so on, "Rome is burning," she told the NYU conference. "Violence against women, lack of peace, especially in the Middle East, the havoc of hate, the ravished environment—these are burning issues. Sometimes I wake up and ask myself, 'What am I doing in this little, little box?'" She believes that issues of concern to religious women should not be narrowly focused, agreeing with other Jewish feminists in this chapter that the main goal is to connect religious reform to the wider world. She calls this challenge "the next agenda."[128]

* * *

Since the founding of Ezrat Nashim, religious Jewish feminists have opened the doors of Judaism to women's more equal participation and a new female spirituality based on women's experiences. Directly influenced by the women's liberation movement, they applied feminist visions of social change to religious life, demonstrating the possibility of radical transformation within a faith tradition.

Like women's liberationists, these women were compelled to activism because of their awareness of gender oppression, especially regarding their religious heritage. Moments of exclusion and marginality that they experienced served as spark plugs to the later feminist revolution. Participation in social movements of the era—civil rights, welfare and housing rights, freedom for Soviet Jewry—also helped to initiate their interest in protest and activism. By the 1970s, they were able to use the new vocabulary of feminism to channel their rage at sexism into a rebellion against religious patriarchy.

That rebellion took several different directions. Working to ordain women as rabbis, pressing for more egalitarian practices across denominations, and creating new liturgies, rituals, and midrash, these women ushered in innovative forms of religious thought and practice. Because of their contributions, women would no longer be "peripheral Jews," without their own spiritual identities. In bringing feminism and tradition into dialogue with each other, these women and their colleagues transformed Jewish religious life.

At times, however, these women's multiple loyalties became difficult to sustain. As the narratives in this chapter reveal, Jewish feminists uncovered myriad forms of gender bias on the part of friends and families, teachers and colleagues, lovers and husbands, against whom they had to take a stand. Institutions of Jewish life generally—synagogues, community centers, schools, seminaries, federations, councils—also came under assault for their patriarchal practices. Although blunted by these feminists' strong Jewish backgrounds and relationships, conflict was unavoidable. But bolstered by women's communities that they helped to organize, Jewish feminists succeeded in changing the nature of the conversation.

The difficulties of bridging Jewish and feminist identities were particularly arduous within Orthodoxy, in which feminist individualism had been regarded as a threat to community survival. Yet as Blu Greenberg's story underscores, "a mild-mannered yeshiva girl" could "find happiness among the feminists," despite initial ambivalence.[129] Even within the more liberal denominations, the compatibility between feminism and Judaism was not automatic. Not all religious pioneers were feminists, as Rebecca Alpert's story discloses, even when they broke barriers and widened access. The Jewish feminist movement did not have a central address, in Paula Hyman's formulation; nor were perspectives unitary.[130] Martha Ackelsberg and Judith Plaskow encountered such profound differences at B'not Esh that they initially despaired of finding common ground even within their own community. Yet with hard work, the divergences among members became a source of growth rather than dissension.[131]

Important contrasts existed between religious and secular Jewish feminists as well, reflected in the failure of the jointly founded Jewish Feminist Organization. Another set of differences separated religious feminists from women's liberationists, who generally considered Judaism as irrelevant or dismissed it as irrevocably patriarchal. These worlds rarely came into contact. The separation lessened discomforts felt by Jewish feminists at anti-Jewish attitudes in the wider women's movement, but it also cut off occasions for collaboration.

The women discussed in this chapter took unusual steps to create opportunities for cross-fertilization. Martha Ackelsberg's, Judith Plaskow's, and Rebecca Alpert's work with secular feminists and LGBT communities, a Jewish-Arab Dialogue Group in which Greenberg participated, and the coalitions that Laura Geller formed with university feminist centers exemplify such efforts. Religious Jewish feminists rejected the dichotomies that had made women less than male Jews, remaining sensitive to inequalities elsewhere. "The gift of the Jewish feminist movement is noting who is on the outside," Geller remarked, prodding religious women to use the enhanced spirituality that the movement has created to work toward a fuller humanity for all people.[132]

"Feminism is the crucible for modern Judaism," Susannah Heschel observed in the introduction to her 1983 anthology.[133] Having put in motion a powerful set of changes that have given women a voice inside the synagogue, pioneering Jewish feminists remain poised to push forward further transformations, inside and outside traditional religious spaces. The agenda remains unfinished, but in Jewish feminism's powerful confrontation with an ancient tradition that had marginalized women, it has already chalked up many victories.

6

"Jewish Women Have Their Noses Shortened"

Secular Feminists Fight Assimilation

Secular Jewish feminists participated in several organizations that joined feminism and Jewish life in the late 1960s and 1970s. Among the most noteworthy of these were Brooklyn Bridge, Chutzpah, and the Jewish Feminist Organization, the latter of which was created after the first two Jewish feminist conferences held in New York in the early 1970s. The Jewish feminist magazine *Lilith* was launched in 1976. Secular feminists targeted sexism within the mixed-gender organizations of the Jewish Left and the Jewish establishment, attempting to create new amalgams of identity that erased hierarchical gender distinctions.

Some of these women had not been Jewish identified, but as they became increasingly uncomfortable as Jews in New Left organizations and women's liberation groups, they sought Jewish affiliations. Along with the process of consciousness-raising inspired by the women's movement, the 1967 Six-Day War, eliciting both strong praise and denunciations of Israel, was a precipitating factor in triggering Jewish identification.

At a time when the American student movement was coalescing against the U.S. war in Vietnam, the 1967 war in the Middle East polarized young Jewish radicals. Israel, the David against the Goliath forces of Egypt, Jordan, and Syria surprised the world with its swift and decisive victory. Young American Jews, both veterans of Zionist youth movements and those who had not felt any previous connection to the Jewish community or to Israel, found themselves identifying with Israel. "Weeping with joy" at the liberation of the Western Wall, they were surprised to discover "how deeply touched they were by Israel's prewar trauma and its swift reprieve from destruction." Few had imagined that they had strong feelings about Israel. "There was practically audible cheering in the neighborhood," added Cheryl Moch, one of the founders of the Jewish radical collective Brooklyn Bridge. "I was raised to believe that Jewish men went like sheep to the slaughter, that they weren't manly. There was a shame factor being Jewish growing up in the fifties and sixties. But all it took [to change it] was the Six-Day War."[1]

But other young radicals believed that Israel emerged from the war as an "oppressor," a "tool of American imperialism."[2] These men and women considered pro-Zionist views "chauvinistic" and counterrevolutionary.[3] At the 1967 National Conference for New Politics in Chicago in late summer, a majority of participants supported the anti-Zionist resolution that condemned Israel as an "imperialist aggressor."[4] The same conference that had shaken Shulamith Firestone and Jo Freeman with its disregard for women's issues became a defining moment for Jewish radicals who acquiesced in anti-Israel denunciations and those who were stunned by them.

Some Jewish radicals, trying to find explanations for the hostile attitudes to Jews and Israel and to align their own "feelings with their politics," began to meet in small groups to discuss Jewish issues.[5] The events of June 1967 put a halt to their "ethnic amnesia"; they could no longer ignore the fact of their Jewish difference. "We were still radicals, Socialists, opposed to the war, exploitation and racism, committed to building a new society. But we were also, we now perceived, Jews. What did that mean? What was the significance of this new consciousness?"[6] "What identity should American Jews develop?"[7]

As a result of this self-questioning, a new radical Jewish Left came into being. "It happened all over the country," reported Aviva Cantor Zuckoff, a leader in the new movement. "We had a lot of refugees from SDS; people with an intense Jewish background but involved in New Left activities; people with little Jewish background who didn't even know what Chanukah was—but then, all of a sudden, something happened, something turned."[8] In the post-1967 period, thousands of New Left "refugees" drifted in and out of dozens of groups created spontaneously as a consequence of the Left's condemnation of Israel. So many groups formed on and off campus that in 1970 the London-based World Union of Jewish Students (WUJS) created the North American Jewish Students Network, informally called Network, a loose association of several hundred groups in a left-to-right spectrum of what they called "the Jewish movement." By 1972, Network anchored the Jewish Student

Press Service, which provided news and information to at least fifty movement newspapers. It became the sponsoring organization for the 1973 and 1974 Jewish feminist conferences in New York.

Network saw itself as a resource "across the entire political spectrum," in Cantor's words, its goal to stimulate the building of a Jewish student movement by providing resources that could lead to cross-fertilization. Though open to all points of view, Network leaders shared a leftist perspective that acknowledged the centrality of concerns about Israel to Jewish identity. What they had most in common was their "separation struggle with the New Left . . . and with the Jewish community."[9]

Network and its associated groups adopted a varied agenda, defending Israel and Zionism but criticizing Israeli occupation policies; publishing underground newspapers; and calling for the establishment of Jewish Studies programs, freedom for Soviet Jewry, and a more open, democratic, and pluralistic Jewish community. By 1973, many politically oriented Jewish leftist groups had folded or moved on to other issues, sometimes aligning with religious-oriented Jewish radicals. The demarcation between the Jewish Left and religious Jewish radicals was not firm, but *havurah* and countercultural religious organizations were generally less focused on Israel than was the Jewish Left.[10]

However innovative the Jewish student movement's vision for Jewish youth leadership, it recapitulated the male-dominated organizational structure of the Jewish establishment. There had been more than three men for every woman present at the North American Jewish Students Network convention in the fall of 1970, with gender ratios even more disproportionate on its governing boards and steering committees. "Sitting at a board meeting, we are addressed as 'gentleman,'" Vivian Silver Salowitz wrote of the new movement. "We are expected to record the minutes of a meeting."[11]

To Cantor, the creation of a new kind of Jewish feminism was the Jewish Left's most important legacy. Many women in its organizations came to identify as Jewish feminists, although they did not necessarily designate themselves as "secular."[12] I use this term to distinguish these activists from those of Ezrat Nashim and other religious Jewish rebels.

A five-day conference at a meeting-camp facility in Zieglerville, Pennsylvania, in September 1971 served as one of Jewish feminism's most important "click" moments. Organized by the World Union of

Jewish Students, the conference brought together over 250 Jewish student activists from around the world, half of them from the U.S. and representing diverse political and religious views, with the express purpose of exploring cultural forms and lifestyles emerging in the Jewish student community.[13] It was the first time that women from the new North American Jewish Student Network and those from the countercultural *havurot* encountered one another. Exhilarated by their common interests and eager to reconcile their differences, the women met together for a few days to discuss their concerns.

The men, however, were "annoyed that the women had 'separated themselves,'" as Cantor told the story. To "mollify" them, the women agreed to present the issues they had discussed in caucus to the whole group. "There the men, from left to right on the movement's political spectrum, shouted them down, hurled verbal insults, and loudly and angrily charged that the changes the women wanted were 'bad for the Jews.'"[14] Resembling events at the National Conference for New Politics and the Nixon counter-inaugural when New Left men insulted women participants, triggering their desire to organize independently, women at Zieglerville had their consciousness raised.

Six months after the Zieglerville gathering, one hundred women from a variety of groups under the umbrella of Network came together to explore sexism in Jewish life. Network women, supported by Ezrat Nashim and members of the radical Jewish collective Brooklyn Bridge, began to plan the first National Conference of Jewish Women at the Hotel McAlpin in 1973, which Blu Greenberg keynoted.

The women and their allies organized a second gathering—this one a National Conference on Jewish Women and Men—that took place in New York City in April 1974, titled "Changing Sex Roles in Jewish Life: Past Expectations, Future Implications." The conference included a wide variety of participants, from "radical lesbian vegetarians to ultra-orthodox women," as one newspaper put it, and men as well as women, in the hope that if men attended the conference, they "would see the injustice of the many restrictions placed on Jewish women" and join the women in their work. The event led to the establishment of the Jewish Feminist Organization (JFO), dedicated to the "full, direct and equal participation of women at all levels of Jewish life—communal, religious, educational, and political."[15] Its governing board consisted of a representative from each of four regions: Cheryl Moch from the East, Maralee Gordon from the Midwest, Diane Gelon from the West, and Brona Brown from Canada. At its launch, the JFO attracted one thousand paid members.[16]

The approach to working for greater women's rights within the Jewish community took two forms. While religiously identified Jewish feminists targeted inequality in synagogues and seminaries, secular Jewish feminists focused on what Cantor called "the assimilation game," seeing danger in the fact that "Jewish women have their noses shortened and bleach their hair to conform to the Anglo-Saxon ideal of beauty, or at least, minimize their Jewish differences." Cantor wondered "why so many Jews were so anti-Israel, why they were deserting the community, why they assimilate." Assimilation meant a loss of positive Jewish connection, an often-internalized sense of oppression that weakened identity. "Feminism was the missing piece of the puzzle," said Cantor, "because you can't understand the experience of Jewish exile without understanding the status of women."[17]

Like black women, Latinas, and other feminists giving voice to their collective identities, secular Jewish feminists linked their struggle as Jewish women fighting patriarchal institutions to larger campaigns against racism, sexism, and capitalism. To be fully aware of themselves as Jewish women was a first step toward engaging the multiple causes of oppression. As Jewish women, they could fight broad feminist and social justice struggles while addressing issues of primary concern to them as Jews. They saw no sharp divide between particularist and universalist interests.

In this regard, secular Jewish women were among the early groups of feminists who embraced identity politics, asserting themselves as a distinctive social group based on shared ethnic and/or class and gender background and interests. They considered themselves Jewish women as well as feminists, emphasizing dual components of a hybrid identity, neither of which could remain dormant or neglected. Such a declaration was a departure for secular feminists who had come to political consciousness on the left, where identifications with Jewishness had been rare.

The secular feminists insisted that Jewish women's sexuality and economic circumstances be taken seriously. The 1973 NJWC had been

Figure 6.1. Cheryl Moch and congresswoman Bella Abzug, Jewish Feminist Organization, April 1975, Photo by Diane Gelon.

disrupted by a demonstration by working-class and gay women, angry that there were no lesbian speakers on the program and that the cost of the conference prevented poorer Jewish women from attending.[18] According to conference coordinator Sheryl Baron Nestel, the turn to "respectability" at the cost of "inclusivity" had been an unintended consequence of the difficulty of raising funds for the NJWC. "So convinced were we that what we were doing was revolutionary that we were unable to see the ways in which the conference, despite being an important and empowering event, also reinforced the normative boundaries of American Jewish life."[19]

The lesson of inclusion demanded by the protesters was not lost on participants, with the result that the platform of the Jewish Feminist Organization that sprang from the 1974 conference incorporated a demand for the full participation of gay women and men in Jewish religious and secular communities.[20] As the Jewish feminist movement evolved in the 1970s and 1980s, lesbian women played a significant role, especially in fighting anti-Semitism in the women's movement.

Often newly radicalized as Jews, the secular feminists had an immense task before them and, in these early years of raised consciousness, few identifiable resources. Like women's liberationists and religious Jewish feminists, they formed consciousness-raising groups, raising uncomfortable issues and spawning new interventions. In some cases, their feminism developed in gender-mixed groups such as the Chicago collective Chutzpah or New York's Brooklyn Bridge.

According to Tamara Cohen, the secular Jewish feminists were an "overlooked bridge," bringing feminism to the Jewish mainstream and Jewish feminism to the Left. Cohen emphasizes the structural disadvantages that many of these women faced as middle- and lower-class women, often with little Jewish education and in conflict with men and sometimes with women empowered by their class, educational status, and Jewish knowledge. In comparison to Ezrat Nashim's battle against religious hierarchies, these women's war against assimilation and cultural stereotypes appeared less media worthy and urgent.[21]

But secular Jewish feminists can claim considerable success. Facing confrontations and even vilification, they showed great courage. They brought focus to the twin problems of assimilation and stereotyping as special trials for Jewish women, not only for Jews more broadly. Their challenges to the established order encouraged change, even if it occurred slowly and partially. In marking gender inequality and ethnic neglect as Jewish feminist issues, they opened a pathway to equity that complemented the efforts of religious feminists. Rebelling against the limits of their roles as good Jewish daughters, wives, sisters, and friends, secular Jewish feminists joined at the frontlines of social change.

Aviva Cantor: "Oppression of Amerika's Jews"

Aviva Cantor did not start out as a radical, she told a Boston journalist who interviewed her after the publication of her 1995 book *Jewish Women / Jewish Men: The Legacy of Patriarchy in Jewish Life*, a sweeping feminist analysis of Jewish history, culture, and psychology.[22] But she became one. Born in the Bronx in 1940, Cantor grew up as the only child of a fervently Zionist father, Joseph Cantor, an immigrant from what is now Belarus, and Naomi Friedman Cantor, born and orphaned in Russian Poland and raised in Toronto.[23] Joseph studied at the Volozhin Yeshiva, described by his daughter as the "Harvard of the yeshiva world," but was thwarted in his desire to immigrate to Palestine when he could not obtain an entry permit from the British Mandatory government there. He went to the United States instead, attended the Brooklyn College of Pharmacy, and bought a corner drugstore in the Bronx, where his wife served as salesclerk.

Cantor's parents were traditional, though not strictly observant Jews, and they sent Aviva to Ramaz, a modern Orthodox day school on the Upper East Side of Manhattan, where she received an excellent Jewish elementary and secondary education. Although going from a "middle-middle-class" family in the East Bronx to the mostly upper-middle-class school proved to be socially difficult, Cantor felt lucky to be grounded in Jewish texts and traditions; she graduated valedictorian of her class.[24]

Cantor went on to Barnard College, taking two middle years of study at the Hebrew University in Jerusalem. Graduating from Barnard in 1961, she received a master's degree from the Columbia Graduate School of Journalism two years later and launched her career as a reporter working for the U.S. bureau of the *London Jewish Chronicle*. That journalistic work connected her to the incipient Jewish student movement and the world of Radical Zionist politics and journalism. In 1966, she married Murray Zuckoff, a socialist writer born on the Lower East Side. Three years later, Zuckoff became the editor of the Jewish Telegraphic Agency, a post he held for some twenty years, covering Israel, black-Jewish relations, the American Jewish community, and other issues concerning Jews.[25]

By the late 1960s, Cantor had become deeply involved with a politically active group of student and young-adult Zionists. She was one of the founders of Young Americans for Progressive Israel (YAPI), an offshoot of Americans for Progressive Israel (API), which was part of the World Union of Mapam (left-wing Zionists), a group that included and supported the left-wing Zionist youth movement Hashomer Hatzair. Created in 1965, YAPI became part of the growing student antiwar movement. After the Six-Day War, Jewish radical refugees from the New Left found their way to the YAPI offices, where they joined Zionist activists to create the ideological infrastructure for what they called "Radical Zionism."[26] They renamed their organization the Jewish Liberation Project (JLP) and in 1969 began publishing the *Jewish Liberation Journal*, with Cantor as editor. Cantor was also the only woman elected to the steering committee of the newly launched North American Students Network.

Cantor strikingly articulated the ideology of the new Radical Zionist youth movement in her *Journal* pieces. In an article titled "Oppression of Amerika's Jews" in the periodical's second year, Cantor outlined the case against assimilation, targeting the comfort zone of many nonidentified Jewish radicals, including radical feminists. Her attack was couched in terms that drew on standard New Left anticapitalist rhetoric, as well as the ethnic and gender pride of the Black Power and feminist movements. Cantor repeatedly referred to women's liberation as she made the case that Jews needed to embrace their distinctiveness in order to fight invisibility, marginality, and oppression.

For Cantor, assimilation was one of the greatest problems of the Jewish Diaspora, a signpost of intentional amnesia about Jewish roots that derived from Jews' adaptation of the dominant culture and the ruling elite's anti-Semitism. Negative attitudes about Jewish identity caused Jews to attempt to "'pass' as 'whites,' . . . clinging helplessly to the status quo, rejecting the ethics of Jewish life." Uninformed about the causes of discrimination, many Jews blamed themselves for their oppression, internalizing the attitude that being different—being Jewish—was "bad," "regressive," "reactionary." Internalized oppression made Jews feel guilty about being together; the "most terrible of all terrible accusations" was that Jews were "clannish." Consequently, "any prideful Jewish identification or action" was interpreted as Jewish chauvinism. "Keeping people powerless by keeping them apart" went hand in hand with "cultural deprivation"—the absence of anything "positively Jewish" in young Jews' education and experiences, similar to how women had been denied their authentic histories.[27]

Negative views of behavior that was excessively Jewish targeted Jewish women: the worst insult was to tell a young Jewish woman that she was "talking like a Jewish fishwife" when she was expressing her feelings. The derision extended to Jewish feminists. "When women get together to discuss their oppression," Cantor claimed, "those opposing women's liberation try to intimidate them by saying they're all a bunch of dykes."[28]

Cantor zeroed in on how the Jews of the radical Left, "when criticizing Amerikan Jews, always mention the mink coats." What they did

not see was the "spiritual nakedness" underneath, the spiritual and cultural poverty that drove many Jewish youth to embrace "Zen, astrology,
drugs, left sectarianism, encounter groups, scientology, psychoanalysis,"
which is "as oppressive and dehumanizing in its own way as is physical
poverty." The process of liberation had to begin with an understanding
of assimilationist pressures and losing authentic identity.[29]

Cantor and her comrades also blamed the Jewish establishment
(dubbed WASHs, for White Anglo-Saxon Hebrews) and the non-
Jewish power elite for these problems. This "plutocracy of wealthy
men" dispensed Jewish people's money on projects that "appealed to
the big givers, without finding out what the rest of the Jews need and
want."[30] To protest such policies and to transform the Jewish public into
a democratic community, the radicals moved beyond writing articles
to direct action. Influenced by New Left confrontation tactics, a group
called Concerned Jewish Students interrupted the annual meeting of
the General Assembly of the Council of Jewish Federations in Boston,
in November 1969. Hillel Levine, a young rabbi then studying for his
Ph.D. at Yale, took the podium to speak for the protesters, criticizing
the elders for their belief in melting-pot ideals.[31] The protest resulted in
the council's forming a funding body to address the students' concerns.

The following year, Network groups organized primarily by the Jewish Liberation Project took over the offices of the Jewish Federation of
New York after the federation refused Network's demands for funding youth projects and for greater accountability. Forty-five movement
activists (the "Federation 45") were arrested after the one-day sit-in in
April, the first such action in the Jewish community.[32] It was a moment
that Cantor proudly recalls, and she regrets that similar demonstrations
faded from the Radical Jewish activist arsenal.

At the New York University "Women's Liberation and Jewish Identity" conference, Cantor explained the differences between Radical
Zionists and Radical Jews. Radical Zionists held that Zionism was the
national liberation movement of the Jewish people and that Israel was
essential to Jewish survival. They were the first group to champion
the two-state solution and supported Israeli comrades struggling to
resolve the Israeli-Palestinian conflict. In contrast, Radical Jews, as non-
Zionists, believed "that it would be too bad if Israel were wiped off the
map, but it had probably been a mistake to create it. Their position was

that Jewish survival didn't depend on Israel and that the Diaspora was a positive thing."[33]

Despite these differences, Cantor believes that Radical Jews and Radical Zionists made common cause in their opposition to the New Left's anti-Jewish stance. For the New Left, "Jews could not be revolutionary as long as they remained conscious Jews because all Jews were middle-class oppressors. To reject being an oppressor, a Jew had to reject being Jewish." For Cantor, the fundamental problem was whether young men and women needed to give up their identities as radical activists if they chose "the Jewish cause." "Could they be revolutionaries and at the same time pro-Israel and committed Jews?"[34] Radical Jewish feminists asked another question: could they be committed Jews while protesting gender inequality in the Jewish community?

By the late 1960s, women in both the Radical Jewish and Radical Zionist camps had begun to address issues of sexism and female subordination raised by women's liberationists. Although the roots of Jewish feminism were multiple, Cantor believes that Jewish feminism primarily "sprang out of the Jewish movement and shared its anti-assimilationist ethos."[35] Joining religious Jewish women with interests in gender equality, they heralded the birth of a new Jewish feminism.

At the NYU conference, Cantor explained that about 30 percent of the individuals in the Jewish movement were women and that Network welcomed women "who were politically assertive." "But the atmosphere was extremely male oriented." She recalled that at the Zieglerville conference, "it became shockingly apparent, very shocking, that the men . . . would not support feminism. Influenced by the women's liberation movement, groups of Jewish women started to meet." Soon the feminists in the Jewish movement "began to see Jewish life through feminist eyes."[36]

Cantor recalls her own feminist "click" moment. While wandering through a bookstore, she picked up a copy of Beverly Jones and Judith Brown's 1968 pamphlet *Toward a Female Liberation Movement*. Reading it, she experienced "a flash of recognition and identification and promptly became a feminist."[37] Jones and Brown were white civil rights activists and women's liberationists in Gainesville, Florida, whose "Florida Paper," an early statement of the pro-woman, radical feminist position, had a transformative effect on the emerging women's movement.[38]

After reading their pamphlet, Cantor undertook the study that resulted in the publication of her bibliography of Jewish women in 1979 (the first in the field) and, later, her comprehensive study of male-dominated Jewish life, *Jewish Women / Jewish Men.* She also co-founded a Jewish women's consciousness-raising group, which met for several years to explore what it meant to be a Jewish woman and, as Cantor put it, "how our Jewish background made us what we are."[39]

Cantor identified an important difference between the Jewish feminists' response to their male comrades' derisive behavior and that of some women's liberation activists to sexism within the New Left. "The shock—and the sexism in the movement generally—did not propel the [Jewish] women to drop out, regroup, and create a separate women's movement as women in the New Left had done," she noted. "Deeply influenced by the women's liberation movement, they already defined themselves as feminists and could discuss their situation in feminist terms."[40] They could combat sexism within the Jewish movement without divorcing themselves entirely from it.

But confronting the secular Jewish community posed significant difficulties. Cantor saw the Jewish establishment as deeply suspicious of Jewish feminists, regarding the 1973 National Conference of Jewish Women as "horrible": "It was just after the Six-Day War and you had the Black Power movement, hippies, and other leftists spouting anti-Zionism. I think people saw us and thought it's like the 10 plagues . . . sex, drugs, rock n' roll, the new left, now us."[41] Ending Jewish women's powerlessness would have required challenging the male-dominated and "totally undemocratic" Jewish establishment power structure, a difficult effort since in the post-1967 "circle the wagons" mood, Jewish feminists were "already being condemned as enemies of the Jewish people for voicing any kind of criticism." They had few allies. The large Jewish women's volunteer organizations seemed hostile to feminism, and the "general women's movement was not interested in Jewish feminism, nor did it extend any assistance to its advocates," failing to challenge anti-Semitism when it "shamefully" spewed forth at the UN World Conferences on Women that started in 1975.[42]

Cantor's furious response in December 1971 to the women's liberation paper *RAT: Subterranean News,* which had published an anti-Israel editorial, contrasted with her more tempered reaction to what she called the "hysterical anti-Semitism" of male movement Jews at Ziegler-ville a few months earlier.[43] Begun in 1968, *RAT*, a New York–based, male-run underground newspaper, had been popular for its coverage of far-left politics and culture. In January 1970, it was taken over by a radical feminist collective, an action that was regarded as a breakthrough in relations between radical women and men.[44] Soon after, the collective published a now-classic essay by Robin Morgan titled "Goodbye to All That," one of the first radical feminist pieces to call for an absolute break with the male Left: "Goodbye, goodbye forever . . . counterfeit Left, counterfeit, male-dominated, cracked-glass-mirror reflection of the Amerikan Nightmare. Women are the real left."[45]

Cantor met with the RAT collective when they asked about reprinting one of her articles, and she had persuaded them to retain her paragraphs on Zionism, which they had wanted to eliminate. Thus, she was shocked by the group's subsequent editorial calling for the destruction of Israel on the grounds it would be best for "the revolution."[46] While Cantor had not expected the RAT women to take a pro-Israel position, "opposing the *existence* of Israel" was another story. "To deny to the Jews what is acceptable for every other nation" was anti-Semitic and "racist," running counter to RAT's democratic, pluralist goals. The "Jewish sisters" in the collective who had signed the editorial (or probably were "pushed" into it, Cantor suggested, "so bad is our oppression") were no doubt "terrified of confronting the meaning of Israel for them as Jews." RAT had "not said 'goodby [*sic*]' to all that," Cantor charged, but lusted for a "last desperate grab for male approval." The collective had "betrayed the women's movement and all it stands for." Cantor ended with a stark pronouncement that revealed the significant distance between Radical Zionist women and radical feminists at this time. "Your editorial calling for the destruction of my homeland, my instrumentality of national liberation, declares you to be my enemy. You have joined the ranks of my oppressors and I cannot call you sisters anymore."

With the exception of the Israel issue, Cantor in fact had a great deal in common with RAT and other radical feminist groups. Like Robin Morgan, she held capitalist "Amerika" and its oppressive ruling elite responsible for social evils, articulating a relentless critique of "the establishment" and class privilege. Cantor also admired the demonstrations that brought national attention to radical feminist causes, a style that she contrasted with the more conciliatory approach of Jewish feminists "who used words as weapons."[47] In *Jewish Women / Jewish Men*, she took Jewish feminists to task for the lack of "fire and ire," which she saw as rooted in the classic Jewish fear of "separation and abandonment." If Jewish women critiqued the Jewish establishment too strongly, they might be perceived as causing disunity and threatening the community, resulting in their own rejection "from the fold."[48] Cantor understood the reasons for the "lack of righteous anger" that could kindle public action: for Jewish women to take on the Jewish establishment would have constituted "high-octane role breaking."[49] But she nonetheless viewed their hesitancy as a flaw within Jewish feminism. Less confrontational and less political than the Jewish women in women's liberation, in many respects Jewish feminists were less effective.

Cantor believed that radical feminists could provide Jewish women the tools to overcome their anxieties about not being "nice Jewish girls" if they confronted sexist power structures.[50] Cantor had few such anxieties herself, as evidenced in 1976, when as associate editor of *Hadassah Magazine*, she ran afoul of the male executive editor, who chastised her for embarrassing the magazine by changing such sexist language as "seminal contribution" to "germinal contribution." The editor threatened to fire her if she continued with such practices, but Cantor stood her ground, arguing that Jewish women should not be "slavishly submissive to a dictionary in a knee-jerk reaction" that made them collaborators in discrimination.[51]

Yet as Cantor's strong criticism of the *RAT* editors reveals, the connection between radical feminism and Jewish feminism remained fraught. There was work to do. Jewish feminists sought to raise consciousness about Jewish issues among women's liberationists, suggesting, for example, that *Women: A Journal of Liberation* do a special issue on ethnic and racial differences that would include a piece on Jewish women. The editors agreed that the magazine should reach out to "non-WASP" women different from themselves.[52] Jewish women understood the importance of connecting to feminist circles. It would be "hard to get to other Jewish women," a friend wrote to Cantor, "if we separate ourselves from this mass movement that 'conscious' Jewish women have already joined." She asked Cantor to send an essay on Jewish women to be included in a National Organization of Women anthology.[53]

But who were these "conscious" Jewish women? Even Cantor did not know for sure, pointing out in one of her essays how little was known about the Jewishness of such notable feminist leaders as Betty Friedan, Gloria Steinem, and Bella Abzug. She emphasized that, beyond these spokeswomen chosen by the media, the movement could claim many other important leaders, including such "non-Jews" as Kate Millet, Robin Morgan, Susan Brownmiller, and Shirley Chisholm, seemingly ignorant of the fact that both Morgan and Brownmiller were Jewish.[54] As Cantor's mistake reveals, the presence and activism of Jewish women in second-wave feminism was little recognized at the time.

An indicator that Jewish feminism was becoming known to at least some radical feminists is seen in an invitation from Ann Snitow and Rachel Blau DuPlessis to Cantor in the early 1990s to contribute to an anthology they were editing about the experiences of second-wave feminist leaders. Busy with other commitments, Cantor was unable to contribute to their volume, *The Feminist Memoir Project*, but it is noteworthy that she was one of the feminist activists whose story the editors hoped to include.[55]

Susan Weidman Schneider: *Lilith*—Beyond Superwoman, "Doctor, . . . Tightrope Walker, Challah Baker, . . . Zionist Stalwart"

"How would you like to be involved with a Jewish feminist magazine?" Aviva Cantor asked Susan Weidman Schneider, then a young mother who was writing freelance for *Hadassah Magazine* and other magazines. "I sort of ran with it," Schneider recalls.[56] An English major who had graduated from Brandeis a decade earlier, Schneider had spent her academic career looking at English literature written by men. Cantor and Schneider, with editor-writers Batya Bauman, Susan Dworkin, Amy Stone, Ethel Fenig, Eleanor Faust-Levy, and the late Elenore Lester, met at the second National Conference on Jewish Women at the McAlpin to plan a publication that would give voice to Jewish women. Schneider credits Cantor with the original idea but believes that the "conversation of a collective" has sustained *Lilith*, the magazine they created, for over forty years. Schneider and Cantor jointly served as *Lilith*'s editors for a decade, but when differences between them could not be resolved,

Cantor left the magazine and Schneider continued as executive editor. Schneider says that even when people tell her "you are Lilith," the magazine still seems to her to be a collective.[57]

At the time of *Lilith*'s launch in 1976, the Jewish press, almost entirely led by men, rejected or belittled the nascent feminist movement. Equally distressing to Schneider was the fact that the mainstream feminist press "scorned Jewish women's issues as parochial or, worse, antifeminist, because they sprang from [Jewish women's] attachment to a patriarchal religion." Either Jewish women were considered "people of privilege" who had bought into the establishment or who "had not suffered enough" if they identified as Jews. "If this is a religion that treats women like second-class citizens, vote with your feet. Why stay connected to a religion that does not appreciate women?"[58] This "parallel marginalization" spurred *Lilith*'s founding group to challenge the negative aspects of Jewish law and popular culture that circumscribed women's lives.[59]

While Schneider believes that her coming to the founding and editorship of *Lilith* was accidental, she acknowledges that her family background shaped her positive Jewish identity and the belief in possibilities for women that put her on the path to Jewish feminism. Schneider was born into a tightly knit Jewish community in Winnipeg, Ontario, in 1944. While well assimilated, Jews made up only 10 percent of the prairie city's population and possessed a significant "rootednesss" in their own culture. On both sides of Schneider's family, there was a sense of "being plugged into the important issues of Jewish life."[60]

Schneider's great-grandparents, who settled the family in Saskatchewan Province and farmed there for several years, were Zionists who made aliyah to Israel in 1904. Her mother, born in Winnipeg, grew up speaking Yiddish and acting in the Yiddish theater. Her mother's involvement with Jewish culture passed on to Susan, who grew up "with a tremendous comfort level" with Jewishness and an affirmation of women's capabilities, passions, and interests. Schneider studied at Hebrew school in her Conservative synagogue and had a Friday-night bat mitzvah, not reading from the Torah as boys did, but she felt no difference in the education afforded to girls and boys. Opportunities for girls to participate in youth-group activities laid the groundwork for her later involvements in collective life.

At Brandeis University in the early 1960s, Schneider found a number of additional female role models, including Socialist Zionist author Marie Syrkin of the English department, one of the university's first woman professors. The faculty as a whole respected female students: "there were so many smart women that the professors would have been ridiculous to disparage them." But despite the university's Jewish background, Brandeis was "a very easy place not to be Jewish."[61] Schneider's Jewish identity went underground; she spent time tutoring African American children and becoming involved in early antiwar protests.

Schneider married in 1969, four years after her college graduation, spending a year on a Native American reservation with her husband, Bruce, then a medical student, and another year in Israel. On her return, she wrote about the work-life balance in Israel, which she contrasted favorably to the situation in the U.S. Her articles brought her to the attention of Aviva Cantor, then editing *Hadassah Magazine*, and she got in on the ground floor—or, rather, as she calls it, "the subbasement" floor—of the emerging Jewish feminist magazine project.[62]

Schneider recognized that it was a propitious time to launch a journal reflecting the emergence of Jewish feminism. "As the women's liberation movement has had an increasing appeal for women of all ages and all walks of life," she explained in 1974, "many Jewish women firm in their Jewish identity felt a growing need to apply their new consciousness of themselves as women to their lives as Jews."[63] In addition, changes in traditional attitudes toward women in Judaism were drawing secular women, alienated from Jewish tradition, back to Jewish concerns. They had to confront problematic issues within Judaism but also the double messages and stereotypes they had received throughout their lives relating to education, family life, gender norms, and achievement. *Lilith* emerged two years later as the first publication "exploring the changing roles and expectations of women in the full spectrum of Jewish life."[64] In Schneider's view, "so much energy was emanating from Jewish women's films and music and conferences and liturgies and task forces that we felt we were discovering—or encountering or uncovering—a whole new continent that had been submerged in our collective unconscious."[65] But this material had not been chronicled or transmitted to a wider public.

The first issue of *Lilith* in fall 1976 showcased the multiple angles the magazine would adopt to present Jewish women's achievements and the issues facing them. Schneider described the magazine's first cover as an "artist's version of the Jewish superwoman, who managed to amalgamate almost all possible roles: doctor, server of chicken soup, scholar, tightrope walker, challah baker, incipient mother, Zionist stalwart." The mix prescribed the pattern that the magazine hoped to follow: "challenging how Jewish law shapes women's lives; touching on the ways popular culture articulates images of Jewish women; truth-telling about individual women's lives, inflected by the idea that if we only spoke out loud our deepest realities, all wrongs would be righted." Over time, she believes the magazine came to present not just the superwoman on a tightrope but more nuanced, grounded, and "uncomfortably ambiguous" portraits of the complex lives of Jewish women.[66] The editors put a premium on "midwifing" emerging authors' viewpoints, exerting "horizontal" rather than hierarchical power to encourage a variety of perspectives, including those of Jewish women who had been most marginalized.[67]

Over the magazine's long history, *Lilith* has explored issues of concern to Jewish women and Jewish feminists in both the secular and religious spheres. With a dual mission of engaging feminists in issues of Jewish interest and heightening the feminist consciousness of Jewish women, it has produced hard-hitting examinations of sexism in the Jewish community and offered stories on such diverse topics as feminist Jewish rituals, lesbianism, Ethiopian women in Israel, "Jewish hair," Jewish mothers, Jewish philanthropy, reproductive rights, and much more. *Lilith* also presents fiction, art, and other cultural work by Jewish women, as well as features on political and community events.

Schneider explored the diverse issues of Jewish feminism in her 1984 volume *Jewish and Female*, a comprehensive sourcebook; she has also written on intermarriage and Jewish women's philanthropy.[68] But her primary work has been as executive editor of *Lilith*. She believes that over the four decades of the magazine's existence, despite differences among branches of the Jewish feminist movement—liberal and radical, secular and religious—there has been a "connective tissue," a kind of "elastic band which holds [Jewish women] more loosely or more tightly," depending on the issue or circumstance.[69]

Figure 6.2. Amy Stone and Barbara Taff of *Lilith* magazine demonstrate for the Equal Rights Amendment, August 1977. Courtesy of the Robert D. Farber University Archives & Special Collections Department, Brandeis University.

The Women of Brooklyn Bridge and Chutzpah

The two most important secular Jewish collectives to spawn Jewish feminist groups were New York's Brooklyn Bridge, founded in 1970 and disbanded two years later, and Chutzpah, a Chicago collective that lasted from 1972 to 1981. The women who joined these groups were often less consciously identified as Jews than were Radical Zionist women such as Cantor and some *Lilith* founders. Not knowing where the path would lead, they came to Brooklyn Bridge and Chutzpah to band with others interested in exploring often-inchoate Jewish identities.

Like the Jewish Liberation Project, Brooklyn Bridge and Chutzpah saw themselves as "bringing Left concerns to the Jewish community and Jewish concerns to the Left community." Their views were rooted in a socialist critique of capitalism and political empire building as well as a ruthless critique of the Jewish establishment. Denouncing militarism, imperialism, racism, and sexism within the broader society, they hoped that their focus on the Jewish community would involve "revitalizing and transforming what it meant to be a Jew in America."[70]

Members of both groups recognized that their coming out as Jews had been deeply influenced by the struggles against race and gender oppression of the late 1960s and early 1970s. Chutzpah members Miriam Socoloff and Henry Balser described what they had learned "from the women's, gay, and black liberation movements": "if we do not demand our right to self-determination the Left is not going to acknowledge our right to exist as a Jewish people."[71] The commitment to make themselves into Jewish-identified leftists carried a responsibility to fight against the entwined roots of sexism, elitism, and privilege within Jewish communal and religious institutions. In "Who We Are," written for the magazine *Chutzpah* in the summer of 1973, group members declared, "we oppose reactionary aspects of organized religion; the delegation of women to second class roles; the cult of worship for the checkbook, superficial commitment to civil rights and social action that mask a real racism within the community."[72]

According to Michael Staub's study of post–Cold War Jewish liberalism, Jewish groups such as Brooklyn Bridge and Chutzpah differed from Radical Zionist groups such as the Jewish Liberation Project in the way they combined a traditional version of prophetic Judaism with New Left concerns about diversity. "As Jews we carry a vision rising out of our tradition of a radical and inclusive social justice," ran an editorial in the inaugural issue of the *Brooklyn Bridge*. The statement articulated strong Jewish pride but at the same time made common cause with racial and other minorities."[73]

Opposition to the New Left's attitudes toward Israel and the Jewish establishment helped to bring radicals together. They had grown furious "at expressions of total support for Arab states and Palestinian guerillas in their call for Israel's destruction." "Reluctantly, we realized that many leftists we had worked with closely showed no awareness of Jewish oppression and no concern for Jewish survival. We realized that this was anti-semitism and decided to fight it. We would oppose persecution of Jews and work for the survival, self-determination, and cultural flowering of our people. We would maintain the best values and skills of the Left and the counter-culture. Now *that* was Chutzpah!"[74]

These views motivated Chutzpah members to create a new politics of engagement around Jewish issues and to establish a community where they enjoyed the support of like-minded Jewish radicals. In an unusual step, the entire collective started group therapy together in 1973, seeking to reject artificial dichotomies such as "therapy and politics" as well as "Jewish/leftist, gay/Jewish, pro-Israel/anti-imperialist" splits.[75] A few years later, six couples moved into a communal house, where they raised their growing families together for nine years. Though the collective officially disbanded in 1981, participants met informally for another three decades.[76]

Despite shared values of group members, women in Brooklyn Bridge and Chutzpah found it challenging to navigate a place for themselves as Jewish feminists. Cheryl Moch of Brooklyn Bridge, Susan Schechter and Maralee Gordon of Chutzpah, and Ruth Balser of Boston, who also published in its newspaper, illuminated the problems of being Jewish and female on the radical Left in the 1970s.

Cheryl Moch: "We Are Coming Home"

The New York Jewish Women's Group, formed in 1970 out of the gender-mixed Brooklyn Bridge collective, was the first Jewish women's consciousness-raising group on record. A few of the initial dozen members had participated in the emerging women's liberation movement and began to see a link between the internalized oppressions they experienced as Jews and as women. Their group examined the ways the women had masked or denied their identities as Jews, embarrassed by what they viewed as Jewish privilege, the politics of the Jewish establishment, or the low status of Jews within their social worlds. In an article called "Self-Hate" in the first issue of *Brooklyn Bridge*, New Yorker Cheryl Moch described her identity confusions: "I knew . . . that being a

Jewish girl from Flatbush was not the hippest, most right-on thing to be. I tortured myself . . . trying to create a false identity."[77]

Moch had been a founder of the Brooklyn Bridge collective, along with her husband and Lee Weiner, the so-called quiet member of the notorious Chicago Seven. When Moch, then twenty, heard about Weiner's idea for a Jewish collective, she was intrigued. For Moch, who had a secular upbringing in Brooklyn, such a group would provide the opportunity to explore her Jewish roots while still participating in "overthrowing the government."[78]

Moch was born in 1950 in East Flatbush. Her parents were neither synagogue members nor Zionists; being Jewish meant enjoying the ubiquitous delicatessens, not being religious. "My mother didn't receive any religious education whatsoever," Moch told me, "so she had nothing to pass on. We didn't learn anything." Her father's family had come to the U.S. as Reform Jews in the 1860s; he knew no Yiddish and had little cultural heritage. His uncles had married Catholics and raised their children in that faith. While her maternal grandfather was religious, he held his faith privately and did not draw his grandchildren in.

Despite the family's assimilation, Cheryl's older and younger sister became interested in Judaism. Although Cheryl's mother found synagogue "boring," she sent all three girls to Hebrew school; only the youngest sister stayed, until she was "turned off" by the gender inequalities of the liturgy and social events.[79] Moch's older sister went to Israel after the Six-Day War, intending to make aliyah. Already a leftist, a "major hippie," and married by the age of nineteen, Moch, then traveling through Europe with her husband, went to Israel to say good-bye to her sister and wound up staying for six months on a kibbutz in the Negev. It was a formative experience. "You can't go to Israel in 1969 and not fall in love with it," Moch recalled.[80] She began to ask herself questions about Israel and the Jewish past. When she returned to the U.S. to complete her last two years at City College in New York, she started taking courses in a program in Jewish studies that had just begun under the direction of Rabbi Israel (Yitz) Greenberg and the noted Holocaust survivor, author, and educator Elie Wiesel.

Moch framed her puzzlement about her own Jewish identity within courses taught by charismatic teachers and enthusiastically joined Weiner and other radicals in starting Brooklyn Bridge. The name was a "metaphor, a symbol," she said. "We wanted to organize a Jewish community" in ways that imitated the Black Panthers or communities organized by Puerto Ricans. "Jews would have the Brooklyn Bridge. . . . Jews had left Brooklyn, and now they were coming back to their roots." The collective announced in the first issue of its newsletter, "We have been running away too long, cutting ourselves off from our roots too long, and that has stunted us. We are coming home to Brooklyn . . . to begin building a new world, and to be Jewish."[81]

Despite the camaraderie that Moch and the women of Brooklyn Bridge shared with their male friends, they recoiled from the sexism on the Jewish Left and sought to discover themselves as Jewish women. They describe the difficulties of the process in *Brooklyn Bridge*: "We sat in a circle, forced smiles on our faces. Twelve women with histories of struggling to be free, to be whole—in the movement, in women's liberation." But it seemed "outlandish" to get together to talk about what it meant to be a Jewish woman: "it hurt us, it scared us to talk about it; we lapsed into silence again and again." As women—"white, middle-class, neurotics"—they were "anything but Jewish." The "Jewish woman went to Hadassah meetings," which they themselves were trying to escape, along with the "hypocrisy, the lifestyle, the ineffectual pain": "Why were we walking back into it now?"[82]

But gradually the women began to talk about the issues that brought them together: "anti-semitic slurs, . . . emotional turmoil, the need to be someplace that belonged to you, the recognition of the oppression our mothers and fathers took out on us and tried to warn us about. We felt Jewish, we just weren't sure what that meant." Puzzling especially about the female dimension of their Jewish identities, they rejected Philip Roth's stereotypical "Sophie Portnoy" and "New York-intellectual-radical-hip" in equal parts. Then, they said, "we unembarrassed each other of our experiences as Jewess—olive-skinned, dark-haired, temptress, bitch. And of Miami Beach Jews with too much jewelry and too loud voices. Those were the stereotypes that had scared us all our lives, that made us all quake when we told others we were in a Jewish women's group." Eventually, after a "minor class war" that occurred when the "oppression of a doctor's daughter sounded trivial to that of the taxicab driver's daughter," the women began to understand what divided them. "Discovering our oppression as Jewish women and of finding some way to free ourselves. Warmth and joy grew between us." They were ready to combat the "male chauvinism of Jewish men" but also to affirm who they were as Jewish women. Although they knew they would remain in the U.S. and fight for Jewish women here, they even talked about "going to Jerusalem."[83]

Founding the New York Jewish Women's Group, these radical feminists began to explore the "ethnic . . . Jewish issues" that had not been touched in the regular women's movement, despite its strong representation of Jewish women: the "self-hatred, . . . hair, . . . the women having nose jobs." The group created pamphlets on these issues, and its members, eleven of whom had come out as lesbians before the group disbanded in 1972, penned articles for *Brooklyn Bridge* and the women's liberation paper *RAT*, the first signs within the women's movement of a new Jewish-identified radical feminism.[84] Some may have contributed to the commentary in *RAT* that so enraged Aviva Cantor.

Employed at the American Jewish Congress at the time as a youth organizer, Cheryl Moch played a significant role in organizing the National Feminist Jewish Conferences of 1973 and 1974, and she became a founding board member of the short-lived Jewish Feminist Organization. But she was disappointed in the religious direction that Jewish feminism took after the conferences and discouraged because it seemed that the Jewish organizational structure was not about to be radicalized. Moving on to work in the arts as photographer and playwright, she "left the community."[85]

Ruth Balser: "Liberation of a Jewish Radical"

Ruth Balser became active in civil rights and peace groups starting in high school and continuing when she went off to college at the University of Rochester in 1965, where she helped to form an SDS chapter that opposed the war in Vietnam and supported the rights of African Americans. After college, Balser moved to Boston, where she joined Bread and Roses, living in a women's commune with her sister, Diane. At the suggestion of her brother, Henry, she wrote an article for the Chutzpah paper about being a Jewish radical in the early 1970s, which appeared later in Chutzpah's anthology.

Balser's piece strikingly articulated the difficulties of reconciling feminist and Jewish sensibilities. "Being Jewish was one of the major reasons for becoming active" in the civil rights and antiwar movements, Balser wrote. Whether waged against American Indians, blacks, or the Vietnamese, "genocide is genocide," and as a Jew, she felt "personally threatened by it." Yet in college, she was teased for occasionally going to services with relatives; as a good Marxist, she should have known that religion was the "opiate of the masses." She learned "to repress a part of [her] identity that had always been so important."[86]

Balser determined to "no longer devote so much energy to a movement dedicated to the liberation of everyone but" her. So she became active in women's liberation. But "sadly and painfully," Balser learned, "while so much else about me was supported by the women's movement, my Jewishness was still unacceptable. There was a lot of talk about the high percentage of Jews in the movement but that statement was always presented either accusingly or jokingly. It was never dealt with in a way that might have helped us to understand it or that might have helped us to feel good." Balser wrote of other women's condemnation of an "aggressive, outspoken, and at least superficially self-assured" style of behavior that they considered "oppressive and elitist." Commonly associated with Jewish women, this style seemed an outcome of Jewish women's need to survive. But the women's group members rejected it in favor of more middle-class, WASP-like values: "be quiet, be polite, be restrained. I, as a loudmouth, Jewish woman, began to feel there was no place for me."[87]

Balser was also concerned with some feminists' celebration of Palestinian militant Leila Khaled, who hijacked a passenger jet in 1969. Like Diane, who had protested when her women's commune hung up posters of Khaled, Ruth believed that supporting anti-Zionism and the violent methods of the Palestine Liberation Organization (PLO) could stir up anti-Semitism. As the worldwide campaign to support Soviet refuseniks in their struggle to emigrate from the USSR unfolded, the issue of Soviet Jewry became another difficult topic for her. At a women's meeting, when Ruth pointed out that the group "supported every oppressed group in the world" except Soviet Jewry, one of her "so-called sisters" told her that the struggle for Soviet Jewry was "reactionary."[88]

Balser recalled a major struggle at one large women's meeting when some members of a Jewish study group, enthusiastic about exploring their individual and collective pasts, were called out by other women's liberationists on the ground that "Jewish activity made the women's movement appear 'Zionist,' despite the fact that [the women] knew nothing of [the study group's] positions on the Middle East." The study group was told that any focus on Jewishness made it "appear that the women's movement supported the existence of a radical Jewish movement—and they personally couldn't support this since any such movement was potentially, if not already, racist and reactionary."[89]

Balser's concerns about the problems of Jewish identity within the women's liberation movement were colored by her views about anti-Semitism, which she saw as quite prevalent; "anyone Jewish" could recount painful experiences. When her campus SDS group performed antiwar actions, for example, it received anti-Semitic phone calls. Once, when she was marching down Massachusetts Avenue in Cambridge protesting the U.S. blockade of North Vietnam, "an MIT student opened up his window and unfurled a ten-foot banner with a swastika, apparently in protest against their demonstration." In "academic" discussions, she was told it was the Jews' fault for being persecuted: "we set it up by insisting on being different!"[90]

Like Cantor and Moch, Balser regarded assimilation as a significant problem for Jewish women radicals. "In the United States, being different is a crime. Therefore we get nose jobs, we straighten our hair, we change our names, we forget the language of our grandparents. In short, we hate ourselves. We hate ourselves to fulfill the American Dream, but that kind of a dream is a nightmare." Because fighting assimilation meant declaring Jewish women's difference as Jews, an unwelcome act within the radical Left and the women's movement, Balser considered a separate Jewish movement. A "humane democratic movement which is also self-consciously Jewish" could make the Jewish world more open while providing a countervailing force to the Left's apparent rejection of Jewish-identified issues and values. Above all, such a movement could help Jewish radicals "feel proud and loving" of themselves and each other.[91]

Balser sought opportunities to come together with Jewish women, participating in teaching a course on Jewish women at the Cambridge women's center and attending the first National Conference on Jewish Women at the McAlpin in 1973. She went on to receive a Ph.D. in clinical psychology from NYU and to a career as mental health professional. Balser has been a member of the Massachusetts State Legislature since 1999, working to advance human rights, women's rights, and other progressive causes. She helped create a women's empowerment project for the Boston-Haifa Exchange and has found other ways to bring together her lifelong interests in feminist and Jewish issues.[92]

Susan Schechter: "The Most Joyous Gathering"

Even among other women's liberationists with uncertain Jewish identities, Susan Schechter's ambivalence was striking. A feminist psychotherapist in Chicago who became part of the Chutzpah collective in 1975, Schechter grew up in St. Louis and went to Washington University. The mentoring she received from friends, relatives, and a particular rabbi became a source of strength and fostered a commitment to social activism.[93] Yet from the time she was a child in Sunday school, the knowledge of Jewish persecution had left her feeling "terrorized"; she pretended to be anything else—Greek, Italian, Spanish—until she came to terms with the "psychic complications" of being Jewish.[94]

Schechter, in her twenties, still believed that Jews were an "oppressed group," but now she considered that a major threat to her identity came from the American Left, which she saw as increasingly anti-Semitic. On a Fourth of July march to protest U.S. imperialism and racism in the early 1970s, she was afraid she would be "thrown out" because of her pro-Israel views. "Why do so few of you say that Jews, like Palestinians, have a right to self-determination?" she queried movement colleagues.[95]

On Fourth of July weekend in 1975, Schechter and Maralee Gordon of Chutzpah attended the National Conference on Socialist Feminism at Antioch College in Yellow Springs, Ohio, where close to two thousand women came together to turn women's liberation analysis "into action" by building a broad-based movement. Concerned about the problems they encountered in defining themselves as socialist feminists and as Jews, Schechter and Gordon convened a Jewish women's caucus. When the workshop notice did not appear on the listings of small group meetings, Schechter suspected the omission was deliberate and might have been "anti-semitic." Some women thought that a meeting for Jewish women was "ridiculous." "I'll go to the caucus just to get a good laugh," said one. But twenty women showed up; more said they would have come if they had known about the meeting. An "enormous sense of solidarity" and common themes emerged: "the fear that affirming a Jewish identity tainted our credibility with the Left; our concern for Israel and a sense that pro-Israeli sentiment would be attacked as racist-Zionist-imperialist; our disappointments with the organized Jewish community and with the Left."[96] Previously intimidated and isolated, several of the women "came out Jewish" for the first time.

Schechter believed that it was essential for the movement as a whole, and not just Jewish women, "to recognize the particular oppression of Jews."[97] The caucus distributed to the conference a "beginning statement" focused on the women's feelings of discomfort within the movement, citing the difficulty of declaring their positive identities as Jews in the context of the women's and socialist movements, as well as their determination to fight anti-Semitism "and all forms of racist domination." The statement mentioned the class position of Jews as an issue that needed to be clarified and revised, as did ideas about Zionism. The caucus had discussed the fact that while stereotypes of wealthy Jews abounded, few socialist feminists knew much about working-class Jews.[98]

Despite the exhilaration of being together, Schechter "sensed that everyone was scared. Thoughts of being hissed at for affirming Israel's right to exist or laughed at for 'making a big deal over being Jewish'" made her "tremendously uncomfortable." But Jews' and non-Jews' response to the statement was generally positive and respectful. Schechter felt excited to have taken a stance as a Jew and viewed the Jewish women's caucus as "the most joyous gathering" in which she had participated. However brief its existence, the caucus enabled her to become more self-assured in talking about Jewish issues within the women's movement, though she still felt "defensive and fearful." But now, she said, "instead of withdrawing, I keep talking."[99]

Schechter went home determined to follow up on this positive moment. With Maralee Gordon, she started a study group to explore issues raised by the Jewish women's caucus: anti-Semitism, Zionism, and class differences in the women's movement. She also put together a mailing list that included Chicago-area Jewish feminists and other emerging leaders in the Jewish feminist movement. Strikingly, it contains the names of two Jewish leaders of the women's liberation movement who had not been publicly identified with Jewish feminism: Shulamith Firestone and Ellen Willis. Schechter may have believed that the two women would be interested in the issues raised by the Jewish women who attended the caucus they organized at the socialist feminist conference, suspecting an affinity between these leaders of the broader women's liberation movement and those moving toward a Jewish feminist identification.

Yet Schechter found it difficult to bring her Jewish and leftist identities into harmony. At the end of the year, she wrote an article for *Chutzpah* in which she acknowledged the "double binds"—the "paradoxical and maddening, i.e., mutually contradictory sets of messages"—that she experienced as a Jewish leftist feminist. Her enemies were both "real and imagined"; external oppression had "merged into the internal." Anti-Semitism existed, and it was necessary to confront the real enemies of the Jewish people; but how much of the problem could be attributed to her own shame, self-consciousness, and confusion about who she was? Despite the closeness she felt with other Jews as they explored their identities and culture, Schechter confessed that "it still does not make up for the grief": "Sometimes I say to myself, 'Who needs all this pain and suffering? Who wants to identify with all of this'? . . . Enough of sadness, rage, and terror." Just as she did not want to admit her Jewish identity as a child and pretended to be something else, even now, she acknowledged, "sometimes I still don't."[100]

Schechter's struggles to come to terms with her Jewish identity are especially interesting in light of her professional work with victims of domestic abuse. At the time of her involvement with Chutzpah, Schechter served as the director of women's services at the Chicago Loop YWCA, working with rape victims and battered women, and was responsible for creating the first shelter for abused women in the city. In 1982, she published her groundbreaking book *Women and Male Violence: The Visions and Struggles of the Battered Women's Movement*, a history and analysis of early efforts against domestic violence.[101]

Schechter's work on this issue in fact derived from her association with the Chicago Women's Liberation Union School—the pioneering organization started by the "Gang of Four" and their associates. Read-ing Virginia Woolf's *A Room of One's Own* in her first class at the school was one of many revelatory moments in CWLU courses "on every-thing from literature to car repair to socialist feminist theory," Schech-ter recalled. Because of the CWLU, she went to work with the Chicago Abused Women's Coalition, organizing the first shelter in Chicago and giving speeches and writing about violence against women. "Without the Women"s Liberation Union and the larger feminist movement sur-rounding it," she wrote, "*Women and Male Violence* would not exist."[102]

A decade after *Women and Male Violence*, Schechter and journal-ist Ann Jones wrote *When Love Goes Wrong: What to Do When You Can't Do Anything Right*, a self-help guide for battered women.[103] When Schechter and her husband, Allen Steinberg, moved to Boston in the late 1990s, she started AWAKE (Advocacy for Women and Children in Emergencies), the first domestic-violence program in a children's hospital and the first fruit of her attempts to link child-protective and domestic-violence systems. Before her death from cancer in 2004, she had done much to accomplish that goal.

Schechter's leadership in the movement revolutionized institutional practices while empowering abused women by strengthening grass-roots activism; she put a premium on women speaking and acting for themselves, rather than through professionals, and worked to enable them to develop the courage they would need to fight tough battles against their abusers and the system that perpetuated their victimhood. Her strategies shaped the early battered women's movement, and col-leagues credit her vision for many of its significant achievements over several decades.[104] It is hard to imagine Susan Schechter, who had been my neighbor and friend in Boston, as afraid, "terribly alone and unpro-tected," even "terrorized," as she had once felt about her own Jewish identity. (Later in her life, when she moved with her family to Iowa, she felt much less conflicted about her Jewish identity and became an activ-ist in the local Jewish community.)[105] Perhaps the struggle to overcome her own doubts and fears helped her to empathize with the terrors of abused women and to assist them in overcoming them.

Schechter was acutely aware that shelters were places where the "intersectionality of gender, race, ethnicity, class, and language" came together, as one scholar wrote about her contributions.[106] She worked hard to help residents, staff, and other providers overcome the stereotypes that accompanied this diversity of background, an ongoing struggle that was particularly important to her. This, too, may have been a legacy of her struggle to understand and express her Jewishness in an environment that was often hostile. Women who suffered the indignities of rape and abuse had far more challenging circumstances to confront than she did, but recognizing the inherent importance of multiple heritages and backgrounds was one way to provide them with the dignity and the strength they needed to fight their enemies on the outside as well as their own demons.

Maralee Gordon: "How Do We Break Out of This Situation of Inequality?"

After attending the National Conference on Socialist Feminism with Schechter, Maralee Gordon turned her attention as a radical Jew to breaking down Jewish patriarchy rather than fighting sexism, in its most violent forms, in the broader society. But she shared Schechter's concerns with anti-Semitism in the women's liberation movement.

Gordon, a founding member of Chutzpah, had been active in the Chicago radical movement before she recognized a need to affiliate with Jewish peers. She grew up in the suburban community of Glencoe, Illinois, across the street from a synagogue, where the family went to Friday-night services. Gordon found them dry and boring compared to the active Judaism she came to know during her years at a Jewish camp as camper and counselor. This experience framed her vision of Jewish community and became a driving force in her life choices. Born in the late 1940s, she said, "the Jewish came first because there was no 'feminist' when I was growing up."[107] But as she matured, her discovery of Judaism's patriarchal attitudes toward women threatened this primary identity.

Gordon went to Brandeis, where she took courses in Jewish education. Graduating in 1970, her time there overlapped with the intense days of the student and antiwar protest movements. Gordon organized the Jewish Activists League, a campus group that picketed the national convention of the Council of Jewish Federations and Welfare in Boston to protest its funding priorities.[108]

Disillusioned with the Jewish establishment, Gordon gravitated toward leftist activism. After college, she worked on the *Chicago Seed*, an underground newspaper, and lived in a women's commune. Wanting a Jewish community, she was also drawn to a new radical Jewish group in Chicago, Am Chai, but after a year of meetings, she found herself uncomfortable in the male-dominated group, where she was not taken as seriously as her male counterparts. The situation was different at the *Chicago Seed*, where the men seemed more willingly to listen to women. In December 1971, Gordon and the women of Am Chai began to meet to raise their own consciousness, and although they came from different backgrounds (some Jewishly knowledgeable, some not) and proposed different strategies (study or activism), they found common ground in identifying the subordination of women as a key element in Jewish tradition, impacting Jews "who never set foot inside a synagogue" as well as the most religious ones. At the beginning, they were essentially a consciousness-raising "rap group," talking about "Jewish mothers, monogamy, how one can be Jewish without following the traditional oppressive roles, and having children—single or married."[109] The group included both gay and straight women.

Despite Gordon's need for Jewish community, Judaism's sexist message threatened her Jewish identity. "If a choice were necessary between "second-class Jew or full-fledged human being," Gordon wrote in *Chutzpah* in 1973, she would not hesitate: "I would not hesitate to preserve and maintain my strength and dignity as a woman, even if it meant sacrificing my identity as a Jew."[110] At the same time, she acknowledged that it was Judaism and Jewish culture, especially its heritage of "social justice and messianism," which inspired her radical politics. As a Jewish feminist who wanted to give equal weight to both parts of her identity, Gordon, like Schechter, felt trapped in a double bind. "How do we break out of this situation of inequality, this situation of women's lives being controlled by men's culture, without abandoning the very culture itself?" she asked.[111]

In the aftermath of the Ohio Socialist Feminist Conference, Gordon co-founded the Jewish feminist caucus and study group with Susan Schechter. But she did not find serious conflict between women's movement ideology and her Jewish ties in Chicago. The Chicago Women's Liberation Union accepted her courses on women in the Bible and women in Judaism at its Women's Liberation School. Chicago-area Jewish feminists held one of the first women's seders in 1972. Gordon and other Chicago Jewish feminists edited *Lilith's Rib*, an offprint newsletter that circulated from 1973 to 1975, its purpose to put Jewish feminists in touch with each other. Its very first issue contained Aviva Cantor's "Jewish Women's Haggada."

The CWLU, the Jewish women's study group, the Chutzpah collective, and *Lilith's Rib* made a great deal of difference as Gordon continued to struggle to reconcile the varied aspects of her identity. "*Chutzpah* was looking at the Jewish world and at the world from a leftist perspective, looking at anti-Semitism in the world, looking at anti-Semitism on the left, looking at strong Jewish identity, . . . looking at class consciousness in terms of the Jewish community." Chutzpah's women were examining the subordinate place of women within Jewish culture and religion. With these communities helping her to find her way, Gordon could proclaim, "I have finally come to terms with my identity. . . . I feel positive about being a Jewish woman within a historical and cultural perspective. It's where I focus my political energy in terms of socialist politics and feminist organizing."[112]

But it was a different story when it came to religion and the Jewish "way of life"; there Gordon felt "bog[ged] down." She continued her childhood habit of synagogue worship, but it took all her self-control not to run out in "feminist frustration." Though drawn to the idea of becoming a rabbi, starting a *havurah*, or taking a role in the world of Jewish education, she felt that "anything enmeshed with religious Judaism is so enmeshed with patriarchy" that she could go no further. Here, too, women working with each other to create a "female-affirming" space within Judaism would be necessary in order to work for equality within the tradition and to develop "quality and substance."[113] Reforms in language, liturgy, and ritual were essential to make Judaism into a tradition that women could embrace. Jewish women needed "to tell each other what it means to be self-determined Jewish women, to give each other support, . . . and to celebrate together [their] Jewish womanhood."[114]

Just as Gordon did not want to choose between her feminism and Judaism, neither did she see a strict dividing line between the secular and religious. In the next few decades, as a wife and mother of three, she became involved in Jewish education, trying to reform and democratize local synagogues and to eliminate patriarchal elements. By the end of the 1990s, she acknowledged that her passion lay on the other side of the pulpit, and she entered a nontraditional rabbinical seminary, benefiting from the numerous reforms made by groups of Jewish women who had done what she hoped for—create a feminist revolution within Judaism. In 2001, some forty years after the founding of the Chutzpah collective and just about an equal time since the ordination of the first female rabbi in 1972, Gordon became a rabbi.

* * *

Gordon's path differed from some of the other women discussed in this chapter, who did not veer from the secular course around which they united as Jewish feminists in the 1970s and 1980s. For others, secular or religious motivations could be paramount at different times in their lives. All of the women found common cause in their beliefs in gender equality and women's freedom and their attempt to express their feminism as part of Jewish life. For some, the journey from Jewish activist to identified Jewish feminist came relatively smoothly after their awakenings within the women's movement. For those who had little background as Jews or who had deliberately rejected the Jewish establishment, the journey to Jewish feminism was more uneven. They had to get to know themselves as Jews as well as feminist activists, confronting negative images about Jews and Israel that were then rampant on the left. They also needed to address the internalized prejudice that had led many of them to distance themselves from the distasteful stereotypes about Jewish girls and women with which they had grown up.

As opposed to the women's liberationists who dedicated themselves to the attainment of universal women's and human rights, the secular Jewish feminists concentrated their efforts on the particularities of Jewish experience, fighting assimilation as well as patriarchy. On occasion, this led them to face off with women's liberationists with whom they had much in common as well as male comrades. Aviva Cantor's denunciation of the anti-Zionist position of the *RAT* editors and the painful, revealing *Chutzpah* writings of Susan Schechter, Ruth Balser, and Maralee Gordon expose the bumpy course of what later in the decade was expressed as identity politics: the coming together around aspects of group identity that could divide women from each other. The stories in this chapter record the sorrow and anger Jewish feminists experienced during the initial phases of the politics of difference within the women's movement.

To declare oneself as a Jewish feminist within the folds of the radical feminist movement in the 1970s was not easy. It often meant grappling with negative associations about Jewish women and all Jews and speaking out against anti-Semitism and anti-Zionism. The secular Jewish feminists were among the first feminists to do so. Even though the Jewish Feminist Organization ended quickly, the common denominator that joined feminist and Jewish identities was realized in *Lilith* magazine and other writings by Jewish feminists, as well as some of the collectives that began in this period. Over time, the perspectives shaped in these new organizations and writings inaugurated significant changes in the Jewish community. Their entanglement with the radical feminist movement is another aspect of the interesting but little-known history of late twentieth-century Jewish feminist activism.

7

"For God's Sake, Comb Your Hair!
You Look like a Vilde Chaye"

Jewish Lesbian Feminists Explore the Politics of Identity

Lesbian feminism emerged as a significant outgrowth of radical feminism by 1970. Lesbians were dissatisfied with their invisibility within radical feminism and with being considered "threats" to the liberal women's movement and created a distinct politics, developing theories, publications, organizations, and coalitions to promote their agendas. They were interested not only in cultural and lifestyle changes but also in the broad transformation of social relations, patriarchal culture, and gender and sexual norms. Their innovations in theory and practice signaled new directions in the radical feminist movement and resulted in lasting changes.[1]

Just as feminism had become a portal into religious Judaism for previously unidentified Jewish feminists, lesbianism became another channel into a deepening Jewishness for women alienated from their Jewish identities and interested in exploring woman-woman relationships. For Jewish women, it was a particularly useful anchor, as Melanie Kaye/ Kantrowitz explained: "As Jewish women, we are often blamed for our strength. When I became a lesbian and no longer had to care what men, Jewish or otherwise, thought of me, I came into my power. As a lesbian I learned fast and ecstatically that women liked me to be strong. I began to enjoy, build, and relax into my full self."[2] These identities developed over time, as lesbian feminist activists became aware of their Jewishness in the context of a lesbian feminist movement that, to their surprise, often harbored anti-Jewish feelings.

Jewish lesbian groups began to coalesce in the mid- and late 1970s. One of the first groups came together spontaneously at the Michigan Womyn's Music Festival in 1976—"somebody just called a session and said, 'let's get together as Jewish lesbians.'" Grassroots groups also formed in Los Angeles, San Francisco, New York, Boston, and Chicago, as well as in such smaller cities as Madison, Wisconsin, and Ithaca, New York. In addition to Di Vilde Chayes (Yiddish: the wild beasts), the subject of this chapter, the movement included such colorfully named groups as Needless Worry, Nashim (Hebrew: women), Dyke Shabbas, the Balebustehs (Yiddish: the bossy women), and Di Yiddishe Shvestern (Yiddish: the Jewish sisters).[3]

Jewish lesbians shared many commonalities with nonlesbian Jewish feminists, although the struggle of Jewish lesbians to be accepted among straight Jewish communities involved particularly fierce struggles. Sometimes Jewish lesbian and straight women came into direct conflict, yet both were engaged in exploring the personal and political meanings of linked oppressions. "In proper Jewish tradition," Evelyn Torton Beck explained in the introduction to her important 1982 book *Nice Jewish Girls: A Lesbian Anthology*, "we ask many questions. It is our way of coming to know. . . . How are we, as Jews, different from each other? . . . How have we internalized myths and stereotypes, particularly about Jewish women? What similarities do we share with lesbians from other ethnic groups?" The desire of Jewish lesbians to be "all of who we are" in a world that was homophobic and anti-Semitic was the common theme of the book.[4]

Di Vilde Chayes, formed by Beck and half a dozen other Jewish lesbians in 1982, provided a safe space within which members could discuss difficult topics regarding Jewish lesbian identity. Though it lasted less than two years, Di Vilde Chayes explicitly confronted anti-Semitism, within and outside the radical feminist movement. Its seven members, who were writers, editors, and publishers, lived in dispersed locations, so they could not gather regularly. Yet they became a support group for each other as they grappled with the interrelated issues of Jewish/lesbian identity and anti-Semitism. The chapter focuses on the Jewish stories of five collective members—Evelyn Torton Beck, Gloria Greenfield, Irena Klepfisz, Melanie Kaye/Kantrowitz, and Adrienne Rich—whose public writings during this period provide context for Di Vilde Chayes' ideas. Bernice Mennis and Nancy Bereano were the other group members.[5]

Di Vilde Chayes was closely associated with *Nice Jewish Girls*, which contained contributions from all the collective members with the exception of Bereano. The anthology "grew out of the political ferment and activism of developing the Jewish lesbian feminist consciousness," Beck recalled. At the time, Jews were silent about homosexuality; according to Beck, "the juxtaposition of Jew and lesbian was so unthinkable it seemed absurd." When Beck's mother's tried to broach the idea of her lesbianism to her rabbi, he replied that it could not possibly be true. That is why the title of the anthology was so important, Beck believes. "We were Nice Jewish Girls AND lesbians, which of course made us NOT NICE."[6] "The entire anthology is an act of resistance," Gloria Greenfield wrote in a cover blurb for the book.

Nice Jewish Girls benefited from the encouragement of the Jewish lesbian community, and in turn, it became a major impetus to creating and nurturing a Jewish lesbian consciousness within the lesbian feminist movement.[7] The book sold ten thousand copies in less than a year and made an enormous impact on the women's community. Moving beyond Ashkenazi and US boundaries, it included contributions from Rachel Wahba, a Sephardic/Arabic Jewish immigrant, and Savina Teubal, of Syrian descent, who grew up in Argentina, and from Marcia Freedman and Shelly Horwitz, Americans who had made aliyah to Israel.[8]

In Beck's preface to the second edition (1989), she spoke of the lively discussions the book had generated. Several consciousness-raising lesbian groups were established in its wake, and a Jewish lesbian newsletter, *Shehechiatnu* (a feminized version of the Jewish blessing *shehechianu*), was put out in different cities following the book's publication. Non-Jewish women also began to form groups to deal with their own anti-Semitism.[9]

Some Jewish lesbian feminists had already played notable roles in the lesbian and Jewish feminist movements. Photographer Joan Biren (or JEB), co-founder of the Furies, an early 1970s lesbian collective, published her early work documenting the lesbian movement in the group's newspaper. Batya Bauman, co-founder of *Lilith*, wrote a piece in the magazine's 1976 inaugural issue linking her lesbian, feminist, and Jewish identities.[10]

Autonomous groups of Jewish feminists, lesbian feminists, and Jewish lesbian feminists came to function within and alongside the general feminist movement. Paralleling the views of religious Jewish feminists, Melanie Kaye/Kantrowitz explained that the collective was a natural, authentic form for Jewish women because in Jewish life, "the community, not the individual, is the unit of solution." "Judaism specifically incorporates time for each individual to make private prayer, allows for a huge range of debate and disagreement. But one is not truly Jewish alone: one is Jewish in community with others. Problems are conceived of in collective terms, and solutions likewise."[11]

For the women of Di Vilde Chayes, the invisibility of Jewish women within the feminist movement was a consequence of the movement's conscious universalism. In a piece for *Womannews* in 1981, Irena Klepfisz suggested another reason: low self-esteem led Jewish women to internalize anti-Semitism, contributing to their silence about their Jewish roots. Klepfisz remarked on the large proportion of Jewish women in the feminist movement and their fear in naming themselves as Jews. For these women, "the number of Jews active in the movement is not a source of pride, but rather a source of embarrassment, something to be played down, something to be minimized."[12]

Klepfisz and other Di Vilde Chayes members saw the invisibility of Jewish women as lesbians and as feminists as a major factor in what they named as anti-Semitism. By linking homophobia and anti-Semitism and urging lesbian Jewish feminists to make themselves visible as Jews and as lesbians, the collective raised consciousness about the multiple forms of discrimination to which Jewish women were subject. Participation in the group emboldened them to create new platforms of expression and take public stances. Members began to speak about their Jewish beliefs and values. Such influential writings as those contained in Kaye/Kantrowitz and Klepfisz's anthology *The Tribe of Dina* came out of their collaboration.[13]

For Jewish lesbians, becoming visible as Jews and becoming visible as lesbians were linked processes. "Jewish invisibility is a symptom of anti-Semitism as surely as lesbian invisibility is a symptom of homophobia," Beck wrote in *Nice Jewish Girls*.[14] The alternative—hiding in the closet— led to oppression. Yet Beck believed that it was much more fearful to declare herself a Jew in lesbian circles than a lesbian in the Jewish world. This was striking, because for Beck as for Klepfisz, child survivors of the Holocaust, Jewishness was a core identity. Such an inbred sense of Jewish selfhood was not the case for Kaye/Kantrowitz and Adrienne Rich, who grew up as assimilated Jews. Though identity struggles of Di Vilde Chayes members varied, for all, coming out as Jews within the feminist movement paralleled their claiming sexual identities. Understanding marginalization in one venue promoted greater understanding of other displacements.

But marginality had its limits. As Beck wrote in *Nice Jewish Girls*, "if you tried to claim both identities—publicly and politically—you were exceeding the limits of what was permitted to the marginal. You were in danger of being perceived as ridiculous—and threatening."[15] Acknowledging multiple oppressions multiplied the risks of embarrassment and vilification. "It is a radical act to be willing to identify publicly as a Jew and a lesbian," Beck declared. Rich called it "dangerous."[16]

Evelyn Torton Beck: "Making Ourselves Visible as Jews"

"I was born in 1933 in Vienna, Austria, the year Hitler came to power; his shadow shadowed me." So Evelyn Torton Beck began the narrative of her life as a Jewish lesbian feminist at the NYU "Women's Liberation and Jewish Identity" conference. The Holocaust framed Beck's early life and memories. Her father, born in Poland, had served in the Austro-Hungarian army, but in 1938, in her presence, he was arrested by two SS men, taken from their home, and sent to Dachau and Buchenwald. Beck's mother, born in Vienna, was proud of the fact that she had stayed in school until sixteen, longer than most girls of her social class. As an Austrian Jew, she felt a sense of social superiority to eastern European Jews, although she married one. So, in a sense, Beck related, "I come from an intermarriage among Jews."[17]

Beck did not have a strong religious education, even though her father, whom she called a "benign patriarch," believed in tradition. Although he was not Orthodox, he went to shul often and observed the holidays, although he did not make them meaningful to his children. Beck's mother, who had little Jewish education, wanted desperately to believe, but the murder of her mother and other family members in the camps made that difficult, if not impossible. Having been raised in patriarchal, anti-Semitic Vienna at the turn of the twentieth century, she was as ambivalent about being a Jew as she was about being a woman. This heritage was passed down to Beck, who continued to battle against the tensions that these identities engendered, but they lessened or even resolved when she became involved in Jewish lesbian feminist activism.[18]

After Beck's father was arrested and sent to the concentration camps, where he was tortured and made to do slave labor for a year, the family was evicted from its home and sent to live in one room in the ghetto. Beck was thrown out of kindergarten, called "dirty Jew," and shunned by her playmates. Within a year, her father was inexplicably released, perhaps because of money the Gestapo collected daily from her mother, as it did from all relatives of the imprisoned who could afford it. Beck also thinks her mother may have used her as a kind of bait: "I was very pretty and did not look Jewish. I had green eyes, blond curls," she remembered. "It felt as if she wanted me to smile and kind of flirt with the guards so that maybe they would release my father; and for all I know, it worked."[19]

One day, miraculously, in 1939, her father reappeared. The family was able to get visas to Italy but had to leave Beck's grandmother and other relatives behind. All perished at Auschwitz. The fact that Beck was saved, while her beloved grandmother died, became part of the burden that she brought with her when the family resettled in the United States after a distant relative agreed to take them in.

The family started over in Brooklyn. It was not fun being a "greenhorn," Beck recalled, "wearing only hand-me-down clothes and sitting for hours in clinics, waiting to be served by hospitals that took in poor people." Beck compensated by being an excellent student; she still has an essay she wrote in German titled "I Survived It All by Reading." "I don't know when I first got the idea that all that had happened to my family had anything to do with being Jewish," she said. But she described what seemed likely to her: "The early injustices that I suffered through and observed had everything to do with the way I saw myself as a woman and as a Jew. These experiences . . . fueled my impulse to create a better world that has then formed my entire life, wherever I've been."[20]

In the U.S., Beck's father tried to make a traditional Jew out of her, sending her to afternoon Talmud Torah, but she hated the rabbis' rigidity and quickly dropped out. She preferred the socialist-Yiddishist Shalem Aleichem Folkshule that she next attended, with its vision of a Jewish homeland in a world of peace and its woman teacher. She can still see herself at twelve or thirteen, collecting money for the Jewish National Fund on the subways—hiding in the back, but when train stopped, she would step into the middle and call out in the loudest voice she could muster, "Ladies and gentlemen . . . ," and a plea for donations would follow.[21]

Shortly after arriving in Brooklyn, Beck joined the Socialist Zionist group Hashomer Hatzair, whose idealism had given her a sense of hope. The time there remains a pivotal experience in her life. Israel, not yet a state, was her utopia. "There was a real sense of purpose to what we were doing," she recalled. "I loved Hashomer Hatzair with its vision of equality. We had strong women leaders; we shared our clothing, we shared our money, we also shared cigarettes."[22] And she loved dancing all night. Beck dreamed of making aliyah to Israel, but her father's Zionism stopped at the thought of his daughter's moving so far away. Later, she became active in a more moderate Zionist group. These early years of Jewish activism shaped her sense of purpose, even though for a time, Jewish identity was no longer central to her life.

Living at home, Beck went to Brooklyn College; she tried the Hillel Society but found the group too "bourgeois" for her Bohemian, prefeminist sensibilities, its Judaism lacking meaning. She quickly married, the expected path even for young rebels. "I was only able to get out of my parental home when I got married," she said, "out of my house into my husband's house." Like her mother, she also "intermarried," but to a red-diaper baby, the son of Jewish communists.[23]

Beck's husband helped her find a scholarship to Yale, where, as a Brooklyn Jew, she felt very alien, but she completed her master's degree. It was at Williams College, where her husband took a job because she had unexpectedly gotten pregnant, that she first encountered WASP anti-Semitism—the powers that be lodged the only other Jew on the faculty in their home. Her first child, a daughter, was born there. Living in that New England Protestant environment made her more self-conscious about being a Jew, but it was not a comfortable identity. When, after a year in New Orleans and a travel fellowship around Europe, Beck's husband took a job at the University of Wisconsin, she returned to graduate school, doing her Ph.D. dissertation on the impact of Yiddish theater on the work of Franz Kafka.[24] Clearly Jewish themes called to her.

After Beck had revived her study of Yiddish in her doctoral work, she was introduced to Isaac Bashevis Singer when he was a visiting professor at Wisconsin, and he soon asked her to become his translator. She agreed, not realizing that she was one of an army of women translators of his work. She later published the first feminist critique of his work, pointing to the many ways in which he used gender stereotypes to characterize and vilify women.[25] Beck's growing interest in Yiddish led her to take her first activist role in the academy, spearheading a petition to create a section on Yiddish language and literature within the prestigious Modern Language Association. The petition succeeded; the section was approved in 1975 and has continued to flourish. "I am the grandmother of Yiddish in the MLA," Beck said with pride.[26]

Beck spent two years as a visiting professor at the University of Maryland after her book on Kafka was published, then went to the University of Wisconsin with a joint appointment in comparative literature and German. She became part of a team that developed the Women's Studies Program, creating courses on the full spectrum of Jewish women's lives as well as courses on lesbian culture and minority women.

Beck and her husband divorced in the early 1970s. Encouraged by feminism's normalization of women's love for women, she came out as a lesbian, an identity that she had feared was hers when she was an adolescent but that was so unthinkable in the context of her growing up that she decided she was not one.

Beck's activism in lesbian feminist communities strengthened her Jewish identity, to which she returned incrementally through her research and teaching and as a result of the anti-Semitism she experienced in feminist movements. Her recovery of Jewish identity was deeply impacted by feminism, as the Judaism with which she had grown up left little room for women's agency. When she had a son, for example, her father and husband fought about whether he should be circumcised. Beck was not part of that conversation: "it's like I didn't exist."[27] As a feminist, she understood why this incident so traumatized her and why she had to leave patriarchal Judaism behind.

In 1978, Beck attended her first official public gathering of Jewish lesbians as part of the Wisconsin regional meeting of the National Lesbian Feminist Organization. At the beginning, the groups had no agenda other than for the women to affirm that "they were not only lesbians but also Jewish." But the assertion of lesbian identity had ripple effects. The "tearing away of a veil, that recognition that you are, in fact, really different," connected these dual experiences of marginality. It is a "less radical outsidership to be a Jew," Beck asserted, "but . . . you are in fact, really different, even in a subculture."[28]

Beyond marginality, Beck suggested a more positive association between lesbianism and Jewish women's identity, differentiating Jewish lesbian feminists from nonlesbian Jewish feminists. "What it means to affirm a lesbian identity is a kind of full and total acceptance of the female," a reaffirmation of Jewish women's experiences. Jewish culture fostered a "lesbian way of being-in-the-world" that encouraged Jewish women to be affectionate and physical with each other. There was a "whole female culture" in Jewish families and a much-appreciated tradition of female accomplishment in Jewish history linked to radical social change.[29]

Yet Beck recognized the danger inherent in making visible links between Jewishness and lesbianism. "As soon as you begin to say, 'We are active in this movement and we are lesbians,' straight feminists might fear a 'Lesbian takeover.'" "Making ourselves visible as Jews" also posed a threat. "You don't have much space between being invisible as Jews or being too visible as Jews"; the possibilities for stereotyping and exclusion were ever present. The lesbian feminist movement ought to have been a "place of refuge" for identified Jewish women, but Beck had not yet found a safe place there. Perhaps it was because lesbian Jewish women were more willing to be in touch with their oppressions that they seemed more sensitive to prejudice and anti-Semitism than other feminists were.[30]

Like several other members of Di Vilde Chayes, Beck experienced several fraught confrontations over anti-Semitism and racism at feminist conferences. In June 1983, the National Women's Studies Association (NWSA), in order "to face troubling divisions within its own movement," devoted a plenary session at its fifth annual conference at Ohio State University to the subject of "racism and anti-Semitism in the women's movement." In addition to Beck, the session included Arab philosopher Azizah al-Hibri; the black feminist writer, editor, and critic Barbara Smith; Carol Lee Sanchez of San Francisco State University; and Minnie Bruce Pratt, editor of *Feminary*. Many of the two thousand delegates at the conference attended the racism/anti-Semitism session—the most emotionally compelling and "potentially volatile" of its plenaries.[31]

Speaking as the only Jew on the panel, Beck admitted that she had never been "as terrified" as she had been at the prospect of speaking at NWSA "as a Jew." "I could attribute it to my being an immigrant survivor who lived under Hitler," she said, "but that would be wrong. I would bet that many or even most American Jews would feel equally afraid if they were in my place. This fear is never extinguished entirely, even in times of relative safety. My parallel: Jews live with a subliminal fear of encountering anti-Semitism the way women live with the fear of rape." As a Jewishly identified Jew, she felt she could become a "lightning rod for the anti-Jewish feeling which often bubbles beneath a surface which denies its existence." This was the way anti-Semitism operated, making Jews feel "that it is not OK to talk about anti-Semitism in and of itself, and it is also not OK to talk about it in the same breath as racism."[32]

In the presentation, Beck described fifteen markers of anti-Semitism, ranging from "obvious forms" (bombing, beatings, graffiti, slurs, and stereotypes) to subtle ones (holding double standards, trivializing Jewish oppression, not respecting cultural differences, making Jews invisible). She included the problems of equating Jews with Israel and "making the term 'Zionist' mean only the worst kind of fanatic." She observed feminists' "verbal jujitsu" around the term, condemning NWSA for refusing to amend its constitution to oppose "anti-Semitism" unless it specifically referred to "Arabs and Jews." Beck supported the recognition of anti-Arab prejudice, but as a separate form of racism. According to all dictionaries and common usage, Beck insisted, "anti-Semitism means prejudice and hatred against *Jews*. . . . If it takes the term 'Jew-hating' to make the NWSA take a clear position, so be it. As a Jew I will not feel safe here, and will not believe in the NWSA's commitment to stop Jew-hating, if it does not do so." NWSA did not alter the preamble as Beck had urged: it chose to define anti-Semitism in its constitution as an oppression directed "against both Arabs and Jews."[33]

Anti-Semitism was not easy to discuss. In 1985, at a feminist studies conference in Milwaukee, where Beck gave a paper about the subject, hostile and demeaning remarks were repeatedly directed at "you Jews." Yet the attack received barely any comment from "paralyzed" audience members, about one-third of whom may have been Jewish, and was absent in an account of the event in a feminist multicultural text.[34] Beck described the difficulty of including Jewish themes in feminist discourse. "First, there is the fear of attack that produces a protective silence; second, is the fear of being perceived as too 'demanding,' 'pushy,' or 'politically incorrect.' Third, and possibly more than any other factor, the fear of being excluded keeps Jewish women silent. Speaking and writing about explicitly Jewish themes (or even including them substantially) raises the worry that the work will be perceived as marginal, and therefore not as widely read and discussed."[35] With Jews invisible and excluded, the "'benign' anti-Semitism of indifference and insensitivity" took over. Feminists categorized Jews with a radical "otherness" that was denied at the very moment it was created. "If Jews do not fit in," Beck worried, "it is quite likely that other groups may not fit into the conceptual framework we have constructed."[36]

Yet Beck maintained her optimism. "Across the U.S. and in many other parts of the world, Jewish lesbian-feminist communities were in the process of coming together; their very existence was exhilarating and inspired hope that by organizing around our differences, would come unity, and that our feminist projects, in all their complexity, would succeed."[37]

Gloria Greenfield: "Standing Up in Defiance"

The idea for *Nice Jewish Girls* was born when Gloria Greenfield attended Beck's workshop on Jewish lesbian feminists at the 1979 National Women's Studies annual conference and passed Beck a note asking if she would like to put together an anthology around this topic. Three years prior, Greenfield, along with friends Pat McGloin and Marianne Rubenstein, founded Persephone Press in the attic of their Watertown, Massachusetts, home. Within a few years, the press was "making waves in the bookselling community," according to one report, and had become "one of the leading specialized independent publishers in the nation."[38] Publishing fiction, poetry, and anthologies on feminist topics, the press created an innovative list that sold well at home and abroad. At the UN World Conference on Women in Copenhagen in 1980, Persephone was featured as the leading lesbian feminist publisher in the world, its list including important works by women of color and Jewish women.

Greenfield had been raised with a strong Jewish identity. Born in Coney Island in 1950 to Sol and Marilyn Greenfield, she was five when her family became eligible for a home loan available to World War II veterans. With her parents, paternal grandmother, and sister, Greenfield left their housing project in Greenpoint and moved into a home in a working-class neighborhood on the "wrong side of the tracks" in Bay Shore, Long Island.[39] Before learning how to sew her own clothes in middle school, Greenfield often felt self-conscious, wearing the cast-off clothes that her mother had picked up at synagogue rummage sales. Neither of her parents had graduated from high school, but they instilled a strong work ethic in their two daughters. Her father worked two jobs, driving a cab during the day and working as an attendant at Pilgrim State Hospital at night. Her mother worked on assembly lines prior to becoming a custodian at Greenfield's high school. When a roller rink was built in Bay Shore, Greenfield's parents took on additional part-time jobs at the roller rink so that their daughters could take private roller-skating lessons. Greenfield mixed easily with the wealthier classmates at school and at the Reform synagogue, where she and her sister received financial assistance to attend religious school.

Just as growing up as the child of working-class Jews in the Long Island suburbs felt "weird," Greenfield's Jewish upbringing as the daughter of a self-identified, strongly Jewish-identified atheist father and observant mother seemed "schizophrenic." Her mother lit Shabbat candles every Friday night, attended synagogue, changed the dishes at Passover, and followed the Jewish calendar. She had grown up on the Lower East Side and with her siblings had run a newsstand at the end of the Williamsburg Bridge on Delancey Street. Her father, who had grown up in New York's densely populated Jewish neighborhood of Williamsburg, rebelled against his family's religious observance. Nonetheless, Greenfield's sense of class dissonance was accompanied by childhood feelings of religious belonging.

Greenfield's father was an ardent Zionist who raised his youngest daughter with the belief that Israel was "essential" and central to Jewish identity. "If Israel is ever in trouble," he told her, "you go there and you fight." She was also told that anti-Semitism must be confronted wherever and whenever it appeared: "You don't disappear into the woodwork; you stand up and fight when necessary. . . . My father taught me that to be a Jew meant that you held a responsibility for the Jewish people." When another usher at the roller rink called her father a "dirty Jew" in front of Greenfield and her sister, her father responded by breaking his arm. "While that was the end of our roller-skating lessons," said Greenfield, "it was a memorable demonstration on fighting back." Later in middle school, when a classmate called Greenfield a "dirty kike" and pushed her into the lockers, Greenfield fought back. Although she and the girl both got suspended, her father was proud of her: there were no gender issues involved in defending herself as a Jew. Her role models were Jewish resistance fighters. "To be Jewish meant standing up in defiance. . . . I was proud to be Jewish."[40]

Greenfield entered college at the State University of New York (SUNY) at Oswego in 1968, at the height of the student movement. At first, she was involved with New Left male activists in the antiwar movement and for an academic year was president of the campus Hillel chapter. But soon she developed a feminist consciousness, majoring in women's studies and communications. She became a feminist activist, creating the radical feminist group Women for a New World, which ran a multipurpose women's center. The group also started AWARE (the Alliance of Women Against Repression Education) at SUNY. AWARE held a statewide conference in Oswego in 1972, with Robin Morgan as the keynote speak. Morgan became Greenfield's mentor, and the two were close for half a dozen years. Greenfield also performed in the radical feminist theater troupe We Are the Women Your Father Warned You About.

Most notorious of Greenfield's feminist groups was the Red Rag Regime, an underground collective that went out on "payback" actions, visiting the homes of men accused of harassment or violence against women. Red Rag left its signature poster—a red woman's fist against a purple background—along with soiled sanitary napkins or tampons, as a sign that the Regime would be watching them, as well as such other "gifts" as flattened auto tires and broken raw eggs. "The tactic . . . proves to be very effective in dealing with male politicos," the collective wrote in a press release. "Since [the men] try to be politically hip, they tend to react defensively, apologetically, and cowardly. . . . Amazing what eggs, a nice symbol of women's fertility, could do to change a boy's mind."[41] The intention was not to hurt, said Greenfield, but to frighten and embarrass.

Greenfield married while she was in college, but she left the marriage after it became clear that her husband did not want children. Soon after, she made the transition from radical feminist to radical lesbian feminist. After graduating from SUNY Oswego, she moved to Boston to study the history of women at the Goddard-Cambridge Graduate Program in Social Change. Several other radical feminist collective members from Oswego relocated to Boston, and with Greenfield, they formed the Pomegranate Grove collective. When they discovered that Boston was less tolerant than Oswego about feminist graffiti, the collective redirected its energy toward productive outcomes. With other activists, Pomegranate Grove helped establish a women-only martial-arts school in Boston.

The Pomegranate Grove collective became engaged with the women's spirituality movement, in which Robin Morgan played an important role. In a keynote address at a lesbian feminist conference in Los Angeles in 1973, Morgan helped to initiate the merging of feminist politics with women's spirituality, identifying herself as a witch whose powers drew from the ancient art of Wicca.[42] Morgan introduced Greenfield to Morgan McFarland, an Englishwoman who was building circles of Dianic healers throughout the U.S. Under McFarland's tutelage, Greenfield trained as a Dianic priestess named Persephone, for whom the press is named.

The collective organized the first national conference on women's spirituality, titled "Through the Looking Glass: A Gynergenetic Experience." Held in Boston on April 24–26, 1976, the event attracted over fifteen hundred women. Dozens of feminist icons—including Mary Daly, Emily Culpepper, and Z. Budapest—led sessions on such subjects as Amazons and gynocracy, the "covenant of the goddess," "starting covens, groups and circles," spiritual music done in a coven ("moon jam"), and feminist theater and art. There were also discussion groups for feminist astrologers, palm readers, and tarotists.[43] Persephone Press was launched at the conference, with the release of its first book, *A Feminist Tarot*, co-authored by Sally Gearhart and Susan Rennie.

After the conference, Pomegranate Grove reexamined its engagement in the women's spirituality movement. It decided to focus instead

Figure 7.1. Pat McGloin and Gloria Greenfield, founders of Persephone Press, at Boston Pride March. Courtesy of Gloria Greenfield.

on growing Persephone Press, with the goal of creating books that could serve as "organizing tools printed to promote consciousness-raising and social change." Within half a dozen years, it had implemented its mission.[44] Persephone served as an outlet for radical feminist voices at a crucial time in the movement and became one of the giants of feminist business. Most of its titles were in the forefront of lesbian feminist thought.

In Greenfield's reflection on the eighteen months that she was involved with the women's spirituality movement prior to starting Persephone, she explained, "I always identified myself during that period as being a Jewish woman," but because she saw religion as the tool of patriarchy, she could not reconcile her feelings as a Jew with radical feminism. The press provided her the opportunity to engage authors who explored critical feminist issues, including race, religion, and ethnicity. "We were committed to publishing works by Jewish women and by women of color. . . . But we had a list of isms that we would not publish. We would not publish anything that was classist or racist or anti-Semitic."[45]

Persephone Press developed an impressive booklist consisting of anthologies, fiction, and poetry.[46] Its 1981 anthology *This Bridge Called My Back: Writings by Radical Women of Color*, edited by Cherríe Moraga and Gloria E. Anzaldúa, a groundbreaking collection of writings from Chicanas, black women, and Asian and Native Americans, challenged racism within radical feminism; it remains one of the most cited books of feminist theorizing. *Nice Jewish Girls* similarly used the anthology format to examine contested issues within feminism, exposing multiple viewpoints of grassroots activists, writers, and scholars. Like *Bridge*, it enjoyed a breakthrough success, becoming an organizing tool for Jewish lesbian feminists.

Greenfield had begun to feel that as Persephone Press grew, the pace of anti-Semitic incidents—some blatant, some subtle—involving authors had increased. On one occasion, a non-Jewish author reprimanded her for her love of Israel; other authors mentioned that they were concerned about her traveling to Europe for research on anti-Semitism, which they feared would take her attention away from antiracism work. She felt the sting of similar incidents.

In the summer of 1982, Greenfield decided to withdraw from Di Vilde Chayes, whose members included several Persephone authors. In a resignation letter, she explained that her decision had nothing to do with personal feelings about members. But she hoped that leaving Di Vilde Chayes would facilitate a healthier relationship between Di Vilde Chayes' authors and herself as publisher.

Persephone Press closed within a year. One rift that contributed to its shutdown concerned a novel written by Jan Clausen, a white, non-Jewish lesbian feminist. Greenfield and McGloin were shocked at what they perceived to be anti-Semitic stereotypes in the manuscript that Clausen submitted, and they abruptly canceled her contract, a decision that angered several Persephone authors, among them several women of color. Although these authors vehemently defended Clausen, Greenfield and McGloin stood their ground.[47]

Financial exigencies also contributed to the press's dissolution. Greenfield and McGloin were unable to come up with capital to print the spring 1983 list. The publishers were disappointed that authors and others in the feminist community did not rally to their support, and they felt that the sacrifices they had made to maintain the press no longer seemed worthwhile. After the press's demise in May 1983, a few authors took back the rights to their respective books. Greenfield and McGloin placed some titles with other small presses, and Boston-based Beacon Press took over the remainder of Persephone's list.[48]

Greenfield continued to speak out against anti-Semitism within the feminist movement. In July 1983, she guest edited a special issue of the feminist newsmagazine *Sojourner* about Jewish women. After receiving letters from Jewish women all over the country in response to her request for information about their experiences of anti-Semitism, she wrote an essay titled "The Tools of Guilt and Intimidation" for the issue. The article reported respondents' belief that anti-Semitism was growing, as well as Greenfield's sense that Jewish women had been complicit in silencing protests against it because of self-hate, scapegoating, or fears of confrontation.[49] Jewish women did not want their reputations to suffer in the way that Greenfield's had: she was being labeled as a "movement creep" for her outspokenness concerning anti-Jewish prejudice. "The pain kept repeating," said Greenfield, "each time I hear of yet another Jewish woman having a nervous breakdown resulting from the movement's response to her confronting anti-Semitism." It was "behavior modification": "If you don't behave as a 'good' Jew (i.e., 'good' Jews are concerned with everyone else's oppression at the expense of their own; 'bad' Jews act greedily with concern for their own oppression), then you won't be admitted into the sorority. And your confrontation with anti-Semitism will be met with dismissing comments such as 'oh, it's just that loud-mouthed Jew'; or 'here they go again, trying to dominate the issues'; or 'she is just trying to cover up her own complicity with classism, racism, and imperialism by talking about anti-Semitism.'"[50]

The *Sojourner* issue and an address Greenfield gave on anti-Semitism in the women's movement, in June 1983 at the San Francisco Lesbian and Gay Rally, marked her departure from radical feminism—what she called her own "goodbye to all that." "I had decided that I needed to 'go home,'" she explained in a statement to the Jewish Women's Archive decades later. "I was making a conscious decision to change my primary identity from 'Jewish radical feminist' to 'feminist Jew.' I declared that for me, confronting sexism within the Jewish community would be more life-affirming and productive than continuing to fight anti-Semitism from inside of the women's movement, which was supposed to be committed to the liberation and safeguarding of *all* women. It was clear to me that even though the radical feminist community claimed to have disengaged politically from the male Left, it did not purge itself of the Left's virulent and historical anti-Semitism."[51]

Greenfield never again identified with the feminist movement; being a Jew and a Zionist have remained her principal identities. She remarried in 1985; she and her husband are the parents of a daughter and two sons. After working as a senior manager in a Fortune 500 company for six years, she pursued graduate work in Jewish philosophy and since has served as a consultant to the Jewish community, a Jewish educator, an Israel advocate, and a documentary filmmaker. Her film credits include *The Case for Israel: Democracy's Outpost* (2008), *Unmasked Judeophobia* (2011), and *Body and Soul: The State of the Jewish Nation* (2014). Her films have been translated into a dozen languages.

Greenfield said that she is a combatant in the wars against the hatred of Jews and the Jewish state, focusing her passion and determination on the defense of Israel and world Jewry: "I've always been a Zionist. And proud to be a Jew. . . . And for me being a Jew isn't an opportunity to be one step away from being white."[52] Greenfield affirms that she is not evading her whiteness by claiming her Jewishness but adding to it, in effect answering those who deride Jewish feminists for complaining about anti-Semitism rather than focusing on racism per se. She makes no apologies for her stance, which she distinguishes from that of Jews and non-Jews who take what she considers an anti-Semitic, anti-Zionist position by criticizing Israel's insistence on its right to defend its borders and its citizens.

Irena Klepfisz and Melanie Kaye/Kantrowitz: "Danger as the Shared Jewish Identity"

Evelyn Beck contacted Irena Klepfisz, and Gloria Greenfield reached out to Melanie Kaye/Kantrowitz, asking them to contribute to *Nice Jewish Girls*. The invitation to Klepfisz came because Beck knew her as a Holocaust survivor, but Klepfisz hesitated, acknowledging that her feelings as an American Jew were not "completely clear." As a lesbian, moreover, she felt like an outsider; she considered the women's movement homophobic, knowing many lesbians who were afraid to come out. She believed that the Jewish women's movement was similarly unwelcoming, seeing publications such as *Lilith* as "mainstream" and unconcerned with lesbian issues. Her sense of herself as an American Jewish lesbian remained "tangled and interlocked."[53]

Melanie Kaye/Kantrowitz, raised in Brooklyn where everyone was Jewish, also hesitated. Kaye/Kantrowitz had not thought much about her Jewish identity until she was well into her thirties. Her father had changed his family name, Kantrowitz, to Kaye, a few years before she was born (because "Kantrowitz was too long, too hard to say"), and she had grown up without a conscious connection to her heritage.[54] By 1980, she began to identify herself as Jewish and reclaimed the family name—it was "like coming out."[55]

Like Klepfisz, Kaye/Kantrowitz believed lesbian Jewish feminism contained elements of danger. While Klepfisz felt especially vulnerable as a lesbian in the women's movement, Kaye/Kantrowitz emphasized her invisibility as a Jew in the non-Jewish communities in which she lived after college. Neither she nor Klepfisz identified with religious Jewish feminists. How could Jewish feminists identify religiously when Jewish patriarchal values subsumed Jewish ethics? Nor could she understand the glue that bound secular Jewish feminists together.

Though active in the feminist and lesbian movements, both Klepfisz and Kaye/Kantrowitz had silenced important parts of their composite identities, unable to bring the whole into alignment. "When you think about what it means to be Jewish," Kaye/Kantrowitz acknowledged in a 1982 interview, "you think of persecution. The only possible escape dangled before you is to erase your being Jewish. If you could only not be who you are . . ." Klepfisz agreed: "It was very hard to deal with my self-hate as a white woman and say, 'I'm proud to be a Jew.' I couldn't fit those two things together somehow."[56]

The two women recognized that Beck's anthology presented opportunities for them to claim fuller identities and to publicly declare themselves as Jewish lesbian feminists. Both decided to contribute to the anthology, and through this work and participation in the Di Vilde Chayes collective, each woman articulated Jewish lesbian experience and problematized anti-Semitism and internal oppression as issues for the lesbian feminist movement.

* * *

Irena Klepfisz was born in the Warsaw Ghetto in 1941. When she was two, her father, a resistance fighter, died in the Warsaw Ghetto Uprising. Klepfisz escaped with her mother to the Polish countryside, where they survived by concealing their Jewish identities; Klepfisz learned Polish in a convent where she was hidden. After the war, she and her mother lived briefly in Lodz, Poland, then emigrated to Sweden, moving to the United States in 1949, when Klepfisz was eight. Irena learned Swedish, but Polish remained the language of her family and community.

Klepfisz grew up in the Bronx, where she and her mother experienced great poverty in their first years as immigrants. As a child—the only surviving member of her father's family—she felt "old with terror and the brutality, the haphazardness of survival." For the survivors with whom she grew up, the Holocaust never ended: her mother stacked "shelves and shelves of food—just in case." Klepfisz agonized over her visibility as a Jew: "over the fact that I lived in a Jewish neighborhood, . . . [that] at a moment's notice I could be found, identified, rounded up." Being Jewish was "dangerous, something to be hidden." America became "a source of pain," a place where Klepfisz was completely isolated, "different, the greenhorn, the survivor."[57]

While the Holocaust remained present, Klepfisz felt robbed of a true sense of mourning because Americans "commercialized" it, "metaphored [it] out of reality," rendering it devoid of meaning.[58] There was no connection between the American Jewish world and the "*yidishe shive*" (Yiddish environment) of her background. "Though the students in my public school were probably 95 percent Jewish, *not once* . . . do I remember a single teacher—Jew or gentile—discuss a Jewish topic or issue, holiday, leader."[59]

The erasure of Jewishness continued for Klepfisz at City College: "Nothing encouraged us to look to our homes and backgrounds for cultural resources worthy of preservation. The message was just the opposite: we were to erase all traces of who we were and where we came from." Klepfisz and other students from the Bronx or Brooklyn had to take four required semesters of speech to divest them of their working-class Jewish accents. "What were we supposed to think after such lessons . . . ? Were we supposed to be proud?"[60]

Klepfisz chose to study American writers rather than the Jewish authors in whom she was interested, feeling it was safer, but she persuaded distinguished Yiddish linguist Max Weinrich, then teaching German at City College, to offer a Yiddish course to her and a few others. Yiddish literature, which she had been introduced to at her childhood shul, became a powerful influence, with its political vision. Yet American and English literature dominated her studies. In 1970, she received her Ph.D. in English from the University of Chicago, doing her dissertation on George Eliot. Her two worlds remained "mutually exclusive."[61]

Feminism was also absent from Klepfisz's academic life. She regretted never having had any women professors and recalled a pivotal moment when, after reading Kate Millet's *Sexual Politics* in 1970, a married friend of hers became indignant, questioning why she "was the one washing the toilet." But Klepfisz considered herself nonpolitical; the feminist activism of the Chicago Women's Liberation Union did not touch her.[62] As she became involved in the "non-Jewish environment" of lesbian feminism, the absorption of feminism into her politics transformed the socialism and *yidishkayt* of her youth. "Needless to say," she wrote, "many of the feminists and lesbians I worked with were Jews; but our focus was never on Jewish issues."[63] In 1976, with Elly Bulkin, Jan Clausen, and Rima Shore, she founded the feminist-lesbian literary magazine *Conditions*, maintained and published by a lesbian collective.

The decision to write for *Nice Jewish Girls* became a milestone in the development of Klepfisz's Jewish feminist identity: "History stepped in again. . . . The women's movement began to take notice of Jewish issues." Klepfisz led workshops on Jewish identity and on anti-Semitism, meeting many women who knew no Jewish history or culture. "Still, they yearned: How can I be Jewish? Is being Jewish more than just *feeling* Jewish? What should I study? Where should I go? Like me, many of them were not drawn to religion or ritual; they were looking for *secular* answers."[64]

Klepfisz hoped to provide them. Although sensitive to the problem of lesbian invisibility, she recognized the necessity of bringing straight Jewish women and lesbian women together around issues of common concern, especially anti-Semitism. She acknowledged that straight women could feel disparaged and isolated at lesbian events and called on Di Vilde Chayes and other lesbians to remember their common Jewishness and create alliances among different kinds of Jewish women.[65]

Figure 7.2. Melanie Kaye/Kantrowitz and Irena Klepfisz at a Di Vilde Chayes gathering, 1982. Courtesy of Gloria Greenfield.

Klepfisz provided a strong voice raising consciousness on the issue of anti-Semitism. In her article "Anti-Semitism in the Lesbian/Feminist Movement," which appeared in *Womannews* in 1981 as well as in the opening section of *Nice Jewish Girls*, she explained that anti-Semitism took more forms than "the overt, undeniably inexcusable painted swastika on a Jewish gravestone or a synagogue wall"; it was sometimes "elusive and difficult to pinpoint, for it is the anti-Semitism either of omission or one which trivializes the Jewish experience and Jewish oppression."[66] She felt it imperative to confront Jewish self-hatred as well as Gentile anti-Semitism. Having been told, "Jews are too pushy, too aggressive, . . . that they control everything," Jewish lesbian feminists kept silent about their Jewishness, fearing to confront what threatened them. "How is such hesitancy possible among women who have passionately devoted themselves to fighting every form of oppression?" She was clear about naming the problem: "Any attempt to draw attention away from one's Jewishness is an internalization of anti-Semitism." Klepfisz called on Jewish and non-Jewish women to ask themselves hard questions in order to identify sources of "shame, conflict, doubt, and anti-Semitism" in themselves. "Like any other ideology of oppression," anti-Semitism "must never be tolerated, must never be hushed up, must never be ignored. It must always be exposed and resisted."[67]

Later in life, Klepfisz was able to combine the disparate worlds of her childhood, bringing together *yidishkayt* and American politics. In her poetry and translations of Yiddish authors, she encouraged the reclamation of secular Jewish culture. She is the author of several books of poetry and prose, including *Keeper of Accounts*, published by Persephone Press, as well as of *A Few Words in the Mother Tongue: Poems Selected and New, 1971–1990* and *Dreams of an Insomniac: Jewish Feminist Essays and Diatribes*, and she has translated the works of Kadya Molodowsky and other women Yiddish poets.[68] She also taught women's studies at Barnard College, specializing in the history and literature of Jewish women.

* * *

While the Holocaust was the single most important event in Klepfisz's identity, it did not play a large role in shaping Melanie Kaye/Kantrowitz, although she had relatives who perished in the concentration camps. The civil rights movement and the antiauthoritarian values of her parents were much more significant in motivating Kaye/Kantrowitz's activism.

Kantrowitz was born in 1945 in the Flatbush section of Brooklyn, where "everyone," or almost everyone, was Jewish. "Jewish was the air I breathed, . . . everything I took for granted." But, she said, it was "nothing I articulated."[69] She did not flaunt her Jewishness. "Sometime around ninth grade," she wrote in her essay for Beck's anthology, "words like *yenta shmatte bubbe* began to embarrass me. . . . [They] marked, stripped, and revealed me. I came from people who talked *like that*," including parents who had a "six-days-plus-two-nights-work-week" in "the store," selling bras and girdles. "I came from them and would be stuck with their lives." Being Jewish meant "being lower class"; getting an education "meant moving up in the world and no longer being Jewish." She wanted to aim higher—"museums, foreign films, and an escape from Brooklyn."[70]

Yet despite the lower-class accents and aspirations that characterized the Brooklyn Jews Kaye/Kantrowitz knew, she respected her parents' values. While not political activists, both "had definite opinions
about right and wrong," which they passed on to her, such as "the Ten
Commandments." Her father joined the Young Communist League as
a teenager during the Depression; though he did not consider himself political, he was definitely left leaning. Kaye/Kantrowitz's mother,
who circulated petitions against the Korean War and strongly opposed
McCarthyism, was an even greater influence. As PTA president of Melanie's junior high school, she fought to bring blacklisted performers to
the annual PTA meeting. Kaye/Kantrowitz's favorite story was how her
mother stood up for her, when during a shelter drill in her kindergarten class, the young girl frightened her classmates by telling them that
the drill was "not a game," as the teacher said, but intended to protect
them from bombs that "burned and killed" people. When the principal
scolded her mother for discussing these facts with a girl so young, her
mother insisted that she could not lie, defending her daughter as "class
conscience and rebel."[71]

Kaye/Kantrowitz appreciated her parents as models. "I have yet to
find [them] wanting," she said. "This was my Jewish upbringing as much
as the candles we lit for Hanukah, or the seders." Her family was not
observant. To them, "breaking religious observance was progressive,
the opposite of superstitious": "When we ate on Yom Kippur, it never
occurred to me that this was un-Jewish. I knew I was a Jew. I knew
Hitler had been evil. I knew Negroes—we said then—had been slaves
and that was evil too. I knew prejudice was wrong, stupid. I knew Jews
believed in freedom and justice."[72] But she did not yet view her parents'
ethics, and her own rapidly forming ones, as Jewish.

In 1963, at age seventeen, Kaye/Kantrowitz went to work for the Harlem Education Project, tutoring African American students and participating in creating freedom schools and other actions to help the
neighborhood. The experience was formative. She became "intensely
focused on white racism, utterly unaware of racism against Jews, or
of the possibility of Jewish danger (the Holocaust was eons ago, irrelevant)." It was years before she understood how her upbringing had
"primed" her for this commitment.[73] At the time, she felt that her
"being *Jewish* had nothing to do with it." "Being Jewish *meant* being

white," an identity that she thought she might escape through her naïve, "unexamined empathy with oppression." In Harlem, as a teenager, she thought she could elude the world of her upbringing: "Flatbush, my parents' clothing store, the world of working- and lower-middle-class Jews, a world I thought of as *materialistic*." She was the kind of Jew, she said, "who didn't feel afraid, ashamed, joyful, grieving, according to the fate and/or behavior of Jews. Who didn't see Jews as 'my people.'"[74]

After graduating from City College, Kaye/Kantrowitz left New York to do graduate work at the University of California at Berkeley, wanting to get away from her family, her people, "to be part of the radical politics developing on the West Coast." Being a Jew at Berkeley had little resonance, although she was surprised that the Brooklyn-Jewish accent that once designated her as "lower class" now marked her "as one of those smart Jews from New York." Involved in the antiwar and student movements, she was not moved by Jewish political issues and did not notice the 1967 Middle East war or identify with Israel. Like Eva in Tillie Olsen's *Tell Me a Riddle*, Kaye/Kantrowitz marked "none" next to religion on a questionnaire she filled out at that time.[75]

Kaye/Kantrowitz also resisted identifying as a Jew within the feminist movement. At a feminist conference in Portland, Oregon, where she moved in 1972, a woman told her that she did not like Jews who were "loud and pushy and aggressive." Stunned, Kaye/Kantrowitz revealed that she was Jewish. In 1975, at the National Conference on Socialist Feminism in Yellow Springs, Ohio, she avoided the opportunity to attend the Jewish caucus called by Susan Schechter and Maralee Gordon. "I couldn't relate to it. I went to a workshop on economics instead."[76] Later she would understand what she did not see then: "that however I thought about or related to my identity and my history, I could no more walk free of these than I could be genderless."[77]

For seven years in Portland, Kaye/Kantrowitz felt like an "alien" in a "wrong city, the wrong part of the world." She rejected religious Jews and the Jewish women who met Friday nights to "schmooze." Later she understood her hesitancy as the way "the mind resists threatening information."[78] But slowly she began to develop a Jewish consciousness, manifesting itself in an interest in Jewish immigrant history and the Holocaust.

Kaye/Kantrowitz moved to New Mexico for a teaching job in 1979; there her "close people" were "almost all lesbians, mostly not Jewish." Her acceptance of Jewishness grew. "The more outside of a Jewish ambiance I was, the more conscious I became of Jewishness." Recognizing how much she needed Jews, Kaye/Kantrowitz began to find Jewish women everywhere. "So Melanie, what's with all the Jewish?" her father asked her in 1982, the year *Nice Jewish Girls* was published. By then, she was fully aware of her hunger for what she described as "home, kin, for *my people*," and of growing anti-Semitism. Decades later would she understand that her previous "rebellion had been enacted simultaneously by thousands of young Jews; that it was in fact a collective Jewish rebellion, articulated in a classically Jewish fashion."[79]

Like Klepfisz, Kaye/Kantrowitz continued to work on issues of anti-Semitism and racism, combining political activism with writing and teaching. In addition to *The Tribe of Dina: A Jewish Women's Anthology*, which she co-edited with Klepfisz, her books include *My Jewish Face & Other Stories*; *The Issue Is Power: Essays on Women, Jews, Violence, and Resistance*; and *The Colors of Jews: Racial Politics and Radical Diasporism*. She taught urban studies at Queens College, where she directed the Worker Education Extension Center, and has worked with New Jewish Agenda and Jews for Racial and Economic Justice.

At the NYU "Women's Liberation and Jewish Identity" conference, Kaye/Kantrowitz distinguished between "minimalist" Jews and "non-Jewish Jews," aligning herself with the latter, whom she sees as "boundary crossers" and "rebels," transcending a narrow, constricting Jewishness but belonging to Jewish tradition.[80] She prefers the term "Diasporists" for people such as herself who recognize Jewish "identity as simultaneously rock, forged under centuries of pressure, and water, infinitely flexible."[81]

Adrienne Rich: "Dear Schvesters"

Irena Klepfisz took the initiative in assembling a group of women interested in meeting to discuss topics of concern to Jewish lesbian feminists. Most had become visible to each other while working on articles for *Nice Jewish Girls* or other lesbian and feminist publications.[82] Klepfisz suggested the group's purpose in an early letter: to do "political work around anti-Semitism in the movement, and to focus and try to understand Jewish–Third world relations in the movement and outside." After exploring the idea with Beck, Kaye/Kantrowitz, and Bernice Mennis, she contacted Gloria Greenfield, Adrienne Rich, and Nancy Bereano, who agreed to join the new group. They called themselves "Di Vilde Chayes," a name that Beck's mother called her when she looked unkempt or acted inappropriately for a girl, like a "wild beast."[83] In an interview at the time, Klepfisz and Kaye/Kantrowitz acknowledged that in books such as *This Bridge Called My Back*, "women of color laid the groundwork" for bringing cultural differences to the forefront of the feminist movement, inspiring Jewish women to explore such topics as anti-Semitism and internal oppression.[84]

Like the early women's liberationists collectives and the newer groups organized by women of color, Di Vilde Chayes aimed to combine consciousness-raising with action. In an unpublished piece, members explained the feelings that led them to join together: "[to] understand what was going on inside ourselves and in the outside world; and based on that understanding, to act in that outside world. The group was a way out of our individual and isolated powerless howlings. . . . It was a way of taking our personal understandings and developing a political vision."[85]

The women had been aware that issues involving Jewish identity and anti-Semitism had been missing from political analysis, but by themselves, they were isolated and afraid, choked by "the fear that had something to do with self-preservation, with not betraying one's past or one's family or one's self." Joining together empowered them, creating "joy at the awakening of one's proud Jewish identity." The group was a way to explore the women's "individual Jewish histories": "our incorporation of myths and stereotypes; a way of unraveling the often unconscious layers of harm and damage that prejudice and oppression create."[86]

Di Vilde Chayes' political vision was "informed by Jewishness in its very framework": "our Jewishness as our feminism, becoming a way of viewing, a new lens through which to see ourselves and the world around us." They hoped that the retrieval of Jewish heritage could spur collective action. Yet they recognized a negative commonality they shared with women's liberationists. "With feminism, and now with Jewishness, the beginning of self-definition and assertion are often met with laughter and trivialization, criticism, and/or anger, as if in defining ourselves we are ruining a happy family, dividing a united front."[87] They expected consciousness-raising and political action as Jewish lesbian feminists to be difficult. To persist would require support from both Jewish and non-Jewish friends.

As Di Vilde Chayes began its meetings in February, Adrienne Rich outlined her goals for the group: "Dear Schvesters: Thinking about what a Jewish Lesbian group/cell/collective/study group/action group/network or combination of these, might be. . . . I want to be part . . . of a Jewish/lesbian/feminist group which can develop an analysis of anti-Semitism and Jewish identity for ourselves and for the feminist movement and which will also relentlessly keep this in with what we already understand of racism, class injustice woman-hating, homophobia."[88]

Rich felt that she had a lot of work to do "simply to feel and understand" both her "existence and oppression as a Jew." When Beck invited her to contribute to *Nice Jewish Girls*, she at first declined, but after thinking over the issues for a year, Rich wrote "Split at the Root" for the anthology.[89] The essay spoke of the profound difficulties of focusing on different oppressions at the same time. "Sometimes I feel I have seen too long from too many disconnected angles," Rich wrote memorably in the now-classic essay, "white, Jewish, anti-Semite, racist, anti-racist, once-married lesbian, middle-class, feminist, exmatriate Southerner, *split at the root*: that I will never bring them whole."[90]

The daughter of an assimilated Jewish father and Gentile mother, both from the South, Rich grew up in a Christian world, shaped by external anti-Semitism, her father's self-hatred, and his "Jewish pride." She married a Harvard man who was from eastern European stock— the "wrong kind of Jew"—and she never felt Jewish pride as writer, wife, or mother.[91] While the civil rights movement felt deeply personal to her, "in the world of Jewish assimilationist and liberal politics . . . things were far less clear. . . . Anti-Semitism went almost unmentioned. It was even possible to view anti-Semitism as a reactionary agenda, a concern of *Commentary* magazine, or later, the Jewish Defense League." Although Judaism was "yet another strand of patriarchy," she always added mentally, "if Jews had to wear yellow stars again, I too would wear one."[92]

Rich's sitting down to write about herself as a Jew seemed a "dangerous act" that filled her with "fear and shame." Her essay had "no conclusions": "I would have liked, in this essay, to bring together the meanings of anti-Semitism and racism as I have experienced them and as I believe they intersect in the world beyond my life. But I'm not able to do this yet. I feel the tension as I think, make notes: if you really look at one reality, the other will waver and disperse."[93]

Di Vilde Chayes' formation offered "another beginning," analogous to the founding moments of radical feminism. "In some ways this feels to me like the early 1970s when we were rushing about searching for the lost, out-of-print, hard-to-come-by information we needed," she wrote to her Di Vilde Chayes sisters, "the books gathering dust in libraries, the history we didn't know. We exchange bibliographies, follow off leads in other bibliographies. We start trying to name what is happening. We make lists . . . of Jewish women fiction writers in America and are shocked at how few we find. We start . . . reversing stereotypes, claiming our strengths. At the same time, within the very movement where this is happening, we have to confront unexamined bigotry, old Leftist attitudes, etc." Given the historical exigencies of the times and the coming together of Di Vilde Chayes, along with work done by other *Nice Jewish Girls* contributors, Rich felt that her own perspectives were "changing, opening out." "I am glad that each of you exists," she told the Schvesters.[94]

A few months after the founding of Di Vilde Chayes, Klepfisz and Kaye/Kantrowitz attended a Memorial Day Jewish Feminist Conference in San Francisco, representing the group. Drawing nearly one thousand women, including some two hundred non-Jews, the conference drew attention to Jewish issues within the feminist community. The large number of attendees allowed Jewish women to connect to their own identities while continuing to see themselves a part of a broader community. Reporting to Di Vilde Chayes, Klepfisz and Kaye/Kantrowitz described their "overwhelming feeling of joy" at being "out" as Jews at the event. "You did not have to worry about being 'too' Jewish, about feeding into Jewish stereotypes, about taking up too much space, too much time, too much energy by asking others to focus on your 'selfish' Jewish concerns. You did not have to worry about being 'paranoid' when describing anti-Semitic experiences and situations. About being 'clannish' for feeling glad and excited at connecting with other Jewish women."[95] Yet despite their euphoria, Klepfisz and Kaye/Kantrowitz

Figure 7.3. Jewish lesbians at Women's Pentagon Action, November 1981. Photo © 2017 JEB (Joan E. Biren).

observed with concern that when it came to the Israel issue, conference goers were deeply divided, with each side expressing "visceral antagonism" toward the other.[96]

"We Had Not Planned to Be a Group Focused Only on Israel"

The conflict among feminists over Israel was reflected in Di Vilde Chayes' war of words with Women Against Imperialism (WAI), a San Francisco anti-imperialist group. In a pamphlet in the spring of 1982, WAI called on "Progressive Jewish women" to oppose "Zionist Israel . . . one of imperialism's most important bastions of white supremacy."[97] A WAI letter to the women's movement at about the same time declared that opposing Zionism was an inherent component of the fight against worldwide imperialism. "We as women do not confront some separate structure of oppression, but the same imperialist system whose bedrock is the oppression of colonized nations inside the US and around the world. If we want to participate in fundamentally changing this system, to be part of building a society where genocide, women's oppression, anti-semitism and class exploitation can no longer exist, then we need to actively side with Palestinian, Black, Chicano-Mexicano, Puerto Rican, Native American and all national liberation struggles which are leading the fight to take this empire apart."[98] Troubled by the Jewish Feminist Conference that Klepfisz and Kaye/Kantrowitz attended in San Francisco, WAI asked, "What does it mean that a thousand Jewish women can gather and not condemn Zionism?" Not to break with Zionism meant "sacrificing our principles and allowing a racist politics to gain ground in our movement for women's and lesbian liberation."[99]

In a letter printed in *off our backs* in spring/summer 1982, Di Vilde Chayes rejected WAI's charge that "Zionism is racism." While it disapproved of the Israeli government's occupation policies, Di Vilde Chayes wrote that none of its criticisms denied Israel's right to exist. Rather, it asserted, *"Zionism is one strategy against anti-Semitism and for Jewish survival."* Because anti-Zionism demanded the "dissolution of the State of Israel," which it believed would require the destruction of Jews within Israel and the removal of a refuge for Jews suffering persecution elsewhere, Di Vilde Chayes argued that it would lead to an increase of anti-Semitism throughout the world. *"Anti-Zionism is anti-Semitism."* To state that it is "not as serious as other oppressions is to imply that Jews have no right to complain until we are marched to the gas chamber."[100]

Further disagreements came when Israel invaded southern Lebanon to destroy a Palestinian guerrilla force in early June, setting off the first Israel-Lebanon war. Following the attempted assassination of the Israeli ambassador in London, Israel attacked PLO targets in Lebanon and sent ground troops into Lebanon in a mission named "Operation Peace for the Galilee." In an attempt to root out the militants, Christian Phalangists who were Israel's Lebanese allies murdered between seven hundred and two thousand Palestinian and Lebanese civilians in the refugee camps of Sabra and Shatila, suspected of being PLO strongholds. The massacres received worldwide condemnation, including protests by millions of Israelis who demonstrated against the war and the Israeli generals believed to have enabled the killings.

Labeling the war a "genocide against the Arab peoples of Palestine and Lebanon," WAI called on the women's movement to join the condemnation of the war and further challenge Israel's right to exist. In a letter printed in feminist outlets in the fall, Di Vilde Chayes called the Lebanon war a "terrible event" and criticized Israel's bombing of civilian installations. But it rejected WAI's characterizations of Israel as "the new Nazi state, and of the invasion as the worst thing any nation had ever done," allegations that scapegoated Israel for the horrors in Lebanon and "for all crimes of imperialism." Such protests falsely presented Israeli policy as monolithic, omitting the historical context of the war, and contributed to an intense climate of anti-Semitism. Di Vilde Chayes members insisted that they could not choose one part of their identity "at the expense of another as if they are . . . mutually exclusive," as in the past they had been forced to choose between "lesbian and Jew, Jew and anti-racist, anti-racist and Zionist." They claimed their "right as Zionists to condemn Israel aggression in Beirut," and at the same time, they claimed their "right as Jews to confront and resist all forms of anti-Semitism which exploits criticism of current Israeli policy."[101]

off our backs published pages of letters about the exchanges between Di Vilde Chayes and Women Against Imperialism. Some writers praised Di Vilde Chayes, condemning WAI's statements as anti-Semitic and criticizing *off our backs* for printing them. Other correspondents, such as noted biologist Ruth Hubbard, denied Di Vilde Chayes' claim that anti-Zionism was racism. Several feminists wrote to oppose the either/ or choice that the groups offered. The controversy escalated.[102]

Irena Klepfisz noted that issues had "quickly . . . evolved, unraveled, and developed"; by the early 1980s, questions about Israel began to overwhelm other women's movement concerns.[103] In an unpublished account, Di Vilde Chayes acknowledged, "We had not planned to be a group focused only on Israel. We are Diaspora Jews whose lives center on this continent. But events forced our hand."[104] "I did not know how to switch my focus away from anti-Semitism, from the wounds of the Holocaust, from my work on strengthening Jewish identity," Klepfisz admitted. "Israel has taken over my life."[105] Only later, on a trip to Israel that Klepfisz took with Kaye/Kantrowitz in 1984–1985 to find material for their anthology *The Tribe of Dina*, did Klepfisz find a more comfortable political space, convinced that it was possible to be "strongly Jewish identified, to believe in the necessity of the State of Israel, and to fight for Palestinian rights."[106] By 1984, Adrienne Rich had also become a strong supporter of Palestinian liberation, questioning Zionism. By that time, Gloria Greenfield had left radical feminism behind, despairing of its willingness to support Israel and confront anti-Semitism and anti-Zionism.

In Klepfisz's view, "confusion and ignorance" about Israel influenced the decision to suspend Di Vilde Chayes. Some members believed that lacking the sophistication to deal with the complex Middle East situation, it would be better to become informed on their own. There were other considerations. Living in different areas made it difficult for members to meet, especially after Rich moved to the West Coast, while competing professional priorities grew more troublesome. Di Vilde Chayes disbanded in 1983.[107] But the women's explorations together had strengthened links to the Jewish aspects of their experience and bolstered their aspirations to claim a place for Jewish feminism in "multi-racial feminist identity politics," in Rich's words.[108]

Jewish and Black Women Confront Racism and Anti-Semitism

Lesbian feminists played a significant role in opening dialogues between Jewish women and non-Jewish women as the intensification of identity politics strained longtime alliances. As the radical feminist coalition of the early movement fragmented, black and Jewish women, who had often found themselves working for the same causes, brought accusations of anti-Semitism and racism against each other. Yet they attempted to understand each other's perspectives and experiences.

In 1983, Elly Bulkin invited Barbara Smith and Minnie Bruce Pratt, a black non-Jewish woman and a white non-Jewish woman who were also both lesbian feminists, to join her in engaging the topics of racism and anti-Semitism in print, an idea that had developed out of the rancorous plenary session on anti-Semitism and racism that took place at the 1983 NWSA conference that had so traumatized Evelyn Torton Beck. Bulkin, Smith, and Pratt's collaboration resulted in the 1984 publication *Yours in Struggle: Three Feminist Perspectives on Anti-Semitism and Racism*.[109] Sections of the book were excerpted in major feminist publications, and it received much attention within the movement.[110]

Minnie Bruce Pratt's essay, the shortest in the volume, described the author's childhood as a white southerner who did not understand the dynamics of white privilege and was totally ignorant of anti-Semitism.[111] The major confrontation in the book was between Barbara Smith and Elly Bulkin. The women agreed that while the impact of prejudice and oppression had often made blacks and Jews "practical and ideological allies," relationships between them had been increasingly marked by "contradictory and ambivalent feelings, both negative and positive, distrust simultaneously mixed with a desire for acceptance; and deep resentment and heavy expectations about the other group's behavior."[112]

Smith's chapter, "Between a Rock and a Hard Place: Relationships between Black and Jewish Women," acknowledged that addressing anti-Semitism set her up to look like a "woman of color overly concerned about 'white' issues." She confessed that her experiences with Jewish women had been "terrorizing" and admitted that she was anti-Semitic, largely because she had been brought up to be suspicious of whites. But Smith charged that in Jewish women's efforts to combat anti-Semitism, they had exercised racism toward black women. She urged black women to understand that they shared commonalities with Jewish women, included being oppressed by the white majority.[113]

Bulkin viewed her essay primarily as a "dialogue among Jewish women" rather than an attempt to persuade black women of her positions. It began with an account of her personal history: she was an Ashkenazi Jew, daughter of an immigrant father and New York–born mother, raised in the Bronx with an early exposure to the Jewish radical tradition. Drawn to antiracist work, Bulkin made no "analogous commitment to fighting Jewish oppression"; she associated her antiracist activism with her "lack of a strong Jewish identity." By the late 1970s, she realized that she did not have to choose between political affinities but could work against anti-Semitism and racism simultaneously.[114]

Bulkin acknowledged the debt that Jewish women owed to women of color, whose identity struggles had framed a new feminist politics based on group solidarity and cultural identity. Yet she pointed out that for black women, Jewishness in America had become "synonymous with whiteness," which she argued was a false equation, given the existence of a minority of Jews of color and the fact that even the majority of Jews stood outside the dominant Protestant mainstream. Bulkin also disputed the idea that all Jews enjoyed class privilege; many were poor and working class. And she rejected the notion that anti-Semitism was a "historical aberration" that was "past and done." African Americans needed to understand Jewish diversity and recognize that anti-Semitism was a real threat, just as Jews needed to understand the specificities of black experience and racism. The only way to address anti-Semitism and antiblack racism was to avoid "comparative oppressions" and "cycles of competition," instead seeing each oppression as unique and specific.[115] Bulkin ended the book with the image of a community of Jewish feminists sharing a positive sense of their own identities as the locus of change.

One indication of such a community came that year when Jewish feminists urged the National Women's Studies Association to give official status to a Jewish Women's Caucus. "Jews are mocked, despised, feared and scapegoated by both the Christian majority in the United States and other religious/cultural/ethnic groups," the women wrote, arguing that caucus status was needed "to raise and maintain the consciousness of NWSA members about Jewish issues."[116] NWSA agreed and in 1984 officially recognized the Jewish Women's Caucus. The caucus worked to keep feminists cognizant of the dangers of "anti-Jewish feeling" and to put Jewish issues on the association's agenda.[117]

The work against anti-Semitism continued in print as well. In *The Tribe of Dina*, Kaye/Kantrowitz and Klepfisz included "*In Gerang* / In Struggle: A Handbook for Recognizing and Resisting Anti-Semitism and for Building Jewish Identity and Pride," written with Bernice Mennis.[118] Identifying strategies of anti-Semitism and resistance and providing some one hundred exercises, the authors called for vigilance, practice, and discussion. At a time when few in the feminist movement or on the left called attention to these problems, this forthright condemnation of anti-Jewish prejudice stands out for its activist engagement with the issue.

* * *

The members of Di Vilde Chayes and other Jewish lesbians brought the concern about "the Other" into new projects in the 1980s, becoming a focal point for Jewish antiracist work. Many Jewish lesbians had experience with multiracial lesbian groups; some desired to incorporate lovers who were non-Jewish or minority women. While Jewish lesbian groups faced divisions over class, ethnicity, race, and religion, they often emerged with important skills in coalition building. Historian Faith Rogow observes that diversity within Jewish lesbian communities sparked genuine creativity.[119]

Kaye/Kantrowitz voiced a common sentiment when she averred that reaching out beyond Jewish communities did not negate the necessity for "a gathering of one's people." "Who will stick up for me if I don't respect myself enough to stand up for myself? . . . Here is our beginning. Have we been for ourselves sufficiently already? Do we even know who ourselves are?"[120] Klepfisz agreed: "A Jew didn't separate herself from her people, even when she could."[121]

In 1988, Adrienne Rich and colleagues started a Jewish feminist newsletter, *Gesher* (Hebrew: bridge), for the National Feminist Task Force of New Jewish Agenda, the progressive Jewish action group. Two years later, the newsletter became the independent Jewish feminist journal *Bridges*, "a converging point" for the "diversity of Jewish women's voices that are often from the margin," according to editor Claire Kinberg. In focusing on Jewish experience, *Bridges* hoped to enhance "connection to others" and become an explicitly Jewish participant in a multiethnic feminist movement.[122]

Former Di Vilde Chayes members played a role in Jews for Racial and Economic Justice (JREJ), an organization dedicated to promoting social justice in New York City; JREJ was founded in 1990 by Melanie Kaye/Kantrowitz and other progressive Jews. Its mission statement declares about the work of the organization, "It contradicts our own sense of 'otherness,' and is a revolutionary act of solidarity with our neighbors-in-struggle." The group cited Jewish tradition in its rationale: "[The JREJ] stands in opposition to assimilation, and to both the idea that Jewish liberation is not worthy of struggle, and that Jews can find a separate justice for ourselves."[123] Though JREJ was not explicitly feminist, Kaye/Kantrowitz, who became founding director in 1992, observed that the organization "modeled feminist activism" and was led by mostly female directors and a female staff.[124]

Irena Klepfisz served as executive director of the progressive, multi-issue New Jewish Agenda (NJA) from 1990 to 1992. During her tenure, the NJA organized the Jewish contingent for a Washington, D.C., march against the first Iraqi war and sponsored a conference on anti-Semitism and racism, with civil rights leader Julian Bond as keynote speaker.[125]

"How each of us shapes our life, shapes history," Klepfisz remarked in a 1989 speech.[126] With the activism and writings of lesbian Jewish feminists such as Klepfisz, Beck, Rich, Kaye/Kantrowitz, Greenfield, Bulkin, and many others represented in the anthologies *Nice Jewish Girls* and *The Tribe of Dina*; in journals such as *Sinister Wisdom*, *Conditions*, *Common Lives / Lesbian Lives*, and *off our backs*; and in Jewish periodicals such as *Genesis 2*, *Lilith*, *Schmate*, *Gesher*, and *Bridges*, Jewish feminism came to include the "coming out" of Jewish women as Jewish lesbians within the feminist movement.[127] Their bridge-building work provided a foundation for synthesizing the complex identities of Jewish women, creating excitement, new visions, and directions for change.

8

"Rise above the World's Nasty Squabbles"

International Dimensions of Jewish Feminism

Beginning in 1975, the first of three international UN World Conferences on Women signaled a new political direction for the women's movement. As the first phases of radical feminism shifted from universalist goals, locally based collectives, and grassroots organizing to new forms of institution and theory building and an emphasis on particularist identity politics, American feminism came increasingly to be shaped by events on the world stage as well as at home.

The new direction for the movement had significant consequences for Jewish women, many of whom realized that they could not act as feminists in isolation from a wider, international arena. Many came to a new sense of themselves as Jewish feminists, determined to foster Jewish assertiveness and self-defense on their own, but they also began to develop strategies for coalition building all over the world. Their objectives differed from those of earlier women's liberationists who focused primarily on eradicating sexism in American society or Jewish feminists who challenged patriarchy in American Jewish religious and communal life. Adopting the dual strategy of challenging both sexism and anti-Semitism, they moved outward from individual and locally based identities, becoming Jewish-women-in-the world.

Between 1975 and 1985, the three women's conferences, part of the United Nations Decade for Women, stimulated a significant movement toward global feminism that arose in the developing world and global South. Most scholars and activists evaluated the UN conferences held in Mexico City, Copenhagen, and Nairobi as a victory for the "universality of women's rights" and "the coming of age" of the international women's movement, a "launch pad for an array of global feminisms."[1] Because of the prominence of the Israeli-Palestinian issues at each event, however, the UN conferences had consequences for Jewish women worldwide that controverted more positive outcomes. The idea of "Zionism is racism," linking Israeli policies to South African apartheid, pervaded each conference. In July 1975, the UN women's conference in Mexico City passed a Zionism-is-racism resolution that became the template for Resolution 3379, passed by the UN General Assembly four months later (revoked only in 1991). In 1980, the UN women's conference in Copenhagen adopted a "Program of Action" that called for the elimination of Zionism. The Nairobi conference in 1985 failed to endorse a Zionism-is-racism resolution after a closely contested platform fight.

For women's liberationists who had resisted or ignored their identities as Jewish women, the contentious Zionism question became a pathway to claim their Jewishness. The public pronouncements of Betty Friedan, writers Esther (E. M.) Broner and Letty Cottin Pogrebin, and psychologist Phyllis Chesler typify this reclamation. Friedan had never explicitly addressed Jewish feminist issues.[2] But after attending the Mexico City conference, she openly named herself a Zionist and Jewish feminist. Broner and Chesler, who participated in the Copenhagen and Nairobi conferences, attempted to mitigate polemical attacks against Jews and Israel, strategizing with international groups of Jewish women and establishing dialogues with Arab and black women at home. They also announced their Jewishness in public forums. Affected by the conferences as well, Pogrebin became radicalized as a Jew, declaring herself a Jewish feminist. Her eleven-page essay on anti-Semitism in the women's movement for the June 1982 of *Ms.* was the magazine's most commented on article to date, triggering an important conversation on the subject.

Some women's liberationists, such as Alix Kates Shulman, considered these women as "uptown" feminists as opposed to "downtown" radicals like themselves who focused primarily on consciousness-raising about gender and male dominance, but both groups offered compelling visions and strategies for gender equality.[3] Broner, Chesler, and Pogrebin were members of the New York "seder sisters," who initiated an influential feminist Passover seder in 1976.[4] Inspired by the feminist Haggadah that Broner and Nomi Nimrod created in Israel the previous year after a women's seder they initiated with Marcia Freedman, the New York seder became a positive reinforcement of Jewish women's history and traditions and modeled women's Passover celebrations throughout the U.S.[5]

Figure 8.1.New York women's seder: Esther Broner, center; to her left, Letty Cottin Pogrebin and Martha Ackelsberg; to her right, Edith Isaac-Rose and Adrienne Cooper. Photo by Joan L. Roth.

Marcia Freedman personifies a new kind of transnational Jewish radical feminist. American born but living in Israel for fourteen years before she returned to the United States, Freedman started the first battered women's shelter in Israel, campaigning for abortion rights, peace, and lesbian rights. She was a prime mover behind Israel's women's movement and served for four years in the Israeli Knesset, engaged with diverse national and international issues. Shaped by her extended encounter with Israel as an Israeli citizen, Freedman's Jewish feminism incorporated global dimensions.[6]

This chapter outlines the new ways in which international events, including the three UN women's conferences and the establishment of alliances with Israeli feminists, impacted Jewish women's identities in the late 1970s and 1980s. It tells the story of these influences on Marcia Freedman and American-born peace activist Galia Golan, who also made aliyah to Israel, and on Friedan, Pogrebin, Broner, and Chesler. Their stories suggest how controversies around anti-Semitism and Zionism at home and abroad shocked Jewish women into a realization that feminists needed to confront issues that they had previously ignored.

Many of these women embarked on new journeys toward self-understanding, taking them toward membership in the community of Jewish feminist activists. At the same time, they attempted to show their support for the wider feminist movement, urging Jewish women to work to "protect pluralism within the women's movement."[7] As Jewish-women-in-the-world, they hoped to create networks of activists, reaching out from "home" across boundaries of race, religion, ethnicity, and sexuality to reestablish feminist connections. Women's liberationists and Jewish feminists discussed earlier, among them Heather Booth, Ellen Willis, Diane Balser, Blu Greenberg, Irena Klepfisz, and Susan Weidman Schneider, also participated in the growing internationalism of the movement.

Driven by the deep fissures over Israel among feminists and progressives, and internally within the Jewish community, Jewish issues took on new urgency in these decades. Concern with anti-Semitism within the women's movement reflected the escalation of rhetoric regarding Israel and Zionism as well as increases in stereotyping and vilification of Jews. The attention paid to these issues by feminists, a good many of whom had not previously identified as Jews, suggests a coming to consciousness as Jews that was fraught with possibility and risk. Claiming identities as Jews publicly as well as privately meant engaging in parts of themselves that for reasons of fear, self-protection, internalized prejudice, indifference, or rebellion had previously been buried or minimized.

Some women on the left allied themselves with anti-Zionism, which they argued was not a contradiction to their Jewishness but a component of an anticolonialist worldview. Supporting the Palestinian freedom movement, groups such as Women Against Imperialism opposed the Jewish state as a manifestation of "racist settler colonialism." They targeted writings and gatherings of Jewish feminists, regretting that "Zionism is gaining more and more legitimacy in the US women's movement and the white left."[8] Criticizing American Jewish feminists' "identity work," these and other anti-Zionist women declared that failure to denounce the Israeli state rendered anticolonial alliances impossible. Their perspectives stood in contrast to those of more identified Jewish feminists, who even when they criticized Israeli policies, did not deny Israel's right to exist.[9]

Betty Friedan and Marcia Freedman: Mexico City, 1975

In June 1975, almost halfway through the period that the UN General Assembly had proclaimed International Women's Year, thousands of women converged on Mexico City. About twelve hundred were official delegates, mainly elite women and men, tasked with drawing up an official conference document. Another six thousand women, leaders at the grassroots level, attended the NGO tribune, a boisterous assembly marked by conflicts and disruptions. According to historian Jocelyn Olcott, the tribune was among the first of its kind, "the beginning of the NGO-ization of activism," a "watershed moment in transnational feminism." After Mexico City, "women would see their concerns as linked to a larger web of global issues," and "global policymakers could no longer ignore women." Yet the Mexico City conference served as a "petri dish for the conflicts that roiled the global 1970s."[10]

Fireworks between women from the West and those from Third World countries began immediately as delegates and NGOs debated the three key issues of International Women's Year: equality, development, and peace. In general, Western women were concerned about economic disparities between women and men, while Third World women focused more on gender and sexual oppression. Class factors as well as regional differences between industrial North and developing global South nations played a major role in shaping these perspectives, dividing elite and middle-class women from working-class and poor women across and within geographical boundaries.[11]

The makeup of the conference politicized issues. Many of the formal delegations were headed by first ladies, with men constituting almost 30 percent of delegates. Another anomaly was the numerical predominance of the Third World representatives, who caucused separately. The final declaration of the Mexico City conference was written entirely by women from Asia, Africa, Latin America, and the Middle East. The national interests of the governments of member states rather than the women's movements in these countries generally determined proceedings at the official conference.

Amid a complex agenda relating to the status of women, family, technology, education, health, and employment, the issue of Zionism attracted disproportionate attention. Throughout the two-week conference, delegates and NGO Tribune participants vilified Israel as a racist regime and denounced Zionism, which they analogized to apartheid, the beginnings of an association that would last well past Mexico City.[12]

The presence of Egyptian first lady Jihan Sadat and her Israeli counterpart Leah Rabin among the official delegates contributed to the polarized atmosphere. When it was Rabin's turn to speak at one session, two-thirds of the women present walked out. Outraged at the action, Betty Friedan, who led the American delegation to the tribune, walked the length of the hall to shake Mrs. Rabin's hand. A Nigerian woman expressed her indignation: "Is the conference supposed to be for the women of the world when they tell me, an African, to walk out on a woman because she is from Israel—when will they walk out on me because I am an African?"[13]

The systematic condemnation of Zionism was reflected in the preamble of the conference's final "Declaration of Mexico on the Equality of Women" and its call to action in Paragraph 26: "Women and men together should eliminate colonialism, neo-colonialism, imperialism, foreign domination and occupation, zionism, *apartheid*, racial discrimination, the acquisition of land by force and the recognition of such acquisition, since such practices inflict incalculable suffering on women, men and children."[14] Congresswoman Bella Abzug, a member of the official delegation, spoke out against the declaration, but to no avail, and the unorganized Jewish delegates were largely helpless. The anti-Zionist plank passed after a procedural change allowed a simple majority vote, as did the official declaration, with only the U.S., Israel, and Denmark voting no.[15] The conference also ratified Resolution 32, which censured Israel for the oppression of Palestinian and Arab women and called for the eradication of Zionism.

For Betty Friedan, the NGO Tribune was one of the "most painful experiences" of her life. Before the event, she received a letter with a warning: "not to speak 'where I was not wanted' or I would be denounced 'first as an American and then as a Jew.'" At the conference, when microphones were turned off and speakers shouted down, it seemed to her "fascist," "the menace of the goosestep." With horror, she saw "bands of organized disrupters led by armed men" break up meetings, "shouting slogans against imperialism and 'Zionism.'" "Followed by gunmen" and under attack, Friedan was hustled out of the hall by several women from Detroit. "My life was threatened," she said, but "when the delegate from Israel tried to speak, I took other American women . . . across the whole hall, and shook [her] hand. . . . And I have spoken out strongly on the part of Israel ever since."[16]

Friedan had been subject to anti-Semitic and antifeminist attacks in the past. Right-wing and fundamentalist opponents of abortion rights and the Equal Rights Amendment accused feminism of being a "Jewish-led 'Zionist' plot, and Friedan had received bomb threats addressed to her Jewish-sounding full name, "Betty Naomi Goldstein Freidan."[17] Despite her distaste for patriarchal Judaism, Friedan had never eschewed her Jewish roots but had not previously identified with Zionism. In 1973, she returned from a visit to Israel disappointed that Prime Minister Golda Meir refused to meet with her, viewing her as an "American witch of women's liberation who might possibly infect Israeli women."[18]

In Mexico City two years later, Friedan headed a NOW-led Feminist Caucus that stoked fears among Third World participants of U.S. cultural imperialism. According to Jocelyn Olcott, Friedan emerged as a "caricature, a flattened symbol of equality-based liberal feminism," flouting gender conventions. Olcott reports that "the fascination with her purported manliness took on a low-grade anti-Semitism," with the Mexican press identifying her by a "dizzying array of Semitic names."[19]

The disturbing Mexico City experiences integrated Friedan's two "embattled identities," making her aware of Jews' vulnerability. Returning home, she organized vigorously against the Zionism-is-racism UN resolution (3379). "All my life I have fought for justice," she proclaimed in New York, "but I have never been a Zionist until today."[20] She later explained that it was the "new strength and authenticity of women as Jews, and Jews as women, which feminism has brought that enables them to combat the use of feminism itself as an anti-Semitic political tool."[21]

Friedan attributed a growing backlash against women's rights to what she saw as the failure of feminism at Mexico City and the triumph of the "new doctrine of moralistic anti-Semitism . . . Zionism as racism." In the U.S., right-wing antifeminists vociferously attacked the women fighting to pass the Equal Rights Amendment as "a scraggly coalition of dykes and kikes, . . . fat, ugly, stringy-haired lesbians in droopy t-shirts,

Figure 8.2. Betty Friedan at NGO tribune at the UN World Conference on Women, Mexico City, June 1975. Photo by Bettye Lane. Courtesy of the Schlesinger Library, Radcliffe Institute, Harvard University.

fanatical Jewesses, and loud-mouthed minorities."[22] Friedan viewed anti-Semitism as a political tool wielded against feminism, noting that anti-Zionist diatribes had been much more dominant at the Mexico City women's conference than at other UN gatherings. This hampered women's global progress, which men in charge resisted in every way possible. "And the whole travesty could be blamed on the Jews!"[23]

Because of Mexico City, Friedan's Judaism and her feminism were aligning: "the further I go to say 'all that I am I will not deny,' and to use my passion and my strength for women, the more I begin to get very profoundly involved in my own Judaism, in whatever origins are mine as a Jew, and in speaking out in terms of Jewish identity." She urged Jewish women to take action to combat feminism as anti-Semitism: "Women as Jews, Jews as women, have learned in their gut, 'if I am not for myself, who will be for me (and who can I truly be for). If I am only for myself, who am I?"[24]

At least one group followed suit. The Mexico City conference proved to be a tipping point for Hadassah, America's largest Jewish women's organization. "Until that time we were standoffish about women's issues," declared Bernice Tannenbaum, who as Hadassah's president represented the organization at the UN women's conferences in Copenhagen and Nairobi. The Mexico City and subsequent UN "Zionism is racism" resolution led Hadassah to seek greater outreach to women's organizations.[25]

Israelis were less surprised by anti-Zionism at the Mexico City conference than the Americans were. Marcia Freedman gave a moving speech after the conference, asserting that Mexico City was "but a dress rehearsal" for the use of the "Zionism is racism" charge in the propaganda war waged by Arab states against Israel. But she declared, "As an Israeli and as a feminist, I cannot take it more seriously than that, nor do I think it deserves to be taken more seriously than that." She called on the PLO to recognize the legitimacy of Israel but urged the Israeli government to recognize the right of Palestinian people to self-determination, categorizing both objectives as broadly feminist, part of a liberation movement "that transcends national, socio-economic, and ethnic boundaries, and perhaps even denies them. The feminist vision is . . . ultimately a vision of one world."[26]

* * *

Marcia Prince Freedman was the daughter of a New Jersey homemaker mother and labor-organizer father, a Communist Party member who raised her to pay attention to social class and power relationships, lessons that she was later able to translate into a gender analysis. Unusually for a communist, her father was also an energetic Zionist, proud that his daughter won an American Jewish Congress essay contest that sent her to Israel in 1956 while still in high school, but he opposed her taking up residence there when she fell in love with the country.

After graduating from Bennington College in 1960, Freedman married and had a child. She earned a master's degree in philosophy, putting her Ph.D. on hold; instead she typed her husband's dissertation ("five times"). She accompanied him to Israel in 1967, shortly after the Arab-Israeli War, when her husband received a fellowship from the University of Haifa. She began to read "Simone de Beauvoir, Betty Friedan, Shulamith Firestone, Ellen Willis, Charlotte Bunch, Kate Millett." Her consciousness raised, she started Israel's first women's liberation group after teaching a course on the subject at Haifa University.[27]

Though Freedman was ultimately disillusioned with Israeli politics, initially she was exhilarated by the country's attempts to become a "full-fledged social democracy."[28] Being part of the dominant group was another attraction. In the U..S, she said, "I had such a minority mentality." With a "well-developed political head" inherited from her father, Freedman grew up alienated from non-Jews, "rich people"—"whoever it was." The Holocaust loomed large, and in her teenage years, she just "read and read and read and read" about it. Her consciousness of anti-Semitism was strong. If she were in a group of people who did not know her, she would "say something that would indicate to them that [she] was Jewish so that they wouldn't embarrass themselves by being anti-Semitic." This consciousness gave her "a certain historical understanding of persecution and therefore of oppression and suppression and domination." She believes that the awareness of anti-Semitism was built into Jews identity as Jews: "The more [identity] we have [as Jews] the more easily that slides into other kinds of activism."[29]

In Israel, though, "all of this Jewish self-consciousness just fell away." In a sea of Jews, she no longer felt peculiar. "I stopped being *the* Jew."[30] Freedman's feminist identity now occupied the foreground, and she became an outspoken feminist pioneer in her adopted country. As part of the dominant culture, it was easy for her to see the "contradictions between a feminist and being identified as a Jew."[31] Unlike in the U.S., where many issues raised by radical feminists had already entered the mainstream, in Israel the problems that Freedman raised, especially those connected to a woman's body—"rape, beatings, incest, teenage prostitution, breast cancer prevention, fertility management, abortions"—were "enveloped in a conspiracy of silence."[32]

American Jewish feminists, including Letty Cottin Pogrebin, Phyllis Chesler, Lilly Rivlin, Pauline Bart, Leah Novick, Melanie Kaye/Kantrowitz, Irena Klepfisz, and Esther Broner (Freedman's "guide and mentor and sister and best friend") provided crucial support, helping to validate the Israeli movement. "As soon as there was an address they were all making pilgrimages," Freedman remarked. They brought word of the growing Israeli women's movement "back to American Jewish feminists, who were just beginning to explore Jewish identity" and for whom the existence of a feminist movement in Israel was a "point of pride."[33]

To much of Israeli society, however, feminism seemed to be an extremist movement and an "*American import.*" Freedman acknowledged that Israeli feminism drew heavily on the Western feminist model in terms of its universalism, radical vision, and confrontation tactics—"noisy demonstrations at rabbinical courts, political gatherings and beauty pageants," disrupting conferences and government sessions. In the Knesset, to which Freedman was elected on the line of the Civil Rights Party, she was considered a "radical extremist" for her "unseemly subject matter"—women's and peace issues.[34] When she left the Knesset, after her marriage had ended, she came out as a lesbian, continuing her feminist work.

After Freedman's return to the U.S. in 1981, she relearned "what it is to be in the minority, to be self-conscious, vulnerable and somewhat frightened and to relearn about anti-Semitism"; she "became a Jew again."[35] Freedman resided in Berkeley, California, where she worked with Israeli/Palestinian and American women's peace groups. In 2002, she became founding president of Brit Tzedek v'Shalom, the Jewish peace group that lobbied for a two-state solution. She continued to spend extended periods of time in Israel fighting for women's rights. But, alienated from mainstream politics in both countries, Freedman never felt completely at home there or in the Diaspora.

"Most of us, as feminists, find ourselves in an adversary position vis-à-vis our governments, our economies, and our cultures," Freedman maintained. "We may want to love them, but experience and accumulated wisdom teaches us that we cannot. This is no less true for Jewish feminists vis-à-vis Israel than it is for American feminists vis-à-vis the United States."[36] Her identity as a Jewish feminist provided her with the greatest sense of community and belonging.

Phyllis Chesler and Letty Cottin Pogrebin: Copenhagen, 1980

After Mexico City, Jewish feminists determined to prepare strategically for the 1980 mid-decade UN women's conference, to be held during the last two weeks of July in Copenhagen. American Jewish women went to the conference with their "eyes open," expecting the official sessions to be politicized against Israel but hoping to interact with other Jewish women to share their experiences of American feminism and "swap

Figure 8.3. UN women's conference meets in Copenhagen, July 1980. UN Photo / Per Jacobsen.

solutions" to neutralize anti-Jewish attacks. Yet once again, Jewish women who opposed anti-Zionist measures found themselves outsiders to the global women's movement.[37] Because of polarizing Middle East issues at both NGO Forum and official meetings, Copenhagen became the most contentious of the three UN Women's Decade conferences.

Delegates from 136 countries took part in the official conference held at the Bella Center on the outskirts of town, with approximately seventy-two hundred women participating in sessions at the NGO Forum at the University of Copenhagen's Amager Center two miles away. As in Mexico City's NGO Tribune, these more spontaneous discussions constituted a parallel conference, creating "oppositional processes" "where the real concerns of women did not get lost in the elite structures of UN programs."[38]

Anti-Zionist sentiment was even more prevalent in Copenhagen than in Mexico City. Third World representatives from the Group of 77, supported by delegates from the eastern European bloc, "used every opportunity to insert a condemnation of 'zionism' into the Programme of Action and separate resolutions," while western European and North American participants "insisted that the 'political' arguments over 'zionism' detracted from the 'real' work of the meetings, the consideration of women's concerns."[39]

To Betty Friedan, the "only news that came out of Copenhagen" was "Zionism-is-racism," as much to "prevent any real world organization on women's rights as to voice another attack on Israel."[40] Friedan was outraged that at the government meetings, where the only important vote was on the Zionism-is-racism resolution, "men were flown in from many capitals to replace the women delegates who had been allowed to sit there during the meaningless pious resolutions on women's rights."[41]

Three paragraphs out of the 287-paragraph "Program of Action" concerned with Israel and the Middle East were the most highly contested elements of the official conference. Paragraph 2 referred to the Mexico City declaration, including the original language calling Zionism a form of racism. Paragraph 5 stated the importance of the struggle to eliminate "Zionism," along with the evils of "imperialism, colonialism, neo-colonialism, . . . racism, racial discrimination, apartheid, hegemonism, and foreign occupation, domination and oppression." Paragraph 244 declared that assistance to Palestinian women should be provided through the UN in cooperation with the Palestinian Liberation Organization, a change from the previous policy. Because all three paragraphs were contrary to U.S. foreign policy, the U.S. delegation voted against approving the entire "World Plan of Action." But the plan sailed through with only Canada, Australia, and Israel joining the U.S. in opposing it.[42] Only one paragraph focused on feminism, and the single reference to "sexism" appeared in a footnote.[43]

A U.S. resolution on racial discrimination caused special anguish between American Jewish and African American women, pitting long-time allies against each other. Originally submitted to the U.S. delegation by the Black Caucus headed by Dorothy Height, the distinguished president of the National Council of Negro Women, the resolution condemned race discrimination. But the U.S. withdrew the resolution when an amendment calling Zionism a form of racism was tacked on. When the motion to defeat the amendment failed, the U.S. voted against the resolution. American black women felt betrayed. The resolution was adopted, however, and Third World women viewed its passage as a validation of the importance of racism as a feminist issue.[44] To many Jewish women, the fact that the final resolution condemning racial discrimination contained the bitterly familiar "Zionism-is-racism" plank seemed "another victory for anti-Semitism."[45]

Both at official sessions and at NGO Forum panels, Israeli delegates found themselves "outmaneuvered and outshouted," often having to leave the defense of Zionism to Americans.[46] Shulamit Aloni, a prominent Knesset member from the Citizens' Rights Movement, dismissed much of the anti-Zionist invective as "associated anti-Semitically with Judaism, and not with Israel." Yet the attacks disheartened her. One of the most prominent attacks came from Leila Khaled, the two-time airplane hijacker who headed the Palestinian delegation and whom Aloni offered to debate. "I'll talk to her only through a gun," Khaled told reporters; "we speak to the world with words, but to Israel only through weapons."[47] Despite the harsh anti-Zionist rhetoric, Aloni held that women's issues such as rape and domestic abuse were discussed at the conference in informative ways.[48]

Naomi Chazan expressed similar views. The daughter of Zina Harman, who, like Naomi, became a Knesset member, and Israel's long-time ambassador to the United States, Avraham Harman, Chazan spent many years in the U.S. before completing her doctorate at Hebrew University; she was one of Israel's leading feminist and peace activists. Chazan denounced the association of Zionism with racism, suggesting that Jews abhorred apartheid as "demeaning to the just cause of black people and an insult to the Jewish people, because it is intrinsically anti-Semitic."[49] Yet she observed that the anti-Jewish, anti-Israel atmosphere at Copenhagen was not found in official conference documents.[50] While Chazan did not excuse Arab women's anti-Israel rhetoric, she thought that the denunciation of Zionism at Copenhagen resembled the "pro-forma" declarations at every international gathering in the 1970s.[51]

While not in attendance, Marcia Freedman noted the difference in American and Israeli Jewish feminists' perceptions. "Israeli feminists were invigorated, not bothered, or barely aware of the confrontation over Zionism." Freedman explained that Israeli feminists were united on "gut issues concerning women" but were deeply divided over the Palestine conflict. "The translation of anti-Zionism into anti-Semitism" was not automatic. "For Israelis, myself included," she concluded, "anti-Zionist resolutions at UN conferences are among the small disturbances in life. They are not taken too seriously in Israel, and they are not taken too seriously anywhere else in the world."[52]

American Jewish women were more alarmed. Helen Lewis of the National Council of Jewish Women observed that while she experienced deep insults to her identity as an American, a Jew, and a woman at the conference, it was only on the level of her Jewishness that she felt her very existence threatened. She understood "what it might have been like to have observed the rise of Hitlerism in the 1930s. . . . There were enemies all over the place."[53] Esther Broner noted how men used women for their own political purposes. Divided by male politics, women acted as separate nations, blaming Israel by rote. "If Israel were not in our midst, the nations seemed to say, then there would be no wife-battering, no child abuse, no sexual slave trade, no illiteracy, no malnutrition, no refugees, and no war."[54]

Broner believed that all Jewish women, not only Israelis and Zionists, were stigmatized at Copenhagen, where "three terms were used interchangeably—feminist / Jew / New York woman." "Perhaps the Jew/ feminist represented an internationalism, a unity that is anathema to those who would separate us. . . . Perhaps it was the woman, the Jew, the scapegoat refusing to be banished into the desert yet again."[55] While Broner felt that Jewish women were not completely victimized because of their assertiveness, she "never felt such a minority," she told Pogrebin. "My Black friends here shrug and say, 'The PLO is a fact of life. Anti-Semitism is a fact of life.' . . . Danger is always arising."[56]

Phyllis Chesler encountered anti-Israel rhetoric at a United Nations (UNITAR) symposium called "Creative Women in Changing Societies" that she organized in Oslo shortly before the Copenhagen conference.[57] There, Jewish women faced "a barrage of accusation" from creative artists all over the world. "You cannot sit down at the table with the Israeli unless you have a knife. You stab her under the table. You stab her over the table," proclaimed an Egyptian doctor at the event.[58] Chesler noted other anti-Semitic remarks she heard from UN officers. Broner, who with Robin Morgan was a member of the U.S. contingent, asked, "Do we make them nervous, we curly, dark-haired, voluble women, used to CR groups and to making our own ambience?"[59]

Despite the chilling revelations at Oslo, Chesler found the UN conference at Copenhagen worse, leading her to write an account of her experiences for *Lilith* magazine, titled "Sisterhood Is Powerful . . . Unless You're Jewish," under the pseudonym "Regina Schreiber," a name suggested by *Lilith*'s Aviva Cantor.[60] Copenhagen created a "paralysis of fear, shame and disbelief" for Jews, Chesler charged. But rather than confronting the anti-Jewish attackers, Jewish women at the conference who were "not yet" feminists were silenced by the harsh vitriol. It was nothing less than a "psychological pogrom. When talking about Copenhagen six months later they would cry, stop speaking." In Copenhagen, wrote Chesler, "I saw my grandmother's wig askew and her legs in the air and Cossacks riding off. And nobody noticed and nobody cared."[61] The experience of trauma that she described at Copenhagen, which she analogized to a rape in Russia, was particularly shocking in the context of a women's conference.

Yet there were attempts at building bridges. At one early-morning caucus, Bella Abzug and Robin Morgan, the latter of whom had credibility with Arab women because of her Third World activism, brought Arab and Jewish women together. Morgan reported, "We did not solve the Middle East [crisis]," but "that magic happened where people embrace and cry."[62] Morgan reflected on the widening dimensions of the international women's movement in her 1984 anthology *Sisterhood Is Global*, a sequel to her landmark collection *Sisterhood Is Powerful*, and started the Sisterhood Is Global Institute that same year. She wrote about Palestinian women in Israel five years later in her book *The Demon Lover*.[63]

To Broner and Chesler, the lesson of Copenhagen was clear: "Don't go alone. Build bridges and networks."[64] They and New York City colleagues formed Feminists Against Anti-Semitism in 1981. Its steering committee included "seder sisters" Letty Cottin Pogrebin, Lilly Rivlin, Broner, and Chesler; Batya Bauman, Aviva Cantor, and Susan Weidman Schneider of *Lilith*; scholars Paula Hyman and Judith Plaskow; and Lesley Hazleton, Vivian Scheinmann, and Shelley Neiderbach. "We are a group of Jewish feminists who are extremely concerned about the spread of anti-Semitism," they announced, "both within the women's movement and in the world at large."[65] The group supported members' concerns about growing anti-Jewish prejudice, offering solidarity and strengthening female and Jewish group identities. "This was the inception," Esther Broner noted. "C-R groups of Jewish women met, some for the first time, realizing their heritage, acknowledging their fears."[66]

Women from the group presented the panel "Anti-Semitism: The Unacknowledged Racism" at the spring 1981 National Women's Studies Conference in Storrs, Connecticut. Drawing an audience of three hundred, the panel included Esther Broner, Phyllis Chesler, Andrea Dworkin, Paula Hyman, and Judith Plaskow. For Chesler, the panel was a defining moment. It was at this event that she "came out as a Zionist": "I proclaimed to my peer group of academic feminists that I was a Zionist in the same way that they were all feminists."[67]

* * *

Born in 1940 to an Orthodox Jewish family in Borough Park, Brooklyn, Phyllis Chesler had been a Zionist from the age of eight, when she joined the socialist-Zionist youth movement Hashomer Hatzair and then the left-wing Ein Harod, with its vision of Arabs and Jews living collectively on the land. Zionism "seemed a vision of liberation, liberation from family life—the many curfews and demands—and perhaps spiritual liberation as well." She had been the "smartest boy" within her Hebrew school but could not have the bat mitzvah that she wanted or become the rabbi that she hoped to be.[68]

After experiencing the second-class treatment of women within Judaism, Chesler largely forgot about being Jewish and became a feminist. She co-founded the Association for Women in Psychology in 1969, taught one of the first women's studies courses, gave the keynote speech at the first feminist conference on rape, and co-founded the National Women's Health Network. In 1972, she published *Women and Madness*, which was a critical and a popular success, eventually selling three and a half million copies.[69]

When Chesler began to encounter anti-Semitism within the movement, she decided to become publicly Jewish. "Goaded by anti-Semitism on the left and among radical feminists," she began wearing an oversized Jewish star to proclaim her identity. Consequently, she said, "within the bosom of the feminist movement . . . I found that I was treated and recognized as a Jewish feminist, and not as a feminist-in-the abstract."[70] She took her return to Jewish identity to the NWSA conference at Storrs, announcing her Zionism there, even though she believed she would encounter harsh criticism of Israel.

With Pogrebin and others, Chesler also participated in the Black-Jewish Women's Dialogue in New York, a group that worked for ten years to learn to "hear one another out." Another post-Copenhagen dialogue developed between religious women of varying faith traditions who were alarmed that the conference had turned into a disaster because of the domination of male politics. Anti-Semitism at the UN sessions became part of the agenda as these women convened several conferences to discuss women's struggles within their traditions.[71]

The discussion was taken up in Israel, too, where Chesler journeyed after Copenhagen, trying to get the government's permission to "coordinate a radical feminist conference," as she told Broner. Chesler was featured in a series of front-page interviews about anti-Semitism as well. But the attempt to raise awareness was not easy, either abroad or back in the U.S., where Chesler faced repeated questions from feminists: "Why did I care so much about Israel? Was I paranoid about anti-Semitism?"[72]

Accusations that Jewish women overdramatized the events of Copenhagen came from within the women's movement in the U.S. and organized women's groups. Although many American Jewish women "invariably reported having been traumatized" at the conference, according to Helen Lewis, few others understood the significance of the anti-Zionist dynamics.[73] Some felt the sting of criticism from anti-Zionist and non-Zionist Jewish women, who did not agree that the conference's focus on Zionism had hijacked grassroots feminist concerns. Nor did they equate anti-Zionism with anti-Semitism, arguing that the former was essential to censure Israel's oppression of Palestinians. These feminists denied that anti-Zionists had oppressed Jewish attendees. According to one non-Jewish American observer, the "Americans and Israelis were the ones doing the intimidating."[74] Bitter feelings abounded, impairing the hopes for feminist unity.

The U.S. faced mounting but ultimately unsuccessful pressure to reverse its vote against the Copenhagen "Program of Action." Concerned that the campaigns mounted by local chapters of the United Nations Association and various women's groups were "pok[ing] their noses under the tent of the women's movement" to "win converts" to their cause, the Leadership Conference of National Jewish Women's Organizations and the Jewish Women's Network argued that the women's movement should not be used "as an instrument of attack against one another" on women's "*survival* issues." Rather, Jewish women needed to intensify their understanding of Zionism as a "Jewish survival issue," helping others to understand their loyalties both as feminists and as Jews.[75]

The Copenhagen conference made clear to the women of the established American Jewish community that there was a gap between their organizations and the feminist movement. They recognized that Jewish women were active in the women's movement but that few had credentials in the organized Jewish community, "and vice versa." The trauma of the UN conferences indicated that a united front against anti-Jewish attacks would benefit all Jewish women. Organization leaders advised their members to "increase their participation and visibility in the women's movement," interacting with "unorganized" Jewish women as a "means of strengthening one another."[76]

* * *

For pioneering second-wave feminist Letty Cottin Pogrebin, Mexico City had been "the initial 'click'" that started her on her life "as a Jewish-feminist." The Copenhagen conference seemed an "even worse quagmire." Worried that "*feminism might be helping to empower some women who hate Jews,*" Pogrebin recognized how difficult it was for "Gentile women [to] feel Jewish fears and see the world through Jewish eyes unless Jews made them do it." She felt she "had to get into the act." Her article in the June 1982 issue of *Ms.* on anti-Semitism in the women's movement was an attempt to "decode" the experiences of Jewish women at the UN conferences and "help to make sure they never happen again."[77]

A founder and editor of *Ms.*, Pogrebin was the author of several books on parenting and gender, the editor of the anthology *Stories for Free Children*, and the consulting editor for Marlo Thomas's feminist albums and children's books promoting gender neutrality, *Free to Be . . . You and Me* and *Free to Be . . . A Family*. Pogrebin's father had been a scion of the Jewish community, so she was Jewishly knowledgeable, but she had become alienated from Jewish religion because of its patriarchal elements and authoritarianism. Discarding her "ethnic self" and concentrating on her displacement as a woman, "being a Jew was irrelevant to anything [she] was doing professionally or socially," she wrote in her 1991 memoir *Deborah, Golda, and Me: Being Female and Jewish in America.* "Even while the private me was wrestling with religious misogyny—the public me was going about her business with no Jewish identity whatsoever. . . . I was a universalist feminist. I was working for equality for all women, so why single out one group? I belonged to no Jewish organizations or synagogue, and felt only the most distant connection to 'the Jewish community.' If asked to join, I probably would have said, No thanks, I have my hands full being a woman."[78]

The "seesaw" on which Pogrebin weighed the balance of her Jewish and female identities recalibrated itself after the Mexico City conference passed the "Zionism is racism" resolution. That event "radicalized" Pogrebin "as a Jew," she recalled, making it obvious that "though feminism had taken on its shoulders the fight against racism, antisemitism wasn't even on its radar screen": "Worse yet, some of my supposed feminist friends were antisemites. I learned that a sister could, when the survival of Israel was at stake, become an enemy. That patriarchy wasn't the only force wreaking havoc in the human community. That other feminists could be the problem, not the solution—precisely because 'woman' wasn't my only significant identity. I was also a Jew."[79]

Pogrebin took her first trip to Israel in 1976 and marked the start of her life as a "*Jewish*-feminist."[80] She began to look at the world through "multiple prisms"—"not just a writer *and* a woman but a writer, a woman *and* a Jew." Her *Ms.* essay, based on eighteen months of research, became the turning point in this "journey of discovery and transformation," catapulting the subject of anti-Semitism from the fringes of the radical feminist movement into the center of mainstream liberal feminism.[81] "You have put this issue on the agenda of the women's movement as well as the larger society, which has never addressed it seriously," Aviva Cantor wrote to Pogrebin.[82]

Pogrebin laid out her findings in five sections that presented problems "basic to Jews and sisterhood." Problem 1, "Failure to See the Parallels," suggested the many ways that anti-Semitism and sexism went side by side. Problem 2, "The Big Squeeze: Anti-Semitism from the Right and from the Left," acknowledged the dangerous tactics of overt anti-Semitic violence from the "lunatic right" as well as "radical myopia," the anti-Zionist, anti-Jewish, and anti-Semitic leanings of leftists. Problem 3, "The Three I's," discussed "invisibility"—"the omission of Jewish reality from feminist consciousness"; "insult"—slurs, Jew-baiting, and outright persecution; and "internalized oppression" or "Jewish self-hatred," perhaps "the most pernicious anti-Semitism of all."[83] Problem 4, "Religion, Gods, and Goddesses—The 5,000-Year-Old Misunderstanding," and Problem 5, "Black-Jewish Relations," reflected strands of evolving feminism that blamed Judaism, and Jewish women, for the twin evils of religious patriarchy and white racism.[84]

Pogrebin 's article became a cause célèbre. Close to three hundred letters arrived at *Ms.*, all but twenty supporting her, with many corroborating the prevalence of feminist anti-Semitism. *Ms.* published only three letters, all challenging Pogrebin. One letter came from ten feminist scholars, all Jewish but none Jewishly identified. Another came from African American novelist Alice Walker, who was formerly married to a Jewish man. The last was from Janice Murphy, coordinator of the Middle East Resource Center in Washington, D.C.

Pogrebin considered the letter from ten academics—four historians (Ellen DuBois, Barbara Epstein, Temma Kaplan, Judith Walkowitz), a sociologist (Judith Stacey), a psychologist (Diane Erhensaft), an anthropologist (Rayna Rapp), a German scholar (Bluma Goldstein), and two English scholars (Deborah Rosenfelt and Jane Gurko)—the most disturbing. The scholars chided Pogrebin for equating anti-Zionism and anti-Semitism, arguing that "Jewish opposition to the Zionist vision and Zionist politics" had a "long, honorable tradition" and that accusations of anti-Semitism made against legitimate criticisms of Zionism were examples of the tendency to "psychologize dissent," a consequence of the "preoccupation with forms of internalized oppression."[85] Pogrebin believed that such attitudes were a "selective feminism," revealing "Jewish negativity and shame." She called it "Jewish identity resistance" and pronounced herself more concerned about its trajectory than the long-term effects of Christian anti-Semitism.[86]

Esther Broner and Galia Golan: Nairobi, 1985

Attitudes toward Israel hardened after the 1982 war in Lebanon. Anti-Semitic attacks against Jewish institutions escalated in Europe. Jewish feminists in the U.S. increasingly confronted verbal assaults they deemed anti-Semitic. Looking toward the 1985 UN women's conference

Figure 8.4. UN women's conference, Nairobi, July 1985. UN Photo / Milton Grant.

in Nairobi, American Jewish women planned proactive steps to defend Israelis and themselves.

The issue was complicated by radical Jewish feminists' mistrust of the Jewish establishment. Outside the women's network, many of its organizations remained male dominated. "The Jewish men are willing to fund us if we say presumably anti-feminist things," Phyllis Chesler wrote to Esther Broner, "but are not willing to fund us to teach them feminism."[87] Broner drafted a "Petition for International Sisterhood" to be presented at Nairobi, which demanded that women not be used as pawns in male-dominated politics, linking Jewish women's stance as Jews to larger, universalist goals. "We who have initiated this petition identify ourselves as women, Jews, and nationals of the United States," she wrote. "But we share a love of justice and ethics with women everywhere."[88] A writer best known for her 1978 novel *A Weave of Women*, about American and Israeli feminists who create a new society in Jerusalem, Broner also created new rituals for women's life passages and Jewish events. She brought her creative spirituality to the tasks of peace making, creating ceremonies to bring women together in dialogue groups and at the UN conferences.

In July 1984, Broner delivered the keynote address in Paris to an international meeting of seventeen Jewish women's organizations, representing sixteen countries and three million Jewish women, who had gathered to prepare for the conference. "You will be learning during this conference invaluable tactics, sadly necessary for the belligerence we will encounter in Nairobi," she told them. "You will learn to attack and counter-attack, a karate approach to diplomacy. We are preparing to meet the enemy." The meeting produced a unanimous resolution that the UN take steps to prevent the Nairobi conference from becoming "a forum for anti-Western, anti-Israel, anti-Jewish rhetoric and resolutions."[89] The women conducted simulation games designed to teach them how to respond to verbal attacks and other disruptions.

Other groundwork for Nairobi involved bridge building between Palestinian and Jewish women. Reena Bernards and Christie Balka, executive director and national co-chair of the progressive, multi-issue New Jewish Agenda (NJA); Gail Pressberg, director of Middle East programs at the American Friends Service Committee; Letty Cottin Pogrebin of *Ms.*; and Israeli feminist Alice Shalvi formed a Dialogue Group to improve relationships between Jewish and Arab women. The women were invited to discuss their grievances together and build a basis for improved communication. Even within the Jewish community, discussion of the Israeli-Palestinian issue was difficult. Bernards and Balka challenged the belief that the way to build a unified international women's movement was to suppress discussion of divisive issues. They were convinced that the women's movement could be united despite Zionist/anti-Zionist controversies.[90]

With twenty-five hundred official delegates and fourteen thousand women participating in the NGO Forum, Nairobi was the largest of the three UN women's conferences. The conference coincided with the high point of the antiapartheid movement. Multiple panels and demonstrations focused on apartheid, with anti-Zionism a linked issue.[91] Almost four hundred Jewish women attended, nearly five times the number at Copenhagen. A Jewish women's caucus met daily to discuss strategies and counter misinformation. Each Jewish woman was instructed to "make peace" with other Jewish women, no matter the organization she represented, to create a united front.[92]

Broner went as part of a team from the New York Black-Jewish Dialogue Group, hoping to use her dialoguing skills. She needed them, especially at a contentious panel on Arab/Jewish women that took place in the NGO Forum's Peace Tent. It might have been more accurately called the "A Council of War," Broner remarked, in spite of rules for acceptable conduct. At the panel, Israeli and American Jewish women were loudly shouted down as they attempted to defend against charges of Zionism as racism. The panel consisted of Fawzia Hassouna, a Palestinian; Selma James, an anti-Zionist Jewish woman from Britain; Deena Metzer, an American from California; and Galia Golan, a founder of Peace Now and a Russian expert in the Political Science Department of Hebrew University. Golan and Hassouna met before the panel to find ways to manage what they expected would be rancorous proceedings. Golan gave a conciliatory speech, excoriating extremism, and presented the Peace Now two-state proposal. She told the audience that she came from the "Zionist peace movement," which wanted the Palestinians to "understand the traumatization of [the] Jewish people" while calling for "negotiation to be based on the principle that Palestinians also have rights." Hassouna bluntly talked of the West Bank's "apartheid system" and of Israel as an "illegitimate country." Despite this condemnation, Golan believed that she and Hassouna made it through their talks in a civilized fashion.[93]

But the critique of the British Jewish panelist was explosive. "Zionism is not Judaism," she asserted, but the practice of "imperialism and racism." Israel, born as insurance against the concentration camps, had become "the same concentration camp." The question-and-answer session brought more diatribes from Arab women and Jewish anti-Zionists. Broner insisted that she and Bella Abzug be allowed to respond. Broner took the mike first, warning about "the danger of the death of meaning" when Israel was likened to Nazi Germany and its soldiers called "Hitler Youth." Then a furious Abzug gave an impassioned defense: "The Zionist movement is a liberation movement," she avowed. "I learned about human rights, about socialism, from Zionism."[94]

The hostility was so great that Golan, who had immigrated to Israel from the U.S. in 1966 and fought on the front lines in the Six-Day War, could not remain. She picked up the tent canvas, unable to handle the overwhelming hatred, and escaped its confines. Later, weeping in the arms of Broner, she declared that it was "all of no use." Broner consoled her, insisting, "This is only Act One. We have to stay for the rest of the drama."[95]

Golan's appeal against extremism had come from personal experience. At a Peace Now rally opposing Israel's invasion of Lebanon a few years earlier, Jewish extremists had thrown a hand grenade that destroyed Golan's car and killed a friend who was demonstrating with her. She knew the cost of terrorism firsthand, dedicating her career to peace activism and to scholarship. Born in 1938 in Cincinnati, Ohio, Golan grew up as a secular Jew, living in Miami Beach, Forest Hills, New York, and other cities with sizeable Jewish populations. But she disliked the minority status of being Jewish and found little connection to synagogue-centered Jewish life. After her uncle converted to Catholicism when Galia was in high school, she, too, considered conversion, attracted by Saint Augustine and Catholic philosophers. At Brandeis University, where she studied political philosophy with Herbert Marcuse, a young rabbi (Blu Greenberg's husband, Yitz Greenberg) deterred her conversion desires by suggesting she had a "Jewish soul." Golan discovered the truth of his speculation doing graduate work in Paris, where she interacted with Jewish friends from Europe, Africa, and the Middle East. Jews, she realized, were an international people, and this sense of Jewish peoplehood attracted her to Israel. The emotions of the Six-Day War turned her into a Zionist, but she was a "critical Zionist," not a religious or nationalist one, embracing the causes of women's rights, human rights, and peace.[96] Nairobi tested her equanimity, but she remained committed to a Jewish-Arab political solution that she believed women could foster. Despite the enmity that she experienced at the Nairobi conference, she appreciated the fact that Jewish and Palestinian women came together in its aftermath.

The New Jewish Agenda's Bernards and Balka organized a post-conference coalition of Palestinian and Jewish women in Israel in which Golan participated. But their session at the Nairobi NGO Forum, co-sponsored by the American Friends Service Committee, had been difficult.[97] At the session "Israeli and Palestinian Women in Dialogue: A Search for Peace," attended by some five hundred women, Israeli peace activist Lisa Blum, who had emigrated from the U.S., and Palestinian Mary Khass, a preschool worker from the refugee camps in Gaza, presented their groups' positions. Organized to minimize disruption, the guidelines for the session specified that "Israel will not be singled out as a unique violator of human rights. Nor will the Palestine Liberation Organization be singled out as a terrorist organization."[98]

But the agreed-on rules broke down as audience members shouted their grievances against Israel, repeatedly bringing up the Nazi analogy.[99] "It was a firestorm," remembered Diane Balser, who had been a member of Boston's Bread and Roses and who co-chaired the session. "We were booed and heckled." *The Protocols of Zion* were cited; Jews were accused of collaborating with Nazis in their own destruction. Perhaps it was the friendship between a Palestinian and an Israeli woman, on top of the idea of a two-state solution, that was so deeply controversial.[100] The "unrelenting attacks on Israel's right to exist" left "a bitter aftertaste with Jewish women," the NJA women agreed, yet despite the hostility, they believed that Forum sessions contributed to the feeling that women could work together. "I found a hunger for contact on all sides," Balka commented, so "NJA intends to persist in this dialogue."[101]

Although the bitter atmosphere at the forum caused the majority of Jewish women to avoid most workshops dealing with the Middle East, hopeful moments did occur, such as the events that took place at one Egypt-Israel session after an anti-Israel chant broke out. Broner told the story: "The American black women in the audience rise and begin singing, 'We shall overcome,' until the Arab women, surprised, [became] quiet. And two Kenyan women rise in rage: 'We are here in Nairobi to make peace, and we're here as women.'"[102]

American feminists were also surprised by the official UN plenum. Hammering out the final conference text, "Forward-Looking Strategies," delegates became involved in a debate over Paragraph 95, which contained a statement about "Zionism is racism" that the U.S. and some western European nations would not support. Consensus seemed remote after a proposed compromise failed. The Jewish women's group debated what to do. Betty Friedan, who had been a daily presence under the Peace Tent, urged them to continue to lobby delegates.[103]

Despite the bleak mood, "strange things" happened, reported Broner, when a Kenyan delegate objected to the inclusion of Zionism as a "major obstacle" to women's progress in Paragraph 95. After a five-hour recess, Iran retracted the motion, and the PLO agreed to more generalized terminology. An amended document was passed. Broner admitted, "Israel is not yet the beloved of the nations. . . . But the women of the world have said that there are causes and issues that rise above the world's nasty squabbles, and it is these . . . issues—these hopes, really— that they have here endorsed. There is dancing in the aisles. The women of the world have spoken with one voice, and Israel is not excluded from the jubilation."[104]

To the U.S. delegation, the replacement of the word "Zionist" in the official conference document with the phrase "all other forms of . . . racial discrimination" was a major victory. Americans left the conference believing that despite anti-American and anti-Zionist sentiment, they had witnessed the birth of a truly international women's movement.[105] This time, said Pogrebin, "Jewish women came home battered but not broken."[106]

Friedan also considered the "breakthrough" at Nairobi significant. Nairobi marked the emergence of the "world's women to new political autonomy, and their effective refusal to let anti-Semitism be used as a political tool to block their advance to equality worldwide." She took pride in Jewish women's refusal to "embrace the passive victim role," which together with the "revulsion of other women against anti-Semitism" played a role in defeating the authoritarian forces that had successfully pitted anti-Semitism and antifeminism against each other at the Mexico City and Copenhagen conferences. Friedan was hopeful that the victory over the "strange congruence" of these negative forces might be a harbinger for "Jewish survival in the world's women's movement and the larger values of feminism."[107] For Christie Balka, too, the resolution's defeat signaled that Jewish feminists could "work in coalition with other women on the basis of both the positive values of Judaism and our shared experiences and commitment to each other as women." It allowed "Jewish women to define ourselves in relation to global feminism."[108]

Yet Balka was chastened at how widespread anti-Zionist sentiment had been. Although the "Zionism is racism" resolution was defeated, "no nation passed up the opportunity to criticize Israel." Balka had not anticipated that such scrutiny would be limited to Israel: "a selective morality on South Africa and other issues appeared to be in force." She acknowledged, "Regardless of the reasons why each of us traveled to Kenya as Jewish women, our identity once there was defined to a great extent by anti-Semitism. What we do in the world—write books for Jewish women, fight for women's equality within traditional Judaism, create rituals for women, make films for women, fight for women's health care, organize women workers, battered women, lesbians, older women—all of this and the power it represents seemed to matter much less than the fact that we were Jews."[109]

There was a silver lining: the forging of stronger bonds between American and Israeli Jewish women. Americans came to understand the threats and hostility facing Israelis and offered support and models of organization and feminist activism. Israeli women, more seasoned to anti-Zionist rhetoric, welcomed the new allies, providing examples of courage and resistance. These alliances prospered in years to come.

The New Jewish Agenda dialogue at Nairobi spawned the creation of the Jerusalem Link, the first Israeli and Palestinian women's joint peace venture, composed of Bat Shalom in West Jerusalem and the Jerusalem Women's Center in East Jerusalem. The initiative continued for a number of years. Galia Golan believed that the meetings between Jews and Arabs caused the Palestinian women to modify their earlier "absolutist rhetoric." She had hope for the future.[110]

"The Empowerment of Jewish Women": Jerusalem, 1988

Israel's most important women's advocacy group, the Israel Women's Network (IWN), had been founded in the summer of 1984, following a U.S.-Israel Dialogue in Jerusalem organized by the American Jewish Congress on the subject of "woman as Jew, Jew as woman." Thirty-two Israeli women participated, including Alice Shalvi, Galia Golan, Naomi Chazan, and Shulamit Aloni. The U.S. delegation, headed by Betty Friedan, counted many prominent Jewish feminists, among them Blu Greenberg and Susan Weidman Schneider.[111]

American feminist support was crucial to the IWN. Israel lacked feminist consciousness at the time, Shalvi observed, despite socialist-Zionist themes of equality and the prominent role of women as early state pioneers. In IWN's first years, the group was almost completely supported by American women, particularly from the New Israel Fund, a dependency that did not trouble Shalvi or her colleagues. "All [Israeli] women's organizations have an arm in the U.S.," she said; "it's the sense of being one people."[112]

The Israel Women's Network, the American Jewish Congress, and the World Jewish Congress worked together on a second initiative, the First International Feminist Conference for the Empowerment of Jewish Women, designed to extend the American-Israeli Jewish feminist network to Jewish women around the world. The groups spent two years planning the conference but were beset by sharp differences. Letty Cottin Pogrebin reported in *Lilith*, "We wrangled over which speakers to invite on what subjects from which countries and how to strike a balance between organizational and unaffiliated women, and between secular and Jewish issues. We almost came to blows about how to accommodate radical feminists and grass roots peace groups and the effect of the intifada on women."[113]

The conference took place in Jerusalem in December 1988, involving 350 Jewish women from over twenty nations, with additional hundreds attending open forums. Helen Suzman, the longtime South African apartheid opponent; Renee Epelbaum, a founder of the Mothers of the Plaza of the Mayo in Argentina; and refusenik Ida Nudel, whom the Soviets had recently permitted to immigrate to Israel, attended. But tensions abounded, with some enraged that the conference omitted discussion of the Intifada, the first Palestinian uprising against the Israeli occupation of Palestinian territories, which erupted in December 1987.

The most hotly debated session came at an evening forum on women and peace, where Galia Golan and Naomi Chazan presented research showing that women were more dovish than men. Veteran SDS and civil rights activist and Chicago Women's Liberation Union pioneer Heather Booth, attending the conference as the head of Chicago's Citizen Action, registered surprise at the level of discord at the emotional session.[114]

Although American women seemed most disturbed at the display of divisiveness among Israeli women, Golan acknowledged a more general anxiety that disagreements could cause participants to lose their "unity as Jewish women." Bella Abzug, who delivered the conference's opening address, reminded attendees that women were there to "change the nature of power." "We're so hungry," Phyllis Chesler agreed. "We're so starved for recognition of our point of view because we don't have it from the outside—from the rabbinate, the Knesset, or Wall Street." Abzug spoke of the common dream of an international Jewish women's network. Alice Shalvi of the IWN concurred: "For 40 years, women have been in the wilderness. . . . We're ready to enter our promised land of a just and equal society. But we have to create it; it's not waiting for us. And women in Israel and the U.S. must be equal partners."[115]

Slated to give the closing "Call to Action," Pogrebin discovered an "intoxicating sisterhood," despite disagreements. Although consensus was not possible, hearing one another's perspectives created a "multi-layered inclusiveness," which was the hallmark of the Jewish feminist struggle: "Each of us wants to be accepted for the woman she is; she refuses to carve herself to fit any mold, even a feminist mold. She insists on her ethnic, religious *and* gender integrity as she sees it." Pogrebin believed the multiplicity of voices fit the complexity of Jewish women's double agenda concerning the struggle against sexism and anti-Semitism. Such issues were serious enough to fight about, said Pogrebin, "and to be Jewish is to be disputatious": "Jews argue because we care. And Jewish feminists argue even more because we have even more to care about."[116]

* * *

On the morning of December 1, 1988, some seventy Jewish women from the First International Jewish Feminist Conference set off on a peaceful march to pray at the Western Wall (Kotel), where women were forbidden to hold service; the vision of women praying there had come from Rivka Haut's pioneering work with Orthodox feminist prayer groups in Brooklyn. Phyllis Chesler received the honor of opening the Torah, and Blu Greenberg was given the first aliyah.[117] With the aid of two women rabbis, the women conducted the service and Torah reading. "We . . . brought sacredness back to the Wall," Broner noted, "while the men on their side roared with rage." "It was an absolute triumph of our human, female spirit over male tyranny," said Chesler.[118]

Broner, Chesler, and Marcia Freedman had dreamed of such a day thirteen years earlier, when they met in a Jerusalem coffee shop with Israeli feminists to plot strategy for integrating the Kotel but they had felt "so pathetic, so powerless."[119] Now, after the three contentious UN conferences and the difficult launch of the International Jewish Feminist Conference, women from different denominations, including secular women, were ready to sacrifice for the unity of the whole, and the prayer service for the Kotel was developed by consensus. The advocacy group Women of the Wall (WOW), consisting of mostly observant Israeli women, was formed at that moment. With its global arm, the International Committee for the Women of the Wall (ICWOW), with many American members, it continues the difficult legal and religious fight for equal prayer rights at the Wall.[120]

American Jewish feminists worked in concert with Israeli feminists in the burgeoning women's peace movement as well. In 1988, "in solidarity with Women in Black and other Israeli and Palestinian women's groups working for peace," Irena Klepfisz, formerly of Di Vilde Chayes, along with activist-poets Grace Paley and Claire Kinberg, founded the Jewish Women's Committee to End the Occupation of the West Bank and Gaza (JWCEO), which supported a two-state solution; they had been encouraged by Lil Moed, an American Jewish feminist who had made aliyah to Israel in 1966 and who had helped to organize SHANI (Israel Women Against the Occupation), formed after the start of the First Intifada.[121]

By 1990, according to Alisa Solomon, there had been an "explosion" of Jewish feminist activism on the Middle East, with women across the United States and in Israel "standing vigil" or meeting with Palestinian women, hoping to find some breakthrough to a peaceful solution.[122] From these beginnings came a diverse, grassroots coalition aimed at reversing what some Jewish feminists viewed as increasingly brutal Israeli policies toward the Palestinians. Some of the protesters declared themselves anti-Zionists yet rejected the label that they were "self-hating" Jews.[123] Others opposed Israeli occupation policies, which they considered unjust, but staunchly defended Israel's right to exist. Outside the peace movement stood Jewish women who were proud feminists but for whom this issue had little or no resonance.

"To Strengthen Jewish Identity in All Its Diversity"

In a speech on Jews and Israel in 1985, Ellen Willis addressed the grow-ing rift among American Jews about Israel. Willis acknowledged the Left's critique of Israel's religious fundamentalism and its military policies, yet she sided with some of the Right's positions, highlighting Israel's vulnerability and the threat of anti-Semitism. In her view, the "deep structure of anti-Semitism that leaves Jews vulnerable to persecu-tion, displacement, and genocide" had not essentially changed.[124]

Willis suggested that by the 1980s, in the United States, and for the Jewish people as a whole, "we are moving in a post-Zionist phase." By this, she meant that it would become increasingly untenable to "define Israel as the basis of Jewish identity or as the realization or central aim of the Jewish project" because of deeply divided views about Israeli militarism, nationalism, and self-defense. Yet Israel and its fate would remain of "vital concern" to Jews, an important focus of Jewish life and culture, and a marker of Jewish identity for Americans.[125]

Willis remained profoundly dedicated to Israel's well-being, labeling herself an "anti-anti-Zionist," as she wrote in her essay, published shortly before her death, in Tony Kushner and Alisa Solomon's 2003 anthology *Wrestling with Zion: Progressive Jewish-American Reponses to the Israeli-Palestinian Conflict*.[126] For her, post-Zionism was not anti-Zionism. She believed that there was a sense in which Israel has to be "Israeli"—"as much or more than Jewish." Willis's relation to Israel was ultimately that "of an outsider, with an intimate stake in what happens to be sure," but still with her "own visions and priorities."[127]

Willis's words notwithstanding, American Jewish feminists found it difficult to distance themselves from the Israel issue. After the UN women's conferences and those in Jerusalem, frameworks of Jewish feminist identity increasingly stretched beyond personal, local, and national sites, so that U.S. Jewish women found it necessary to negotiate the developing terrains of transnational feminism from a Jewish per-spective. Despite Willis's postulation of a post-Zionist phase, it became increasingly difficult for Jewish feminists to ignore global identity issues around Zionism in favor of local ones.

In the face of such challenges, new groups began to engage in Jew-ish feminist consciousness-raising. These associations helped Jewish feminists find new political homes as visible Jews. In "personalizing the political" by connecting Jewish and female experience, they empowered themselves as feminists.

This was not the only precept that the Jewish radical feminists of the 1980s shared with the pioneer women's liberationists. Like the movement founders, they were motivated by their anger at the oppressions of sexism, racism, homophobia, classism, and other structures of domination, seeing their political actions as part of a broad movement to eradicate these interlocking harms. How they meshed these goals with attention to the problems and opportunities of Jewish feminist identity differed for various individuals and groups of women. As the 1990s began, they confronted difficult issues of racism within the feminist movement as well as anti-Semitism and gender, class, and sexual inequalities. The decade witnessed the creation of several organizations and institutions that joined Jewish and feminist impulses, providing new spaces for hybrid identities. Among these groups were *Bridges: A Journal for Jewish Feminists and Their Friends*, which began in 1990, and the Jewish Women's Archive, established in 1995 to collect and promote the stories of Jewish women.

The problem of confronting anti-Semitism and distinguishing it from anti-Zionism remained in the new century. While the struggle for the feminists considered in these chapters had been to bring together the Jewish and feminist aspects of their personalities and heritage, by the 2000s, the ground had shifted, making the integration of feminism and Zionism more urgent and perhaps more difficult than earlier. In 2012, Pogrebin admitted that like Adrienne Rich, she felt "split at the root": "one side of me struggling against the hijacking of feminism for anti-Israel aims, . . . the other side resisting the institutionalized patriarchy and entrenched sexism of Jewish institutions, including those of the Zionist left." Pogrebin believed that Zionism remained to Jews "what feminism is to women—an ongoing struggle for self-determination, dignity, and justice." But for her, integration remained incomplete: "Depending on where I stand, whether as a feminist in Zionism or a Zionist in feminism, one or another essential part of me is likely to feel displaced, denigrated, unseen, or unheard."[128] Other Jewish feminists found connections among feminism, Jewish identity, and Zionism to have been automatic and less problematic. Another, smaller group rejected the Zionist label entirely. Conversations about these positions within the Jewish community and among feminists have been forceful and vigorous.[129]

Differences about Jewish identity that had been covered over in the early stages of women's liberation became redefined not only as negative signposts of identity but as positive aspects of heritage that incorporated diverse backgrounds and welcomed coalition building. In Alisa Solomon's words, by the start of the 1990s, a fair proportion of those who had led the "Jewish identity movement" were becoming activists. The momentum had been building since the 1970s, with "alienated and assimilated Jewish women . . . joining with sisters more rooted in their Jewishness, to strengthen Jewish identity in all its diversity."[130] As they faced continuing challenges, bonds formed with Jewish women at home and abroad vastly aided these efforts. At the same time, Jewish women continued to ally themselves with broader feminist causes and groups, providing ideas and leadership to the changing faces of feminism.

Conclusion

Second-wave feminism in the 1960s and 1970s was a mass movement that brought together thousands of feminist activists from diverse ethno-racial and class backgrounds. These women faced unique historical circumstances shared by men of their generation whom they joined in protest movements challenging racial and social discrimination, the horrific Vietnam War, and establishment values. There is much research to explain why college-age Jewish youth were highly represented in the ranks of these protesters. Among the most often cited reasons were the family values that shaped political identities and the process of educational clustering that brought highly motivated youth in touch with like-minded comrades.[1] These synchronic influences gave members of the 1960s and 1970s generation a vocabulary of discontent that they utilized to fight political and social injustices.

Jewish women flocked to the social movements of these decades in particularly high numbers. The same factors that drove them to enlist in the battles of the New Left led them to revolt against the sexism they found there, often leading the charge. Angry at the neglect of their ideas and contributions and intolerant of bullying, they were determined to fight second-class citizenship even when it meant breaking with men in their communities or from other women in the movement. As we have seen, the multiple types of Jewish stimuli helped them to become such fierce warriors. These were not the sole influences on them. For example, many black women exemplified how to be feminist activists and grassroots leaders in the broader movement. But Jewish backgrounds, ethical imperatives, and networks and associations played a major part in shaping the contributions of Jewish women's liberationists and Jewish feminists.

Concerned with inequalities arising from the linked oppressions of gender, sexuality, class, and race, Jewish women in the women's liberation movement played leading roles in launching a largely successful challenge to sexism. In their fight against the strictures of patriarchy, they were gender universalists who did not prioritize, or even recognize, their ethnic origins as a claim on the most inclusive concerns of sisterhood. Only in later decades did some of them begin deliberately to associate themselves with the Jewish influences that had contributed to their activism. For other women's liberationists, it was the belated awareness of what they perceived as the neglect or threat of anti-Semitism in the feminist movement that led them to acknowledge their Jewishness and seek ties with other Jewish women. But even by the end of the 1980s, when this book concludes, some women's liberationists did not participate in the era's "ethnic revival."[2] For a number of them, it was the conference I convened at NYU and the probing interviews I conducted with them that belatedly summoned up these associations or, as Vivian Rothstein put it, "instigated" these connections.[3] And in a few cases in this book, Jewish identity remained a matter of private admission, hidden from public scrutiny, or denied completely.

As distinct from what might be called the "feminism-primary" Jewish women featured in part 1 of *Jewish Radical Feminists*, the Jewish-identified feminists who appear in part 2 believed that the liberation of Jewish women required the overthrow of patriarchal institutions within Jewish culture. Attempting to align the Jewish aspects of their identities with their feminist commitments, in many ways they were "hyphenated" feminists, seeking the feminist transformation of Jewish institutions.

The first Jewish feminist groups, religious and secular, came to awareness shortly after the founding of the early women's liberation groups in the late 1960s. They fought against sexism within Jewish religious practices and the Jewish community, including their marginalization by male colleagues in the Jewish Renewal and student movements. Schooled in feminist activism by their associations with women's liberation leaders and texts and women's study groups, Jewish-identified feminists came from homes with high Jewish content and practice but also those with little Jewish background. As they sought to eradicate the religious, social, and sexual inequities of American Jewish life, they created new models of Jewish feminism that drew on disparate elements of the traditions that they had encountered in their formal and informal education.

The transformations that both groups of women did much to initiate unfolded largely through community, the matrix of change common to women's liberationists and Jewish feminists. Drawn to the collectives in this book and other organizations, these feminist pioneers discovered that in listening to each other they could hear their own voices. Their joint discourses provided the seeds for strategies and actions that empowered their generation. As Linda Gordon reminds us, "collective" was a sacred word for the women's movement.[4] How well that framework fit with the communal thrust of Jewish political tradition. While the movement exhibited the inevitable tensions between communitarianism and individualism that befell other utopian experiments, the stories in this book reveal that women's liberation and Jewish feminism were inherently collective dramas infused by the energies of unique persons. The synergies produced by strong, assertive feminists when they came together enabled the movement to flourish, diversify, and transform.

The biographical narratives in the book illuminate the manifold ways of being Jewish and feminist that were enacted and expressed by members of women's liberation and Jewish feminist collectives. Each model is a disparate amalgam, shaped in varying measures by heritage, personality, and social and historical location. Together they suggest a catalogue of personas and offer new information about the construction of what we now see as intersectional identities. Diversity within the feminist movement was marked within each of the two major divisions described in this book. Even among feminist groups with shared perspectives and common educational and activist pasts, the range, depth, and variety of Jewish backgrounds is striking.

The side-by-side profiles in the book reveal the diverse Jewish lives of this feminist generation. Though vital in their influence, for most (but not all) of the women's liberationists, the Jewish factors in these lives remained below the surface, not articulated or a matter of conscious awareness at the time of the 1960s–1970s rebellions. This was the case with Chicago's Gang of Four, who did not discuss their Jewish experiences with each other during their movement activism or in many decades of friendship. Two came from secular Yiddish / Communist Party backgrounds; one came from a Conservative suburban Jewish

family; another had refugee parents from Europe. Their Jewish edu-
cations included classes at Yiddish shul and Hebrew school, informal
education at Labor Zionist camps and Jewish community centers, and
synagogue attendance.

The same variety and substantive immersion in Jewish life and heritage characterize members of the Boston groups described in the book.
While some of the women had the red-diaper-baby backgrounds that
typified Jewish radicals of the New Left, the Jewish credentials that the
women exhibited were more wide ranging. The women of Bread and
Roses Collective #1 had grown up in Reform, Conservative, and Reconstructionist congregations; attended Yiddish shul and Hebrew-school
classes; and had been traumatized by family Holocaust stories and other
Holocaust remembrances. McCarthyism, too, cast its shadow over their
childhoods. Some had been inspired by immigrant ancestors, including
Socialist and Communist Party members, or by independent-minded
activists. Like the Chicago women, they attributed a sense of themselves
as outsiders at least in part to their Jewishness, but they had rarely articulated this belief, acknowledging their gender-determined and often
class-based experiences of marginality much more fully.

The New York women's liberationists also exhibited a breadth of Jewish experiences. In this case, the retreat from Orthodoxy, the physical
and metaphysical experiences of anti-Semitism, and the frustrations of
gender discrimination within Judaism become prominent childhood
inheritances. Like the women's liberationists from Chicago and Boston,
these New York second-wave feminist leaders did not often acknowledge their own Jewishness or recognize the Jewishness of other collective members. If it was present, it simply did not matter.

The Jewish story of the Boston Women's Health Book Collective
begins in a similar fashion but unfolds differently. Here, too, a plethora
of Jewish backgrounds stands in bold relief against a shared feminist
milieu. The Jewish configuration of the OBOS collective includes a lifelong observant Jew; a member who had attended an Orthodox Hebrew
day school in a working-class community; a child Holocaust survivor
influenced by a brief, early exposure to Orthodox religion; two daughters of labor union or Communist Party activists, one of whom later
embraced kabbalah and Buddhist mysticism; and one woman who identified no Jewish background, except the threat of anti-Semitism. These

diverse factors contributed to the women's lives as activists in tandem with motivations they shared with non-Jewish feminist collaborators. A "eureka" moment several years into the collective's life marked a sudden recognition of the disproportionate number of Jewish women among the founders, a matter of surprise at such a prominent though hitherto unremarked kinship. Because the women shared work and family times and because of the very public embrace of Judaism by one of the collective's leading members, the observant Esther Rome, Jewishness became a glue that cemented the women's bonds. Like the Jewish members, the non-Jewish founders of OBOS considered the group's Jewishness a positive factor in maintaining the social fabric of the collective, contributing to its continuity and productivity.

The portraits in part 2 of this book fill in the gallery of Jewish women active in the 1960s–1980s women's movement. As with the women's liberationists in part 1, there is no single prototype for these pioneering Jewish feminists, who were among the first in their generation to confront sexism within Jewish religious and communal life. Some religious feminists came from observant homes across the denominational spectrum; others came from homes with little religious content, and their religious inclinations, shaped by feminism, were self-determined. Secular Jewish feminists supported the goals of their religious peers but directed their energies elsewhere. Their backgrounds also exhibit diverse Jewish influences: day schools, Hebrew after-school programs, Jewish camps, travel to Israel, and Holocaust connections including experience as survivors and refugees. The knowledge and networks resulting from these Jewish influences provided a base for Jewish feminists' explosive decision to challenge the patriarchal foundations of Jewish life and thought. Direct contact with women's liberation leaders, immersion in the movement's groups, and contact with its foundational texts and ideas provided momentum that drove the women's campaigns. Educated and strengthened by the movement, they brought feminism to the Jewish mainstream and Jewish feminism to the Left—efforts that were complementary rather than separate and competing alternatives.

Although the integration of feminism and Jewishness was far from seamless, feminism served as a "portal" into Judaism for many Jewish women, as Blu Greenberg suggested, encouraging them to probe their own religious tradition and confront its oppressive elements.[5] Feminism also encouraged secular women to uncover aspects of Jewish life that could empower them to respect their heritage and name themselves as Jewish feminists, as it did for Adrienne Rich, who wrote of the ways in which the movement allowed her to find the "starved Jew" in herself.[6] Their assault on the assimilatory mode of American Judaism challenged both the Jewish establishment and women's liberationists who espoused a politics of universalism. While established Jewish community leaders often considered these Jewish-identified feminists to be a "loyal opposition," their demands to remedy injustices created unavoidable tensions.[7] Conflicts between women's liberationists and Jewish feminists could become severe as well.

Yet connections between women in these groups inspired creative thinking and actions. Encountering Naomi Weisstein at a Yale University graduate lecture became a turning point for theology student Judith Plaskow, instigating her feminism. Courses on socialist feminist theory at the Chicago Women's Liberation Union School motivated the pioneering domestic-abuse work of Susan Schechter of the Chutzpah collective. Maralee Gordon taught courses on Jewish women at the CWLU School in the early 1970s, as did Ruth Balser at the Cambridge Women's Center, enabling cross-fertilization.

For many, however, the journey to claim a Jewish feminist identity was fraught with uncertainty. Some feared reactions from friends, family, feminist colleagues, and the Jewish community. Quite a number described their naming of themselves as Jewish feminists as a "coming out," parallel to declaring forbidden sexual identities. In the face of such anxieties, the support offered by feminist and Jewish groups was enormous, providing opportunities for growth and the courage to explore difficult questions.

To varying extents, Jewish feminists pushed up against negative attitudes toward their identification as religious women, radical Jews, or Zionists. Within much of the women's movement and the radical Left more generally, Israel was treated with suspicion, not as an ally of Third World liberation movements with which feminists increasingly sought to align their politics. The question of whether feminists could be Zionists that would roil the feminist movement in the 2000s first emerged in the global feminist movement during the 1970s and 1980s, making the alliance between Jewish radicalism and feminism increasingly difficult.

As Jewish feminists encountered identity politics within the movement, some became aware of their difference and isolation from other feminists. For the women of Di Vilde Chayes and other secular feminists, the confluence of concerns around anti-Semitism, anti-Zionism, and racism took center stage, making it difficult to reconcile Jewish identities with feminist sisterhood. While coalition building remained a desired goal, the complexities of identity politics impeded collaboration and connection.

Jewish women did not share uniform attitudes toward Israel, Zionism, or anti-Semitism. Differences existed among Jewish-identified feminists, as well as between them and women's liberationists. Views could shift even within a particular group, seen when several members of Di Vilde Chayes began to question their previous views about Israel. Much as Jewish feminists exhibited a wide variety of Jewish backgrounds, so they also demonstrated many shades of opinion regarding Zionism, anti-Zionism, and anti-Semitism.

Yet, despite this spectrum of opinions and experiences, the women featured in this book recognized characteristics that they shared with other Jewish women in their collectives and the movement, even though, in the case of the women's liberationists, many did not acknowledge these connections publicly or even to themselves. A sense of themselves as outsiders—or, more precisely, the dual experience of being outsiders and insiders—was a critical factor shared by many groups. While acknowledging the class and racial advantages accruing to many Jews in the postwar period, the women nonetheless perceived themselves as different from other Americans. Being Jewish accentuated the sense of marginality they felt as women in a masculinist, Christian-dominated society. Yet within leftist movements and multicultural communities, Jewish roots did not confer status as an oppressed or marginalized group, nor was Jewish difference recognized among those who might ally with women of color. Declaring themselves feminists committed to the radical restructuring of Jewish life could threaten the women's standing within both Jewish and feminist circles. The simultaneous experience of Jews as insiders and outsiders, as "both victims of and members of a privileged class," as Cheryl Greenberg has put it, highlights the complex, shifting, and voluntary nature of identity and contributes to the broad project of multicultural understanding.[8]

Women's liberationists and Jewish feminists saw another common trait in their own assertiveness and candor. Often described as pushy, loud, aggressive, and unfeminine, the women in this book recast the negative terms that others applied to their behavioral style as appropriate responses to demeaning and inequitable treatment. The double marginality that they experienced as women and as Jews called forth their willingness to forcefully fight for equality. In this respect, some Jewish feminists found the example of women of color particularly inspiring.

Concomitant to the women's outspokenness, the willingness to challenge authority characterized generations of Jewish women before them as well as Jewish female activists of their cohort. Paula Doress-Worters found role models in Jewish women in Bread and Roses who "weren't self-conscious about being perceived as too aggressive, or too loud," their confidence giving them a platform to effect social change.[9] Blu Greenberg was influenced by her Orthodox mother's "need for truth and justice" and her demand for tough criticism, which became models for her own difficult challenges to tradition.[10] While not unique to Jewish women's liberationists and Jewish feminists, such qualities appeared widely among them and were cited by many narrators in this book as group descriptors.

Many feminists drew attention to Jewish women's affinity for critical thinking as a key aspect of their movement participation. While not exclusive to Jewish women in women's liberation, where exploration of life experiences became the primary mode for raising consciousness, critical thinking was an aspect of Jewish culture that had been passed on through many generations. Judaism's valorization of intellectual questioning and creativity, its propensity for argument and debate, and its openness to multiple interpretations stemmed from ancient rabbinical tradition. While some critics thought that "excessive intellectualization" might have been problematic for Jews, the emphasis on teaching and learning—the idea that Jews were "People of the Book"—remained a highly regarded component of twentieth- and twenty-first-century Jewish culture.[11]

For radical feminist Ellen Willis, critical skepticism was the essence of Jewishness, a by-product of the Diaspora Jew's living between two worlds. As the "perennial doubter, the archetypal outsider," this feminist

Jew used her experience of betweenness to probe and challenge not only inherited ways of thinking but also the canards of comrades and leftist associates.[12] Norma Swenson, a non-Jewish founder of OBOS, recognized the trait as a paramount feature of her Jewish co-founders' approach to problematic issues of women's health. Encouraging analysis both of Judaism itself and of the world, Judaism's engagement with critical thinking helped to stimulate feminists to rethink problematic aspects of their lives and invent creative solutions.

A final correspondence among women's liberationists and Jewish feminists in this work is the role played by Jewish values. This category is quite amorphous, reflecting ethical tenets gleaned from the varied backgrounds and experiences that activists recalled as they reinterpreted their motivations years later. Social justice ideals—humane and compassionate treatment for every person, empathy for and identification with the oppressed, the duty to act righteously—were the most frequently cited values, but they emerged from different starting points.

For both women's liberationists and Jewish feminists, religious sources provided a strong foundation for social justice activism. Heather Booth's confirmation text, the Book of Amos ("let justice flow like a river and righteousness like a mighty stream"), framed her lifelong allegiance to the prophetic tradition. Meredith Tax, confirmed in a Reform synagogue, absorbed what she saw as "ethical Judaism" there. Hillel's principle—"that which is hateful to you, do not do to your neighbor"—and the prophetic injunction to "do justice, love mercy, and walk humbly" became lifelong commitments.[13] Similar "words of the prophets calling us to justice and social engagement" motivated theologian Judith Plaskow, although she thought her Reform-synagogue education otherwise uninspiring.[14] Rabbi Laura Geller, who also grew up Reform, became fascinated by the connection of justice to morality, and later, she too studied Christian and then Jewish ethics in her search for answers. Orthodox yeshiva student Arlene Agus located encouragement for her activism in the Hebrew Bible and the Jewish prayer book, in which she found evidence of "communal unity" and a rationale for struggling for greater spiritual equality for women.[15] The Torah also gave Blu Greenberg her faith and encouragement for eventually challenging women's religious inequalities.

Secular radicalism was another influence on the social justice ideals of feminist Jews. Like other 1960s activists, many of their parents were Yiddishists, trade unionists, socialists, or Communist Party members. Amy Kesselman, schooled in her parents' progressive Jewish politics, typified this group. The secular community shul that her parents helped to found provided her with "a hatred of dictators and Jew haters, a belief in struggle," and gave her a "connection with downtrodden people," a message reinforced by her family, whose holiday seders always included the spiritual "Go Down Moses." The "rabid anti-clericalism" of Naomi Weisstein's mother and grandfather and her mother's anarchist radicalism similarly influenced her political development.[16] For Miriam Hawley, "social justice was the family religion," imparted by her parents, Communist Party members who were active in the Rosenbergs' defense.[17]

For several women in this book, Zionism offered a set of values related to social justice, independence, and Jewish liberation. Vivian Rothstein's immersion in Hashomer Hatzair, the Labor Zionist youth movement, schooled her in the values of feminist equality, commitment to a social movement, and the need to take action "rather than be acted upon."[18] Hashomer Hatzair's vision of equality and strong women leaders were also pivotal for Evelyn Torton Beck, shaping her sense of purpose. For Martha Ackelsberg, the daughter of Zionists, Zionism meant an engagement with the ideals of Jewish peoplehood and a lifelong commitment to collective life, the subject of much of her scholarship and activism. As a founder of Young Americans for Progressive Israel and a member of other Zionist groups, Aviva Cantor prioritized the goals of Jewish peoplehood, working to expand the reach of Radical Zionism within the U.S. Gloria Greenfield ascertained from her father, a passionate Zionist, that Israel was central to Jewish identity and that all Jews must fight for its survival.

The importance of remembering history as a route to meaning, identity formation, and continuity emerges as another central node in the constellation of Jewish values discussed in this book. For Jews, collective memory is crucial to understanding self and tradition, an essential component of knowledge and of political and social action. The many Holocaust themes that echo through these narratives indicate its significance in forming the women's earliest views about Judaism as well as their determination to remember and engage with these stories. Becoming activists who actively combatted the evils of prejudice and terror was a response to this early learning. Whether it was the stories that Shulamith Firestone, Michele Clark, and Diane Balser heard from survivors in their families and neighborhoods or read in schoolbooks and encyclopedias, or the freighted silences of parents such as those of Meredith Tax who refused to discuss its horrors, or the actual encounters with Nazism experienced by Vilunya Diskin, Evelyn Torton Beck, and Irena Klepfisz as child refugees, the Holocaust loomed large in the women's memories. In linking them to Jews' tragic past, it led them to recognize and attempt to thwart the oppression of others. Writer Susan Brownmiller, author of the landmark treatise *Against Our Will*, retrospectively acknowledged that her awareness of rape as a systemic violation of women had been profoundly influenced by the murders of Jews in the Shoah.[19] Vivian Rothstein, a daughter of refugee parents, believed that growing up in a refugee community positioned her as an outsider, enabling her to become an observer and, often, critic of American culture.

While Jewish heritage shaped feminists' worldview and helped lead them to activism, they rejected those aspects of the tradition they found oppressive. The rigidity of Firestone's Orthodox upbringing alienated her from Judaism and led her to imagine a different kind of utopian community. Kesselman disliked what she saw as the tribal exclusiveness of Jews, their "blind loyalty to a group."[20] Marya Levenson and Tax abhorred the materialism of their synagogues and some affluent suburban communities. For these and other reasons, feminists discarded or suppressed their Jewish identities, at least temporarily. Their resentment toward repressive and stultifying aspects of their childhood environments prompted pioneering innovations in feminism.

The patriarchal elements of Jewish tradition also accounted for Jewish women's disaffection from Judaism. Like non-Jewish feminists, many Jewish women in the movement rejected religion as inherently tainted by sexism and therefore unacceptable and irrelevant to their lives. The association of Jewishness with a religion unsympathetic to women could carry over to Jewish culture more broadly. Ezrat Nashim and other Jewish feminists used the tools of second-wave feminism and the springboards to activism derived from their Jewish experiences to challenge the tenets and practices of Judaism that had consigned women to secondary roles. Their transformative work, as well as secular feminists' assaults on sexism in the Jewish establishment, made it easier for Jewish women to identify as both Jewish and feminist.

Between the late 1960s and the late 1980s, when this book concludes, second-wave feminism had moved from its early focus on universal sisterhood to an orientation toward identity politics, emphasizing strong collective group identities as the basis of political analysis and social action. By 1990, a multiculturalism that emphasized race-based diversity had succeeded identity politics as the preferred rubric for expressing difference, inducing feminist and ethnic reconsiderations of identity along a more pluralistic, multidimensional spectrum.[21] Although numerous scholars believed that Jews were excluded from the multicultural paradigm, others saw a place for Jewish experience as a "liminal border case, neither inside nor outside—or better, both inside and outside," with the capacity to broaden the intersectional framework.[22]

Most of the Jewish feminists in the book foregrounded the Jewish aspects of their identities, whereas women's liberationists often expunged the Jewish components of their identities or let them lie dormant. Sometimes they were "ghosts," invisible but present.[23] But even the most homogeneous identity-based communities showed a wide array of "mutually constructing multiple aspects of fluid and porous identities," as political theorist Marla Brettschneider has defined intersectionality, with elements of gender, sexuality, class, and generation complementing the frames of ethnic culture and/or religion.[24]

The historically diverse experiences of Jewish women in this book demonstrate the multiple ways in which Jewish women brought together the Jewish and feminist aspects of their experiences along with class, generational, sexual, regional, religious, and other perspectives. We see their lives unfolding along these interlocking frames, exposing the simultaneous axes of belonging, commitment, and influence that shaped their participation in the women's movement and with which they effected change in their own lives and those of many others. The women's identities were complex, fluid, and multisided. Together they illustrate the wide range of identities among their cohort and the continuous shifting of identity over the course of their own lives.

Beyond the significance of the stories of the women in this book to the construction and meaning of individual lives, they deserve to be recognized as important parts of the larger twentieth-century narratives of the history of feminism and Judaism. These women's struggles, contributions, failures, and achievements point to new ways of thinking about these remarkable decades.

Epilogue

Gender relations throughout the United States were radically trans-formed during the two decades discussed in this book. By the 1990s, new directions in the movement suggested a so-called third wave of feminism based on cultural rather than political liberation, yet as is the case with earlier women's movements, it makes more sense to recognize a continuing chain of feminist actions over the course of the century rather than discrete, disconnected periods of short-term activism. These activities continued into the 1990s and the twenty-first century, when many of the radical feminists discussed in this book maintained their original focus on political organizing. Rather than individual change, often regarded as the hallmark of 1990s feminism, these women kept their eyes on the collective goals that had motivated women's liberation. Solidarity and social action continued to exert a powerful force on their vision of a socially just and egalitarian future; younger colleagues drawn into feminism benefited from their examples and contributions.[1]

The women's liberationists chronicled in this book achieved many of their goals, even when the social movement they helped to lead had been recast and reimagined. In their innovative writings, their imagina-tive approaches to difficult social problems, and their assertive political and social leadership, they continued to follow the dictates of *tikkun olam*, sometimes without conscious awareness of Jewish influences on their actions. The many books they authored, the organizations they founded, and the varied campaigns they ran indicate a remarkable level of engagement in civic and intellectual life over half a century and an abiding commitment to feminist change. By 1990, Jewish feminists, too, had achieved considerable success within Jewish religious and commu-nal life as well as in the broader society. These women's accomplish-ments provided examples to younger generations of the possibilities of living an integrated life that joins Jewish, American, and feminist social activism in positive ways.

Twenty-first-century Jewish women have faced identity struggles of their own, but because of Jewish feminist role models, many of whom had been conflicted about their Jewish identities, the younger women's efforts to form unified personalities have seemed less fraught than those of preceding generations. New organizations such as the Jewish Women's Archive, formed in 1995 to chronicle the diverse histories of North American Jewish women, and Mayyim Hayyim, created in 2004 to offer modern approaches to the *mikveh* and other spiritual resources, helped to uncover traditions that inspired young women to become change agents in their own lives. Although these women faced new perplexities embodied in contemporary life, they did not need to engage in the deep, often bitter struggles of Jewish women's liberationists and early Jewish feminists to find partners, mentors, and comrades on the journey to integrate the manifold aspects of selfhood.

How twenty-first century women regard the effects of the women's movement on their lives was the subject of the last panel at my NYU conference. The stories narrated by the five participants and panel chair, spanning some twenty years in age, point to larger patterns of activism and identity construction. The first three stories, from Tamara Cohen, Judith Rosenbaum, and Jaclyn Friedman, come from women born in the early 1970s who were about forty years of age at the time of the conference. The last three stories come from women in their twenties who were born in the mid-1980s: Nona Willis Aronowitz, Collier Meyerson, and Irin Carmon. I close this book with their snapshots of contemporary feminist and Jewish activism.

Tamara Cohen: "What It Meant to Be a Jew and a Woman in New York City in the Early Nineties"

Tamara Cohen, born in 1971, is a socially committed, feminist activist rabbi, writer, and poet whose roots in Jewish feminism are deep.[2] Cohen's father babysat while her mother attended the first Jewish feminist conference in 1973. Cohen was raised by "a mother transformed by feminism and Jewish feminism"; when she got her period, she was given the gift of *Our Bodies, Ourselves*, *The Tribe of Dina* (edited by Melanie Kaye/Kantrowitz and Irena Klepfisz), and Marge Piercy's *The Moon Is Always Female*. Yet she never took feminism for granted,

Figure E.1. Tamara Cohen, Collier Meyerson, Nona Willis Aronowitz, Irin Carmon, Jaclyn Friedman, and Judith Rosenbaum, NYU conference panel, April 2011. Courtesy of Judith Rosenbaum.

watching the struggles of her mother and others of her generation unfold around her.

At Barnard College in the early 1990s, the struggles of gay and black students drew Cohen's attention, taking her activism to places that her "mother's feminism had not gone." She was personally transformed by coming out as a lesbian in the context of identity politics and AIDS activism and also by her discovery of her own "white-skin privilege." "Betwixt and between," Cohen tried to figure out where she belonged, situating herself as "a Jewish feminist and a feminist Jew" who felt a sense of "otherness from white Protestant culture" along with a desire to create bonds with other groups. She co-founded a rape crisis center on campus, protested Columbia's gentrification in Harlem, and became a vocal activist in the campaign to ordain gays and lesbians at the Jewish Theological Seminary. Yet she felt "split at the root," in Adrienne Rich's formulation, feeling ashamed in some sense "at being a religious person," unsure about how to bring her Jewishness into the social spaces of activism, how "to take up the mantle of feminist transformation within Judaism," how to ally with others in the "external world" for social justice causes. Such was the "what it meant to be a Jew and a woman in New York City in the early nineties."

Cohen emerged from these beginnings to fashion a second-generation identity as feminist daughter that creatively synthesized her multiple concerns. She went on to earn a master's degree in women's history, writing a thesis on the rise of Jewish feminism; worked as director of Multicultural and Diversity Affairs and LGBT Affairs at the University of Florida; served as program director at Ma'yan, the Jewish Women's Project in Manhattan; and became a founding board member of Brit Tzedek v'Shalom. In 2014, she was ordained as a Reconstructionist rabbi, in which position she writes and lectures widely on topics relating to diversity, Jewish feminism, and spirituality.

Judith Rosenbaum: "Jewishness and Feminism Were Indistinguishable"

An educator, historian, and feminist activist, Judith Rosenbaum is now executive director of the Jewish Women's Archive (JWA). Like Tamara Cohen, Rosenbaum was born into Jewish feminism. The daughter of Paula Hyman, a pioneer of the movement, and a physician father, Rosenbaum often heard that her mother discovered that she was pregnant with her at the 1973 Jewish feminist conference. Rosenbaum grew up thinking that "all Jews were feminists and that all feminists were Jews"; feminism was as central a Jewish practice "as eating matzo at Passover. . . . It was as much a part of Jewish experience to have women gathering in your living room on Sunday night for feminist consciousness-raising as going to synagogue." To have this totally "coherent, organic" vision of the unity of feminism and Judaism was a "tremendous birthright."

Rosenbaum's journey as a Jewish feminist involved stepping out of the particularities of Jewish experience that she learned as a child, even with its inherent feminist content, and moving more directly to engage with the concerns of a wider world. Though she felt like a "freak" in high school as a self-conscious Jewish feminist, she experienced little conflict between the "Jewish and women's center" worlds at college. But by the time Rosenbaum got to graduate school, Jewish feminism seemed to have narrowed and did not feel sufficiently engaged with the breadth of issues fundamental to women's lives. Rosenbaum's dissertation on the history of American women's health activism examined how feminism had dealt with issues of women's embodiment. Though her work included the stories of many Jewish participants involved in the women's health movement, she did not explicitly address their Jewishness. In graduate school, integral parts of her own identity—that once "organic" connection between feminism and Jewishness—remained silent, invisible.

Rosenbaum sought to make that connection whole again in her career as public educator. As director of public history and then executive director of the JWA, she has developed creative ways to integrate the narratives of feminism and of Jewish activism, found innovative approaches to online learning, and forged links with community partners and with users of various ages, backgrounds, interests. Most recently, JWA has begun cultivating the leadership of female-identified Jewish teens to shape conversations in their communities, through the Rising Voices Fellowship. Working from the core of Jewish feminism that centers her own identity, Rosenbaum aspires to create broad-based coalitions and partnerships that can acknowledge a changing movement that is not monolithic but rather exults in a new diversity and wider intelligence.

Jaclyn Friedman: "A Daughter of Women's Liberation"

Jaclyn Friedman, founder and former executive director of Women, Action, and the Media, a nonprofit lobbying group for gender justice in the mass media, is the author of several best-selling books about empowering women's sexuality and is a popular opinion writer on these subjects.

Friedman was born in 1971 to largely apolitical parents in New Jersey but grew up with strong Jewish feminist leanings, in part because her rabbi was Sally Priesand, the first American woman rabbi. Ordained by the Reform movement in 1972, the year of Friedman's birth, Priesand was Friedman's first feminist role model. Growing up, Friedman did not realize that Priesand was a feminist "rock star": "She was just my rabbi. It was very subtle; I wouldn't have told you then that I was learning about feminism, but I was." Friedman loves to tell the story of a young boy in the congregation, which also had a female cantor, who asked his parents if boys could be rabbis too.[3]

As a teenager, Friedman became involved in the New Jersey Reform Jewish youth group the Jersey Federation of Temple Youth (JFTY). JFTY incorporated Priesand's teachings into the social justice framework that guided nearly everything it did, and Friedman credits this influence with shaping her viewpoint on social issues and teaching her to become a leader and an activist. There she formed her vision, and she learned how to organize, how to collaborate, how to see campaigns through to completion. "My social justice framework comes from Judaism," she said. "Judaism is also often my touchstone; if I feel like the work is getting overwhelming, or I don't feel like I'm getting anywhere, or I want to give up I remember: 'It is not yours to complete the work, neither is it yours to desist from it.' That's from the *Pirkei Avot*. We would sing the Hebrew version, *Lo Alecha*, at camp all the time, and it's never left me."[4]

Friedman went to Wesleyan University, where she was active in student government, but it was the experience of sexual assault that changed her life, leading her to become an advocate for the reform of institutional responses to sexual violence. In her thirties, she founded Women, Action, and the Media, dedicated to fighting against rape and sexual violence and to helping women to reclaim sexual pleasure. Her 2009 book, co-edited with Jessica Valenti, *Yes Means Yes: Visions of Female Sexual Power and a World without Rape*, was ranked number eleven on *Ms.* magazine's "Top 100 Feminist Nonfiction of All Time" list. In 2017, she published *Unscrewed: Women, Sex, Power and How to Stop Letting the System Screw Us All*, a call for women to move from individualistic models to collective action to create the structural changes needed for female sexual empowerment.[5]

Friedman celebrated the Jewish holidays, performed rituals, and identified Jewishly but had no formal connections to the Jewish world or to Jewish feminism. In her late thirties, however, Judaism started to pull her back. The "Women's Liberation and Jewish Identity" conference helped her to locate herself in a tradition she had not understood. "The history of Jewish women in feminism is largely invisible, which is why that conference was so meaningful," she observed. "I suddenly understood, 'Oh, I make sense in this context. This is not accidental.'"

Connecting to the Jewish past via these narratives of feminist activism suggests a channel of engagement for contemporary Jews.

Nona Willis Aronowitz: "A New-York-to-the-Core Jewish Feminist"

Nona Willis Aronowitz is a journalist and feminist author. Born in 1984, she is the daughter of cultural critic and feminist pioneer Ellen Willis and radical sociologist Stanley Aronowitz. Willis Aronowitz grew up in Greenwich Village, where "cultural Jewishness was in the water." This kind of secular Jewishness, modeled by her mother, focused on a heady "cerebral transcendence" and the pursuit of social justice. During many summers at Camp Kinderland, which was founded by leftist Jewish activists, Willis Aronowitz was further exposed to the Jewish social justice tradition; it was a "through line" in her life.

Becoming a feminist was a more deliberate quest for Willis Aronowitz. Ellen Willis passed away in 2006, just as her daughter graduated from Wesleyan. While at college, Willis Aronowitz had felt alienated from the male-led, more conservative Jewish community she encountered there, but she felt no need to question the feminist and socialist upbringing of her youth. In the wake of her mother's death, however, amid the outpouring of love she received from her mother's friends and admirers, she wondered about her own connection to that tradition. She also began to question whether feminism mattered much beyond the circle of New York's Upper West Side and Greenwich Village, where she had grown up in a special, lefty "bubble." With a friend, Emma Bee Bernstein, a Camp Kinderland alumna with a Jewish, feminist mother who had grown up in a similar environment, she set out on a road trip to dozens of cities across the U.S. to find out about "how young women grapple with the concepts of freedom, equality, joy, ambition, sex, and love—whether they call it 'feminism' or not." "We took our Jewishness along the way," Willis Aronowitz said, interacting with women from different backgrounds, classes, regions, races, and religions all over the country. Many of her previous ideas about feminism were shattered. Learning about the multiplicity of desires and experiences that this younger generation brought to the fateful term was an "aha" moment that taught her about the variability of feminism while reaffirming its relatedness to her own life. Chronicling her generation's perspectives as her mother did of hers, she wrote *Girldrive: Criss-Crossing America, Redefining Feminism* with Bernstein.[6] In 2014, she edited an anthology of her mother's criticism, *The Essential Ellen Willis*.

Willis Aronowitz appreciates the intellectual richness of the Jewish tradition, particularly acknowledging the contributions of her mother and her mother's friends. While she considers herself spiritually Jewish, in many ways, feminism is the cornerstone of her belief system. "To be culturally Jewish means you have your religion be feminism," she said, but "also be a Jew at the same exact time, and still be an atheist."

Collier Meyerson: "About Being a Woman of Color in a Religion That Can Sometimes Shut You Out of It"

Collier Meyerson is a writer, reporter, blogger, and producer. She has been a national reporter for MSNBC / NBC News and a visiting fellow at Yale Law School's Program for the Study of Reproductive Justice.

A biracial Jew who grew up on the Upper West Side of New York, Meyerson worked for the multiracial Jewish organization Be'chol Lashon for several years after graduating from Macalaster College in 2007. She brought her special background into this work and her creative efforts as a spokesperson for Jews like her. Collier's birth mother was Jewish, and she was adopted by a black non-Jewish mother and white Ashkenazi Jewish father. Her parents intentionally created a combination of African American and Jewish cultures so that Meyerson would not be "confused or ashamed" about her background. As a child, living on Manhattan's West Side, she studied at the Dance Theater of Harlem, a historically black dance school, and learned Yiddish language and Jewish culture at her synagogue.

With Meyerson's New York background and the summers she spent with her friend Nona Willis Aronowitz at Camp Kinderland, where most campers were Jewish, she grew up with an "innate" sensibility of Jewishness and feminism. But her skin color separated her from other young Jewish feminists for whom the issue of "white privilege" often became the center of probing identity issues. Meyerson experienced the pain of race-based discrimination early on. She chose to be Jewish at the age of ten, when her parents urged her to "practice something," leaving the choice of religious faith open to her. But after three years of preparing for her bat mitzvah at Hebrew School, synagogue representatives told her she could not hold the ceremony there because she had a black, presumably non-Jewish, mother. Although they relented when her quick-witted mother mentioned that her biological mother was Jewish, Meyerson left the faith, hurt and angry, from then on taking part in her aunt's seders "begrudgingly." Another upsetting incident occurred after college, when a dinner guest at her home found it difficult to believe that someone who did not "look Jewish" could know Hebrew prayers and songs as well as she did.[7]

Interested in efforts "to expand the (often) projected narrow definition of what 'Jewish' looks like," Meyerson turned her attention to being a woman of color "in a religion that can sometimes shut you out of it," hoping to start conversations that could expand the acceptance of diversity within Judaism. She was especially interested in the relationship between whiteness and women, starting the popular blog *Carefree White Girl*. Are Jews considered "carefree white girls?" she has been asked frequently. Meyerson's experience makes it clear that Jewish feminism has many colors. She is part of the current generation of outspoken young women hoping to transform narrow definitions that prescribe what normative Jewish feminists act and look like. More recently, she has come to define herself as a "mulatto," "creating a clan" with friends from similar backgrounds, with whom she feels completely at home.[8]

Meyerson writes regularly for *Fusion*, with an emphasis on the topics of race and politics, and is a contributor to the *New Yorker* and other magazines.[9] Her multicultural, multiracial background provides her an unusual perch from which to comment on deeply contested intergroup matters.

Irin Carmon: "How Do We Maintain That Sense of Otherness and Responsibility towards Social Justice?"

Irin Carmon, born in Israel in 1983, is a feminist journalist who co-authored the best-selling 2105 book about the U.S. Supreme Court justice Ruth Bader Ginsburg, *Notorious RBG: The Life and Times of Ruth Bader Ginsburg*.[10] Carmon considers herself "mostly Israeli." She immigrated to the U.S. with her parents when she was two but journeyed back and forth between Israel and America with her parents for much of her childhood. As an Israeli who grew up without any kind of religious framework, she believed her experiences were different from those of other young feminists on the NYU panel.

Carmon identified three kinds of Jewish influences on her feminist work: those affecting her as a reader, as an immigrant, and as a person of "considerable privilege." The Jewish tradition of learning and education played a primary role, allowing her to understand and empathize with the way lives were lived, the injustices suffered by many people and groups. Despite her lack of direct contact with second-wave feminists, she gained a formidable feminist education through reading the texts they created, with Jewish feminist authors primary among them.

The immigrant experience was also formative. Her parents found Americans Jews baffling, and so, generally, did Carmon, who had never been to a Shabbat service and did not understand the sort of "cultural inflections that people think of as Jewish." Basically she did not feel "at home" with American Jews until college. As a result of her confusion, she developed an interest in Jewish peoplehood and, as a writer, spent a lot of time trying to find Jews in unusual places such as Alabama, Cuba, and Brazil.

Carmon's own mobility and status as a citizen of three countries—Israel, the U.S., and (through her grandmother) Germany—led her to see herself as part of a privileged minority that possesses the economic and social underpinnings to guarantee its contemporary security and well-being. This, of course, is a new position for Jews, unlike the fragility that derived from their perennial sense of otherness but that also sparked their characteristic sympathy for the underdog. Carmon asks, "How do we maintain that sense of otherness and responsibility towards social justice when we become privileged and powerful members of society?"

* * *

Carmon's question allies with the core frames of radical feminism, which began as a movement that was not supposed to be parochial or particularistic. The feminist issues that most strongly motivate Carmon and her fellow panelists are the universal ones that apply to the widest swath of their contemporaries. So, too, for these six women, the broadest issues within Jewish life and Jewish feminism are the ones that they see as most meaningful. Their passionate call to pluralism, inclusion, and diversity stands as an emblem of what these younger generations want from a feminism that is integrated with Jewishness in the contemporary world.

Inclusivity and pluralism might be watchwords for beginning a conversation among young Jewish feminists and others in their generation about the Israeli-Palestinian conflict, one of the most pressing issues on the global agenda today. As this issue has complicated Jewish feminist identities for the young women's feminist forbears, so it roils contemporary discussions of Jewishness and of feminism. But as Judith Rosenbaum, Collier Meyerson, and Nona Willis Aronowitz pointed out in their remarks, feminist understandings of power and trauma and of relationships with the "Other," combined with a characteristic Jewish intellectual curiosity, can generate better, more open conversations among the Jewish community and feminists alike. Feminist leadership in the peace movement continues to be one of the most promising international developments of recent times, Tamara Cohen added, especially regarding Israel and Palestine. Israeli-born Irin Carmon admitted to compartmentalizing the politics of Israel apart from identity issues relating to Jewish life. She shares Ellen Willis's caution about Americans insinuating themselves into the politics of a land where they do not live, but she acknowledges the complexity of these issues and the advantage of openness and inclusiveness as Jewish women of many different stripes attempt to engage politically and ethically on such a deeply divisive matter. As Jaclyn Friedman's work reminds us, social justice for women must involve both personal and political empowerment across differences, a conviction that owes much to the insights of radical second-wave feminists.

The views of these women reflect the broad societal changes that have occurred within their generation's life cycles. These include the growing racial and ethnic diversity of the United States, an openness to change, and a confident liberalism based on a willingness to participate in the political process, although on their own terms.[11] Such demographic and political factors correlate especially well to women who came of age after the 1980s and who identify as feminists. Even in a period that saw a shift toward postmodern and even so-called postfeminist discourse, young women claimed feminist identities in growing numbers. This group is more diverse in matters of race, ethnicity, income, and education than were their second-wave forbears, demographic factors that shaped their inclusive worldview and political perspectives.[12]

But the women's attitudes also reflect the special legacy they have inherited as young Jewish feminists. Their values and worldviews were influenced in part by those who came before—their actual and metaphorical mothers. How these young women define their identities, find community with other young feminist women, and connect with contemporary social movements is a product both of their generational context and the shaping forces of the past, including Jewish feminist role models.

The difficulties of affirming and integrating multiple aspects of feminist identity, without denying, devaluing, or displacing component parts, have not been erased, to be sure. Even the most positively identified younger Jewish feminists must still confront complex problems of sexism and anti-Semitism and the divisive global politics around Israel and Palestine. But the revolutions started by women's liberationists and Jewish feminists provide a secure foundation for continuing attempts to come to grips with the troubling problems related to the heterogeneous elements of their mixed identities. The achievements of Jewish radical feminism must be placed on the historical record, for they can surely inspire the struggles of the present.

ACKNOWLEDGMENTS

Just as the women's movement was a collective project, so too was this book. I am enormously grateful to the dozens of women's liberationists and Jewish feminists who took this journey with me and whose stories fill this book. My deepest appreciation goes to Martha Ackelsberg, Arlene Agus, Rebecca Alpert, Nona Willis Aronowitz, Diane Balser, Ruth Balser, Evelyn Torton Beck, Heather Booth, Susan Brownmiller, Aviva Cantor, Irin Carmon, Phyllis Chesler, Michele Clark, Tamara Cohen, Vilunya Diskin, Joan Ditzion, Paula Doress-Worters, Marcia Freedman, Jaclyn Friedman, Laura Geller, Galia Golan, Linda Gordon, Maralee Gordon, Blu Greenberg, Gloria Greenfield, Miriam Hawley, Melanie Kaye/Kantrowitz, Amy Kesselman, Irena Klepfisz, Marya Levenson, Collier Meyerson, Cheryl Moch, Judy Norsigian, Grey Osterud, Jane Pincus, Judith Plaskow, Letty Cottin Pogrebin, Judith Rosenbaum, Vivian Rothstein, Wendy Sanford, Susan Weidman Schneider, Alix Kates Shulman, Norma Swenson, Meredith Tax, and Marilyn Webb, as well as the late Rosalyn Baxandall, Esther Broner, Betty Friedan, Shulamith Firestone, Adrienne Rich, Esther Rome, Susan Schechter, Naomi Weisstein, and Ellen Willis.

My research for the book began in earnest during a fellowship year spent as the Goldstein-Goren Research Scholar at the Goldstein-Goren Center for American History at New York University. Thanks to Hasia Diner of the Center for this opportunity and for continued encouragement and to Shira Kohn and Rachel Kranson for a conference and subsequent book co-edited with Hasia: *A Postwar Jewish Feminist Mystique: Jewish Women in Postwar America*. My article for their anthology became a prelude to this book.

That article concerned the Jewishness of the Gang of Four Chicago radical feminists, Amy Kesselman, Heather Booth, Vivian Rothstein, and Naomi Weisstein. Their group conversations with me, emails, and correspondence exposed the richness of this topic and led me to probe the general topic further. Over the ensuing years, these women gifted me with their attentiveness and respect for this evolving history. I am fortunate that the other narrators in this book emulated the enthusiasm and engagement I encountered with the Gang of Four.

Thanks also to Stanley Aronowitz, Phineas Baxandall, Jesse Lemisch, Judah Rome, Nathan Rome, Laya Firestone Seghi, Aaron and Ruth Seidman, and Allen Steinberg for insights and memories of their family members. I am grateful to Wini Breines, Sandra Butler, Nancy Chodorow, Vicki Gabriner, Nan Geffen, Susannah Heschel, Robin Morgan, Rochelle Ruthchild, Ann Snitow, and Pamela Berger for sharing information and stories with me.

Participants in the "Women's Liberation and Jewish Identity" conference that I organized in 2011 at NYU provided experiential accounts and generated a deep well of enthusiasm. In addition to the previously named women, I thank the historians' panel composed of Ellen Du Bois, Linda Gordon, Alice Kessler-Harris, and Ruth Rosen, as well as Gloria Feldt, Idit Klein, Yavilah McCoy, Debra Schultz, and Chava Weissler for their participation. Thanks to Jennifer Young for providing assistance with conference logistics. The Spencer Foundation cosponsored the conference as part of its Initiative on Civic Learning and Civic Action; thanks especially to Susan Dauber.

The Jewish feminist seminar I convened for a year in Boston after the NYU conference, hosted by the Jewish Women's Archive, also provided illumination. Thanks to Susannah Heschel for suggesting this follow-up and for the contributions of participants including Diane Balser, Rivka Neriya-Ben Shahar, Paula Doress-Worters, Janet Freedman, Miriam Hawley, Yavilah McCoy, Keren McGinity, Gail Reimer, Judith Rosenbaum, and Susan Schnur. The opportunity to present portions of this book at seminars at the Center for Jewish History in New York, Brandeis University's Mandel Center for the Humanities, the Seminar for Contemporary Jewish Life, the Close Looking Series of the University Archives & Special Collections Department, and Brandeis's History Department Faculty / Graduate Student Seminar and at various sessions of the Association for Jewish Studies, the Association for Israel Studies, the Berkshire Conference for the History of Women, the Harvard Conference on Public Intellectuals, and the Stanford Conference on the

Jewish 1968 and Its Legacies helped crystallize my ideas. Thanks to Janet Giele, Karen Hansen, Jonathan Krasner, Jon Levison, Tony Michels, Riv-Ellen Prell, Joseph Reimer, Jonathan Sarna, and Beryl Satter for their helpful comments. I also benefited from presenting material from the book at Brandeis's BOLLI Program, the Brandeis Women's Studies Research Center, and various synagogues. Comments of reviewers for NYU Press and for *American Jewish History*, where an article derived from the book appeared, were especially discerning.

I have been fortunate to have a wonderful group of research assistants during the course of my work on this book. Thanks to the Hadassah-Brandeis Institute at Brandeis University and to Debby Olins, who directs its Gilda Slifka Intern Program, for arranging these summer assistantships and to Aislinn Betancourt, Leora Jackson, Danya Lagos, Amanda Sharick, Noaem Shurin, and Hannah Sutin for their energetic participation in varied tasks. The Women's, Gender, and Sexuality Program at Brandeis University sponsored Jara Connell's and Kendra McKinney's work as my graduate research assistants, and NYU's Goldstein-Goren Program sponsored Adena Silberstein.

My colleagues in the American Studies Program and the Women's, Gender, and Sexuality Studies Program at Brandeis University have provided constant intellectual stimulation and support, as have faculty in the other programs with which I have been affiliated: the African- and Afro-American Studies Department, the Education Program, the History Department, and the Program in Creativity, the Arts, and Social Transformation. I owe incredible gratitude to Angie Simeone, Charity Adams-Brzuchalski, Cheryl Sweeney and Melanie Zoltan of the American Studies Program for their assistance.

Librarians and archivists at the American Jewish Historical Society, the Robert Farber University & Special Collections Department at Brandeis, the Sally Bingham Center for Women's History and Culture at Duke University, the Arthur and Elizabeth Schlesinger Library on the History of Women in America at the Radcliffe Institute, the Sophia Smith Collection of Women's History at Smith College, and the Tamiment Library at New York University provided expert assistance. Thanks also to Cassandra Berman for finding materials in the Brandeis Collections and to the women of the Redstockings Women's Liberation

Archives for Action. In London, Gail Chester, Jeanette Copperman, and Sheila Shulman provided useful perspectives on related issues. The staff of the Jewish Women's Archive has been helpful in innumerable ways.

Joan Biren, Virginia Blaisdell, Janie Eisenberg, Jo Freeman, and Joan L. Roth have created an irreplaceable record of the women's liberation movement in their extraordinary photos; I thank them for their help in this project. Filmmakers Mary Dore and Susie Rivo also generously shared photos of women's liberation and Jewish feminist events. A special thanks goes to Virginia Blaisdell for her time and creative efforts concerning the book cover.

For over thirty years, I have been a member of a unique feminist biography group. The conversations I have had with Fran Malino, Megan Marshall, Susan Quinn, Judith Tick, Roberta Wollons—and now, from afar, Lois Rudnick—have greatly enhanced my well-being over this long period as well as the writing of this book.

Susan Ware, who was a member of a prior women's biography group with me, read and commented on every draft of this book, as she has done with other of my books over many years. I have benefited enormously from Susan's knowledge about women's history and the task of writing women's lives. I thank her for her intellectual generosity, her wisdom, and her sustaining friendship. Grey Osterud also provided remarkably insightful comments on the entire manuscript. Thanks to Gail Reimer for perceptive readings on the manuscript and to Evelyn Torton Beck, Stephen J. Whitfield, and Erica Harth for their helpful comments on various chapters. I am grateful to Sharon Feiman-Nemser, Louis Nemser, Barbara Haber, Nancy Gertner, Carol and Ilan Troen, Karen Klein, Pamela Allara, and Elinor Fuchs for their support and advice.

At NYU Press, Eric Zinner's astute guidance and creative ideas, aided by Alisha Nadkarni and Dolma Ombodykow on NYU's editorial team, helped bring the book to fruition. Andrew Katz provided remarkable copyediting. My wonderful Ph.D. student Sascha Cohen helped with proofreading.

My son-in-law Dan Meagher came to my rescue innumerable times in connection with the technical and photographic aspects of this project. Thanks to Dan for his skills and cheerful willingness to lend a hand.

My daughters, Lauren and Rachel, are always inspirations to me, especially when I think of the ways they reflect their generation's feminist perspectives and their proud sense of themselves as Jewish women. Thank you to Lauren and Carl and Rachel and Dan for the gifts of Tillie and Max, who fill our lives with laughter, joy, and amazement.

My husband, Steve, my partner for almost fifty years, has always been ready to talk with me about the issues that frame this book, testing and challenging my theories, responding to my questions and enthusiasms. I owe him the deepest gratitude for his own enthusiasm and patience.

NOTES

ARCHIVES CONSULTED

American Jewish History Archives, Center for Jewish History, New York, NY

Arthur and Elizabeth Schlesinger Library on the History of Women in America, Radcliffe Institute for Advanced Study at Harvard University, Cambridge, MA

Chicago Women's Liberation Union, Herstory Project, www.cwluherstory.org

Jewish Women's Archive, http://jwa.org

Library Special Collections, University of California at Los Angeles, Los Angeles, CA

Redstockings Women's Liberation Archives for Action, New York, NY, www.redstockings.org

Robert D. Farber University Archives & Special Collections Department, Brandeis University, Waltham, MA

Sallie Bingham Center for Women's History and Culture, Duke University, Durham, NC

Sophia Smith Collection, Smith College, Northampton, MA

Tamiment Library, New York University, New York, NY

INTRODUCTION

1. Naomi Weisstein, "Chicago '60s: Ecstasy as Our Guide," *Ms.*, September–October 1990; also quoted in Susan Brownmiller, *In Our Time: Memoir of a Revolution* (New York: Delta/Dell, 2000), 18.

2. Naomi Weisstein, conference call with author (with Amy Kesselman, Heather Booth, and Vivian Rothstein), August 9, 2008.

3. Exceptions include Dina Pinsky's sociological study *Jewish Feminists: Complex Identities and Activist Lives* (Urbana: University of Illinois Press, 2010) and articles by Paula E. Hyman, "Jewish Feminism Faces the American Women's Movement: Convergence and Divergence," in Deborah Dash Moore, ed., *American Jewish Identity Politics* (Ann Arbor: University of Michigan Press, 2008), 221–240; and Daniel Horowitz, "Jewish Women Remaking American Feminism / Women Remaking American Judaism: Reflections on the Life of Betty Friedan," in Hasia Diner, Shira Kohn, and Rachel Kranson, eds., *A Jewish Feminine Mystique? Jewish Women in Postwar America* (New Brunswick, NJ: Rutgers University Press, 2010), 235–256. On women's liberation generally, see Brownmiller, *In Our Time*; Sara Evans, *Personal Politics: The Roots of Women's Liberation in the Civil Rights Movement and the New Left* (New York: Vintage Books, 1979); Alice Echols, *Daring to Be Bad: Radical Feminism in America* (Minneapolis: University of Minnesota

Press, 1989); Rachel Blau DuPlessis and Ann Snitow, eds., *The Feminist Memoir Project: Voices from Women's Liberation* (1998; repr., New Brunswick, NJ: Rutgers University Press, 2007); Alice Echols, *Shaky Ground: The Sixties and Its Aftershocks* (New York: Columbia University Press, 2002); Ruth Rosen, *The World Split Open: How the Modern Women's Movement Changed America* (New York: Penguin Books, 2000); Estelle B. Freedman, *No Turning Back: The History of Feminism and the Future of Women* (New York: Ballantine, 2002); Sara M. Evans, *Tidal Wave: How Women Changed America at Century's End* (New York: Free Press, 2003); Benita Roth, *Separate Roads to Feminism: Black, Chicana, and White Feminist Movements in America's Second Wave* (New York: Cambridge University Press, 2004); Winifred Breines, *The Trouble between Us: An Uneasy History of White and Black Women in the Feminist Movement* (New York: Oxford University Press, 2006); Nancy A. Hewitt, ed., *No Permanent Waves: Recasting Histories of U.S. Feminism* (New Brunswick, NJ: Rutgers University Press, 2010); Dorothy Sue Cobble, Linda Gordon, and Astrid Henry, *Feminism Unfinished: A Short, Surprising History of American Women's Movements* (New York: Norton, 2014).

4. Sara M. Evans, foreword to Stephanie Gilmore, ed., *Feminist Coalitions: Historical Perspectives on Second-Wave Feminism in the United States* (Urbana: University of Illinois Press, 2008), viii; Gilmore, "Thinking about Feminist Coalitions," ibid., 5.

5. "Women's Liberation and Jewish Identity: Uncovering a Legacy of Innovation, Activism, and Social Change," conference at NYU Skirball Center for Judaic Studies, April 10–11, 2011 (hereafter WLJIC).

6. The historians' panel at the conference included Ellen DuBois, Linda Gordon, Alice Kessler-Harris, and Ruth Rosen, all of whom had participated in the women's liberation movement.

7. Nancy Whittier, *Feminist Generations: The Persistence of the Radical Women's Movement* (Philadelphia: Temple University Press, 1995), 55–56.

8. See, for example, Steven M. Cohen and Arnold M. Eisen, *The Jew Within: Self, Family, and Community in America* (Bloomington: Indiana University Press, 2000).

9. Heather Booth, remarks at "Re-Joyce: Women Changing the World, a Symposium in Honor of Joyce Antler," Brandeis University, October 17, 2015.

10. See, for example, Susan A. Glenn, *Daughters of the Shtetl: Life and Labor in the Immigrant Generation* (Ithaca, NY: Cornell University Press, 1990); Hadassa Kosak, *Cultures of Opposition: Jewish Immigrant Workers, New York City, 1881–1905* (Albany: State University of New York Press, 2000); Joyce Antler, *The Journey Home: How Jewish Women Shaped Modern America* (New York: Schocken Books, 1997); Melissa Klapper, *Ballots, Babies, and Banners of Peace: American Jewish Women's Activism, 1890–1940* (New York: NYU Press, 2013).

11. On 1960s youth activism, see Rebecca A. Klatch, *A Generation Divided: The New Left, the New Right, and the 1960s* (Berkeley: University of California Press, 1999); Paul Buhle, ed., *History and the New Left: Madison, Wisconsin, 1950–1970* (Philadelphia: Temple University Press, 1990); Mark Oppenheimer, *Knocking on*

Heaven's Door: American Religion in the Age of Counterculture (New Haven, CT: Yale University Press, 2003).

12. Klapper, *Ballots, Babies, and Banners of Peace*, 122–123, 133.

13. On maternalism, see Theda Skocpol, *Protecting Soldiers and Mothers: The Political Origins of Social Policy in the United States* (Cambridge, MA: Harvard University Press, 1992); Molly Ladd-Taylor, *Mother-Work: Child Welfare and the State, 1890–1930* (Urbana: University of Illinois Press, 1994); Rebecca Jo Plant, *MOM: The Transformation of Motherhood in Modern America* (Chicago: University of Chicago Press, 2010).

14. On gender and Jewish identity, see Paula E. Hyman, "Gender and the Shaping of Modern Jewish Identities," *Jewish Social Studies* 8, nos. 2–3 (2002): 153–161; Hyman, *Gender and Assimilation in Modern Jewish History: The Roles and Representation of Women* (Seattle: University of Washington Press, 1995); and Marion A. Kaplan and Deborah Dash Moore, eds., *Gender and Jewish History* (Bloomington: Indiana University Press, 2011).

15. I use "Judaism" primarily to connote religious aspects of Jewish life, and "Jewishness" to refer to matters of culture and ethnicity more broadly, but I follow Jonathan Sarna in noting the interrelationship between "Judaism as a faith" and "Jews as a people." See Jonathan D. Sarna, *American Judaism* (New Haven, CT: Yale University Press, 2005), xvi–xvii.

16. See Mark Rudd, "Why Were There So Many Jews in SDS? (or, The Ordeal of Civility)," talk presented at the New Mexico Jewish Historical Society, November 2005, available at www.markrudd.com; Todd Gitlin, "50 Years since the 60s," *Forward*, May 14, 2012; Philip Mendes, "'We Are All German Jews': Exploring the Prominence of Jews in the New Left," *Melilah: Manchester Journal of Jewish Studies* 6 (2009): 1–17.

17. David A. Hollinger, "Communalist and Dispersionist Approaches to American Jewish History in an Increasingly Post-Jewish Era," *American Jewish History* 95, no. 1 (2009): 4, 11. The "Scholars' Forum: American Jewish History and American Historical Writing" in this issue includes responses to Hollinger's article by Hasia R. Diner, Alan M. Kraut, Paula E. Hyman, and Tony Michels, as well as a rejoinder by Hollinger (33–78).

18. For an early view of the movement, see Jo Freeman, "The Women's Liberation Movement: Its Origin, Structure, and Ideas" (1970), available at www.jofreeman.com. Also see Echols, *Daring to Be Bad*, 6–11.

19. Thanks to Sonia Fuentes for information about Jewish women in NOW.

20. See Susannah Heschel, "Jewish Studies as Counterhistory," in David Biale, Michael Galchinsky, and Susannah Heschel, eds., *Insider/Outsider: American Jews and Multiculturalism* (Berkeley: University of California Press, 1998), 113.

21. Among the many writings of religious Jewish feminists are Elizabeth Koltun, ed., *The Jewish Woman: New Perspectives* (New York: Schocken Books, 1976); Anne Lapidus Lerner, "'Who Hath Not Made Me a Man': The Movement for Equal Rights for Women in American Jewry," *American Jewish Year Book* 77 (1977):

3–38; Susannah Heschel, ed., *On Being a Jewish Feminist: A Reader* (New York: Schocken Books, 1983); Judith Plaskow, with Donna Berman, eds., *The Coming of Lilith: Essays on Feminism, Judaism, and Sexual Ethics, 1972–2003* (Boston: Beacon, 2005); Steven Martin Cohen, "American Jewish Feminism: A Study in Conflicts and Compromises," *American Behavioral Scientist* 23, no. 4 (1980): 531–532; Riv-Ellen Prell, *Prayer & Community: The Havurah in American Judaism* (Detroit: Wayne State University Press, 1989); and Sylvia Barack Fishman, *A Breath of Life: Feminism in the American Jewish Community* (Hanover, NH: University of New England Press, 1995).

22. See Aviva Cantor, "Halcyon Days: The Sixties Movement," *culturefront*, Winter 1997, 59; and Aviva Cantor Zuckoff, "Oppression of Amerika's Jews," *Jewish Liberation Journal* 1, no. 8 (1970).

23. Writings of secular Jewish feminists include Aviva Cantor, *Jewish Women / Jewish Men: The Legacy of Patriarchy in Jewish Life* (San Francisco: HarperCollins, 1995). On the Jewish Left, see Michael E. Staub, *Torn at the Roots: The Crisis of Jewish Liberalism in Postwar America* (New York: Columbia University Press, 2002); and Staub, ed., *The Jewish 1960s: An American Sourcebook* (Waltham, MA: Brandeis University Press, 2004).

24. Rachel Kranson, "'To Be a Jew on America's Terms Is Not to Be a Jew at All': The Jewish Counterculture's Critique of Middle-Class Affluence," *Journal of Jewish Identities* 8, no. 2 (2015): 61; Staub, *Torn at the Roots*, 208–209.

25. Evelyn Torton Beck, ed., *Nice Jewish Girls: A Lesbian Anthology*, rev. ed. (Boston: Beacon, 1989).

26. Evelyn Torton Beck, "The Politics of Jewish Invisibility," *NWSA Journal* 1, no. 1 (1988): 97.

27. Alisa Solomon, "Building a Movement: Jewish Feminists Speak Out on Israel," *Bridges* 1, no. 1 (1990): 44.

28. On anti-Semitism in American life generally, see David A. Gerber, ed., *Anti-Semitism in American History* (Urbana: University of Illinois Press, 1987); Leonard Dinnerstein, *Antisemitism in America* (New York: Oxford University Press, 1994).

29. See Evelyn Torton Beck, "No More Masks: Anti-Semitism as Jew-Hating," *Women's Studies Quarterly* 11, no. 3 (1983): 13; Melanie Kaye/Kantrowitz and Irena Klepfisz with Bernice Mennis, "*In Gerang* / In Struggle," in Kaye/Kantrowitz and Klepfisz, eds., *The Tribe of Dina* (Boston: Beacon, 1989), 304–316; Elly Bulkin, Minnie Bruce Pratt, and Barbara Smith, *Yours in Struggle: Three Feminist Perspectives on Anti-Semitism and Racism* (1984; repr., Ithaca, NY: Firebrand Books, 1988); and Letty Cottin Pogrebin, *Deborah, Golda, and Me: Being Female and Jewish in America* (New York: Crown, 1991), chap. 11 (203–234).

30. On Jewish women in international perspective, see Marjorie N. Feld, *Nations Divided: American Jews and the Struggle over Apartheid* (New York: Palgrave Macmillan, 2014); and Nelly Las, *Jewish Voices in Feminism: Transnational Perspectives* (Lincoln: University of Nebraska Press, 2015).

31. Recent works that focus on anti-Zionism include Keith Feldman, *A Shadow over*

Palestine: The Imperial Life of Race in America (Minneapolis: University of Minnesota Press, 2017); and Brooke Lober, "Conflict and Alliance in the Struggle: Feminist Anti-Imperialism, Palestine Solidarity, and the Jewish Feminist Movement of the Late 20th Century," Ph.D. diss., University of Arizona, 2016.

32. Moore, introduction to *American Jewish Identity Politics*, 8–9.

33. See Debra L. Schultz, *Going South: Jewish Women in the Civil Rights Movement* (New York: NYU Press, 2001).

34. Matthew Frye Jacobson, *Roots Too: White Ethnic Revival in Post–Civil Rights America* (Cambridge, MA: Harvard University Press, 2006), especially chap. 6.

35. Vivian Rothstein, quoted in Joyce Antler, "'Ready to Turn the World Upside Down': Jewish Women and Radical Feminism," in Diner, Kohn, and Kranson, *Jewish Feminine Mystique?*, 219; Paula Doress, quoted in Antler, *Journey Home*, 283.

36. Ezra Mendelsohn, "Jewish Universalism: Some Visual Texts and Subtexts," in Jack Kugelmass, ed., *Key Texts in American Jewish Culture* (New Brunswick, NJ: Rutgers University Press, 2003), 163.

37. David Biale, *Not in the Heavens: The Tradition of Jewish Secular Thought* (Princeton, NJ: Princeton University Press, 2011), 1; Isaac Deutscher, *The Non-Jewish Jew and Other Essays* (Oxford: Oxford University Press, 1968); Deutscher, "Message of the Non-Jewish Jew," Marxists Internet Archive, accessed April 11, 2015, www.marxists.org.

38. Deutscher, "Message of the Non-Jewish Jew."

39. Ibid. On Jewish secularism, see Biale, *Not in the Heavens*; Laura Levitt, "Other Moderns, Other Jews: Revisiting Jewish Secularism in America," in Janet R. Jakobsen and Ann Pellegrini, eds., *Secularisms* (Durham, NC: Duke University Press, 2008), 108–138; Saul L. Goodman, "Jewish Secularism in America," *Judaism* 9, no. 4 (1960): 319–330; Jon Stratton, *Coming Out Jewish: Constructing Ambivalent Identities* (London: Routledge, 2000).

40. Gerald Sorin, "Socialism in the United States," in *Jewish Women: A Comprehensive Historical Encyclopedia*, March 20, 2009, Jewish Women's Archive.

41. Tony Michels, *A Fire in Their Hearts: Yiddish Socialists in New York* (Cambridge, MA: Harvard University Press, 2005), 21–22.

42. See Linda Gordon Kuzmack, *Women's Cause: The Jewish Women's Movement in England and the United States, 1881–1933* (Columbus: Ohio State University Press, 1990). Antler, *Journey Home*.

43. See Leila J. Rupp and Verta Taylor, *Survival in the Doldrums: The American Women's Rights Movement, 1945 to the 1960s* (New York: Oxford University Press, 1987); Klapper, *Ballots, Babies, and Banners of Peace*, 4.

44. Schultz, *Going South*, 5.

45. Eric Herschthal, "The Rabbi Was a 'Freedom Rider,'" *New York Jewish Week*, May 11, 2011, http://jewishweek.timesofisrael.com; Mendes, "We Are All German Jews"; Stephen J. Whitfield, "Famished for Justice: The Jew as Radical," in L. Sandy Maisel, ed., *Jews in American Politics* (Lanham, MD: Rowman and Littlefield, 2001), 222.

46. Rudd, "Why Were There So Many Jews in SDS?"

47. See Horowitz, "Jewish Women Remaking American Feminism"; Antler, *Journey Home*, 259–267; Letty Cottin Pogrebin, "Gloria Steinem," in *Jewish Women: A Comprehensive Historical Encyclopedia*, March 20, 2009, Jewish Women's Archive.

48. See, for example, Cobble, Gordon, and Henry, *Feminism Unfinished*; Leslie Bow, *Asian American Feminisms* (New York: Routledge, 2012); Mary J. Henold, *Catholic and Feminist: The Surprising History of the American Catholic Feminist Movement* (Chapel Hill: University of North Carolina Press, 2008); Joy James and T. Denean Sharpley-Whiting, eds., *The Black Feminist Reader* (Malden, MA: Blackwell, 2000); and Alma Garcia, ed., *Chicana Feminist Thought: The Basic Historical Writings* (New York: Routledge, 1997).

49. Karen Brodkin, *How Jews Became White and What That Says about Race in America* (New Brunswick, NJ: Rutgers University Press, 1998). Also see Eric L. Goldstein, *The Price of Whiteness: Jews, Race, and American Identity* (Princeton, NJ: Princeton University Press, 2006); and Cheryl Greenberg, "'I'm Not White—I'm Jewish': The Racial Politics of American Jews," in Efraim Sicher, ed., *Race, Color, Identity: Rethinking Discourses about "Jews" in the Twenty-First Century* (New York: Berghahn Books, 2013), 5–55.

50. Rudd, "Why Were There So Many Jews in SDS?"; Mendes, "We Are All German Jews." Stanley Rothman and S. Robert Lichter, *Roots of Radicalism: Jews, Christians and the New Left* (New York: Oxford University Press, 1982).

51. See Michels, *Fire in Their Hearts*; Klapper, *Ballots, Babies, and Banners of Peace*.

52. Ellen DuBois, remarks at WLJIC. See Kranson, "To Be a Jew."

53. Audience member, remarks at WLJIC.

54. Heather Booth, interview with author, August 9, 2008; Booth, correspondence with author, August 20, 2008.

55. On "minimalist" Jews, see the discussion in Alice Kessler-Harris, *A Difficult Woman: The Challenging Life and Times of Lillian Hellman* (New York: Bloomsbury, 2011), 141; also Kessler-Harris, remarks at WLJIC.

56. Marla Brettschneider, *Democratic Theorizing from the Margins* (Philadelphia: Temple University Press, 2002), 65; also see Brettschneider, "Critical Attention to Race: Race Segregation and Jewish Feminism," *Bridges* 15, no. 2 (2010): 20–33; and Brettschneider, ed., *The Narrow Bridge: Jewish Views on Multiculturalism* (New Brunswick, NJ: Rutgers University Press, 1996).

57. Audre Lorde, "Learning from the 60s," in *Sister Outsider: Essays and Speeches by Audre Lorde* (Berkeley, CA: Crossing, 2007), 130.

58. On the statement, see the Combahee River Collective home page, accessed July 1, 2017, https://combaheerivercollective.weebly.com. On identity politics, see Barbara Ryan, *Feminism and the Women's Movement: Dynamics of Change in Social Movement, Ideology and Activism* (New York: Routledge, 1992); Roth, *Separate Roads to Feminism*.

59. Kimberlé Williams Crenshaw, "Mapping the Margins: Intersectionality, Identity

Politics, and Violence against Women of Color," in Kimberlé Crenshaw, Neil Gotanda, Gary Peller, and Kendall Thomas, eds., *Critical Race Theory: The Key Writings That Formed the Movement* (New York: New Press, 1995); Bim Adewunmi, "Kimberlé Crenshaw on Intersectionality: 'I Wanted to Come Up with an Everyday Metaphor That Anyone Could Use,'" *New Statesman*, April 2, 2014, www.newstatesman.com:

60. Adewunmi, "Kimberlé Crenshaw on Intersectionality."

61. Beck, "Politics of Invisibility," 101.

62. Goldstein, *Price of Whiteness*, 212, 235; Brodkin, *How Jews Became White*, 2–3; David Biale, "The Melting Pot and Beyond: Jews and the Politics of American Identity," in Biale, Galchinsky, and Heschel, *Insider/Outsider*, 17.

63. Peter McClaren, "White Terror and Oppositional Agency: Towards a Critical Multiculturalism," in David Theo Goldberg, ed., *Multiculturalism: A Critical Reader* (Cambridge, MA: Blackwell, 1994), 1.

64. Goldstein, *Price of Whiteness*, 6.

65. Interview with Andrea Dworkin, *Community News* (Boston), July 19, 1980.

66. Evelyn Torton Beck, interview with Fran Moira, *off our backs*, September 30, 1982.

67. Linda Gordon, "Participatory Democracy from SNCC through Port Huron to Women's Liberation to Occupy: Strengths and Problems of Prefigurative Politics," in Tom Hayden, ed., *Inspiring Participating Democracy Student Movement from Port Huron to Today* (2012; repr., New York Routledge, 2016), 108.

68. See Biale, "Melting Pot and Beyond," 17–33; Heschel, "Jewish Studies as Counterhistory," 101–115; David A. Hollinger, *Postethnic America: Beyond Multiculturalism* (New York: Basic Books, 1995); Shaul Magid, *American Post-Judaism: Identity and Renewal in a Post-ethnic Society* (Bloomington: Indiana University Press, 2013).

69. Bethamie Horowitz, *Connections and Journeys: Assessing Critical Opportunities for Enhancing Jewish Identity* (New York: UJA-Federation of New York, 2000; updated 2003), 183.

70. Stuart Hall, "Cultural Identity and Diaspora," in Jonathan Rutherford, ed., *Identity: Community, Culture, Difference* (London: Lawrence and Wishart, 1990), 225. Also see Stephen J. Whitfield, "Enigmas of Modern Jewish Identity," *Jewish Social Studies* 8, nos. 2–3 (2002): 162–167.

71. Horowitz, *Connections and Journeys*, vii–viii.

72. For early writings on these themes, see Carol Hanisch, "The Personal Is Political," in *Notes from the Second Year: Women's Liberation* (1970), accessed September 27, 2017, http://www.carolhanisch.org/; Susan Brownmiller, "Sisterhood Is Powerful," *New York Times*, March 15, 1970; and Robin Morgan, ed., *Sisterhood Is Powerful: An Anthology of Writings from the Women's Liberation Movement* (New York: Random House, 1970).

73. See Bernd Simon and Bert Klandermans, "Politicized Collective Identity: A Social Psychological Analysis," *American Psychologist* 56, no. 4 (2001): 321.

74. *Pirkei Avot* (Ethics of the Fathers), 2:5, cited in Evelyn Torton Beck, "Naming Is Not a Simple Act: Jewish Lesbian-Feminist Community in the 1980s," in Christie

Balka and Andy Rose, eds., *Twice Blessed: On Being Lesbian, Gay, and Jewish* (Boston: Beacon, 1989), 171–172.

75. Gordon, "Participatory Democracy," 120.

76. Adewunmi, "Kimberly Crenshaw on Intersectionality."

77. As at the time the Jewish membership of collectives in the cities examined came largely or almost entirely from an Ashkenazi background, the interviews reflect this demographic.

78. As a follow-up to the conference, I organized a discussion group of Jewish women's liberationists and Jewish feminists, including several conference participants, which met for a year at the Jewish Women's Archive to examine issues that had arisen at the NYU event.

79. Whittier, *Feminist Generations*, 55–56. On the birth years of second-wave feminists, see Jason Schnittker, Jeremy Freese, and Brian Powell, "Who Are Feminists and What Do They Believe? The Role of Generations," *American Sociological Review* 68, no. 4 (2003): 607–614.

80. In *Roots Too*, Matthew Frye Jacobson comments that the resolution marked the birth of "identity politics" (225), Moore, introduction to *American Jewish Identity Politics*, 1. Also see Kranson, "To Be a Jew," 64–65. On the NCNP, see Renata Adler, "Letter from Palmer House," *New Yorker*, September 23, 1967.

81. Helle Berg and Lisa Rosen Rasmussen, "Prompting Techniques: Researching Subjectivities in Educational History," *Oral History* 40, no. 1 (2012): 91–93.

82. Janet Giele, "Life Stories to Understand Diversity: Variations by Class, Race, and Gender," in Glen H. Elder, Jr., and Janet Z. Giele, eds., *The Craft of Life Course Research* (New York: Guilford, 2009), 238.

83. Ibid.; also see Janet Z. Giele and Glen H. Elder, Jr., "Life Course Studies: Development of a Field," in Giele and Elder, eds., *Methods of Life Course Research: Qualitative and Quantitative Approaches* (Thousand Oaks, CA: Sage, 1998), 5–27.

84. Alison Booth, "Recovery 2.0: Beginning the Collective Biographies of Women Project," *Tulsa Studies in Women's Literature* 28, no. 1 (2009): 17.

85. Simon and Klandermans, "Politicized Collective Identity," 321.

86. Kessler-Harris, remarks at WLJIC.

CHAPTER 1. "READY TO TURN THE WORLD UPSIDE DOWN"

1. Schultz, *Going South*, 22.

2. Amy Kesselman, with Heather Booth, Vivian Rothstein, and Naomi Weisstein, "Our Gang of Four: Female Friendship and Women's Liberation," in DuPlessis and Snitow, *Feminist Memoir Project*, 25–53.

3. Marilyn Webb and Heather Booth convened a women's group in Hyde Park, Chicago, after the SDS meeting in Champaign–Urbana in 1966, but that group met only briefly. Marilyn Webb to author, July 28, 2016. Giardina notes that Poor Black Women, a group organized in 1960, began to develop an analysis of male supremacy in the summer of 1967. It did not call itself a women's liberation group

until the fall 1968, but "it could and perhaps should be considered to have been as early as the Chicago group." Carol Giardina, *Freedom for Women: Forging the Women's Liberation Movement, 1953–1970* (Gainesville: University Press of Florida, 2010), 267n20.

4. Kesselman et al., "Our Gang of Four," 53.

5. See Booth, Kesselman, Rothstein, and Webb, remarks at WLJIC.

6. The phrase "our vision of beloved community" comes from Weisstein, "Chicago '60s," 66.

7. Brownmiller, *In Our Time*, 14–15.

8. Jo Freeman, *The Politics of Women's Liberation* (New York: Longman, 1975), 59.

9. See, for example, Evans, *Personal Politics*, 156–157; Giardina, *Freedom for Women*, 94–97; Linda Gordon, "The Women's Liberation Movement," in Cobble, Gordon, and Henry, *Feminism Unfinished*, 100–102.

10. "'New Politics' Convention to Open Here," *Chicago Tribune*, August 27, 1967.

11. Jo Freeman (aka Joreen), "On the Origins of the Women's Liberation Movement from a Strictly Personal Perspective," 1995, Jo Freeman's website, www.jofreeman. com. A condensed version is in DuPlessis and Snitow, *Feminist Memoir Project*, 171–196. Also see Evans, *Personal Politics*, 198–199; on the New Politics Convention, see 179–80. Jo Freeman wrote several articles under her movement name, "Joreen," a contraction of her two names, but later dropped that name. Also see Giardina, *Freedom for Women*, 128–130.

12. Jesse Lemisch, interview by Susan Brownmiller, October 22, 1994, Susan Brownmiller Papers, Schlesinger Library.

13. Naomi Weisstein, "Self-Interview on the Chicago Women's Liberation Union for Margaret Strobel," 1987, Schlesinger Library, 10–11; Freeman, "On the Origins," 181; Echols, *Daring to Be Bad*, 65–66.

14. Judith Hole and Ellen Levine, *Rebirth of Feminism* (New York: Quadrangle Books, 1971), 115; Giardina, *Freedom for Women*, 130.

15. Weisstein, "Chicago '60s"; also quoted in Brownmiller, *In Our Time*, 18.

16. Evans, *Personal Politics*, 201.

17. Brownmiller, *In Our Time*, 18.

18. See Giardina, *Freedom for Women*, 131–133.

19. Quoted in Ryan, *Feminism and the Women's Movement*, 47. Ann Snitow, interview by author, June 29, 2009.

20. Heather Booth, Evi Goldfield, and Sue Munaker, "Toward a Radical Movement," in Barbara A. Crow, ed., *Radical Feminism: A Documentary Reader* (New York: NYU Press, 2000), 62; Evans, *Personal Politics*, 202.

21. Vivian Rothstein to author, September 19, 2016; Amy Kesselman to author, September 19, 2016; Heather Booth to author, September 19, 2016.

22. Charlotte Bunch, interview by Sara Evans, December 14, 1997, Interview Notes, 1992–97, Sara Evans Papers, Bingham Center.

23. Rosalyn Baxandall to Naomi Weisstein, October 17, 1996, Naomi Weisstein Papers, Schlesinger Library.

24. Echols, *Daring to Be Bad*, 107–114; Brownmiller, *In Our Time*, 52–55.

25. Kesselman et al., "Our Gang of Four." "Divorcing our husbands," quoted in Ashley Eberle, "Breaking with Our Brothers: The Source and Structure of Chicago Women's Liberation in 1960s Activism," *Western Illinois Historical Review* 1 (Spring 2009): 68n28. See Jessie Lemisch, "Sectarian Rage in the New SDS," *History News Network*, January 20, 2007, http://historynewsnetwork.org. Giardina quotes Firestone's remark that West Side was insufficiently feminist (*Freedom for Women*, 134).

26. Naomi Weisstein, Evelyn Goldfield, and Sue Munaker, "A Woman Is a Sometime Thing, or Concerning Capitalism by Removing 51% of Its Commodities," quoted in David Barber, *A Hard Rain Fell: SDS and Why It Failed* (Jackson: University Press of Mississippi, 2010), 110.

27. Booth, Goldfield, and Munaker, "Toward a Radical Movement," 62.

28. Echols, *Daring to Be Bad*, 68; Brownmiller, *In Our Time*, 25; Weisstein, "Self-Interview," 14.

29. Baxandall to Weisstein, October 17, 1996.

30. Evans, *Tidal Wave*, 161; Echols, *Daring to Be Bad*, 68. Among accounts of the break from the New Left, see Ellen Willis, "Women and the Left," in Crow, *Radical Feminism*, 513–515; Echols, *Daring to Be Bad*, 103–137.

31. Kesselman et al., "Our Gang of Four," 42–43.

32. Echols, *Daring to Be Bad*, 67.

33. Kesselman et al., "Our Gang of Four," 30, 42.

34. Jewish Women's Archive, "Heather Booth," accessed July 6, 2014, http://jwa.org. Also see Laura Kaplan, *The Story of Jane: The Legendary Underground Feminist Abortion Service* (Chicago: University of Chicago Press, 1997); and Meredith Stern, "Interview with Heather Booth of the Jane Abortion Service," Justseeds Member Projects, November 13, 2012, http://justseeds.org/.

35. Jewish Women's Archive, "Heather Booth"; Vivian Rothstein and Naomi Weisstein, "Chicago Women's Liberation Union," *Women: A Journal of Liberation* 2, no. 4 (1972): 2–5, available at www.cwluherstory.org.

36. CWLU Herstory, "The Chicago Women's Liberation Rock Band," accessed January 12, 2014, www.cwluherstory.com; Naomi Weisstein, "Days of Celebration and Resistance: The Chicago Women's Liberation Rock Band, 1970–1973," in DuPlessis and Snitow, *Feminist Memoir Project*, 354–55, 361; Jessie Lemisch and Naomi Weisstein, "Remarks on Naomi Weisstein," 1997, www.cwluherstory.com.

37. Lemisch, interview, 37; Naomi Weisstein, "The Chicago Women's Liberation Rock Band, 1970–1973," *New Politics* 15, no. 1, Whole Number 57 (2014), http://newpol.org.

38. Eberle, "Breaking with Our Brothers," 75–76. Also see Margaret Strobel, "Consciousness and Action: Historical Agency in the Chicago Women's Liberation Union," in Judith Kegan Gardiner, ed., *Provoking Agents: Gender and Agency in Theory and Practice* (Urbana: University of Illinois Press, 1995), 52–68; and Strobel, "Organizational Learning in the Chicago Women's Liberation Union," in

Myra Marx Ferree and Patricia Yancy Martin, eds., *Feminist Organizations: Harvest of the New Women's Movement* (Philadelphia: Temple University Press, 1995), 145–164.

39. Kesselman et al., "Our Gang of Four," 28.
40. Ibid., 32.
41. Ibid.
42. Ibid., 26.
43. Ibid., 35. Vivian Rothstein, remarks at WLJIC.
44. Kesselman et al., "Our Gang of Four," 28–29.
45. Ibid., 30–31.
46. Ibid., 33–34.
47. Stern, "Interview with Heather Booth of the Jane Abortion Service."
48. Kesselman et al., "Our Gang of Four," 27–28.
49. Ibid., 35.
50. Ibid., 36.
51. Ibid., 38.
52. Rothstein to author, June 20, 2016.
53. Kesselman et al., "Our Gang of Four," 38.
54. Ibid.
55. Ibid., 39.
56. Ibid., 32.
57. Ibid., 33.
58. Ibid., 25.
59. Kesselman to author, July 31, 2008.
60. Kesselman, Booth, Rothstein, and Weisstein, conference call with author, August 9, 2008.
61. Weisstein, "Self-Interview."
62. Booth, conference call, August 9, 2008.
63. Heather Booth, interview by Sara Evans, November 5, 1972, Chicago, Evans Papers.
64. Rothstein to author, August 1, 2008.
65. Rothstein to author, July 8, 2011.
66. Vivian Rothstein, interview by Sara Evans, July 10, 1973, Chicago, Evans Papers.
67. Ibid.
68. Rothstein to author, July 8, 2011, and June 20, 2016.
69. Ibid.
70. Conference call, August 9, 2008.
71. Booth to author, August 20, 2008.
72. Booth, interview, November 5, 1972.
73. Booth, email to author, August 20, 2008.
74. Kesselman, email to author, July 31, 2008.
75. Rothstein to author, July 8, 2011.
76. Booth, conference call, August 9, 2008.

77. Heather Booth, interview by Sara Evans, July 9, 1973, Chicago, Evans Papers.

78. Kesselman, conference call, August 9, 2008.

79. Weisstein, "My Call to Courage: Tribute to My Mother," Weisstein Papers; Lemisch and Weisstein, "Remarks on Naomi Weisstein."

80. Weisstein, "My Call to Courage."

81. Kesselman, conversation with author, August 9, 2008; Kesselman to author, August 20, 2008.

82. Booth, interview, November 5, 1972.

83. Weisstein, "My Call to Courage."

84. Quoted in Melanie Kaye/Kantrowitz, "Stayed on Freedom: Jews in the Civil Rights Movement and After," in Brettschneider, *Narrow Bridge*, 115.

85. The "Gang of Four" discussed the Holocaust with me in a second conference call on September 13, 2008.

86. Rothstein, remarks at WLJIC.

87. Booth, conference call, September 13, 2008.

88. See Joyce Antler, "The Mother and the Movement: Feminism Constructs the Jewish Mother," chap. 6 in *You Never Call! You Never Write! A History of the Jewish Mother* (New York: Oxford University Press, 2007), 149–167.

89. Weisstein, conference call, August 9, 2008.

90. Weisstein to author, August 18, 2008.

91. Kesselman to author, August 20, 2008.

92. Ibid.

93. Rothstein to author, August 31, 2008.

94. Rothstein, conference call, August 9, 2008.

95. Weisstein, conference call, August 9, 2008.

96. Naomi Weisstein, "All Mountains Moved in Fire: A Personal, Political, and Scientific Memoir of the Early Women's Liberation Movement" (co-written with Candace Lyle Hogan), 1988–1989, 9, Weisstein Papers.

97. Booth to author, June 15, 2016.

98. Rothstein to author, June 20, 2016.

99. See Staub, *Torn at the Roots*, 129–130, 132; Clayborn Carson, "Black-Jewish Universalism in the Era of Identity Politics," in Jack Salzman and Cornell West, eds., *Struggles in the Promised Land: Toward a History of Black Jewish Relations in the United States* (New York: Oxford University Press, 1997), 188–189.

100. Kesselman, remarks at WLJIC.

101. Rothstein, remarks at WLJIC.

102. Booth, Rothstein, and Kesselman, remarks at WLJIC.

103. Emily Sigalow, "'Unconscious Affinities': An Examination of Jewish Women's Involvement in the Chicago West Side Group," paper for Jonathan Sarna, Department of Near Eastern and Judaic Studies, Brandeis University, April 23, 2009.

104. Quoted in "Our Gang of Four: Friendships and Women's Liberation," 1999, CWLU Herstory Project, www.cwluherstory.org. Also see Rothstein and Weisstein, "Chicago Women's Liberation Union"; and Weisstein and Rothstein,

"Chicago Women's Liberation Union: A Detailed Report on the CWLU's Organizing Strategy," 1972, CWLU Herstory Project, www.cwluherstory.org.

105. Rothstein to author, June 20, 2016.

106. Rothstein and Weisstein, "Chicago Women's Liberation Union."

107. Eberle, "Breaking with Our Brothers," 79.

108. Vivian Rothstein, "The Liberation School for Women, a Project of the Chicago Women's Liberation Union," paper presented at "A Revolutionary Moment: Women's Liberation in the Late 1960s and Early 1970s" conference, Boston University, March 28, 2014; Rothstein to author, June 20, 2016.

109. Karen V. Hansen, "Women's Unions and the Search for a Political Identity" (1986), in Hansen and Ilene J. Philipson, eds., *Women, Class, and the Feminist Imagination: A Socialist-Feminist Reader* (Philadelphia: Temple University Press, 1990), 222.

110. Rothstein and Weisstein, "Chicago Women's Liberation Union," 3.

111. Rothstein to author, June 20, 2016.

112. Hansen, "Women's Unions and the Search for a Political Identity," 222.

113. Weisstein, "Self-Interview," 43–44.

114. Brownmiller, *In Our Time*, 60–61.

115. Ibid.; Echols, *Daring to Be Bad*, 67.

116. Weisstein, "Days of Celebration and Resistance," 358–360. See Brownmiller, *In Our Own Time*, 61–62; Evans, *Tidal Wave*, 124.

117. Brownmiller, *In Our Time*, 62.

118. Kesselman et al., "Our Gang of Four," 50; Booth, remarks at WLJIC.

119. Weisstein, draft memoir, 19, 41.

120. Kesselman et al., "Our Gang of Four," 51.

121. Ibid., 52.

122. Ibid., 53.

123. Weisstein's landmark article "Kinder, Kuche, Kirche as Scientific Law: Psychology Constructs the Female," was printed first by the New England Free Press (1968), then in the *Journal of Social Education* 35 (1971) and many other publications. On Weisstein's struggles with sexism in science, see her article "'How Can a Little Girl like You Teach a Great Big Class of Men?' the Chairman Said, and the Other Adventures of a Woman in Science," in Sara Ruddick and Pamela Daniels, eds., *Working It Out: 23 Writers, Artists, Scientists, and Scholars Talk about Their Lives and Work* (New York: Pantheon, 1978). See Joyce Antler, "Naomi Weisstein," in *American National Biography* (New York: Oxford University Press and American Council of Learned Societies, 2018), www.anb.org.

124. Rothstein, remarks at WLJIC.

125. Booth, remarks at WLJIC.

126. Natalie Doss, "The Progressive: For Over Forty Years, Heather Booth Has Worked to Build a Small-D Democracy," *Chicago Weekly*, January 7, 2010, www.chicago weekly.net.

127. Booth, conference call, August 9, 2008.

128. Marilyn Webb, interview by author, June 5, 2009; Webb to author, June 21, 2011.

129. Rosen, *World Split Open*, 134.

130. Ibid.

131. Echols, *Daring to Be Bad*, 117.

132. Shulamith Firestone, "Letter," *Guardian*, February 1, 1969, 12, quoted in Echols, *Daring to Be Bad*, 316n70.

133. Webb to author, August 4, 2016.

134. Rosen, *World Split Open*, 135.

135. On the D.C. Women's Liberation movement, see Anne M. Valk, *Radical Sisters: Second-Wave Feminism and Black Liberation in Washington, DC* (Urbana: University of Illinois Press, 1968), chap. 3. Valk dates the founding of the organization as early 1968, with the group establishing a small membership by the end of 1968 (ibid., 66). Also see Evans, *Tidal Wave*, 98–101.

136. Susan Faludi, "Death of a Revolutionary," *New Yorker*, April 15, 2013, www.new yorker.com.

137. Webb, interview.

138. Ibid.

139. Webb to author, August 4, 2016.

140. Webb, interview.

141. Marilyn Webb, post to Shulie's List, October 5, 2012. Shulie's List was an email listserv created by Firestone's friends after her death on August 28, 2012.

142. Webb to author, June 21, 2011.

143. Michael Walzer, "Universalism and Jewish Values," Twentieth Annual Morgenthau Memorial Lecture on Ethics and Foreign Policy, Carnegie Council for Ethics in International Affairs, May 15, 2001, New York City, available at www.carnegie council.org. Biale notes that it was "through the particular" that Jews such as these came to view the universal. Biale, *Not in the Heavens*, 24.

144. Roth, *Separate Roads to Feminism*, 194–195.

145. Jacobson, *Roots Too*, 288.

CHAPTER 2. "FEMINIST SEXUAL LIBERATIONISTS, ROOTLESS COSMOPOLITAN JEWS"

1. Rosalyn Fraad Baxandall, "Catching the Fire," in DuPlessis and Snitow, *Feminist Memoir Project*, 210.

2. Nona Willis Aronowitz, "The Feminist Manifesto," *Tablet*, October 19, 2012, www .tabletmag.com.

3. Rosen, *World Split Open*, 228–229.

4. Jeffrey S. Gurock, *Jews in Gotham: New York Jews in a Changing City, 1920–2010* (New York: NYU Press, 2012), 5.

5. Rosen, *World Split Open*, 196–197; Echols, *Daring to Be Bad*, 83–84; Ellen Willis, "Radical Feminism and Feminist Radicalism," in *No More Nice Girls: Countercultural Essays* (Hanover, NH: University of New England Press, 1992), 121.

6. Amy Kesselman's recollection, cited in Baxandall, "Catching the Fire," 212; Echols,

Daring to Be Bad, 73; Jo Freeman, "On Shulamith Firestone," *n+1* 15 (2012): 125; Brownmiller, *In Our Time*, 25.

7. Echols, *Daring to Be Bad*, 72–73.

8. Vivian Rothstein, quoted in Clara Bingham, *Witness to the Revolution: Radicals, Resisters, Vets, Hippies and the Year America Lost Its Mind and Found Its Soul* (New York: Random House, 2016), 333.

9. Echols, *Daring to Be Bad*, 138–158; Brownmiller, *In Our Time*, 64, 25.

10. Baxandall, interview by Sara Evans; Faludi, "Death of a Revolutionary."

11. Alice Echols, "'Totally Ready to Go': Shulamith Firestone and *The Dialectic of Sex*," in *Shaky Ground*, 104.

12. Phyllis Chesler, "Shulamith Firestone," Phyllis Chesler Organization, November 12, 2012, http://phyllis-chesler.com; Echols, "Totally Ready to Go," 108.

13. Ellen Willis, "Introduction: Identity Crisis," in *No More Nice Girls*, xx–xxi.

14. Ibid., xiv.

15. See Vivian Gornick, "The Next Great Moment in History Is Theirs," *Village Voice*, November 27, 1969; Gornick and Barbara K. Moran, eds., *Women in Sexist Society: Studies in Power and Powerlessness* (New York: Basic Books, 1971); and Gornick, "Twice an Outsider: On Being Jewish and a Woman," *Tikkun* 4 (March–April 1989): 29–31, 123–125; Morgan, *Sisterhood Is Powerful*; DuPlessis and Snitow, *Feminist Memoir Project*.

16. Carol Hanisch, post to Shulie's List, October 5, 2012.

17. Echols, *Daring to Be Bad*, 73–74.

18. Faludi, "Death of a Revolutionary."

19. Shulamith Firestone, *The Dialectic of Sex: The Case for Feminist Revolution* (New York: Morrow, 1970), 42–43; also quoted in Echols, *Daring to Be Bad*, 79.

20. Baxandall, "Catching the Fire," 212.

21. See Echols, *Daring to Be Bad*, 186–187.

22. Ibid., 192–193.

23. Alix Kates Shulman, "On Shulamith Firestone," *n+1* 15 (2012): 130.

24. This profile is based on Rabbi Tirzah Firestone, *With Roots in Heaven: One Woman's Passionate Journey into the Heart of Her Faith* (New York: Plume Books / Penguin, 1998). Laya Firestone Seghi provided additional information: interview by author, May 27, 2014; and letter to author, July 17, 2017.

25. T. Firestone, *With Roots in Heaven*, 25–26, 33.

26. Ibid., 32.

27. Faludi, "Death of a Revolutionary."

28. T. Firestone, *With Roots in Heaven*, xii.

29. Ibid., xii, 6, 64.

30. Laya Firestone Seghi, remarks at memorial for Shulamith Firestone, St. Mark's Church in the Bowery, Parish Hall, New York, September 23, 2012.

31. Seghi, interview.

32. Ibid.; Seghi to author, July 17, 2017.

33. Faludi, "Death of a Revolutionary."

34. T. Firestone, *With Roots in Heaven*, 36.

35. Baxandall, interview by Sara Evans.

36. S. Firestone, *Dialectic of Sex*, 11, 16, 83, 8.

37. John Leonard, review of *Dialectic of Sex*, *New York Times Book Review*, July 30, 1972, 2, quoted in Margalit Fox, "Shulamit Firestone, Feminist Writer, Dies at 67," *New York Times*, August 30, 2012.

38. Brownmiller, *In Our Own Time*, 151–152.

39. Ann Snitow, interview by author, June 29, 2009. See Snitow, "Feminism and Motherhood: An American Reading," *Feminist Review* 40, no. 1 (1992): 36; and Snitow, "Returning to the Well: Revisiting Shulamith Firestone's *The Dialectic of Sex*," in *The Feminism of Uncertainty: A Gender Diary* (Durham, NC: Duke University Press, 2015), 300.

40. Brownmiller, *In Our Own Time*, 152.

41. S. Firestone, *Dialectic of Sex*, 11–12.

42. Ibid., 149, 8, 146, 11.

43. See Susanna Paasonen, "From Cybernation to Feminization: Firestone and Cyberfeminism," in Mandy Merck and Stella Sandford, eds., *Further Adventures of "The Dialectic of Sex" Critical Essays on Shulamith Firestone* (New York: Palgrave Macmillan, 2010), 69.

44. Firestone, *Dialectic of Sex*, 273–274.

45. Ibid., 117, 261–262.

46. Ibid., 122, 33.

47. Mandy Merck, "Integration, Intersex, and Firestone," in Merck and Sandford, *Further Adventures*, 163, 172.

48. Ibid., 164, 170–174.

49. Firestone, *Dialectic of Sex*, 122.

50. Kate Millet, remarks in "Shulamith Firestone, 1945–2012" (memorial booklet, St. Mark's Church in the Bowery, 2012), 21.

51. Anselma Dell'Olio, quoted in Faludi, "Death of a Revolutionary."

52. Susan Brownmiller to author, July 11, 2016.

53. Shulamith Firestone, *Airless Spaces* (New York: Semiotext(e), 1998).

54. Laya Firestone Seghi, remarks at memorial for Shulamith Firestone, St. Mark's Church in the Bowery, September 23, 2012.

55. Heather Booth, post to Shulie's List, October 3, 2012.

56. Anne Pyne, post to Shulie's List, October 3, 2012.

57. Peggy Dobbins, post to Shulie's List, October 3, 2012. Laya Firestone Seghi noted, "Orthodox boys (and my brother in particular)" repeated the words of the prayer "to flaunt their higher status and ridicule girls," although she has no memory of her brother striking his chest during morning prayers. Seghi to author, July 17, 2017.

58. Anne Pyne, post to Shulie's List, October 5, 2012.

59. Marilyn Webb, post to Shulie's List, October, 4, 2012.

60. Firestone, *Dialectic of Sex*, 243–244.

61. Rosalyn Baxandall, post to Shulie's List, October 4, 2012.

62. Anne Pyne, post to Shulie's List, October 4, 2012.

63. Roxanne Dunbar, post to Shulie's List, October 4, 2012.

64. Anne Pyne, post to Shulie's List, October 3, 2012.

65. Alix Kates Shulman, interview by author, December 19, 2008.

66. On the "limits of liberalism," see Rosen, *World Split Open*, chap. 3; Shulamith Firestone, "The Women's Rights Movement in the U.S.: A New View," *Notes from the First Year*, June 1968, 1–7.

67. Alix Kates Shulman, remarks in "Shulamith Firestone, 1945–2012," 15.

68. Amy Kesselman, interview by author, January 30, 2009.

69. Arlene Agus, interview by author, January 10, 2013.

70. Heather Booth, post to Shulie's List, October 3, 2012.

71. Andrew Klein, remarks in "Shulamith Firestone, 1945–2012," 29.

72. Susan Brownmiller to author, July 11, 2016.

73. Seghi, interview; Seghi to author, July 17, 2017.

74. Seghi, interview.

75. Ellen Willis, "Can a Non-Jew *Listen* to Jews?," *Village Voice*, May 3, 1974.

76. Stanley Aronowitz, interview by author, April 28, 2009. Also see Ann Snitow, "The Politics of Passion: Ellen Willis (1941–2006)," in *Feminism of Uncertainty*, 293–296.

77. Lisa L. Rhodes, *Electric Ladyland: Women and Rock Culture* (Philadelphia: University of Pennsylvania Press, 2005), 90.

78. Ibid., 92.

79. Ibid., 103, 98; Evelyn McDonnell, introduction to McDonnell and Ann Powers, eds., *Rock She Wrote: Women Write about Rock, Pop, and Rap* (New York: Rowman and Littlefield, 1993), 8.

80. Rhodes, *Electric Ladyland*, 103.

81. Ellen Willis, foreword to Echols, *Daring to Be Bad*, vii.

82. Ellen Willis, "Up from Radicalism: A Feminist Journal," *US Magazine*, 1969, in Nona Willis Aronowitz, ed., *The Essential Ellen Willis* (Minneapolis: University of Minnesota Press, 2014), 6, 11–13.

83. Ibid., 15.

84. Echols, *Daring to Be Bad*, 150; Rhodes, *Electric Ladyland*, 130.

85. Echols, *Daring to Be Bad*, 140.

86. Brownmiller's account of the speak-out appeared as a front-page story in the *Village Voice*, March 27, 1969.

87. Rosen, *World Split Open*, 196. Carol Hanisch's paper "The Personal Is Political," published in *Notes from the Second Year*, helped popularize the term. Shulamith Firestone and Anne Koedt, editors of *Notes*, provided the paper's title. See Giardina, *Freedom for Women*, 267n13.

88. Leora Tanenbaum, "Sisterhood, For and Against," *Women's Review of Books* 10, no. 8 (1993): 17.

89. Ibid., 18.

90. Ellen Willis, "Next Year in Jerusalem," *Rolling Stone*, April 1977, reprinted in Nona Willis Aronowitz, ed., *The Essential Ellen Willis* (Minneapolis: University of Minnesota Press, 2014), 132–169. The essay also appears in Ellen Willis, *Beginning to See the Light: Sex, Hope, and Rock-and-Roll* (Hanover, NH: Wesleyan University Press, 1992), 261–317. Page numbers refer to the Aronowitz edition.

91. Sasha Frere-Jones, Emily Gould, and Sara Marcus, Ellen Willis roundtable, March 7, 2012, www.bookforum.com.

92. Willis, "Next Year in Jerusalem," 132, 133–134, 137.

93. Ibid., 137.

94. Ibid., 137–138.

95. Ellen Willis to Michael Willis, September 8, 1975, Ellen Willis Papers, Schlesinger Library.

96. Willis, "Next Year in Jerusalem," 100–101.

97. Ibid., 135, 144–145.

98. Ibid., 152.

99. Ibid., 157–158, 161.

100. Ibid., 168.

101. Ibid., 161.

102. Ibid., 163, 169.

103. Ibid., 168–169.

104. Ellen Willis, "Radical Jews Caught in the Middle," *Village Voice*, February 4–10, 1981, 20.

105. Ibid.

106. Shulman, interview.

107. Willis, "Can a Non-Jew *Listen* to Jews?"

108. Ellen Willis, "The Myth of the Powerful Jew," in *Beginning to See the Light*, 237, 239.

109. Ibid., 235, 237.

110. Ibid., 237; Ellen Willis, "Advice for Survival," review of *The Real Anti-Semitism in America*, by Nathan Perlmutter and Ruth Ann Perlmutter, *New York Times*, October 3, 1982.

111. Ellen Willis, interview by Letty Cottin Pogrebin, n.d., Letty Cottin Pogrebin Papers, Sophia Smith Collection.

112. Willis, "Advice or Survival."

113. Willis, "Myth of the Powerful Jew," 230; Willis, "Advice for Survival."

114. Willis, "Advice for Survival"; Willis, "Radical Jews Caught in the Middle."

115. Willis, "Radical Jews Caught in the Middle," 18.

116. Ibid., 18–19.

117. Ibid., 18.

118. Ibid.

119. Ibid., 20.

120. Ibid.

121. Willis, "Can a Non-Jew *Listen* to Jews?," 23.

122. Ellen Willis, "Why I'm Not for Peace," *Radical Society* 29, no. 1 (April 2002): 13–20.

123. Ellen Willis, "Is There Still a Jewish Question? Why I'm an Anti-Anti-Zionist," in Tony Kushner and Alisa Solomon, eds., *Wrestling with Zion: Progressive Jewish-American Responses to the Israeli-Palestinian Conflict* (New York: Grove, 2003), 226, 229.

124. Willis, "Next Year in Jerusalem," 161.

125. Willis, interview by Pogrebin.

126. Ellen Willis to Michael Willis, September 8, 1975.

127. Shulman, interview.

128. Ibid.; Shulman to author, July 9, 2016.

129. Alix Kates Shulman, remarks at WLJIC.

130. Rosalyn Baxandall, interview by author, April 29, 2009.

131. Julie Fraad, conversation with author, July 20, 2016.

132. Phineas Baxandall to author, July 18, 2016.

133. R. Baxandall, interview.

134. Alix Kates Shulman, "Summer Jew," *Michigan Quarterly Review* 42, no. 1 (2003), reprinted in Shulman, *A Marriage Agreement and Other Essays* (New York: Open Road Media, 2012), 164, 169.

135. Willis, "Myth of the Powerful Jew," 237.

136. Shulman, remarks at WLJIC.

137. Alix Kates Shulman, *A Good Enough Daughter: A Memoir* (New York: Schocken Books, 1990), 99–100; Shulman, interview.

138. Shulman, remarks at WJLIC.

139. Ibid.

140. Shulman, interview.

141. Alix Kates Shulman, remarks in *Makers: Women Who Make America*, documentary, 2013.

142. Ibid.; "An Interview with Alix Kates Shulman / Charlotte Templin," *Missouri Review* 24, no. 1 (2001): 103–121.

143. See Caitlin Flanagan, "How Serfdom Saved the Women's Movement: Dispatches from the Nanny Wars," *Atlantic Monthly*, March 2004, www.theatlantic.com. Also see Alix Shulman's website, www.alixkshulman.com.

144. Kat Stoeffel, "How Second-Wave Feminists Fought Cat-Callers," *New York*, November 26, 2014, http://nymag.com.

145. Alix Kates Shulman, "Sex and Power: Sexual Basis of Radical Feminism," in *Marriage Agreement and Other Essays*, 91.

146. "Interview with Alix Kates Shulman / Charlotte Templin," 105.

147. Bella Book, "An Interview with Alix Kates Shulman," March 15, 2016, Jewish Women's Archive.

148. Alix Kates Shulman, *Burning Questions* (New York: Thunder's Mouth, 1978), 10.

149. "Interview with Alix Kates Shulman / Charlotte Templin," 115.

150. Shulman, interview. See Alix Kates Shulman, *To the Barricades: The Anarchist Life of Emma Goldman* (New York: Thomas Y. Crowell, 1971); and Shulman, ed., *Red Emma Speaks: Selected Writings and Speeches* (New York: Vintage Books, 1972).

151. Alix Kates Shulman, "Living Our Life," in Carol Ascher, Louise DeSalvo, and Sara Ruddick, eds., *Between Women: Biographers, Novelists, Critics, Teachers and Artists Write about Their Work on Women* (Boston: Beacon, 1984), 5, 13. The article was also reprinted in Shulman, *Marriage Agreement*, 137–152.

152. This statement is adapted from Antler, *Journey Home*, 92. See Alice Wexler, *Emma Goldman in America* (Boston: Beacon, 1984), 92; and David Waldstreicher, "Radicalism, Religion, Jewishness: The Case of Emma Goldman," *American Jewish History* 80, no. 1 (1990): 87.

153. Shulman, remarks at WLJIC.

154. Redstockings, "Redstockings Manifesto," July 7, 1969, available at www.red stockings.org.

155. Shulman, remarks at WLJIC.

156. Book, "Interview with Alix Kates Shulman."

157. Susan Brownmiller, interview by author, April 15, 2009.

158. Jewish Women's Archive, "Susan Brownmiller," in "The Feminist Revolution," accessed March 3, 2013, http://jwa.org.

159. Ibid.

160. Susan Brownmiller to author, July 11, 2016.

161. Ibid.

162. Brownmiller, interview.

163. Ibid.

164. Brownmiller, *In Our Time*, 82–94.

165. Brownmiller, *Against Our Will*, 15; New York Public Library, "The New York Public Library's Books of the Century," accessed October 24, 2017, www.nypl.org; Sascha Cohen, "How a Book Changed the Way We Talk about Rape," *Time*, October 7, 2015, http://time.com; accessed September 10, 2017, http://www.nypl.org. For a reappraisal from a radical feminist magazine, see Stevi Jackson, "Against Our Will," *Trouble & Strife* 25 (Summer 1997), www.troubleandstrife.com.

166. Jewish Women's Archive, "Susan Brownmiller."

167. Brownmiller, *In Our Time*, 65.

168. Ibid., 66.

169. Baxandall, interview by author.

170. Robin Morgan, interview by author, March 12, 2013.

171. Brownmiller to author, July 11, 2016.

172. Willis, "Introduction: Identity Crisis," xx–xxi; Baxandall, "Catching the Fire," 210–211.

CHAPTER 3. "CONSCIOUS RADICALS"

1. See Nancy Hawley and Marya Levenson, "Dear Sisters," letter to Bread and Roses, October 8, 1970, Meredith Tax Papers, Bingham Center; and Meredith Tax and Diane Balser, "Draft Internal Statement," n.d., Bread and Roses file, Winifred Breines Papers, Schlesinger Library. On the formation of Bread and Roses, see

Ann Hunter Popkin, "Bread and Roses: An Early Moment in the Development of Socialist-Feminism," Ph.D. diss., Brandeis University, 1978.

2. Evans, *Tidal Wave*, 105.

3. Roxanne Dunbar-Ortiz, *Outlaw Women: Memoir of the War Years, 1960–1975* (Norman: University of Oklahoma Press, 2014), 139.

4. Meredith Tax, "The Sound of One Hand Clapping: Women's Liberation and the Left," *Dissent*, Fall 1998, available at www.meredithtax.org. See Brownmiller, *In Our Time*, 62; and Echols, *Daring to Be Bad*, 158–159.

5. Linda Gordon to author, August 8, 2016; Evans, *Tidal Wave*, 105, 260n18; Gordon, "Participatory Democracy," 116.

6. See Hawley and Levenson, "Dear Sisters."

7. Gordon to author, August 8, 2016; and Gordon, "Participatory Democracy," 118.

8. Bread and Roses organizing document, Grey Osterud Papers, Schlesinger Library. Bread was "money," and roses was "a good life." Hawley and Levenson, "Dear Sisters"; Popkin, "Bread and Roses," 50.

9. Bread and Roses member Ann Hunter Popkin notes a phone chain in January 1970 with two hundred women in twenty-three collectives, plus fifty-seven "at-large" members who were "between collectives." Popkin, "Bread and Roses," 93, 101.

10. Grey Osterud to author, June 28, 2013.

11. The Chicago Women's Liberation Union was born at the Radical Women's Conference in Palatine, Illinois, in October 1969, one month after Bread and Roses organized. Eberle, "Breaking with Our Brothers," 70.

12. Popkin, "Bread and Roses," 211; Meredith Tax, "Preliminary Strategic Suggestions for the Boston Women's Movement," June 14, 1969, Tax Papers; "The Need for a Program, Strategy and Political Organization in the Boston Women's Movement," June 30, 1969, Tax Papers.

13. First draft of the Bread and Roses statement of purpose, cited in Breines, *Trouble between Us*, 98.

14. Tess Ewing, "Bread and Roses," paper presented at "A Revolutionary Moment: Women's Liberation in the Late 1960s and Early 1970s" conference, Boston University, March 27–29, 2014.

15. Gordon, "Participatory Democracy," 116.

16. Meredith Tax, "Caste and Class," quoted in Breines, *Trouble between Us*, 99.

17. "Bread and Roses Is a Women's Liberal Organization," typescript, Bread and Roses, Grey Osterud Papers; Meredith Tax and Diane Balser, "Draft Internal Statement," n.d., Breines Papers; Hawley and Levenson, "Dear Sisters"; Marya Levenson, undated notes, in Levenson's possession.

18. Ewing, "Bread and Roses"; Gordon to author, August 8, 2016.

19. Jean Tepperman, untitled memo, November 4, 1969, Osterud Papers; Meredith Tax, "For the People Hear Us Singing, 'Bread and Roses! Bread and Roses!,'" in DuPlessis and Snitow, *Feminist Memoir Project*, 315.

20. Popkin, "Bread and Roses," 180, 165.
21. Tax, "Sound of One Hand Clapping."
22. Popkin, "Bread and Roses," 96–97.
23. Tax, "Sound of One Hand Clapping."
24. Ewing, "Bread and Roses." Also see Echols, *Daring to Be Bad*, 204.
25. Meredith Tax, "My Questions and Some Tentative Answers," September 14, 1971, Tax Papers.
26. Gordon to author, August 8, 2016; Gordon, "Participatory Democracy," 119–120.
27. Gordon to author, August 8, 2016.
28. The documentary *Left on Pearl*, made by the 888 Women's History Project Collective, tells the story of the takeover and the creation of the women's center. Also see Gordon, "Women's Liberation Movement," 77.
29. See Breines, *Trouble between Us*, 100–103; Gordon to author, August 8, 2016.
30. Bread and Roses Survey Questionnaires, Ann Popkin Papers, 1968–1977, Schlesinger Library.
31. Breines, *Trouble between Us*, 108.
32. The opening lines from Tepperman's "Witch" are,

> They told me
> I smile prettier with my mouth closed.
> They said
> Better cut your hair—
> Long, it's all frizzy,
> looks Jewish. (Tax Papers)

33. Interviews with Bread and Roses members Judy Ullman, Nancy Chodorow, Rivka Gordon, and Rochelle Ruthchild provided additional background and context.
34. Kristine M. Rosenthal, "Women in Transition: An Ethnography of a Women's Liberation Organization as a Case Study of Personal and Cultural Change," Ph.D. diss., Harvard Graduate School of Education, 1972, 19–20; Popkin, "Bread and Roses," chap. 2 (24–41).
35. Popkin, "Bread and Roses," 29–32, 37–41; Darren E. Sherkat and T. Jean Blocker, "The Political Development of Sixties' Activists: Identifying the Influence of Class, Gender and Socialization on Protest Participation," *Social Forces* 72, no. 3 (1994): 833.
36. Popkin, "Bread and Roses," 26–29. Rebecca Klatch finds that 1960s activists of both the Left and the Right "were raised with a consciousness of the political world and encouraged to 'think politically.'" Klatch, *Generation Divided*, 40.
37. Klatch, *Generation Divided*, 40.
38. Popkin, "Bread and Roses," 101–102.
39. Meredith Tax, interview by author, September 11, 2009.
40. Meredith Tax, interview by Kate Weigand, Voice of Feminism Oral History Project, June 11–12, 2004, Sophia Smith Collection, 6.
41. Tax, "For the People Hear Us Singing," 311.
42. Tax, interview by Weigand, 3.

43. Meredith Tax, unpublished memoir, work in progress, 2013, in the author's possession.

44. Ibid.

45. Tax, interview by author.

46. Meredith Tax, "Jewish Identity: From Whitefish Bay to Rivington Street," keynote speech at a women's conference at the JCC, March 6, 1983, available at www .meredithtax.org.

47. Ibid.; Tax, unpublished memoir.

48. Tax to author, June 20, 2016.

49. Meredith Tax, remarks at WLJIC; also posted on Tax's blog, *Taxonomy*, April 12, 2011, www.meredithtax.org.

50. Ibid.

51. Ibid.

52. Tax, "Jewish Identity."

53. Tax, "For the People Hear Us Singing," 311; Tax, remarks at WLJIC.

54. Tax, "Jewish Identity."

55. Tax, "For the People Hear Us Singing," 312.

56. Meredith Tax and Cynthia Michel, "An Open Letter to the Boston Movement," n.d., Osterud Papers.

57. Tax, "For the People Hear Us Singing," 317.

58. Ibid., 318.

59. Tax, interview by author; Tax to author, June 20, 2016.

60. Tax to author, June 20, 2016.

61. Meredith Tax, *The Rising of the Women: Feminist Solidarity and Class Conflict, 1880–1917* (New York: Monthly Review Press, 1980).

62. Meredith Tax, *Rivington Street* (New York: William Morrow, 1982); Tax, *Union Square* (New York: William Morrow, 1988).

63. Tax, interview by author.

64. CARASA was "opposed to linking the question of abortion rights with population control ideas." On the organization's goals, see Meredith Tax's website, http:// meredithtax.org.

65. See Meredith Tax, letter to the editor, *New York Times*, August 21, 2001, Tax Papers.

66. Meredith Tax's website, www.meredithtax.org; Tax, *Double Bind: The Muslim Right the Anglo-American Left, and Universal Human Rights* (London: Centre for Secular Space, 2013); Tax, *A Road Unforeseen: Women Fight the Islamic State* (New York: Bellevue Literary Press, 2016).

67. Meredith Tax, "The False Idol of Land Worship," *Jewish Weekly Forward*, May 10, 2002.

68. Tax, remarks at WLJIC. See Meredith Tax's blog, *Taxonomy*, April 12, 2011, www .meredithtax.org.

69. Gordon to author, August 8, 2016.

70. Gordon, remarks at WLJIC.

71. Ibid.

72. Ibid.

73. Ibid.; Linda Gordon, interview by author, February 9, 2009; Gordon to author, August 8, 2016.

74. Quoted in Evans, *Tidal Wave*, 30; original in Popkin, "Bread and Roses," 98.

75. Gordon, interview.

76. Ibid.

77. Gordon's major books include *Women's Body, Women's Right* (New York: Viking, 1976); *Heroes of Their Own Lives: The Politics and History of Family Violence* (New York: Viking, 1988); *Pitied but Not Entitled: Single Mothers and the History of Welfare, 1890–1935* (New York: Free Press, 1994); *The Great Arizona Orphan Abduction* (Cambridge, MA: Harvard University Press, 1999); *Dorothea Lange: A Life beyond Limits* (New York: Norton, 2010); and *The Second Coming of the KKK: The Ku Klux Klan of the 1920s and the American Political Tradition* (New York: Liveright, 2017).

78. Hawley and Levenson, "Dear Sisters."

79. Marya Levenson, interview by author, June 13, 2011.

80. Ibid.

81. Michele Clark, "Stories from Life: The Bat Mitzvah Mother," *Bridges* 6, no. 1 (1996): 76.

82. Michele Clark, interview by author, November 21, 2012.

83. Ibid.

84. Ibid.

85. Ibid.

86. Ibid.

87. The collective spent a year discussing their mothers as a way of getting over mother-blaming, and because two-thirds of the group were Jewish, the critiques became a tableau of Jewish mother-blaming. Clark, interview.

88. Michele Clark, "Stories from Life: No Shuttle to Central Vermont," *Bridges* 1, no. 2 (1990): 17.

89. Ibid., 18, 20.

90. Grey Osterud, interview by author, July 22, 2010.

91. Ibid.

92. Grey Osterud to author, July 22, 2010.

93. Ibid.

94. Balser is the author of *Sisterhood and Solidarity: Feminism and Labor in Modern Times* (Cambridge, MA: South End, 1987).

95. Diane Balser, remarks at WLJIC.

96. Diane Balser, "Diane Balser, 68, Talks to Susan Schnur: Her Lifelong Feminist-Jewish Politics," *Lilith* 37, no. 1 (2012): 34; Balser, remarks at WLJIC; Diane Balser, interview by author, November 5, 2008.

97. Balser, remarks at WLJIC; Balser, interview.

98. Balser, "Diane Balser, 68, Talks to Susan Schnur," 36.

99. Balser, interview.

100. Balser, "Diane Balser, 68, Talks to Susan Schnur," 36.

101. Ibid.

102. Ibid., 37.

103. Ibid., 39.

104. Balser, remarks at WLJIC.

105. Margaret M. Braungart and Richard C. Braungart, "The Life-Course Development of Left- and Right-Wing Youth Activist Leaders from the 1960s," *Political Psychology* 11 (1990): 243–282; Sherkat and Blocker, "Political Development of Sixties' Activists," 837.

106. Braungart and Braungart, "Life-Course Development," 259.

107. Tax, interview by Weigand, 9.

108. Judy Ullman, interview by author, May 9, 2013.

109. Klatch, *Generation Divided*, 52–57.

110. Ibid., 58.

CHAPTER 4. OUR BODIES AND OUR JEWISH SELVES

1. Susan Wells, *Our Bodies, Ourselves and the Work of Writing* (Stanford, CA: Stanford University Press, 2010), 33.

2. Brownmiller, *In Our Time*, 180.

3. Nancy Miriam Hawley, remarks on "Formative Years: The Birth of *Our Bodies, Ourselves*" panel, with Joan Ditzion, Paula Doress-Worters, and Wendy Sanford, at "A Revolutionary Moment: Women's Liberation in the Late 1960s and Early 1970s" conference, Boston University, March 27–29, 2014.

4. Quoted in Molly M. Ginty, "*Our Bodies, Ourselves* Turns 35 Today," *Women's eNews*, May 4, 2004.

5. Jane Pincus, oral history by Katelyn Lucy, November 29, 2008, Sophia Smith Collection, 8.

6. See Zobeida E. Bonilla, "Including All Women: The All-Embracing 'We' of 'Our Bodies, Ourselves,'" *NWSA Journal* 17, no. 1 (2005): 176.

7. Norma Swenson to author, August 11, 2016.

8. The establishment of an official Founders group took place in 1996, when Sally Whelan, Pamela Morgan, and Elizabeth McMahon-Herrera were added as founders. Our Bodies, Ourselves, "History" and "OBOS Founders," accessed October 24, 2017, www.ourbodiesourselves.org.

9. Jane Pincus and Joan Ditzion, "Preface/Introduction," in Boston Women's Health Book Collective, *The New Our Bodies, Ourselves* (New York: Touchstone / Simon and Schuster, 1984), xi.

10. Swenson to author, August 11, 2016; Kathy Davis, *The Making of "Our Bodies, Ourselves": How Feminism Travels across Borders* (Durham, NC: Duke University Press, 2007), 24. On the Boston Women's Health Book Collective, also see Wells, *Our Bodies, Ourselves and the Work of Writing*; and Sandra Morgen, *Into Our Own Hands: The Women's Health Movement in the United States, 1969–1990*

(New Brunswick, NJ: Rutgers University Press, 2002); Heather Stephenson and Kiki Zeldes, "'Write a Chapter and Change the World': How the Boston Women's Health Book Collective Transformed Women's Health Then—and Now," *American Journal of Public Health* 98, no. 10 (2008): 1741–1745.

11. Nancy Miriam Hawley, remarks at WLJIC.

12. Sanford, quoted in Davis, *Making of "Our Bodies, Ourselves,"* 30.

13. Hilary Salk, Wendy Sanford, Norma Swenson, and Judith Dickson Luce, "The Politics of Women and Medical Care," in Boston Women's Health Book Collective, *New Our Bodies, Ourselves*, 560.

14. Pincus and Ditzion, "Preface/Introduction," xiv.

15. Norma Swenson to author, August 11, 2016.

16. See Wells, *Our Bodies, Ourselves and the Work of Writing*, 7–8.

17. The translation process began in the mid-1970s; a self-published Spanish-language edition appeared in 1977. A new process of cultural adaptation followed the direct translations of this early period. Stephenson and Zeldes, "Write a Chapter and Change the World."

18. See my discussion in *Journey Home*, 282–283.

19. Mary Stern, the founder who moved to Canada, was not Jewish.

20. Hollinger, "Communalist and Dispersionist Approaches."

21. The author conducted interviews with eight founders and the husband, son, brother, and sister-in-law of the late Esther Rome. Two Jewish founders were not interviewed. Ruth Bell Alexander was not interviewed because of reasons of geography. Alexander is the author of *Changing Bodies, Changing Lives: A Book for Teens on Sex and Relationships* and a variety of math-game books for children. Pamela Berger preferred not to be interviewed. A professor of art history and film, Berger wrote and produced *Sorceress*, about a medieval woman healer, and wrote, produced, and directed *Killian's Chronicle*, about an Irish slave who escapes from a Viking ship and is rescued by Native Americans, and *The Imported Bridegroom*, based on a short story by the Yiddish *Forward*'s editor, Abraham Cahan. Berger's scholarly work includes, most recently, *The Crescent on the Temple*, a study of how the Dome of the Rock served as the image of Solomon's Temple in Christian, Muslim, and Jewish art.

22. See Pincus and Ditzion, "Preface/Introduction," xiii.

23. Joan Ditzion and Miriam Hawley, interview by author, August 4, 2016; Swenson to author, August 11, 2016.

24. Boston Women's Health Book Collective, preface to *Our Bodies, Ourselves* (New York: Simon and Schuster, 1973), xiii.

25. See Davis, *Making of "Our Bodies, Ourselves,"* chap. 3.

26. Ibid., 109.

27. Swenson to author, August 11, 2016.

28. Jane Pincus (1998), quoted in Bonilla, "Including Every Woman," 176.

29. Wells, *Our Bodies, Ourselves and the Work of Writing*, 93.

30. The BWHBC came to function as a small nonprofit organization, with no

resemblance to a collective, "let alone a family." Davis, *Making of "Our Bodies, Ourselves,"* 117.

31. See Wells, *Our Bodies, Ourselves and the Work of Writing*, 84.

32. Davis, *Making of "Our Bodies Ourselves,"* 81, 195–196, 200–203.

33. Wendy Kline, "The Making of *Our Bodies, Ourselves*: Rethinking Women's Health and Second-Wave Feminism," in Gilmore, *Feminist Coalitions*, 67–71, 77–79.

34. See Jane Sprague Zones, "Esther Rome," in *Jewish Women: A Comprehensive Historical Encyclopedia*, March 20, 2009, Jewish Women's Archive.

35. This account is based on information from Nathan Rome, interview with author, April 25, 2013; Judah Rome, interview with author, April 30, 2013; and Ruth and Aaron Seidman, interview with author, June 17, 2013.

36. Wendy Sanford, quoted in Sue Woodman, "Esther Rome: Our Bodies, Her Self," *Guardian*, July 7, 1995, 18.

37. Paula Doress-Worters, quoted ibid.

38. Wendy Sanford, "In Memoriam: Esther Rome," *A Gala Celebration—Our Bodies, Ourselves*, March 8, 1996, 24–26.

39. Nathan Rome to author, July 24, 2016.

40. Jane Wegscheider Hyman and Esther R. Rome, in cooperation with the Boston Women's Health Book Collective, *Sacrificing Ourselves for Love: Why Women Compromise Health and Self-Esteem, and How to Stop* (Freedom, CA: Crossing, 1996).

41. Sanford, "In Memoriam," 25.

42. Judah Rome, interview.

43. Nathan Rome, interview.

44. Doress-Worters, quoted in Woodman, "Esther Rome."

45. Judah Rome, interview.

46. Doress-Worters, quoted in Woodman, "Esther Rome," and in Sanford, "In Memoriam," 25.

47. Wendy Sanford, interview by author, September 19, 2013.

48. Doress-Worters, quoted in Woodman, "Esther Rome."

49. Doress-Worters, remarks at WLJIC.

50. Ibid.; Paula Doress-Worters, interview by author, July 23, 2010; Paula Doress-Worters to author, July 9, 2016.

51. Doress-Worters, interview.

52. Ibid.

53. Ibid.

54. Ibid.

55. Doress-Worters to author, April 24, 2016.

56. Doress-Worters, interview.

57. Quoted in Antler, *Journey Home*, 283, from interview by author, January 1996.

58. Doress-Worters, interview.

59. "Vilunya Diskin," OBOS website, accessed April 8, 2013, www.ourbodiesourselves.org.

60. Vilunya Diskin, "Once Orphaned, Thrice Adopted: With the Songs of the Sabbath Echoing," *Jewish Currents*, May 22, 2012.

61. Vilunya Diskin, interview by author, August 4, 2010; Diskin, "Once Orphaned, Thrice Adopted."

62. Diskin, "Once Orphaned, Thrice Adopted."

63. Ibid.; Diskin, interview.

64. Diskin, "Once Orphaned, Thrice Adopted."

65. Diskin, interview.

66. Diskin, "Once Orphaned, Thrice Adopted."

67. Ibid.

68. Ibid.

69. Brownmiller, *In Our Time*, 180.

70. Miriam Hawley, interview by author, February 3, 2009.

71. Hawley, remarks at WLJIC.

72. Hawley, interview.

73. Hawley, remarks at "Formative Years" panel..

74. Hawley, remarks at WLJIC.

75. Jewish Women's Archive, "Nancy Miriam Hawley," accessed July 16, 2015, http://jwa.org.

76. Hawley, interview.

77. Ibid.

78. Hawley, remarks at WLJIC.

79. Joan Ditzion, remarks at "Formative Years" panel.

80. Joan Ditzion, interview by author, June 27, 2013.

81. Ibid.

82. Ibid.

83. Ditzion, remarks at "Formative Years" panel.

84. Ibid.

85. Ditzion, interview.

86. Ibid.

87. Ibid.

88. Jane Pincus, interview by author, July 15, 2013.

89. Ibid.

90. Ibid.; Jane Pincus to author, August 5, 2016.

91. Pincus to author, August 5, 2016.

92. Ibid.

93. Pincus to author, August 5, 2016.

94. John Sullivan, "Plan to Release Notorious Killer Prompts Debate about Insanity," *New York Times*, July 14, 2000, www.nytimes.com.

95. Norma Swenson, interview by author, May 21, 2014.

96. Wendy Sanford, interview by author, September 19, 2013.

97. Ibid.

98. Wendy Sanford, "Bodies: A Memoir," *Narrative*, 1, www.narrativemagazine.com.

99. Ibid., 5; Wendy Sanford, remarks on "Formative Years" panel.

100. Sanford, "Bodies," 4–5, 8, 10, 7.

101. Sanford, interview.

102. Ibid.

103. Sanford, "Bodies," 12.

104. Sanford, interview.

105. Sanford, "Bodies," 12.

106. Sanford, interview.

107. Ibid.

108. Ibid.

109. Ibid.

110. Ibid.

111. Swenson, interview.

112. See Jeffrey Ann Goudie, "Herself Back in Topeka," *Topeka Magazine*, Summer 2011, 42.

113. Swenson, interview.

114. Ibid.

115. Ibid.

116. Ibid.

117. Norma Swenson to author, August 11, 2016.

118. Norma Swenson, "Prague Weekend: Political Memoir," unpublished manuscript, 2014.

119. Norma Swenson, "The Last Passover [1939]," unpublished manuscript, 2014.

120. Swenson, interview; Swenson to author, August 11, 2016.

121. Swenson, interview.

122. Judy Norsigian, interview by author, July 30, 2013.

123. Ibid.

124. Ibid.

125. Ibid.

126. Ibid.

127. Anita Diamant, interview at *Moment* symposium "The Origins of Creativity," November–December 2011, www.momentmag.com.

128. Robbie Pfeufer Kahn, "Taking Our Maternal Bodies Back: *Our Bodies, Ourselves*, and the Boston Women's Health Book Collective," in Joyce Antler and Sari Knopp Biklen, eds., *Changing Education: Women as Radicals and Conservators* (Albany: State University of New York Press, 1990), 121–122.

129. Jacobson, *Roots Too*.

130. Hollinger, *Postethnic America*; Magid, *American Post-Judaism*.

131. Ditzion, interview.

CHAPTER 5. "WE ARE WELL EDUCATED JEWISHLY . . . AND WE ARE GOING TO PRESS YOU"

1. Blu Greenberg, remarks at WLJIC; Blu Greenberg, interview by author, June 29, 2013.

2. Judith Plaskow, "The Jewish Feminist: Conflict in Identities," address delivered to the National Jewish Women's Conference in New York, February 1973, in Koltun, *Jewish Woman*, 3.

3. Hyman, "Jewish Feminism Faces the American Women's Movement," 223. Also see Paula E. Hyman, "Jewish Feminism in the United States," in *Jewish Women: A Comprehensive Historical Encyclopedia*, March 1, 2009, Jewish Women's Archive.

4. Carol Christ, "Community and Ambiguity: A Response from a Companion in the Journey," *Journal of Feminist Studies in Religion* 23, no. 1 (2007): 29.

5. Mary Daly, *The Church and the Second Sex* (New York: Harper and Row, 1968); Daly, *Beyond God the Father: Toward a Philosophy of Women's Liberation* (Boston: Houghton Mifflin, 1973).

6. Hyman, "Jewish Feminism Faces the American Women's Movement," 225.

7. Cohen, "American Jewish Feminism." Also see Pinsky, *Jewish Feminists*.

8. Susan Dworkin, "A Song for Women in Five Questions," *Moment*, May–June 1973, 44, quoted in Ann Lapidus Lerner, "Who Has Not Made Me a Man: The Movement for Equal Rights for Women in American Jewry," *American Jewish Year Book*, 1977, 6.

9. See Rabbi Rebecca Einstein Schorr and Rabbi Alysa Mendelson Graf, eds., *The Sacred Calling: Four Decades of Women in the Rabbinate* (New York: CCAR, 2016); Riv-Ellen Prell, ed., *Women Remaking American Judaism* (Detroit: Wayne State University Press, 2007). Also see Judith Plaskow, "Spirituality in the United States," in *Jewish Women: A Comprehensive Historical Encyclopedia*, March 20, 2009, Jewish Women's Archive.

10. Martha Ackelsberg, interview by author, August 5, 2013.

11. Ibid.

12. Members included Susan Reverby, June Finer, Elaine Archer Cerutti, Barbara Ehrenreich, and Rachel Fruchter.

13. Ackelsberg, interview.

14. See "A Matter of Choice: Women Demand Abortion Rights," *Health-Pac Bulletin*, March 1970.

15. Ackelsberg, interview.

16. Martha Ackelsberg, oral history by Julie Colatrella, April 16, 2010, Documenting Lesbian Lives Oral History Project, Sophia Smith Collection, 25.

17. Ibid.

18. Prell, *Prayer & Community*, 69–70. Also see Mark Oppenheimer, *Knocking on Heaven's Door: American Religion in the Age of Counterculture* (New Haven, CT: Yale University Press, 2003), chap. 3; and Shira Eve Epstein, "The Havurah Movement and Jewish Feminism: Preserving While Re-envisioning Judaism," bachelor's

thesis, Rutgers University, 1999, Shira Eve Epstein Papers, American Jewish Historical Society.

19. Ackelsberg, interview.

20. Alan Silverstein, "The Evolution of Ezrat Nashim," *Conservative Judaism* 30, no. 1 (1975): 41–51; Paula E. Hyman, "Ezrat Nashim and the Emergence of a New Jewish Feminism," in Robert Seltzer and Norman J. Cohen, eds., *The Americanization of the Jews* (New York: NYU Press, 1995), 284–295. Beth Friedman, Toby Gottlieb Brandriss, Judy Hauptman, Ruth Hundert, Judy Samuels, and Susan Shevitz joined in 1972; later members included Eva Fogelman and Tobi Reifman. Martha Ackelsberg to author, November 24, 2017.

21. Ackelsberg, oral history; Epstein, "Havurah Movement," 68.

22. Martha Ackelsberg, "Women at Rabbinical Assembly Seek Full Religious Participation," *Genesis* 2, April 20, 1972.

23. Susan Shevitz, interview by author, April 23, 2014.

24. In 1973, at the request of Bill Novak, then editor of *Response: A Contemporary Jewish Review*, Ezrat Nashim and a number of secular Jewish feminists published *The Jewish Woman*, a special edition of the magazine, edited by Elizabeth Koltun with an introduction by Ackelsberg. A revised edition, edited by Koltun with an expanded introduction by Ackelsberg, appeared three years later as *The Jewish Woman: New Perspectives*. Susannah Heschel's reader *On Being a Jewish Feminist* (New York: Schocken Books) came out in 1983, reflecting a second stage of Jewish feminism. Susannah Heschel, interview by author, June 23, 2009.

25. Martha Ackelsberg, introduction to Koltun, *Jewish Woman*, 9.

26. Martha Ackelsberg, "Feminism: Giving Birth to a New Judaism," *Sh'ma*, September 4, 1981, 2.

27. Martha Ackelsberg, "Spirituality, Community, and Politics: B'not Esh and the Feminist Reconstruction of Judaism," *Journal of Feminist Studies in Religion* 2, no. 2 (1986): 116, 120; Ackelsberg, interview.

28. See Martha Ackelsberg, "How Can a Feminist like Me Enjoy a Liturgy like This?," *Sh'ma* 36, no. 623 (2005): 2; Ackelsberg, "Families and the Jewish Community: A Feminist Perspective," *Response* 14, no. 4 (1985): 5–15; Ackelsberg, "Family or Community?," *Sh'ma* 17, no. 330 (1987): 76–80; and Ackelsberg, "Personal Identities and Collective Visions: Reflections on Being a Jew and a Feminist," lecture at Smith College, 1983, American Jewish Historical Society.

29. Hyman, "Ezrat Nashim," 287, 289; also see Heschel, *On Being a Jewish Feminist*; and Donna Robinson Divine, introduction to lecture by Martha Ackelsberg at Smith College, February 22, 2010; Robinson to author, June 29, 2013.

30. In interviews with fourteen women who were members of Ezrat Nashim from 1971 to 1974, Lianna Levine found eight who were members of Conservative synagogues, four Orthodox, one Lubavitch (Hasidic), and one Reform. Levine, "Women of Ezrat Nashim," paper for Sylvia Barack Fishman, Department of Near Eastern and Judaic Studies, Brandeis University, December 2004. Thanks to Martha Ackelsberg for this reference.

31. Arlene Agus, remarks at WLJIC.

32. Ibid.

33. "After a Decade of Jewish Feminism the Jewry Is Still Out," interview with Paula Hyman and Arlene Agus, *Lilith* 11 (Fall–Winter 1983): 21.

34. Arlene Agus, interview by author, January 10, 2013.

35. Agus has been an adviser to the Jewish Child Care Association and a faculty member at the Skirball Center for Adult Jewish Learning.

36. Agus, interview; Arlene Agus, "Keeping Jewish Creativity Feminist," *Sh'ma* 16, no. 305 (1986): 38–40.

37. Agus, interview.

38. See Susan Shapiro, "Standing Again with Judith Plaskow: A Select Reading of Her Essays," *Journal of Feminist Studies in Religion* 23, no. 1 (2007): 27; Rebecca T. Alpert, "A Prophetic Voice for Truth," *Journal of Feminist Studies in Religion* 23, no. 1 (2007): 8.

39. Judith Plaskow, "*The Coming of Lilith*: A Response," *Journal of Feminist Studies in Religion* 23, no. 1 (2007): 36.

40. See Martha Ackelsberg and Judith Plaskow, "Why We're Not Getting Married," *Lilith* 29 (Fall 2004), http://lilith.org.

41. "Judith Plaskow," in Ann Braude, ed., *Transforming the Faith of Our Fathers: Women Who Changed American Religion* (New York: Palgrave Macmillan, 2004), 220.

42. Judith Plaskow, interview by author, August, 5, 2013; and Judith Plaskow, oral history by Allison Pilatsky, March 22, 2010, Documenting Lesbian Lives Oral History Project.

43. Plaskow, interview.

44. See Alpert, "Prophetic Voice for Truth," 7.

45. Judith Plaskow, *Standing Again at Sinai: Judaism from a Feminist Perspective* (San Francisco: Harper and Row, 1990), xii.

46. Plaskow, oral history.

47. Plaskow, interview; Plaskow, oral history.

48. Plaskow, interview.

49. Ibid.

50. Plaskow, oral history.

51. Ibid.

52. Plaskow, interview; Plaskow, oral history.

53. Judith Plaskow, "Intersections: An Introduction," in Plaskow, *Coming of Lilith*, 7.

54. Plaskow, oral history.

55. Plaskow, interview; Plaskow, "Intersections," 7.

56. Plaskow, oral history; Plaskow, "Intersections," 7.

57. "Judith Plaskow," 221; Plaskow, "Intersections," 7.

58. Plaskow, oral history; "Judith Plaskow," 221.

59. Plaskow, "Intersections," 9.

60. Plaskow, interview.

61. Plaskow, "Intersections," 8.
62. Plaskow, "Coming of Lilith," 28–29.
63. Ibid., 32.
64. Ibid., 31.
65. Judith Plaskow Goldenberg, "The Jewish Feminist: Conflict in Identities," *Response: A Contemporary Jewish Review* 18 (Summer 1973): 12.
66. Plaskow, oral history.
67. Plaskow, "Intersections," 10.
68. Ibid., 11.
69. Plaskow, *Standing Again at Sinai*, 21.
70. Ibid., 59, 71, 119.
71. Ibid., 133, 139–141, 155, 157, 161.
72. Ibid., 210, 237–238.
73. Plaskow, interview.
74. Plaskow, "Intersections," 12.
75. Ibid., 13–14.
76. Plaskow, *Standing Again at Sinai*, xii–xiii.
77. Plaskow, "Coming of Lilith," 35.
78. Plaskow, "Intersections," 15; Plaskow, oral history.
79. Plaskow, "Intersections," 14–15.
80. Judith Plaskow, "Anti-Semitism: The Unacknowledged Racism," in Plaskow, *Coming of Lilith*, 98.
81. Plaskow, interview.
82. Ackelsberg, oral history, 27; Plaskow, oral history, 24.
83. Laura Geller, interview by author, January 9, 2016. Betty Friedan, "Women in the Firing Line," *New York Times*, October 28, 1984, www.nytimescom.
84. Betty Friedan, *Central Conference of Reform Rabbis Yearbook* 89 (1979): 180, quoted in Carole B. Balin, "Reform Rabbis, Betty Friedan, and the Uses of 'Tradition,'" in Michael A. Meyer and David N. Myers, *Between Jewish Tradition and Modernity: Rethinking an Old Opposition* (Detroit: Wayne State University Press, 2014), 289.
85. Geller, interview.
86. Laura Geller, "The Torah of Our Lives," in Gail Twersky Reimer and Judith A. Kates, eds., *Beginning Anew: A Woman's Companion to the High Holy Days* (New York: Simon and Schuster, 1997), 263–264.
87. Laura Geller, "Reactions to a Woman Rabbi," in Heschel, *On Being a Jewish Feminist*, 213.
88. Geller, interview.
89. Karla Goldman, "Laura Geller," in *Jewish Women: A Comprehensive Historical Encyclopedia: A Comprehensive Historical Encyclopedia*, March 1, 2009, Jewish Women's Archive; Danielle Berrin, "Rabbi Laura Geller Moves from Senior Rabbi to Study of Aging," *Jewish Journal*, June 22, 2016; Geller, interview.
90. Quoted in Berrin, "Rabbi Laura Geller."

91. Ibid.
92. Rebecca Alpert, interview by author, June 26, 2012.
93. Rebecca Alpert, oral history, Lesbian, Gay, Bisexual and Transgender Religious Archives Network, www.lgbtran.org.
94. Alpert, interview.
95. Alpert, oral history.
96. Rebecca Alpert, remarks at WLJIC; Alpert to author, June 1, 2011.
97. Alpert, remarks at WLJIC.
98. Judy Klemesrud, "Barnard's New Alumnae Tell What They Now Want Out of Life," *New York Times*, June 2, 1971, 36.
99. Alpert, remarks at WLJIC.
100. Ibid.
101. Ibid.
102. Rebecca T. Alpert, "Coming Out of the Closet as Politically Correct," *Tikkun* 11, no. 2 (1996): 61.
103. Rebecca T. Alpert, *Out of Left Field: Jews and Black Baseball* (New York: Oxford University Press, 2011); Alpert, *Religion and Sports: An Introduction and Case Studies* (New York: Columbia University Press, 2015); Alpert, *Like Bread on the Seder Plate: Jewish Lesbians and the Transformation of Tradition* (New York: Columbia University Press 1997); Rebecca T. Alpert, Sue Levi Elwell, and Shirley Idelson, eds., *Lesbian Rabbis: The First Generations* (New Brunswick, NJ: Rutgers University Press, 2001).
104. Alpert, interview.
105. Alpert, interview; Alpert, remarks at WLJIC.
106. Blu Greenberg, remarks at WLJIC.
107. Ibid.
108. Ibid. Also see William Novak, "Talking with Blu Greenberg," *Kerem* 4 (Winter 1995–1996): 34–37.
109. Greenberg, remarks at WLJIC.
110. Blu Greenberg, "Being Jewish: My Life and Work," unpublished manuscript, Blu Greenberg Papers, Schlesinger Library.
111. Blu Greenberg, "How an Orthodox Woman Evolved," 5.
112. Greenberg, "Being Jewish, My Life and Work"; Greenberg, remarks at WLJIC.
113. Greenberg, remarks at WLJIC.
114. Greenberg, "How an Orthodox Woman Evolved"; Greenberg, "Being Jewish."
115. Greenberg, "Being Jewish."
116. Novak, "Talking with Blu Greenberg," 27; Greenberg, "How an Orthodox Woman Evolved," 7.
117. Novak, "Talking with Blu Greenberg," 28.
118. See "Blu Greenberg," in Braude, *Transforming the Faith of Our Fathers*, 249.
119. Beth Mohr, "Jewish Woman Leader Urges Moderate Tack on Feminism," *San Diego Union*, February 9, 1977; Greenberg, "How an Orthodox Woman Evolved," 8.

120. Greenberg, "How an Orthodox Woman Evolved," 8.

121. Greenberg, "Being Jewish."

122. Ibid.

123. Greenberg, remarks at WLJIC.

124. Blu Greenberg, "Betty Friedan: An Appreciation," Jewish Telegraphic Agency, February 8, 2006, www.jta.org.

125. Blu Greenberg, *On Women and Judaism: A View from Tradition* (Philadelphia: Jewish Publication Society of America, 1981).

126. Blu Greenberg, "Jewish Activism in the 80s," unpublished paper, Greenberg Papers; "Blu Greenberg," 255; Novak, "Talking with Blu Greenberg," 35.

127. Greenberg, "Being Jewish."

128. Greenberg, remarks at WLJIC.

129. Greenberg, *On Women and Judaism*, 21.

130. Hyman, "Jewish Feminism Faces the American Women's Movement."

131. Plaskow, "Intersections," 13.

132. Geller, interview.

133. Heschel, introduction to *On Being a Jewish Feminist*, xxiii.

CHAPTER 6. "JEWISH WOMEN HAVE THEIR NOSES SHORTENED"

1. Cheryl Moch, interview by Tamara Cohen, March 14, 2002, quoted in Cohen, "An Overlooked Bridge: Secular Women of the Jewish Left and the Rise of Jewish Feminism," master's thesis, Sarah Lawrence College, 2003, 21.

2. Staub, *Torn at the Roots*, 129; Jack Nusan Porter and Peter Dreier, preface to Porter and Dreier, eds., *Jewish Radicalism: A Selected Anthology* (New York: Grove, 1973), xxvi.

3. Cantor, *Jewish Men / Jewish Women*, 352; Cantor, "Halcyon Days."

4. See Cantor, *Jewish Women / Jewish Men*, 345; Ofira Seliktar, *Divided We Stand: American Jews, Israel, and the Peace Process* (Westport, CT: Praeger, 2002), 27–28.

5. Cantor, *Jewish Women / Jewish Men*, 353; Cantor, "Halcyon Days," 57; Aviva Cantor, remarks at WLJIC.

6. Chaim Rosmarin, "America's New Jewish Left," *New Outlook*, April 1971, 38, quoted in Cohen, "Overlooked Bridge," 21.

7. Cantor, "Halcyon Days," 57.

8. Aviva Cantor, interview by author, February 27, 2009.

9. Cantor, *Jewish Women / Jewish Men*, 354; Cantor, remarks at WLJIC.

10. Cohen, "Overlooked Bridge," 22; Cantor, *Jewish Women / Jewish Men*, 355.

11. Vivian Silber Salowitz, "Sexism in the Jewish Student Community," in Elizabeth Koltun, ed., "The Jewish Woman: An Anthology," special issue, *Response* 18 (Summer 1973): 56.

12. Cantor, *Jewish Women / Jewish Men*, 373; Cantor to author, October 4, 2016.

13. "International Jewish Seminar Attended by 250 Students: First of Kind in U.S.," Jewish Telegraphic Agency, September 3, 1971, www.jta.org. The conference was titled "Jewing It, '32: Encounters in the Month of Ejul."

14. Cantor, *Jewish Women / Jewish Men*, 414.

15. Lindsay Miller, "Jewish Women Seek Identity," *New York Post*, April 1974 (thanks to Cheryl Moch for this clipping); Jewish Women's Archive, "Cheryl Moch," accessed August 20, 2016, http://jwa.org.

16. "Jewish Women Join Forces," *Chutzpah* 7 (Summer–Fall 1974): 1.

17. Aviva Cantor Zuckoff, "Oppression of Amerika's Jews," *Jewish Liberation Journal* 8 (November 1970): 2–4; Leora Tanenbaum, "Was Portnoy Right?," *Boston Phoenix*, October 6, 1995, 5.

18. Fees were waived for those who were unable to pay. Cantor to author, October 4, 2016. See Ruth Balser, "A Collective Identity," *Genesis* 2, March 1973, 10; and Ruth Magder, "The First National Jewish Women's Conference: A Study of the Early Jewish Feminist Movement," senior thesis, History Department, Barnard College, 1991, American Jewish Historical Society.

19. Jewish Women's Archive, "Sheryl Baron Nestel," accessed September 14, 2016, http://jwa.org.

20. See Magder, "First National Jewish Women's Conference"; and Jewish Women's Archive, "Cheryl Moch."

21. Cohen, "Overlooked Bridge"; Jewish Women's Archive, "Cheryl Moch"; Jewish Women's Archive, "Sheryl Baron Nestel."

22. Tanenbaum, "Was Portnoy Right?," 5.

23. Amy F. J. Stone, "Aviva Cantor," in *Jewish Women: A Comprehensive Historical Encyclopedia*, March 1, 2009, Jewish Women's Archive.

24. Cantor, interview.

25. "Obituary: Murray Zuckoff, JTA's Editor for Nearly 20 Years, Dies at 79," Jewish Telegraphic Agency, December 29, 2004, http://www.jta.org.

26. Cantor, "Halcyon Days," 57.

27. Zuckoff, "Oppression of Amerika's Jews," 2–4.

28. Ibid., 3.

29. Ibid., 4.

30. Cantor, remarks at WLJIC.

31. Cantor, *Jewish Women / Jewish Men*, 352; Staub, *Torn at the Roots*, 194–195, 201; Josh Nathan-Kazis, "Treat Jewish Students like the Adults That They Are," *Forward*, December 19, 2007.

32. Cantor, "Halcyon Days," 58–59; Stone, "Aviva Cantor."

33. Cantor, remarks at WLJIC. See Staub, *Torn at the Roots*, chap. 6.

34. Cantor, *Jewish Women / Jewish Men*, 352–353.

35. Ibid., 413.

36. Cantor, remarks at WLJIC.

37. Aviva Cantor, "Jewish Women's Haggadah," in Koltun, *Jewish Woman*, 95.

38. Echols, *Daring to Be Bad*, 62–63.

39. Cantor, "Jewish Women's Haggadah," 95.

40. Ibid.; Cantor, *Jewish Women / Jewish Men*, 414–415.

41. Cantor, quoted in Susan Josephs, "We Are No Longer a Joke," *Jewish Week*, February 13, 1998.
42. Cantor, remarks at WLJIC.
43. Cantor to author, October 3, 2016.
44. Hole and Levine, *Rebirth of Feminism*, 273.
45. Robin Morgan, "Goodbye to All That," in Rosalyn Baxandall and Linda Gordon, eds., *Dear Sisters: Dispatches from the Women's Liberation Movement* (New York: Basic Books, 2000), 57.
46. This and the following quotes are from Cantor's undated typescript, "to the RAT collective," Aviva Cantor Papers, Brandeis University.
47. Cantor to author, October 3, 2016.
48. Cantor, *Jewish Women / Jewish Men*, 423–425.
49. Cantor, remarks at WLJIC.
50. Cantor to author, October 3, 2016; Aviva Cantor, "Notes for Speech at 1998 Reunion (25th Anniversary of 1973)," Cantor Papers.
51. Jesse Zel Lurie to Aviva Cantor, February 12, 1976, and Aviva Cantor to Jesse Zel Lurie, February 13, 1976, Cantor Papers.
52. Jane, for the journal staff (*Women: A Journal of Liberation*), to Bonnie, October 1, 1972, Cantor Papers.
53. Note from Doris to Aviva Cantor, n.d., Cantor Papers.
54. Aviva Cantor, "Jewish Women's Liberation: America—Still Programmed to Be Wives," *Israel Horizons* 21, nos. 3–4 (1973): 12, Cantor Papers.
55. Rachel Blau DuPlessis and Ann Snitow to Aviva Cantor, n.d., Cantor Papers.
56. Susan Weidman Schneider, interview by author, January 29, 2009.
57. Ibid.
58. Ibid.
59. Jewish Women's Archive, "Susan Weidman Schneider," accessed May 25, 2015, http://jwa.org.
60. Schneider, interview.
61. Ibid.
62. Ibid.
63. Untitled typescript, 1974, Lilith Editorial and Administrative Files, Lilith Archives, Brandeis University.
64. Ibid.
65. Jewish Women's Archive, "Susan Weidman Schneider."
66. Ibid.
67. Anne Lapidus Lerner, "Lilith Magazine," in *Jewish Women: A Comprehensive Historical Encyclopedia*, accessed March 20, 2009, Jewish Women's Archive; Susan Schnur, remarks at "Looking Back, Looking Forward: Symposium Celebrating 40 Years of the Lilith Magazine Archives," Brandeis University, March 26, 2017.
68. Susan Weidman Schneider, *Jewish and Female: A Guide and Sourcebook for Today's Jewish Woman* (New York: Touchstone, 1984); Schneider, *Intermarriage:*

The Challenge of Living with Differences between Christians and Jews (New York: Free Press, 1989); Schneider, Arthur B. C. Drache, and Helene Brezinsky, *Head and Heart: A Woman's Guide to Financial Independence* (Pasadena, CA: Trilogy Books, 1991).

69. Schneider, interview.

70. Cohen, "Overlooked Bridge," 24.

71. Miriam Socoloff and Henry Balser, "Jewish, Radical, and Proud," *Chutzpah* 4 (February–March 1973): 17, quoted in Cohen, "Overlooked Bridge," 24–25.

72. Cohen, "Overlooked Bridge," 2.

73. "Revolutionary Jewish Nationalism," *Brooklyn Bridge* 1 (June 1972): 21, quoted in Staub, *Torn at the Roots*, 238–239.

74. Chutzpah Collective, introduction to Steven Lubet, Jeffry (Shaye) Mallow, Adar Rossman, Susan Schechter, Robbie (Sholem) Skeist, and Miriam Socoloff, eds., *Chutzpah: A Jewish Liberation Anthology* (San Francisco: New Glide, 1977), 3, 6. The other members of the Chutzpah Collective were Maralee Gordon, Marian Henriquez Neudel, Myron Perlman, Barbara Pruzan Perlman, and Leo Schlosberg.

75. Ibid., 5–6.

76. Maralee Gordon, interview by author, December 17, 2012.

77. Cheryl Moch, "Self-Hate," *Brooklyn Bridge* 1 (February 1971): 20, quoted in Cohen, "Overlooked Bridge," 31.

78. See Lee Weiner, "Toward a Politics of Revolutionary Nationalism," *Brooklyn Bridge* 1 (May 1971): 5, 14; Cheryl Moch, interview by author, June 5, 2009.

79. Cohen, "Overlooked Bridge," 32–33.

80. Moch, interview by author.

81. "We Are Coming Home," *Brooklyn Bridge* 1 (February 1971), reprinted in Michael E. Staub, ed., *The Jewish 1960s: An American Sourcebook* (Lebanon, NH: Brandeis University Press 2004), 262; Moch, "Self-Hate," 20.

82. "The 5000-Year-Old Woman," *Brooklyn Bridge* 1 (February 1971): 3.

83. Ibid.

84. Cohen, "Overlooked Bridge," 99.

85. Moch, interview by author; also see Jewish Women's Archive, "Cheryl Moch."

86. Ruth Balser, "Liberation of a Jewish Radical," in Lubet et al., *Chutzpah*, 15.

87. Ibid.

88. Ibid., 16.

89. Ibid., 16–17.

90. Ibid., 17.

91. Ibid., 18.

92. Ruth Balser, interview by author, October 12, 2017.

93. Allen Steinberg to author, June 26, 2017.

94. Susan Schechter, "To My Real and Imagined Enemies, and Why I Sometimes Can't Tell You Apart," in Lubet et al., *Chutzpah*, 12–13.

95. Ibid., 13.

96. Susan Schechter, "Solidarity and Self-Respect: Coming Out Jewish at the Socialist Feminist Conference," in Lubet et al., *Chutzpah*, 57.

97. Susan Schechter, handwritten notes, Jewish Women's Caucus, Socialist Feminist Conference, Antioch College, July 4–6, 1976, Susan Schechter Papers, Schlesinger Library.

98. Ibid.

99. Schechter, "Solidarity and Self-Respect," 59. Also see the original *Chutzpah* article about the conference, "Solidarity and Self-Respect: Coming Out Jewish at the Socialist Feminist Conference," *Chutzpah* 9–10 (1975): 1, 4.

100. Schechter, "To My Real and Imagined Enemies: Double-Binds of Being Jewish," *Chutzpah* 12 (1976), American Jewish Historical Society. Also in the *Chutzpah* anthology, "To My Real and Imagined Enemies," 13.

101. Campbell Robertson, "Susan Schechter, 57, Author of Books Exploring Impact of Domestic Violence," obituary, *New York Times*, February 16, 2004.

102. Susan Schechter, "Reflection," in Raquel Kennedy Bergen, Jeffrey L. Edleson, and Claire M. Renzetti, eds., *Violence against Women: Classic Papers* (Boston: Pearson / Allyn and Bacon, 2005), 218.

103. Susan Schechter, *Women and Male Violence: The Visions and Struggles of the Battered Women's Movement* (Boston: South End, 1982); Ann Jones and Susan Schechter, *When Love Goes Wrong: What to Do When You Can't Do Anything Right* (New York: HarperCollins 1992).

104. See Fran S. Danis, "A Tribute to Susan Schechter: The Visions and Struggles of the Battered Women's Movement," *Affilia: Journal of Women and Social Work* 21, no. 3 (2006): 336–341.

105. Steinberg to author, June 26, 2017.

106. Danis, "Tribute to Susan Schechter," 338.

107. M. Gordon, interview.

108. Ibid. On the protest, see Staub, *Torn at the Roots*, 194.

109. "Chicago," *Brooklyn Bridge* 1 (June 1972) 26; Maralee Gordon, "Jewish Women Up from Under," *Chutzpah* 4 (February–March 1973): 8.

110. Gordon, "Jewish Women Up from Under," 9.

111. Ibid.

112. Maralee Gordon, "Feminist Frustration with the Forefathers," in Lubet et al., *Chutzpah*, 148.

113. Ibid., 148–151.

114. Maralee Gordon, "Role Models for Jewish Women," in Lubet et al., *Chutzpah*, 23.

CHAPTER 7. "FOR GOD'S SAKE, COMB YOUR HAIR! YOU LOOK LIKE A VILDE CHAYE"

1. See, for example, Ginny Berson for the Furies, "Beyond Male Power," in Crow, *Radical Feminism*, 163–166; Anne M. Valk, *Living a Feminist Lifestyle: The Intersection of Theory and Action in a Lesbian Feminist Collective*, in Hewitt, *No Permanent Waves*, 225.

2. Melanie Kaye/Kantrowitz, "Some Notes on Jewish Lesbian Identity," in Beck, *Nice Jewish Girls*, 42; Evelyn Torton Beck to author, August 7, 2016.

3. Faith Rogow, "Why Is This Decade Different from All Other Decades? A Look at the Rise of Jewish Lesbian Feminism," *Bridges* 1, no. 1 (1990): 70.

4. Beck to author, August 7, 2016; Evelyn Torton Beck, "Why Is This Book Different from All Other Books?," in Beck, *Nice Jewish Girls*, xxxii.

5. Bereano published the second edition of *Nice Jewish Girls* in 1984, when she was editor of Crossings Press. Mennis taught at Adirondack Community College and co-facilitated a series of workshops on black-Jewish relations at the Women's Center of Brooklyn College.

6. Beck to author, August 7, 2016.

7. *Nice Jewish Girls* became a "catalyst for Jewish feminist energy and a special muse to Jewish lesbian creativity." Rogow, "Why Is This Decade Different from All Other Decades?," 71.

8. See Rachel Wahba, "Some of Us Are Arabic," Beck, *Nice Jewish Girls*, 69–72; Savina Teubal, "A Coat of Many Colors," ibid., 100–103; Shelley Horwitz, "Letter from Jerusalem," ibid., 225–229; and Marcia Freedman, "A Lesbian in the Promised Land," ibid., 230–240.

9. Beck, "Why Is This Book Different from All Other Books?," xii; Beck to author, August 7, 2016.

10. Joan Biren's oral history is in the Voices of Feminism Oral History Project, Sophia Smith Collection. For Bauman, Zionism enabled her positive identification as a Jew, two decades before she came out as a lesbian. Batya Bauman, "Ten Women Tell . . . the Ways We Are," *Lilith* 1 (Winter 1976–1977): 9–10.

11. Melanie Kaye Kantrowitz, "Ani Main, 5749," *Barre-Montpelier Times Argus*, September 22, 1988, 89–90.

12. Irena Klepfisz, "Anti-Semitism in the Lesbian-Feminist Movement," in Beck, *Nice Jewish Girls*, 53.

13. Kaye/Kantrowitz and Klepfisz, *Tribe of Dina*.

14. Beck, "Why Is This Book Different from All Other Books?," xvii.

15. Ibid., xv.

16. Ibid., xxxii; Adrienne Rich, "Split at the Root," in Beck, *Nice Jewish Girls*, 73.

17. Beck, remarks at WLJIC; and Evelyn Torton Beck to author, June 7, 2011.

18. Beck, remarks at WLJIC; Beck to author, June 7, 2011; Evelyn Torton Beck, interview by author, December 22, 2008; Beck to author, August 7, 2016.

19. Beck, remarks at WLJIC; Beck to author, June 7, 2011.

20. Beck, remarks at WLJIC; Beck to author, June 7, 2011.

21. Beck, remarks at WLJIC; Beck to author, June 7, 2011.

22. Beck, remarks at WLJIC; Beck to author, June 7, 2011.

23. Beck, remarks at WLJIC; Beck to author, June 7, 2011.

24. Evelyn Torton Beck, *Kafka and the Yiddish Theater: Its Impact on his Work* (Madison: University of Wisconsin Press, 1972).

25. Evelyn Torton Beck, "The Many Faces of Eve: Women, Yiddish, and Isaac

Bashevis Singer" (Working Papers in Yiddish and East European Jewish Studies, Max Weinreich Center for Advanced Jewish Studies of the YIVO Institute for Jewish Research, 1975).

26. Beck, remarks at WLJIC; Beck to author, June 7, 2011.

27. Beck, remarks at WLJIC; Beck to author, June 7, 2011.

28. Aviva Cantor, "Evelyn Torton Beck," *Lilith* 10 (Winter 1982–1983); Beck to author, August 7, 2016.

29. Cantor, "Evelyn Torton Beck."

30. Ibid.

31. "Conference Report," in "Notes and Letters," *Feminist Studies* 10, no. 2 (1984): 354.

32. Evelyn Torton Beck, "'No More Masks': Anti-Semitism as Jew-Hating," *Women's Studies Quarterly* 11, no. 3 (1983): 11–12.

33. Beck to author, August 7, 2016; Beck, "No More Masks," 13.

34. The panel took place at the "Feminist Studies: Reconstituting Knowledge" conference in Milwaukee, 1985, and was mentioned in Teresa de Lauretis, "Feminist Studies / Critical Studies: Issues, Terms, and Contexts," in Lauretis, ed., *Feminist Studies / Critical Studies* (Bloomington: Indiana University Press, 1989), 7. See Beck, "Politics of Jewish Invisibility," 100–101n21.

35. Beck, "Politics of Jewish Invisibility," 96.

36. Ibid., 101–102. Also see Evelyn Torton Beck, Julie L. Goldberg, and L. Lee Knefelkamp, "Integrating Jewish Issues into the Teaching of Psychology," in Phyllis Bronstein and Kathryn Quina, eds., *Teaching Gender and Multicultural Awareness: Resources for the Psychology Classroom* (Washington, DC: American Psychological Association, 2003), 237–252.

37. Beck to author, August 7, 2016.

38. Shirley Moskow, "An Alternative Press Rewrites the Traditional Success Story," *News-Tribune*, August 5, 1981, Persephone Press Papers, Schlesinger Library.

39. Biographical information comes from Gloria Greenfield, interviews by author, January 15 and February 16, 2009.

40. Greenfield, interview, January 15, 2009; Greenfield also tells the story in "Shedding," in Beck, *Nice Jewish Girls*, 6.

41. Oswego Women's Center, press release, n.d., Gloria Greenfield's personal collection.

42. See Mary Kassian, *The Feminist Gospel: The Movement to Unite Feminism with the Church* (Wheaton, IL: Crossway, 1992).

43. See Jewish Women's Archive, "'Through the Looking Glass' Conference Program, April 1976," http://jwa.org.

44. Pat McGloin, quoted in Evelyn C. White, "Persephone's Success Story Started with Feminist Will," *Seattle Gay News*, July 20–August 2, 1982, Persephone Press Papers.

45. Greenfield, interview, January 15, 2009.

46. Persephone Press's book list included Cherríe Moraga and Gloria Anzaldúa, eds., *This Bridge Called My Back* (1981); Audre Lorde, *Zami* (1982); Michelle Cliff,

Abeng: Claiming an Identity They Taught Me to Despise (1983); Beck, *Nice Jewish Girls*; Irena Klepfisz, *Keeper of Accounts* (1982); Elly Bulkin, *Lesbian Fiction* (1981); Elly Bulkin and Joan Larkin, eds., *Lesbian Poetry* (1981).

47. Jewish Women's Archive, "Gloria Greenfield," accessed October 6, 2012, http:// jwa.org. Because of the incident, Clausen's lover, Elly Bulkin, revised her original sole-authored project, an essay about anti-Semitism, bringing in a white, non-Jewish lesbian feminist and a black lesbian feminist as co-authors of a book about racism and anti-Semitism. See Elly Bulkin, Minnie Bruce Pratt, and Barbara Smith, *Yours in Struggle: Three Feminist Perspectives on Anti-Semitism and Racism* (New York: Firebrand Books, 1984).

48. Pat McGloin and Gloria Z. Greenfield to Persephone authors and editors, "Current Situation," April 13, 1983, Persephone Press Papers; Mary Kay Lefevour, "Persephone Press Folds," *off our backs* 13, no. 10 (1983): 10; Molly Lovelock, "Persephone Press: Why Did It Die?," *Sojourner: The New England Women's Journal of News, Opinions, and the Arts*, September 1983, 4, 18; Greenfield, interview, February 16, 2009.

49. Gloria Greenfield, "The Tools of Guilt and Intimidation," *Sojourner* 8, no. 11 (1983): 4.

50. Ibid.

51. Jewish Women's Archive, "Gloria Greenfield."

52. Greenfield, interview, January 15, 2009.

53. Irena Klepfisz, "Resisting and Surviving America," in Beck, *Nice Jewish Girls*, 114; Irena Klepfisz, interview by author, March 10–11, 2009.

54. Kaye/Kantrowitz, "Some Notes on Jewish Lesbian Identity," 38–39.

55. Jil Clark, "An Act of Resistance," interview with Gloria Greenfield, Melanie Kaye, and Irena Klepfisz, circa 1982, Persephone Papers, Schlesinger Library.

56. Ibid.

57. Klepfisz, "Resisting and Surviving America," 112; Irena Klepfisz, "Secular Jewish Identity: *Yidishkayt* in America," in Kaye/Kantrowitz and Klepfisz, *Tribe of Dina*, 36.

58. Klepfisz, "Secular Jewish Identity," 35–36.

59. Ibid., 36–37.

60. Ibid., 38–39.

61. Ibid., 40.

62. Klepfisz, interview.

63. Klepfisz, "Secular Jewish Identity," 43.

64. Ibid., 43–44.

65. Klepfisz to Dear Vilde Chayes, June 2, 1982, Greenfield's personal collection.

66. Irena Klepfisz, "Anti-Semitism in the Lesbian/Feminist Movement," in *Nice Jewish Girls*, 52.

67. Ibid., 52–54, 55–57.

68. Irena Klepfisz, *Keeper of Accounts* (Watertown, MA: Persephone, 1981); Klepfisz, *A Few Words in the Mother Tongue: Poems Selected and New, 1971–1990* (Portland,

OR: Eighth Mountain, 1991); Klepfisz, *Dreams of an Insomniac: Jewish Feminist Essays and Diatribes* (Portland, OR: Eighth Mountain, 1993).

69. Melanie Kaye/Kantrowitz, "To Be a Radical Jew in the Late 20th Century," in *Issue Is Power*, 94.

70. Kaye/Kantrowitz, "Some Notes on Jewish Lesbian Identity," 39–41; Clark, "Act of Resistance."

71. Kaye/Kantrowitz, "To Be a Radical Jew in the Late 20th Century," 93.

72. Ibid.

73. Ibid., 94.

74. Melanie Kaye/Kantrowitz, "Stayed on Freedom: Jews in the Civil Rights Movement and After," in Brettschneider, *Narrow Bridge*, 107, 109, 111–112.

75. Kaye/Kantrowitz, "To Be a Radical Jew in the Late 20th Century," 94–95.

76. Ibid., 95.

77. Kaye/Kantrowitz, "Stayed on Freedom," 114.

78. Ibid.

79. Ibid., 77, 97, 111–112.

80. Kaye/Kantrowitz, remarks at WLJIC; Kaye/Kantrowitz, "Stayed on Freedom," 112.

81. Melanie Kaye/Kantrowitz, *The Color of Jews: Racial Politics and Radical Diasporism* (Bloomington: Indiana University Press, 2007), 222.

82. "Notes from Di Vilde Chayes: A Jewish Lesbian Feminist Collective," typescript in the possession of Evelyn Torton Beck.

83. Irena Klepfisz to "Schvesters," February 2–7, 1982, Greenfield's personal collection. *Schvesters* is Yiddish for "sisters."

84. Clark, "Act of Resistance."

85. "Notes from Di Vilde Chayes."

86. Ibid.

87. Ibid.

88. Adrienne Rich to "Dear Schvesters," February 18, 1982, Greenfield's personal collection.

89. Beck to author, August 7, 2016.

90. Rich, "Split at the Root," 83.

91. Ibid., 76, 78.

92. Ibid., 81, 83.

93. Ibid., 6, 84.

94. Rich to "Dear Schvesters."

95. Melanie Kaye/Kantrowitz and Irena Klepfisz, "Jewish Feminist Conference: Thoughts and Impressions," *off our backs* 12, no. 8 (1982): 2.

96. Ibid.

97. "Zionism and White Supremacy," *Sojourner* 7, no. 7 (1982): 2–3. See Feldman, *Shadow over Palestine*, 188–189.

98. Women Against Imperialism, "Feminism, Anti-Semitism, and Racism . . . Taking Our Stand against Zionism and White Supremacy," *off our backs* 12, no. 7 (1982): 20.

99. Women Against Imperialism, "Who Are the Real Terrorists? Zionist Israel and the USA!," June 12, 1982, mimeo, Hall-Hoag Collection of Extremist Literature in the United States, Brandeis University Archives, Waltham, MA.

100. Women Against Imperialism, "Feminism, Anti-Semitism, and Racism," 20; Di Vilde Chayes, "What Does Zionism Mean?," *off our backs* 12, no. 7 (1982) 21.

101. See Evelyn Beck, Nancy Bereano, Melanie Kaye/Kantrowitz, and Irena Klepfisz, "Di Vilde Chayes: Zionists Deplore Killings in Lebanon and Criticize Nature of Anti-Israel Protests," *off our backs* 12, no. 9 (1982): 27.

102. Ruth Hubbard, "Theocracy vs. People" (letter), *off our backs* 12, no. 11 (1982): 25–26; Rachael Kamel, "Two Half-Truths Needing a Whole," *off our backs* 12, no. 9 (1982): 28.

103. Irena Klepfisz to author, September 25, 2016.

104. "Notes from Di Vilde Chayes."

105. Klepfisz, "Yom Hashoah, Yom Yerushalayim," 119, 116.

106. Ibid., 119–120.

107. Klepfisz to author, September 25, 2016; Beck to author, August 7, 2016.

108. Adrienne Rich, "Jewish Days and Nights," in Kushner and Solomon, *Wrestling with Zion*, 162.

109. Al-Hibri and Sanchez were not included, and Bulkin replaced Beck, whose panel contribution was printed separately in *Women's Studies Quarterly* along with summaries of the other panelists.

110. See Melanie Kaye/Kantrowitz, "*Yours in Struggle*: In Review," *off our backs* 15, no. 9 (1985): 20. Bulkin published a chapter of the book, titled "Breaking a Cycle," in *off our backs* 14, no. 4 (1984): 14–17.

111. Minnie Bruce Pratt, "Identity: Skin Blood Heart," in Bulkin, Pratt, and Smith, *Yours in Struggle*, 9–63.

112. Barbara Smith, "Between a Rock and a Hard Place: Relationships between Black and Jewish Women," in Bulkin, Pratt, and Smith, *Yours in Struggle*, 71.

113. Ibid., 68–69, 72, 75, 85.

114. Elly Bulkin, "Hard Ground: Jewish Identity, Racism, and Anti-Semitism," in Bulkin, Pratt, and Smith, *Yours in Struggle*, 93–94, 138.

115. Ibid., 98, 110–111, 109, 138, 153.

116. "Statement of Purpose and Justification to the Coordinating Council of NWSA from the Jewish Women's Task Force / Proposed Caucus," 1984, Jewish Women's Caucus Papers, NWSA, Mindy Sue Shapiro's personal collection. It expressed "the irony of having to 'qualify' as an oppressed group" amid "centuries of international Jew-hating and currently, amidst the present era of blatant anti-semitism."

117. In the first years of the Jewish Women's Caucus, Martha Ackelsberg served as its representative to NWSA's Steering Committee. Other members of the caucus included Judith Arcana, Annette Kolodny, and Mindy Sue Shapiro (who served as chair). Jewish Caucus Papers, NWSA, Shapiro's personal collection.

118. Kaye/Kantrowitz and Klepfisz with Mennis, "*In Gerang* / In Struggle." See Penny Rosenwasser, *Hope into Practice: Jewish Women Choosing Justice Despite Our Fears*

(PennyRosewasser.com, 2013), for an example of a recent work on internalized anti-Semitism.

119. Rogow, "Why Is This Decade Different from All Other Decades?," 70.

120. Kaye/Kantrowitz, "To Be a Radical Jew in the Late 20th Century," 102.

121. Klepfisz, *Dreams of an Insomniac*, quoted in Shana Penn, "The Reclamation of *Yidishkayt*," *Women's Review of Books* 8, nos. 10–11 (1991): 46.

122. See Elly Bulkin, "Bridges: A Journal for Jewish Feminists and Our Friends," in *Jewish Women: A Comprehensive Historical Encyclopedia*, March 1, 2009, Jewish Women's Archive; Claire Kinberg, "Challenges of Difference at *Bridges*," in Brettschneider, *Narrow Bridge*, 31; "Feminists Hope Party Will Prevent Collapse of Bridges," *Jewish News of Northern California*, August 20, 1999, www .jweekly.com.

123. Jews for Racial and Economic Justice, "Our Strategic Vision," 2015, www.jfrej.org.

124. Jewish Women's Archive, "Melanie Kaye/Kantrowitz," accessed February 17, 2016, http://jwa.org.

125. Klepfisz to author, September 25, 2016. The November 8–10, 1991, NJA conference, "Carrying It On: A National Conference Organizing against Anti-Semitism and Racism for Jewish Activists and College Students," attracted five hundred participants. Jenney Milner and Donna Spiegelman, "Carrying It On: A Report from the NJA Convergence on Organizing against Racism and Anti-Semitism," *Bridges* 3, no. 1 (1992): 138–147.

126. Irena Klepfisz, "A Jewish Women's Call for Peace—Days of Awe," unpublished speech, quoted in Evelyn Torton Beck, introduction to Klepfisz, *Dreams of an Insomniac*, xxvii.

127. See Rose Katz, "Jewish Feminist Publishing," *Feminist Collections: Women's Studies Library Resources in Wisconsin* 4, no. 2 (1983): 24–26.

CHAPTER 8. "RISE ABOVE THE WORLD'S NASTY SQUABBLES"

1. See Judith Zinsser, "From Mexico to Copenhagen to Nairobi: The United Nations Decade for Women, 1975–1985," *Journal of World History* 13, no. 1 (2002): 140, 142; Kristen Ghodsee, "Revisiting the United Nations Decade for Women: Brief Reflections on Feminism, Capitalism and Cold War Politics in the Early Years of the International Women's Movement," *Women's Studies International Forum* 33 (2010): 3–12; Jane Jaquette, "The 1980 Mid-Decade Conference," in Anne Winslow, ed., *Women, Politics, and the United Nations* (Westport, CT: Greenwood, 1995), 47–48; Jocelyn Olcott, *International Women's Year: The Greatest Consciousness-Raising Event in History* (New York: Oxford University Press, 2017), 5, 15. Also see Lourdes Benaria, "Reflections on the Copenhagen Conference," *Feminist Studies* 7, no. 2 (1981): 335–344.

2. On Betty Friedan and Jewishness, see Antler, *Journey Home*, 259–267; Kirsten Fermaglich, *American Dreams and Nazi Nightmares: Early Holocaust Consciousness and Liberal America, 1957–1965* (Hanover, NH: Brandeis University Press, 2006), chap. 2; Horowitz, "Jewish Women Remaking American Feminism," 235–256.

3. Alix Kates Shulman, interview by author, December 18, 2008.

4. Other seder sisters were Edith Isaac-Rose, Bea Kreloff, Michele Landsberg, and Lily Rivlin. The "seder mothers" included Bella Abzug, Grace Paley, and Gloria Steinem.

5. See E. M. Broner, *The Telling: The Story of a Group of Jewish Women Who Journey to Spirituality through Community and Ceremony* (San Francisco: HarperCollins, 1993).

6. Marcia Freedman, *Exile in the Promised Land: A Memoir* (Ithaca, NY: Firebrand Books, 1990), 234.

7. Helen S. Lewis, "The Copenhagen Conference and Its Aftermath: Implications for a Jewish Women's Agenda," International Council of Jewish Women, January 29, 1981, National Council of Jewish Women Records, Library of Congress, http://wasi.alexanderstreet.com.

8. Lober, "Conflict and Alliance in the Struggle," 173; Women Against Imperialism, "Who Are the Real Terrorists?," quoted ibid., 174.

9. On criticisms of American Jewish feminists' identity work, see Jenny Bourne, "Homelands of the Mind: Jewish Feminism and Identity Politics," *Race & Class* 29, no. 1 (1987): 1–24. Also see Ellen Cantarow, "Zionism, Anti-Semitism and Jewish Identity in the Women's Movement," *Middle East Report* 154 (September–October 1988): 38–43.

10. Jocelyn Olcott, "Globalizing Sisterhood: International Women's Year and the Politics of Representation," in Niall Ferguson, Charles S. Maier, and Erez Manela, eds., *The Shock of the Global: The 1970s in Perspective* (Cambridge, MA: Harvard University Press, 2011), 286–287; Olcott, "Cold War Conflicts and Cheap Cabaret: Sexual Politics at the 1975 United Nations International Women's Year Conference," *Gender & History* 22, no. 3 (2010): 733–754; Olcott, *International Women's Year*, 5, 15.

11. Niliifer Cagatay and Ursula Funk, "Comments," *Signs* 6, no. 4 (1981): 777.

12. See Feld, *Nations Divided*, 91–92.

13. Betty Friedan, "Scary Doings in Mexico City," in *"It Changed My Life": Writings on the Women's Movement* (New York: Norton, 1985), 350.

14. United Nations, "Report of the World Conference of the International Women's Year, Mexico City, 19 June–2 July 1975," paragraph 26, 7; also see paragraphs 23–24, 6.

15. Gil Troy, *Moynihan's Moment: America's Fight against Zionism as Racism* (New York: Oxford University Press, 2013), 84.

16. Ibid.

17. Betty Friedan, "Anti-Semitism as a Political Tool: Its Congruence with Anti-Semitism," 1985, Betty Friedan Papers, Schlesinger Library, 6.

18. Antler, *Journey Home*, 267; Troy, *Moynihan's Moment*, 85.

19. Olcott, *International Women's Year*, 116–121, 126.

20. Bernard Goodwin to Betty Friedan, December 8, 1975, Friedan Papers, quoted in Troy, *Moynihan's Moment*, 178.

21. Troy, *Moynihan's Moment*, 85.

22. Friedan, "Anti-Semitism as a Political Tool," 12.

23. Ibid.

24. Troy, *Moynihan's Moment*, 85.

25. Quoted in Marlin Levin, *It Takes a Dream: The Story of Hadassah* (Jerusalem: Gefen, 1997), 342.

26. Marcia Freedman, "Dear Sisters," letter from the Knesset, October 24, 1975, Freedman Papers, Brandeis University.

27. Freedman, *Exile in the Promised Land*, 42–43, 45; "Marcia Freedman on Israeli Feminism," *off our backs* 13 (March 1983): 18.

28. Marcia Freedman, interview by author, November 8, 1912.

29. Ibid.

30. Ibid.

31. "Marcia Freedman on Israeli Feminism."

32. Tzafu Saar, "The American Woman Who Brought Feminism to Israel," *Haaretz*, August 3, 2010, www.haaretz.com.

33. Freedman, interview; Freedman, "How I Went to Israel and Became an Anglo-Saxon: The American Influence on Second-Wave Israeli Feminism," Brandeis University, 1998–2000, Freedman Papers.

34. Freedman, "How I Went to Israel"; Freedman, interview; Saar, "Woman Who Brought Feminism to Israel," *Haaretz*, March 8, 2010; Freedman, *Exile in the Promised Land*, 55, 59, 97, 105.

35. "Marcia Freedman on Israeli Feminism."

36. Marcia Freedman, "Thoughts on Kenya, 1985," Shirley Joseph Papers, American Jewish Historical Society.

37. See Georgia Dullea, "U.N. World Conference on Women Opens Today in Copenhagen," *New York Times*, July 14, 1980; Helen S. Lewis, "The Copenhagen Conference: An Orchestrated Attack on Zionism," preliminary report to the Jewish Community Council of Greater Washington and to Pioneer Women, August 10, 1980, American Jewish Historical Society; Feld, *Nations Divided*, 93.

38. See Dullea, "U.N. World Conference on Women"; Joan Borsten, "UN Women Join the Anti-Israel Bandwagon," *Jerusalem Post*, n.d.; Judy Krausz, "The Anguish of Copenhagen: Three Israeli Representatives Talk about the Disastrous Women's Conferences," *Pioneer Women*, November 1980, 18–20; Zinsser, "From Mexico to Copenhagen to Nairobi," 139–168; Lois A. West, "The United Nations Women's Conferences and Feminist Politics," in Mary K. Meyer and Elisabeth Prügl, eds., *Gender Politics in Global Governance* (Lanham, MD: Rowman and Littlefield, 1999), 191.

39. Zinsser, "From Mexico to Copenhagen to Nairobi," 152.

40. Betty Friedan, "Afterword to 'Scary Doings in Mexico City,'" in *"It Changed My Life,"* 392.

41. Ibid., 393.

42. Helen S. Lewis, "Reflections on Copenhagen: A Chilling Experience—1980 Conference Seen as Throwback to 1930s," *Pioneer Women*, November 1980, 15–16; "prerequisite for peace" quoted in Troy, *Moynihan's Moment*, 241.

43. United Nations, *Report of the World Conference of the United Nations Decade for Women: Equality, Development and Peace* (New York: United Nations, 1980), 10–11.

44. Selma Baxt to Sheila Mittleman, August 26, 1980, Joseph Papers; Lewis, "Copenhagen Conference and Its Aftermath."

45. Lewis, "Reflections on Copenhagen," 15–16.

46. Judy Krausz, "The Anguish of Copenhagen," *Pioneer Woman*, November 1980, 18; E. M. Broner, "Women: Embraced and Embattled at the UN: Part II," n.d. (circa 1985), E. M. Broner Papers, Brandeis University.

47. Krausz, "Anguish of Copenhagen," 20; Naomi Chazan, "The Women's Movement and Anti-Semitism," typescript, Pogrebin Papers; Chazan, "Anti-Semitism and Politics in the International Women's Movement," paper prepared for the "International Conference on Politics and Anti-Semitism in the Women's Movement: The Road to Nairobi," Paris, July 8–10, 1984, American Jewish Historical Society.

48. Joan Borsten, "Copenhagen Letter: People Listened When Aloni Defended Israel," *Jerusalem Post*, July 25, 1980.

49. "Israel Delegates at UN Conference Call Apartheid Abhorrent," *Los Angeles Times*, July 20, 1985, quoted in Feld, *Nations Divided*, 96.

50. Chazan, "Anti-Semitism and Politics in the International Women's Movement."

51. Ibid.

52. Freedman, "Thoughts on Kenya, 1985."

53. Lewis, "Copenhagen Conference at Its Aftermath."

54. Broner, quoted in Regina Schreiber, "Sisterhood Is Powerful . . . Unless You're Jewish," *Lilith* 8, offprint, June 1981 (prepared for the National Women's Studies Association Meetings, June 1981). Original article: Schreiber, "Copenhagen: One Year Later," *Lilith* 8 (January 31, 1981): 30–35.

55. E. M. Broner, "The Road to Nairobi," paper presented at the International Gathering of Women's Organizations, July 1984, Broner Papers; also printed in *Moment*, November 1984, 35–39.

56. Esther Broner to Letty Cottin Pogrebin, July 13, 1980, Broner Papers.

57. E. M. Broner, "Women: Embraced and Embattled at the UN," 1980, Broner Papers.

58. Broner, "Road to Nairobi."

59. Broner, "Women: Embraced and Embattled at the UN."

60. Phyllis Chesler to author, June 20, 2017.

61. Schreiber, "Sisterhood Is Powerful."

62. Quoted in Feld, *Nations Divided*, 93.

63. Robin Morgan, ed., *Sisterhood Is Global: The International Women's Movement Anthology* (New York: Anchor/Doubleday, 1984); Morgan, *The Demon Lover: On the Sexuality of Terrorism* (New York: Norton, 1989).

64. Esther Broner, "Out of Africa, or, A Sad Thing Happened to Me on the Way to a Happy Ending," 1985, Broner Papers.

65. Batya Bauman, notes from Feminists Against Anti-Semitism meeting, February 22, 1981, Broner Papers.

66. Broner, "Road to Nairobi."

67. George Jochnowitz, "A Conversation with Phyllis Chesler: American Feminist and Zionist Activist," *Midstream* 53, no. 5 (2007): 10.

68. Ibid.; Phyllis Chesler to author, March 21, 2014.

69. Phyllis Chesler, "The Walls Came Tumbling Down: How Jewish Feminists Made History," *On the Issues* 11 (February 28, 1989), www.phyllis-chesler.com.

70. Aviva Cantor Zuckoff, "An Exclusive Interview with Dr. Phyllis Chesler," *Lilith* 1 (Winter 1976–1977): 24; Chesler to author, March 21, 2014.

71. "Hear the Voices of Women of Religious Conviction," *St. Petersburg Times*, January 28, 1984; Doree Lovell and Elsa A. Soldender, "Soul Survivors," *Baltimore Jewish Times*, January 27, 1984; Inge Lederer Gibel, memo, Second Women of Faith in the 80s Conference, November 16, 1983, Greenberg Papers.

72. "Conversation with Phyllis Chesler"; Chesler to Esther Broner, June 27, 1984, Broner Papers.

73. Lewis, "Copenhagen Conference and Its Aftermath."

74. Cantarow, "Zionism, Anti-Semitism and Jewish Identity," 38.

75. Lewis, "Copenhagen Conference and Its Aftermath."

76. Ibid.

77. Pogrebin, *Deborah, Golda, and Me*, 154, 158–159.

78. Ibid., 146, 149.

79. Letty Cottin Pogrebin, "A Writer, a Woman, and a Jew," *Forward*, January 13, 2006.

80. Pogrebin, *Deborah, Golda, and Me*, 154.

81. Pogrebin, "A Writer, a Woman, and a Jew."

82. Cantor to Pogrebin, July 27, 1982, Pogrebin Papers.

83. Pogrebin, *Deborah, Golda, and Me*, 215.

84. Ibid., 223–226.

85. "Letters Forum: Anti-Semitism," *Ms.*, February 1983, 12–13.

86. Pogrebin, *Deborah, Golda, and Me*, 231, 234. A bitter dispute over Jewish identity politics also unfolded in London, where the issues of anti-Semitism, anti-Zionism, and racism in the women's movement emerged in the radical feminist journal *Spare Rib* in the 1980s. See "Women Speak Out against Zionism: If a Woman Calls Herself Feminist She Should Call Herself Anti-Zionist," in the August 1982 issue; Bourne, "Homelands of the Mind"; JF Publications, ed., *A Word in Edgeways: Jewish Feminists Respond* (London: JF Publications, 1988); and Bernice Hausman, "Anti-Semitism in Feminism: Rethinking Identity Politics," *Iowa Journal of Literary Studies* 11 (1991): 85–86.

87. Chesler to Broner, June 27, 1984, Broner Papers.

88. Esther Broner, "A Women's Petition for International Sisterhood to Be Presented at Nairobi, 1985," Broner Papers.

89. Broner, "Road to Nairobi."

90. Christie Balka and Reena Bernards, memo to NJA National Council Representatives, Middle East Task Force and Feminist Contacts re: UN Decade for Women Conference in Nairobi, May 15, 1985, Joseph Papers.

91. See Feld, *Nations Divided*, 96–97.

92. Lena Einhorn, "Being a Jew at the UN Women's Forum in Nairobi," *Bulletin of the International Council of Jewish Women*, March 1986; Connie Kreshtool, "The Road to Nairobi," *Reform Judaism*, Winter 1985–1986, 20, 29; Ruth Cowan, "Nairobi Diary," *Jewish Standard*, August 9, 1985, 3, 25; National Council of Jewish Women, "American Jewish Women Better Prepared at Nairobi," Joseph Papers.

93. Galia Golan, interview by author, March 11, 2015.

94. Broner, "Out of Africa."

95. Esther Broner, "In and Out of Africa, 1985," Broner Papers.

96. Golan, interview.

97. Ezra Berkley Brown, "New Jewish Agenda: A People's History," New Jewish Agenda, accessed July 1, 2017, http://newjewishagenda.net.

98. Ibid. Also see Feld, *Nations Divided*, 96.

99. Ruth Seligman, "Dialogue," *Forum*, July 15, 1985, 7.

100. Balser, "Diane Balser, 68, Talks to Susan Schnur," 37–38; Broner, "In and Out of Africa."

101. Feld, *Nations Divided*, 97, quoting New Jewish Agenda press release, July 23, 1985.

102. Broner, "In and Out of Africa."

103. Shirley Joseph, "'Forward-Looking Strategies': How It Happened," *Moment*, October 28, 1985, 28–29.

104. Broner, "In and Out of Africa."

105. Mary Battiata, "The Feminist Finale," *Washington Post*, July 20, 1985, G1, G5; "Women's Conference Clouded by Hostility toward U.S., Israel," News Wire Service, n.d.; "Nairobi Women's Conference Ending a Decade for Women . . . with Forward Looking Strategies," *off our backs* 15, no. 9 (1985): 1; Ghodsee, "Revisiting the United Nations Decade for Women," 9.

106. Pogrebin, *Deborah, Golda, and Me*, 161, quoted in Feld, *Nations Divided*, 97.

107. Friedan, "Anti-Semitism as a Political Tool."

108. Christie Balka, "Beyond Zionism Is Racism in Nairobi," *Sojourner*, October 1985.

109. Ibid. In "Jewish Women & Nairobi: Another View" in the November 1985 issue of *Sojourner*, Ellen Cantarow responded to Balka's article, questioning whether Zionism should be regarded as the "national liberation movement of the Jewish people" and asking the "implicit question, 'Was Nairobi good, or bad, for the Jews?'" She urged the American women's movement to move beyond its own "chauvinist self-concern" (18–19).

110. Galia Golan, interview; Golan to author, July 10, 2017; E. M. Broner, Mass/Broner Letter, April 11, 1987, Broner Papers.

111. Alice Shalvi, "Israel Women's Network," in *Jewish Women: A Comprehensive Historical Encyclopedia*, March 1, 2009, Jewish Women's Archive.

112. Louise Woo, "Pursuing the Promise of Equality in the Promised Land," *Oakland (CA) Tribune*, March 8, 1987.

113. Letty Cottin Pogrebin, statement, 2011, http://lilith.org.

114. Randi Jo Land, "Peace Is a Women's Issue too," *Jerusalem Post*, December 8, 1988.

115. Randi Jo Land, "Feminists Convene—and Clash on Peace," *Jewish Week*, December 23, 1988.

116. Ibid.

117. The service was prepared by Rivka Haut, Norma Joseph, Rabbi Helene Ferris, and Shulamit Magnus. Phyllis Chesler to author, June 21, 2017. See Phyllis Chesler and Rivka Haut, eds., *Women of the Wall: Claiming Sacred Ground at Judaism's Holy Site* (Woodstock, VT: Jewish Lights, 2002).

118. Phyllis Chesler, "The Walls Came Tumbling Down," *On the Issues* 11 (1989): 11.

119. Ibid., 9.

120. In 2013, several founding members of WOW broke away from the group to form Original Women of the Wall (OWOW), which describes itself as an "independent, autonomous, pluralistic, feminist group." See the group's website: www.originalwow.org. OWOW rejected a compromise that allowed women to pray at a more distant site south of the Western Wall but not at the Kotel.

121. Sherry Gorelick, "Peace Movement in the United States," in *Jewish Women: A Comprehensive Historical Encyclopedia: A Comprehensive Historical Encyclopedia*, March 20, 2009, Jewish Women's Archive.

122. Solomon, "Building a Movement," 42–43.

123. See Feld, *Nations Divided*, 98; Cantarow, "Zionism, Anti-Semitism and Jewish Identity," 43.

124. Ellen Willis, typescript, no title (Speeches on Jews and Israel), n.d. (circa 1985), Willis Papers.

125. Ibid.

126. Willis, "Is There Still a Jewish Question?"

127. Willis, typescript (Speeches on Jews and Israel).

128. Pogrebin, "Zionism, Meet Feminism."

129. Examples of the recent commentary on feminism and Zionism include Emily Shire, "Does Feminism Have Room for Zionists?," *New York Times*, March 7, 2017, www.nytimes.com; and Collier Meyerson, "Can You Be a Zionist and a Feminist? Linda Sarsour Says No," *Nation*, March 13, 2017, www.thenation.com.

130. Solomon, "Building a Movement," 43.

CONCLUSION

1. Klatch, *Generation Divided*; Sherkat and Blocker, "Political Development of Sixties' Activists"; Braungart and Braungart, "Life-Course Development"; Nathan Glazer, *Remembering the Answers: Essays on American Student Revolt* (New York: Basic Books, 1970).

2. Jacobson, *Roots Too.*

3. Rothstein, remarks at WLJIC.

4. Gordon, "Participatory Democracy," 120.

5. Greenberg, interview.

6. Adrienne Rich, "If Not with Others, How?," in *Blood, Bread, and Poetry: Selected Prose, 1979–1985* (New York: Norton, 1986), also quoted in Jacobson, *Roots, Too,* 256.

7. Dworkin, "Song for Women in Five Questions," 44.

8. Cheryl Greenberg, "Pluralism and Its Discontents," in Biale, Heschel, Galchinsky, *Insider/Outsider*, 82.

9. Doress-Worters, interview.

10. Greenberg, "How an Orthodox Woman Evolved," 5.

11. Stephen J. Whitfield comments, "If Jews have been disproportionately radicals, it may because they have been disproportionately intellectuals." Whitfield, "Famished for Justice," 228–229.

12. Willis, "Next Year in Jerusalem," 135.

13. Tax, "False Idol of Land Worship"; Tax, remarks at WLJIC.

14. Plaskow, *Standing Again at Sinai*, 12.

15. Agus, interview.

16. Kesselman et al., "Our Gang of Four," 36.

17. Hawley, remarks at "A Revolutionary Moment."

18. Rothstein to author, June 20, 2016.

19. Brownmiller, *Against Our Will*; and Jewish Women's Archive, "Susan Brownmiller."

20. Kesselman to author, August 20, 2008.

21. Jacobson argues that multiculturalism was in force from the 1970s but emerged as a "coherent phenomenon" only in the 1990s. *Roots Too*, 226–227.

22. David Biale, Michael Galchinsky, and Susannah Heschel, introduction to *Insider/Outsider*, 8. On the exclusion of American Jews from multiculturalism, see Beck, "Politics of Jewish Invisibility"; Pinsky, *Jewish Feminists*, 97; Greenberg, "Pluralism and Its Discontents," in Biale, Galchinsky, and Heschel, *Insider/Outsider*, 82; Hollinger, *Postethnic America*.

23. Lisa E. Bloom, *Jewish Identities in American Feminist Art: Ghosts of Ethnicity* (New York: Routledge, 2006).

24. Marla Brettschneider, *Jewish Feminism and Intersectionality* (Albany: State University of New York, 2016), 8.

EPILOGUE

1. On feminist movement history, see Nancy A. Hewitt, ed., *No Permanent Waves: Recasting Histories of U.S. Feminism* (New Brunswick, NJ: Rutgers University Press, 2010).

2. Profiles of the six women are based on their remarks at the WLJIC panel.

3. See Leah Berkenwald, "Meet Jaclyn Friedman: Jewess with Attitude," June 20, 2011, Jewish Women's Archive.

4. Friedman's citation of this line echoes Alix Kates Schulman's in chapter 2.

5. Jaclyn Friedman and Jessica Valenti, eds., *Yes Means Yes! Visions of Female Sexual Power and a World without Rape* (Berkeley, CA: Seal, 2008); Jaclyn Friedman, *Unscrewed: Women, Sex, Power, and How to Stop Letting the System Screw Us All* (Berkeley, CA: Seal, 2017).

6. Nona Willis Aronowitz and Emma Bee Bernstein, *Girldrive: Criss-Crossing America, Redefining Feminism* (Berkeley, CA: Seal, 2009).

7. See Collier Meyerson, "Reflections on Off and Running," and "Lots of Latkes," Be'chol Lashon, accessed June 14, 2011, www.bechollashon.org.

8. Collier Meyerson, "On Passing, Wishing for Darker Skin, and Finding Your People: A Conversation between Two Mulattos," *Fusion*, June 5, 2015, www.fusion.net.

9. See Collier Meyerson, "Clinton, Sanders, and the Myth of a Monolithic 'Black Vote,'" *New Yorker*, April 15, 2016, www.newyorker.com.

10. Irin Carmon and Shana Knizhnik, *Notorious RBG: The Life and Times of Ruth Bader Ginsburg* (New York: Dey Street Books, 2015).

11. Pew Research Center, "Millennials: Confident. Connected. Open to Change," February 24, 2010, www.pewsocialtrends.org.

12. Catherine Harnois, "Re-presenting Feminisms: Past, Present, and Future," *NWSA Journal* 20, no. 1 (2008): 128.

INDEX

Page numbers in italics refer to illustrations.

ABOUT THE AUTHOR

Joyce Antler is the Samuel J. Lane Professor Emerita of American Jewish History and Culture and Professor Emerita of Women's, Gender, and Sexuality Studies at Brandeis University. She is the author of *You Never Call! You Never Write! A History of the Jewish Mother* (2007) and *The Journey Home: How Jewish Women Shaped Modern America* (1997) and is the author or editor of many other books on American Jewish history and women's history.

Martha Ackelsberg

Rebecca Alpert

Diane Balser

Rosalyn Baxandall

Evelyn Torton Beck

Heather Booth

Esther Broner

Susan Brownmiller

Aviva Cantor

Phyllis Chesler

Michele Clark

Vilunya Diskin

Joan Ditzion

Paula Doress-Worters

Shulamith Firestone

Marcia Freedman

Laura Geller

Galia Golan

Linda Gordon

Maralee Gordon